Population and its problems:
A plain man's guide

Population and its problems:

A plain man's guide

THE WOLFSON COLLEGE
LECTURES 1973

EDITED BY

H. B. PARRY

FELLOW OF WOLFSON COLLEGE, OXFORD
AND
NUFFIELD INSTITUTE FOR MEDICAL RESEARCH, HEADINGTON,
OXFORD

CLARENDON PRESS · OXFORD

1974

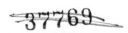

*Oxford University Press, Ely House, London W.*1

GLASGOW   NEW YORK   TORONTO   MELBOURNE   WELLINGTON
CAPE TOWN   IBADAN   NAIROBI   DAR ES SALAAM   LUSAKA   ADDIS ABABA
DELHI   BOMBAY   CALCUTTA   MADRAS   KARACHI   LAHORE   DACCA
KUALA LUMPUR   SINGAPORE   HONG KONG   TOKYO

ISBN 0 19 857380 4

© OXFORD UNIVERSITY PRESS 1974

PRINTED IN GREAT BRITAIN BY
BUTLER & TANNER LTD
FROME AND LONDON

Preface

IT is customary during Hilary term each year for Wolfson College to organize a series of weekly lectures on a topic of broad academic and general interest. As a World Population Conference is being planned for the summer of 1974, it seemed timely to undertake a review of our knowledge of the main determinants of population size. This review comprised a series of principal lectures, together with papers given at a Workshop Discussion Weekend arranged at the end of the lecture series. It was sponsored by Wolfson College jointly with the Professor of Biomathematics, Professor M. S. Bartlett, F.R.S., the Professor of Geography, Professor J. Gottmann, the Regius Professor of Medicine, Professor Sir Richard Doll, F.R.S., the Professor of Social Anthropology, Professor M. Freedman, the Professor of Zoology, Professor J. W. S. Pringle, F.R.S., and the Reader in Physical Anthropology, Dr. G. A. Harrison, at the University of Oxford.

The lecture series was designed to provide the interested non-specialist person with a general, critical introduction to the main factors which determine the size of populations, beginning with animal populations and pre-industrial human societies, and also as an introduction to a detailed survey of the many complex factors which influence and ultimately determine the present-day size of human populations. No attempt was made to cover all aspects of the subject; rather, the lectures were directed to certain fields considered to be central to any proper appraisal of present-day population problems. The lectures provide scholarly introductions to these fields, and, with their key references to the principal relevant literature, allow the interested reader to pursue further any chosen topic. The lectures form Part I of the book.

Part II comprises papers presented at a Workshop Weekend on 16–18 March 1973, which commenced with the last lecture. It was designed to provide a forum for a fuller discussion of certain problems posed by the probable population size of the United Kingdom in the year A.D. 2001. The Workshop allowed the presentation of a series of shorter, more specialist papers before an

invited audience, and an opportunity for discussion in small groups
of topics raised directly or by implication in the lectures. Many of
the papers represent new studies and arise from different academic
disciplines.

Wolfson College is particularly grateful to the joint sponsors for
their support and for making it possible to bring together such a
group of contributors, and to Professor D. V. Glass, F.R.S.,
F.B.A. and Mr. E. Grebenik for their wise suggestions in the
formulation of the lecture series; to Mr. Michael Argyle, Mr. John
Guillebaud, Dr. R. W. Hiorns, Mr. K. E. Hunt, Mr. G. T. Jones,
and Dr. Sheila Callender for acting as rapporteurs of the Workshop sessions; and to Mr. A. Hourani, Fellow of St. Antony's
College, for so kindly arranging for Mr. Musallam's contribution.
The organizers are particularly indebted to Dr. Christopher
Perrins, and to Mrs. Beryl Schweder and the Wolfson College
office staff for their help in making the arrangements.

Professor Glass wishes to thank Dr. S. Thapar and Mr. J.
Hobcraft, who computed data used in his lectures. Dr. Seers
would like to thank Richard Stanton for research assistance. Dr.
Berelson would like to thank his colleagues on the U.S. Population
Council staff, and particularly Dorothy Nortman, K. S. Strikantan,
Jeroen Van Ginneken, and P. John Ross. The Oxford and Reading
Conservation Society would like to thank Cherry Branwell, Jean
Dearnley, and Keith Freeman for help with their survey.

The editor is especially grateful to Mr. F. W. Jessup, C.B.E.,
for his assistance, at very short notice, with the editing.

Oxford   H. B. P.
May, 1973

Contents

Contents   ix

PART I
Population size and its determinants

I.I. Introduction

H. B. PARRY

Wolfson College and Nuffield Institute for Medical Research, Oxford University

MANY aspects of the rapid increases in the human populations of many countries in this century, and especially since 1945, have been widely discussed [1–4]†. The purpose of the lectures contained in this book is to provide a background of critical scientific evidence against which the non-specialist citizen, be he academic or non-academic, may develop an informed view regarding a subject which is central to so many problems—social, economic, and political—now besetting vast regions of the world. It is not intended that these lectures and the following Workshop Discussion should attempt to cover the whole range of considerations relevant to any assessment of world population now and in the centuries to come. Two such assessments have been published recently, and have received wide attention; one by *The Ecologist* [5] and one commissioned by the 'Club of Rome' [6] and based on studies at the Massachusetts Institute of Technology. While there is considerable support from biological scientists [5] for the view that there is serious risk of impending irreversible damage to our environment by population pressures, it is no less clear that many social scientists would dissent from such an extreme view [7]. Furthermore, the projections made in the 1960s of probable trends in the populations of the developed countries may prove to be too high, if the trends calculated from the data of the 1970s in the United Kingdom [8, 9] and elsewhere [10] are borne out by subsequent experience.

It seemed most useful to restrict our survey to those aspects of demography where generally acceptable quantitative scientific knowledge could be assembled and where, if present, important lacunae in our knowledge might be defined. In such a dispassionate review it was hoped to find some guidance in adopting a prudent attitude towards any country's population size and

† Throughout the book references are at the end of each chapter.

population policies. However, if no such guidance should emerge then one must conclude that it is reasonable to await more information, being careful not to prejudge the issue.

During geological time most animal populations have probably come into ecological balance with their environment, although very few examples have been examined in detail [11]. Professor Varley describes from his own work on the winter moth the subtle interplay of many factors—food supply, microclimate, predators, disease, parasitic infestations, and competition between individuals for available resources—which in their total effect determine the winter moth population from year to year in one habitat and stabilize it over a period of years. As Professor Varley goes on to discuss, the removal of one constraint on population, such as predation especially on some higher mammals, or the increase of another, such as infectious disease in human populations, may lead to rapid alterations in numbers. It is perhaps relevant to recall instances of the impact of infectious disease on the populations of Western Europe as recently as the eighteenth century. The population of Marseilles and Provence was devastated by the last great plague epidemic in Western Europe in 1720–2, when many areas lost up to 60 per cent of their population [12]; while Chambers [13] concludes that 60 per cent of all children born in the Vale of Trent in England in the mid-eighteenth century died before adulthood, and he attributes a major component of the increase of population in England in the latter half of the eighteenth century to the decline in mortality from infectious diseases, notably smallpox [14]. Cassen [15] mentions similar situations arising in this century in India.

In human tribal communities there are grounds for supposing a complex of constraints of a socio-religious and economic character, which reinforce the basic population constraints recognized as acting on animal populations, and together tend to stabilize a small population within its traditional territory or support base [16]. Such populations may be termed ecologically stabilized or in ecological equilibrium. The prime difficulty is that few such societies have been studied adequately enough to establish firmly that population stabilization did in fact occur.

Mr. Ardener draws on his experience of African societies since 1945 in emphasizing the difficulties in establishing whether or not any causal relationship exists between group behaviour and the deliberate determination of population within an ethnicity. He wisely draws attention to the many pitfalls which bedevil studies in this field, in which reliable data on the attitudes, motivation and the outcome of sexual activity are so peculiarly difficult to assemble [26, 27]. The implication for studies of complex developed communities is a counsel of caution in making causal inferences to the quantitative impacts of socio-individual factors on population determination.

Furthermore, the difficulties of defining what precisely is meant by the concept of 'population' in a small-scale community underlines an important aspect of population statistics of large-scale developed communities, which are related firmly to the nation-state and based on politically defined territories. These communities, however, represent the sum total of a great many social units whose reproductive performances may vary greatly within a country, and even within a religious sector of a country [17].

Professor Brass surveys the data on population size of nation-states with developed communities, census data, and estimates of world population. He draws attention to the composite nature of a national population enumeration, the inherent difficulties in making forecasts of population trends based on present information, and the lack of information on the many subtle factors determining the completed family size. The latter may vary widely between different sectors of the community, e.g. consider the very high fertility of the Hutterite immigrants in North America. However, the gaps in our knowledge regarding the determinants of completed family size are so extensive that Professor Brass considers it is not practicable to attempt to operate a population policy for a national developed community; we cannot forecast with sufficient accuracy what the population trend is likely to be without or with the policy, and hence we have no satisfactory way of assessing the impact of any explicit population policy. The best we can do is to monitor the population size, to watch for small changes in those parameters which are the most important determinants of future total population size, and update any forecasts of future trends as frequently as possible.

Professor Glass examines in detail the factors which have influenced, and are influencing, the population sizes of developed countries, particularly since 1930, and the frequency with which differing trends tend to be countervailing. He draws attention to the gradual changes in social attitudes towards family limitation, which, in time, have become part 'of customary reproductive behaviour' of large sections of society in the United Kingdom. With improved medical services, the effects of small fluctuations in fertility have become the overriding determinant of future population size. The current period fertility rate of 2·4 live births per woman is likely to lead to a population increase in the United Kingdom of ½ per cent p.a. with a doubling in 150 years; this is surely a sustainable rate of increase. The aim in the United Kingdom (and other developed countries) should be to attain a near-stationary or fluctuating-stationary population, based on the present population size. While there is no formally explicit population policy in the United Kingdom, there is a policy implicit in much social and tax legislation. It is probably prudent to continue in this way, to carry out socially desirable changes—such as reforms in education, the employment of women, and housing—and await their cumulative effect on population trends, whilst also scrutinizing the expanding aspirations of an affluent society [18].

Professor Ohlin provides a critical examination of the principal economic considerations which relate to population size and its impact on the environment in developed countries. He draws attention once again to the very complex and capricious nature of the determinants of fertility and hence to the inherent difficulties of forecasting trends in, and deliberately influencing, population size. The impact of world population size on the environment is not due so much to its rate of increase (1 per cent p.a.) as to the increase in consumer-demand expectation. For non-renewable primary resources and energy, this expectation is increasing at 7 per cent p.a. [19, 20] and carries with it the accompanying pollution and and ecological damage associated with industrial effluents and urban agglomerations [21]. These problems are probably amenable to adequate control, at a price, but the case against economic growth largely rests on an aesthetic judgement as to the desired environment and 'life-style'. Population size is not the crucial determinant: in developed countries, the expected *per capita* consumption of economic resources and the impact of that consumption on environmental aesthetics are vastly more important.

The crux of the problem of population size in developed countries relates to the conservation of resources for posterity; the crux in the developing countries is the decline in present mortality rates and the gross demographic and economic dysequilibria which this decline will cause within a generation.

Professor Seers deals with the problems of the 'poor' developing countries, many of which are showing very rapid rates of population increase. This increase is especially marked in rural communities, and amongst immigrants into urban centres from these communities. In rural areas opportunities for education and the non-domestic employment of women are very limited, and efforts to improve the status of women have made little impact. There may be scope for increasing agricultural yields in favoured areas, but the long-term effects of the introduction of high-yielding cereals, the so-called 'green revolution', seem unlikely to fulfil the original expectations [22]. In these circumstances population policies designed to limit further growth assume great importance; without them economic development and capital accumulation will be unable to keep abreast, let alone move ahead, of the continuing increase of people.

A recurrent comment in the lectures is the importance, for determining reproductive attainment, of the individual's attitudes towards sexuality. There is very great difficulty in obtaining reliable, comprehensive, and quantitative data in this area, which is subject to so many imponderable and very personal decisions. Professor Illsley provides new and penetrating insights into the factors affecting decisions on individual fertility, based on studies in Aberdeen over the last 20 years. In the past such decisions on fertility have been influenced greatly by the socio-religious and politico-economic beliefs of the society, community, or group to which the individual belonged [23, 24, 25], but now decisions on individual fertility represent a response at the personal, as distinct from the group, level. The decisions are taken in pursuit of personal goals constantly varying in character and importance, and indeed are influenced by the individual's current ideology and life-style. In advanced industrialized societies changes in mean completed family size are most likely to result from modification of these preferred personal goals.

The lecture by Dr. Berelson provides a comprehensive review of the programmes of population limitation in many parts of the world, notably in the poorer countries, where (as Professor Seers pointed out) constraints on population growth are very important for future economic and social well-being. The Population Council

of New York, of which Dr. Berelson is President, has played a
dynamic role in the initiation, support, and development of these
programmes, many of which are now achieving most encouraging
results. Dr. Berelson stresses the importance of basic social change
going hand-in-hand with socio-medical methods of fertility control, and indeed the close integration of family-planning programmes with economic development plans. His paper provides a
wealth of data on the implementation of methods of family
limitation, notably those used in the developing countries but many
also of worldwide relevance.

REFERENCES

1. BRASS, W. (1970). The growth of world population. In *Population
   control* (ed. A. Allison), pp. 131–51. Pelican original. Penguin
   Books, Harmondsworth; Int. Monet. Fund and World Bk. Gr.
   (1973). *Fin. Develop.* **10**, No. 4, 2–26.
2. GREBENIK, E. (1972). On controlling population growth. In *Biology
   and the human sciences* (ed. J. W. S. Pringle), pp. 25–48. Clarendon
   Press, Oxford.
3. SPOONER, B. (ed.) (1972). *Population growth: anthropological implications*, pp. xxvi + 425. Mass. Inst. Tech. Press, Cambridge,
   Mass.
4. HARRISON, G. A. and BOYCE, A. J. (eds.) (1972). *The structure of
   human populations*, pp. xiii + 447. Clarendon Press, Oxford.
5. Editors of the *Ecologist* (1972). *A blueprint for survival*, pp. 139.
   Penguin Books, Harmondsworth.
6. MEADOWS, D. H., MEADOWS, D. J., RANDERS, J. and
   BEHRENS, W. W. (1972). *The limits of growth*. Earth Island
   Publications, London.
7. CLARK, C. (1970). The economic and social implications of population control. In *Population control* (ed. A. Allison), pp. 222–37.
   Penguin Books, Harmondsworth.
8. Editorial (1972). What is the future British population?, *Nature,
   Lond.* **240**, 173.
9. Registrar General's Annual Estimates of the Population of England
   and Wales and of Local Authority Areas, 1972. H.M.S.O.,
   London.
10. BERELSON, B. (ed.) (1974). *Population policy in developed countries*,
    in press. The Population Council, New York; [1a], pp. 3–7.
11a. ANDREWARTHA, H. G. (1970). Population growth and control:
     animal populations. In *Population control* (ed. A. Allison), pp.
     45–69. Penguin Books, Harmondsworth; b. SOUTHWOOD,
     T. R. E. (1970). The natural and manipulated control of animal
     populations. In *The optimum population for Britain* (ed. L. R.
     Taylor), pp. 86–102. Academic Press, London.

12. BIRABEN, J. N. (1972). Certain demographic characteristics of the plague epidemic in France, 1720–2. In *Population and social change* (eds. D. V. Glass and R. Revelle), pp. 233–42. Arnold, London.

13. CHAMBERS, J. D. (1972). *Population, economy, and society in pre-industrial England*, pp. xiii + 162. Oxford University Press, London.

14. RAZZELL, P. E. (1973). Population change in eighteenth century England: a re-appraisal. In *Population in industrialization* (ed. M. Drake), pp. 128–56. University Paperback, Methuen, London.

15. CASSEN, R. H. (1974). This volume, pp. 216–43.

16a. BENEDICT, B. (1972). Social regulation of fertility. In *The structure of human populations* (eds. G. A. Harrison and A. J. Boyce), pp. 73–89. Clarendon Press, Oxford; b. DIVALE, W. T. (1972). Systemic population control in the middle and upper paleolithic: Inferences based on contemporary hunter-gatherers. *World Archaeology*, **4**, 223–43.

17. ZELDIN, T. (1974). This volume, pp. 310–15.

18. MISHAN, E. J. (1973). To grow or not to grow, *Encounter* **40**, 9–29.

19. ANON. (1969). *Resources and man:* A study and recommendations by the Committee of Resources and Man of the Division of Earth Sciences, National Academy of Sciences and National Research Council, Washington, D.C. W. H. Freeman, San Francisco, California.

20. AKINS, J. E. (1973) The oil crisis: this time the wolf is here, *Foreign Affairs (Washington, D.C.)*, Winter No. and *Petroleum Inst. Weekly*, 27 March, pp. 1–20.

21. BOYDEN, S. (1972). Ecology in relation to urban population. In *The structure of human populations* (eds. G. A. Harrison and A. J. Boyce), pp. 411–41. Clarendon Press, Oxford.

22a. FRANKEL, F. R. (1971). *India's green revolution*. Princeton University Press, Princeton, N.J.; b. BHAVAGAN, M. R., HARA-SINGH, K., PAYNE, R. and SMITH, D. (1973). *The death of the green revolution*, pp. 13. Declaration Third World Publications, 15 Davey Road, Birmingham, B13 9NT, U.K.

23. NOONAN, J. T., JR. (1972). Intellectual and demographic history. In *Population and social change* (eds. D. V. Glass and R. Revelle), pp. 115–36. Arnold, London.

24. MUSALLAM, B. (1974). This volume, pp. 300–10.

25. ZELDIN, T. (1970). The conflict of moralities: confession, sin and pleasure in the nineteenth century. In *Conflicts in French society: anticlericalism, education and morals in the nineteenth century* (ed. T. Zeldin), pp. 13–50. St. Antony's College, Oxford, Publications No. 1. Allen and Unwin, London.

26. FORD, C. S. and BEACH, F. A. (1951). *Patterns of sexual behaviour*. Harper Bros. and Haeber, New York.

27. LÉVI-STRAUSS, C. (1968). *Structural Anthropology* (trans. C. Jacobson and B. G. Schoepf), pp. xxi + 410. Allen Lane, The Penguin Press, London. See pp. 10 *et seq.*

I.2. Animal populations and their biological constraints

G. C. VARLEY

Hope Professor of Entomology, Oxford University

IT might be thought that man and other animals are so different that population studies of animals can contribute little or nothing to an understanding of human populations; but man depends on plant growth and on other animals for food, just as many other kinds of animals do. In fact, methods used for analysing some insect populations are being usefully modified and applied to populations of birds and mammals, and might help to simplify our understanding of the complexities of human population statistics.

Zoologists like myself take the view that we may be able to discuss more intelligently the problems of human population on the planet Earth if we understand how populations of plants and animals interact. Already we face very big dilemmas, which may become worse if the alleviation of the constraints which now affect us make long-term solutions of future problems more difficult. In this category come those solutions to the problem of human hunger which seek only to provide more food. If more food is the only relief provided now, conditions may be established for bigger and more intractable famines later.

Towards the end of the eighteenth century Malthus became concerned about the rising population of Great Britain, and he predicted that 'misery and vice' would follow unless population increase was halted. In 1801 this persuaded the government of the day to start a census. Since then—some eight generations later—his prediction appears to have been falsified, because, although the population has risen five-fold, living standards have risen. Malthus had failed to foresee the Industrial Revolution. In his day, windmills, waterwheels, and horses provided the main supplements to human muscle. International trade, largely in luxury goods, moved by sail. The use of fossil fuel to run the railways and the steamships transformed this situation, and thus cheap food and heavy goods could be brought from the ends of the earth.

In the face of these enormous changes in transport and the use of fossil fuel, the basic effects of increasing population size are hard to demonstrate. It is from the study of animals that we can get some idea of the effects for which to look. I propose first to examine the constraints on animal populations, and then to tell you something about what Oxford ecologists have learned of some of the animals in Wytham Wood. Lastly, I want to draw some general conclusions and see how they might be applied to the study of human populations.

For small insects like flour beetles we can provide almost ideal

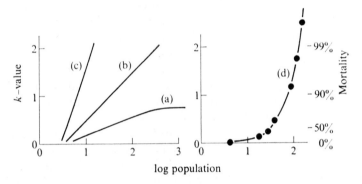

FIG. 1. The killing power or *k*-value measures the adverse effect of a density-dependent factor on a logarithmic scale. The scale on the right is the equivalent percentage mortality. The theoretical curves (a)–(c) represent: (a) undercompensation; (b) exact compensation; (c) over-compensation; (d) Competition for 10 g food by different numbers of larvae of the sheep blowfly shows overcompensation when very crowded. (Data from Nicholson 1954.)

living conditions in a small container. The beetles can be sifted out from the flour and counted at regular intervals, and at each sifting the flour can be renewed. We find that after a generation or two the beetle population rises to a maximum; then there is no further increase and the numbers remain approximately constant. The crowded beetles not only produce far fewer eggs than un-crowded beetles, but they also indulge in cannibalism! Misery and vice have set in, much as Malthus predicted. This crowding acts as a density-dependent factor which affects the population more and more adversely as the population density of the beetles rises.

Density-dependent effects are very important in regulating

animal populations; but not every kind of mortality which increases its relative effect as population density rises will stabilize a population. It is simplest to consider a population which has separate, synchronized generations which can easily be arranged experimentally; suitable real examples are to be found in the many insects with an annual life-cyle. If we express the population on a logarithmic scale it is very convenient to express the mortality caused by crowding by the logarithmic change it causes in the population. This is the *killing power* or *k*-value. When the *k*-value is plotted against the logarithm of the population density on which it acts, a line such as (b) in Fig. 1 represents a density-dependent factor which exactly compensates for population change within the generation. Line (a) undercompensates and line (c) over-compensates for population changes. Nicholson [8] experimented with the sheep blowfly in Australia. On a fixed ration of 10 g of food, the ability of newly hatched larvae to grow and become flies varied with their initial numbers. When the mortality is expressed as the *k*-value and plotted against the logarithm of the initial number (Fig. 1, line (d)) the density-dependent nature of the mortality caused by crowding becomes clear. At high populations there is severe overcompensation. So it is not surprising that when Nicholson performed another kind of population experiment in which a fixed ration of food was added daily to a cage of sheep blowflies, the population was very unstable. Numbers in the cage rose rapidly to 3000 flies (Fig. 2(a)). They laid so many eggs on the small dish of meat that there was insufficient for any larvae to survive. Only when nearly all the adult flies had become too old to lay eggs was the daily egg production low enough for a lot of larvae to grow and form puparia. This new generation began to emerge as flies some time after all the parental flies were dead. The population of puparia graphed in Fig. 2(a) fluctuated with extreme violence because the density-dependent larval mortality grossly overcompensated for population change, and so failed to regulate the population in a stable manner. The population was much more stable when Nicholson killed off 99 per cent of the flies as they became adult (Fig.2 (b)), because this reduced the effective rate of increase to much less than ten-fold per generation. This could be predicted from the form of the curve (d) in Fig. 1.

Predators and their prey tend to reach a fairly stable equilibrium. Game and lions are both abundant in many of the African

National Parks. Where man has interfered, the effects have sometimes been serious. In the Kaibab Forest in Arizona the deer [6] had been more or less in balance with their main predators, the puma and the wolf, but, when these predators were removed, the deer increased twenty-fold and depleted their food supply so severely that they starved in the winter.

Man himself acts as a major predator of many game animals, and they are protected from overexploitation by various restrictions on hunting; there are close seasons, limitation on hunting

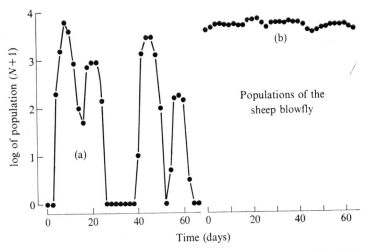

FIG. 2. Populations of the sheep blowfly supplied with 50 g larval food per day. Food for the adult flies was in excess of needs. The population of viable pupae was counted daily. In (a) the emerging flies were added to the population. In (b) only 1 per cent of the merging flies were added and 99 per cent were destroyed.

methods, and so on. Although man is beginning to learn the need to prohibit irresponsible hunting on land, and has been able to plan the exploitation of some island seal colonies by careful management, this is hard to organize where there is no recognized land tenure. At sea, overfishing is widespread, especially in the case of the larger whales which graze the plankton of the southern oceans. When they began to become rare, the whalers' reaction to falling catches was to increase their efforts and to use bigger factory ships and faster craft to carry the harpoon guns. As whaling can remain fairly profitable by exploiting the smaller species of whale, the large species are in serious danger of extinction. Predator and prey can reach a balance only if the predator reduces its hunting when the prey population falls below the equilibrium level.

Fatal diseases are probably important in the regulation of many animal species, but unless a sudden change occurs their effects may go unrecorded. Such diseases may arise from infections by viruses, bacteria, and fungi and from many kinds of parasitic worms. A sudden epidemic of a new disease dramatically changed the status of the rabbit in Australia and in Britain [10]. The myxoma virus was apparently native to South America, and the rabbits there were immune. In Australia, where the rabbits were susceptible, its introduction was catastrophic because the disease was quickly transmitted from one rabbit to another by bloodsucking mosquitoes, but by 1958 the Australian rabbits had largely become immune to the original virus. There is also a possibility that, because the mosquitoes would bite sick rabbits but not dead ones, the method of transmission favoured a benign strain of the virus. Now the rabbits in Australia still suffer from the disease, but it is not often fatal. In Britain, the main carrier of myxomatosis has been the rabbit flea, which is most likely to carry infection to a new rabbit if the host is killed so that the infected flea is forced to seek another live rabbit from which to feed. This has favoured the spread of a relatively virulent form of myxomatosis, and resistance to the disease has developed more slowly than in Australia. The disease is now endemic in Britain, and keeps the rabbit population at a low level in many areas.

A fatal disease of salmon, known as ulcerative dermal necrosis (UDN), was found in South-west Ireland [7] in the winter of 1964–5. Many of the big fish running up the rivers to spawn were found dead. Within 5 years the disease had spread to most salmon rivers in the United Kingdom. There is still disagreement as to the nature of the causative organism, whether it is viral, bacterial, or fungal, because all are found associated with the lesions on the dying fish. It was feared that this disease would seriously reduce the salmon catches, and indeed the figures for the numbers of salmon caught by various means in Scottish waters have shown a fall from 270 000 in 1967, the year by which all the main Scottish rivers were affected, to just over 160 000 in 1971. Is the conclusion justified that the fall in the catch is the result of disease? Unfortunately, other factors enter into the story. Fig. 3 shows that there was a similar fall in the catch recorded between 1959 and 1961 for which disease cannot be held responsible. This inherent variability makes it hard to assess the contribution of the disease, especially as a new factor has appeared in the records. A salmon

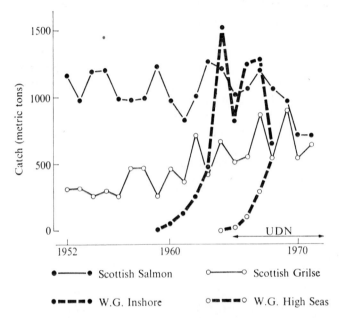

FIG. 3. Changes in salmon catches in Scotland in relation to the salmon disease (UDN). Salmon are the larger fish which have completed the migration to Greenland and back. Grilse are younger smaller fish which have not migrated. Any effect of UDN on the Scottish fishery is obscured by the rapid growth of a fishery in West Greenland (W.G.), which catches feeding salmon of both Canadian and British origin. The basic figures up to 1969 are published in *The Salmon Net* (June 1970), pp. 43–53.

fishing industry has begun at sea off Greenland, and in 1964, 1966, 1967, and 1968 the tonnage caught was greater than the total Scottish catch. (I have no records since then.) If the salmon population is regulated mainly at the juvenile stage in streams, then a severe fall (caused by UDN) in the number of eggs laid might have little effect on the numbers of two-year-old fish going to sea. In contrast, the catching of a percentage of the feeding fish off Greenland might cause a proportionate reduction in the European catch.

Fatal diseases which affect both man and animals are described and documented in a recent book on trypanosomiasis [3]. Trypanosomes are minute protozoa which infect the blood of various mammals. They are endemic in the wild game in parts of Africa and are transmitted by tsetse flies to domestic animals and man. The trypanosomes are usually fatal to horses and to European breeds of cattle, but native cattle are more resistant. In man, the trypanosomes cause sleeping sickness. Ford describes how the accidental introduction of the viral disease rinderpest into Africa about 1889 killed off much of the game and domestic animals over a period of time, and the game did not recover for nearly four decades. The increase of the game made conditions suitable for both a rise and an extension of the tsetse-fly population. In turn, the tsetse fly transmitted trypanosomes to both domestic animals and man, especially in the 1930s when a very serious epidemic of sleeping sickness caused the decay of many West African tribes. In spite of medical and veterinary precautions there are still big tracts of Africa in which the presence of tsetse flies makes livestock farming hazardous.

I now want to come nearer home and tell you something about the animals in Wytham Wood, which came into the possession of the University very largely through the foresight of Charles Elton. There we have an area where many ecologists have been able to study the populations of various creatures, some of which may be familiar to you through the B.B.C. Horizon film 'The Wood'.

Some of the work has been continued by my staff and a series of research students for more than 25 years. We have been able to make census counts of many species [11], and perform experiments of a kind which would be impossible with human populations.

I chose to study the winter moth on oaks at Wytham because the insect has one generation a year and is very abundant, indeed, its caterpillars were numerous enough to defoliate most of the oaks in 1948. The moth is also easy to count [13]. The flightless female moths climb to the tree tops to lay their eggs, and it is easy to trap a sample as they go up the trunks. The fully grown caterpillars spin down from the foliage to pupate in the earth. They can be intercepted in metal trays, their identity checked, and then they can be dissected and examined for parasites. These parasites are similar to those which are used in the biological control of insect pests. They are either parasitic flies, like *Cyzenis*, or parasitic hymenoptera, many different species of which attack the eggs, larvae, and pupae of the winter moth. The results of the caterpillar census can be presented as a histogram, which shows how many of the caterpillars in each year were attacked by different parasites,

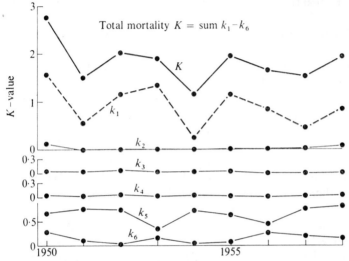

FIG. 4. Key factor analysis of nine life-tables for the winter moth. In the life-tables, six types of mortality act in succession. The killing power of each is expressed on a logarithmic scale as the k-value. k_1 affects eggs and first-stage larvae. k_2–k_4 affect large larvae and are parasitism by *Cyzenis*, miscellaneous parasites, and a protozoan respectively. Pupae die because of pupal predation k_5 and pupal parasitism k_6. The key factor is k_1. Its changes are more than enough to explain the changes in total mortality K.

and demonstrates what a small proportion of them eventually emerged as adults, to be captured in the nets on the tree trunks. But we have found another way to express the results which is more meaningful. When the change in numbers within a genera-tion is expressed on a logarithmic scale, this change represents the killing power of whatever has caused the mortality (the k-value). When we plot a graph [14] of the annual changes in each k-value and of the total generation mortality K, which is the sum of the k-values which have acted in succession (Fig. 4) we, can at once answer the question: What are the most important causes of change in the mortality from generation to generation? We call the biggest variable the key factor. This turned out to be what we have called 'winter disappearance'; this expresses the difference between the number of eggs estimated to have been available in the winter and the number of fully fed larvae which we find in May. We know that this loss is related to the timing of the bud-burst of individual trees and that many newly hatched larvae fail to get food and die because the majority of oak buds open very late, after the winter-moth eggs have hatched. So far we have failed to predict the year-to-year changes in this winter disappearance, but it is clear that winter disappearance contains the key factor which determines population change.

We call this graphical process 'key-factor analysis'. It serves an additional function: we can see which other components of the generation mortality are important, and which are small enough or vary so little that their effect on population change is negligible.

The key factor determines population change. On a logarithmic scale the populations of a number of oak-feeding insects changed in rather similar ways—probably because the same key factor was affecting many of them in the same way—but the populations of the different species were at very different levels. What regulates the level about which the population of each species fluctuates? This is likely to be some density-dependent factor, which we may discover by graphing the k-values against the population density on which they have acted [13]. For the winter moth only one mortality factor—pupal predation—is clearly density-dependent, and we are satisfied that this is largely caused by predatory beetles, with some help from shrews, moles, and mice. Whilst we were investigating the attacks by predators on winter-moth pupae, we also found that some pupae had been parasitized and contained larvae of the ichneumonid wasp *Cratichneumon culex*. We already knew this wasp as an adult insect, because in one year as many as 50 had emerged per square metre and had been counted in our traps; but until then we had no idea that it was a regular parasite of the winter moth.

There has been a lot of argument about the way in which parasitic insects seek their hosts. We knew from experience of biological control that under favourable conditions parasitic insects can regulate a pest species at a low population density, but there was no satisfactory explanation at a theoretical level. The published mathematical theories were too simple, and none gave a realistic description of the kind of thing that was observed. Dr. Hassell, who had worked on *Cyzenis* at Wytham, went to Berkeley in 1968 and analysed with Dr. Huffaker the results of a big experiment with *Nemeritis*, an ichneumonid parasite of the caterpillars of the common flour moth. *Nemeritis* searched for its host caterpillars much less efficiently when crowded than when at a low population density. It had not been suspected that mutual interference between adult parasites could be so important, but when this effect was incorporated into a mathematical model for parasite attack we found that there could be a stable balance between host and parasite [4].

Using this information from California about parasite behaviour we have constructed a population model which describes the changes in the number of winter moth and its two main parasites, the fly *Cyzenis* and the ichneumonid wasp *Cratichneumon*. For each of the parasites we use two constants: the 'quest constant' from local observation and the 'mutual interference constant', fitting the rather inaccurate local observations but based, at least in principle, on the measurements for the other species in California. The pupal predation is represented by a simple density-dependent factor. The key factor, winter disappearance, which we have been unable to describe by any sub-model, is put into the calculations as the observed value. The calculation starts from observed population figures for the three species in 1950, and its outcome matches with surprising accuracy the changes in the populations of winter moth and its two parasites [12]. We had tried many different kinds of model in the hope of matching our observations, but we failed to get a good fit until we included density-dependent effects acting directly on each of the three species concerned.

Other kinds of animal which have been studied at Wytham

The animals at Wytham which have been counted in some detail include the titmice, especially great tits and blue tits, which nest in boxes provided by David Lack and his associates of the Edward Grey Institute of Field Ornithology. In the breeding season titmice feed their young on winter moth and other caterpillars.

The caterpillars of winter moth are fully grown by late May, and after that time the amount of food available to these birds on the oak trees diminishes rapidly to a low level. The reason why oaks provided such an abundant supply of caterpillars only when the leaves were still small did not become clear until Paul Feeny [2], who had been trained in Oxford first as a chemist and then as a zoologist, measured the amount of tannin in oak leaves. The tiny leaves contain little tannin, but by the time they have reached full size 1 per cent of their dry weight is tannin, and the proportion rises to about 5 per cent by the end of the summer. Now tannin reacts with proteins and denatures them. Digestive enzymes are proteins, and Feeny showed that oak tannin added to an artificial diet had a very adverse effect on the digestive processes of caterpillars. This is why almost all species which are common on oak complete their feeding in May or very early in June. The migrant and resident birds which feed on insects have evolved a breeding season which corresponds with this temporary superabundance of food. Krebs [5] has analysed the changing titmouse populations using methods derived from those described for the winter moth; at first sight the key factor appeared to be the varying survival from year to year in the period when the young birds were first independent. Although there was a sign of a feeble density-dependent effect of crowding of nestlings within the nest, there seemed to be no sign that territorial behaviour was density-dependent. Yet when Krebs tested this experimentally the result was entirely unexpected. In an isolated piece of woodland where each bird was recognizable because it was ringed, Krebs had waited until, early in the breeding season, all the pairs of birds had set up territories. Then he removed all the marked titmice. Within a very few days exactly the same number of pairs of birds had reoccupied the territories! This convincingly demonstrated that there must have been a reservoir of birds, which up till then had eluded observation, prevented from occupying the spare nest boxes in the area simply by the territorial behaviour of the resident birds.

Southern [9] counted both tawny owls and their favoured food, the mice and voles, at Wytham. The food requirements of the owls could be estimated, and likewise the amount of food made available by the voles and mice. On the average the owls required 5000 kcal ha^{-1} [11], and the production of the mice and voles was estimated to be only 3000. Only when the small mammals were unusually abundant were there enough to satisfy the owls, which then laid well and reared two or three owlets each. In years when food was scarce, the owls kept alive by eating alternative food such as earthworms, but on this inadequate diet they either laid no eggs, or, if they did, the young starved. From this alone we might expect that the owl population was very dependent on food supply; but the breeding population scarcely varied at all

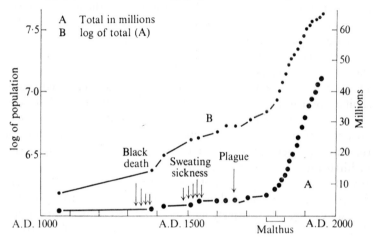

FIG. 5. The population figures in England and Wales before 1800 are from Carr-Saunders [1] and the information about human epidemics from Zinsser [15]. Curve A is the population number in millions. Curve B shows the log of this population number.

from year to year. The owls survived under adverse conditions, but when food was abundant, the excess young owls were driven out by territorial behaviour.

Applications to man

We have seen for animals that both the quality and quantity of available food are very important. We must also distinguish clearly between the factors which cause population change and the factors which regulate population level. It is particularly unfortunate that in economic entomology the word control is used indiscriminately for these two processes. The populations are regulated by density-dependent effects which act either through mortality and changes in birth rate or through mutual interference and territorial behaviour, which lead to emigration.

If we look at the population of England and Wales (Fig. 5) it must be clear that until, in the time of Malthus, a countrywide census was begun in 1801, the figures are based on a few rough estimates from various sources, which can be found in Carr-Saunders [1]. The graph on an arithmetical scale is hard to interpret. When replotted on a logarithmic scale the changes in the rate of exponential growth become clear. There was a very sudden increase in population growth rate at about 1800, but since then the rate has somewhat diminished. An oversimple way to look at the causes of change is to graph the birth rates and death rates. Death rates have fallen fairly steadily as medical knowledge and sanitary precautions have been improved. The birth rate has been subject to much more acute changes. The P.E.P. report of 1947 on population made five projections which seemed reasonable at the time. However, they did not foresee the sudden postwar rise in birth rate, and the actual population has remained well above any of their five projections. Later in 1972 *Population Projections No. 2, 1971–2011* was published by H.M.S.O.; in this publication we can see the relatively enormous effect within a little more than a generation of assuming different fixed values for fertility and mortality.

We have seen that for the winter moth we could identify the main cause of population change by key-factor analysis (Fig. 4). This method has already been adapted for use with birds and mammals in which mature adults have a well-defined breeding season but survive to breed in a number of successive years. The difficulty in applying this approach to human populations is that breeding is not seasonal: perhaps the comparison of a series of cohort life-tables taken to represent the population at intervals of 10 or 20 years might show how far the observed changes in population growth rate since 1800 depend on changes in infant mortality, survival to maturity, age of female parent at peak of reproduction, and completed family size. The population present at any time will also be influenced by the length of the post-reproductive life and by immigration and emigration; all of which could be incorporated into graphs like that shown in Fig. 4.

For animal populations the identification of density-dependent effects is very important. For the winter moth we did not get good agreement with observed population figures until the population model included density-dependent effects acting separately on the winter moth and each of its two main parasites. The identification of density-dependent effects is far more difficult for human populations, because a method of correlation is needed. Of recent times nearly all local human populations have only increased in numbers, and many other essential conditions have also changed monotonically during the same period, so that almost everything measured will be correlated with population change. However, it is impossible to discover by these methods which condition is really causal in determining population size. The long-term problem for man is how to manage his own population so that the very unpleasant density-dependent effects like epidemic disease and famine can be avoided. It is encouraging that observed birth rates are so labile, because it implies that they are now greatly affected by social policy and economic circumstances. For a positive population policy we need to know how social legislation indirectly influences both human behaviour and personal motivation, which determines the age of marriage and the desired family size under present conditions.

REFERENCES

1. CARR-SAUNDERS, A. M. (1922). *The population problem; a study in human evolution*, Clarendon Press, Oxford. pp. 516.
2. FEENY, P. P. (1970). Seasonal changes in oak leaf tannins and nutriments as a cause of spring feeding by winter moth caterpillars, *Ecology* **51**, 565–81.
3. FORD, J. (1971). *The role of the trypanosomiases in African ecology— a study of the tsetse fly problem*, pp. 568. Clarendon Press, Oxford.
4. HASSELL, M. P. and VARLEY, G. C. (1969). A new inductive population model for insect parasites and its bearing on biological control, *Nature, Lond.* **223**, 1133–7.
5. KREBS, J. (1971). Territory and breeding density in the great tit, *Parus major, Ecology* **52**, 2–22.
6. LEOPOLD, A. (1943). Deer irruptions, *Wisc. Conserv. Bull.*, August 1943. (Reprinted in *Wisc. Conserv. Dep. Pub.* **321**, 1–11.)
7. MILLS, D. (1971). *Salmon and trout: a resource, its ecology, conservation and management.* Oliver and Boyd, Edinburgh.
8. NICHOLSON, A. J. (1954). An outline of the dynamics of animal populations, *Aust. J. Zool.* **2**, 9–65.
9. SOUTHERN, H. N. (1970). The natural control of a population of tawny owls (*Strix aluco*), *J. Zool., Lond.* **162**, 197–285.

10. THOMPSON, H. V. and WORDEN, A. N. (1956). *The rabbit*. New Naturalist Monograph No. 13. Collins, London.
11. VARLEY, G. C. (1970). The concept of energy flow applied to a woodland community. In *Animal population in relation to their food requirements*. British Ecological Society Symposium No. 10 (ed. A Watson), pp. 389–404. Blackwell's Scientific Publications, Oxford.
12. —— (1971). The need for life tables for parasites and predators. In *Concepts of pest management*, (eds. R. L. Rabb and F. E. Guthrie), pp. 59–68. Raleigh, North Carolina, U.S.A.
13. —— (1971). The effects of natural predators and parasites on winter moth populations in England, *Proc. Tall Timbers Conference on ecological animal control by habitat management, February 1970*, pp. 103–16. Tallahassee, U.S.A.
14. —— and GRADWELL, G. R. (1960). Key factors in population studies, *J. Anim. Ecol.* **29**, 399–401.
15. ZINSSER, H. (1935). *Rats, lice and history*, pp. i–xii, 1–301. Routledge, London.

I.3. Social anthropology and population

EDWIN ARDENER

Institute of Social Anthropology, Oxford University

Introduction

In any series of lectures on population there comes (somewhere between the animal populations and the great population explosions of relatively recent times) the lecture on supposed small-scale, archaic, or pre-modern human groups. Formerly these would have been boldly called 'primitive' or 'savage' at one of their extremes and 'peasant' at the other. In this series the title originally offered to me was 'Tribal Communities'. Whatever they are termed, the social anthropologist's contribution is commonly, but wrongly, seen in the present context as in some degree historical or pre-historical. In population studies the anthropological subject matter has been seen as a bridge between biological and industrial man.

It would have been easy today, therefore, to survey briefly the range of demographic studies of exotic populations made by social anthropologists and others. But to do that on this occasion would be to repeat some extremely recent publications indeed. In particular: the contributions to the excellent volume edited by Dr. Harrison and Dr. Boyce [30] are, or should be, the essential background reading for much of this lecture series. Fortunately, as far as I am concerned, some of the main topics and many telling ethnographic examples are, as it were, elegantly pre-empted by many of the contributors therein. That leaves me the opportunity to consider some wider questions raised by our researches. There was a time when it was necessary to make some propaganda for quantified demographic studies in social anthropology—for there has been an on-and-off relationship with statistics over the years. That necessity has dwindled away—we are perhaps now in a different danger of mistaking the lessons of the studies we have. Eleven years ago I wrote:

It may be suspected perhaps that in some societies interpreted through institutional and value systems alone, without detailed attention to demographic factors, anthropologists may have sometimes attributed to the fly [travelling on the axle of the chariot] the momentum of the chariot wheel. [4: p. vii].

There was much talk at that time, for example, of the relative roles of matrilineal and patrilineal kinship systems as determinants of marital stability or instability. Demographic data were brought into the discussions. As time went on the marital stability question was subsumed in more powerful anthropological models of alliance and exchange. Using these approaches it is interesting to note that the recent demographic analyses of Chagnon for the Yanomamö of South America [19] are totally different in conception from those done, under the stimulus of Barnes [10], Mitchell [36], and other pioneer specialists, in Africa. In changes of this sort the definition of what is 'demographic' has also changed. Social anthropologists can see these intellectual processes a little more easily in their studies, because they can take nothing for granted in their subject matter. But problems uncovered during the critical period of change in anthropological theory, inspired usually by other than demographic preoccupations, are of quite general interest: Are the entities called 'populations' *names* or *numbers*? If names: named for whom, and by whom? If numbers: counted by whom, and for whom? In asking the questions 'by whom?' and 'for whom?' we also ask in particular: by or for the 'people' concerned? Or by or for the anthropologist or other scientific observer?

The problem of the sorts of entity that populations are could not be better stated (in order, unfortunately, to be put aside) than by Dr. Harrison and Dr. Boyce: 'Because there are many factors determining the ways populations are *defined* . . . the situation may be much more like a *continuum of overlapping categories* than a series of clusters.' They continue: 'However, whilst it is possible to conceptualize populations in these terms, in practical considerations populations *are recognized according to some particular component which is of interest*. And the major components on which interest focuses are demographic, genetic, social, and ecological' [30: p. 3, my italics]. This lecture will occupy the conceptual space between these two sentences. We shall be concerned with the light that anthropological studies can throw on terms like 'determinants of population size', even of 'population' itself. For this week at least, humanity will look slightly more independent of supposed raw demographic trends than I am sure it will look in later lectures, but no less vulnerable because of that. I shall be arguing that all human aggregates have 'folk demographies', on the one hand, and, on the other, that our vast bodies of numerical data do not necessarily build a culture-free or neutral demographic science.

Ethnic self-definition

I may as well say at the outset then that there is no entity that 'tribal community' consistently labels. There is already a considerable literature on 'tribe' and 'tribalism' [25, 37, 13, 20]. The term 'ethnicity' has of late risen from the ruins of controversy [12, 42, 5]. But new 'ethnicities' are not simply old 'tribes' writ large. To some lay persons they seem to deserve the adjective 'atavistic' rather than 'primitive'—often seated in cities as much as in jungles [20]. So let us begin with the question: If we do not know what a tribal community is, how can we say anything sensible about its population? You might well try the answer that commonsense approximations already exist which at least throw light on the question. For example, General Custer made a supposedly adequate estimate of the number of Sioux. I shall agree that demographic statements have been attached to tribal labels. I shall suggest that it is not accidental that our evidence derives from the preoccupations of Custer rather than from the requirements of Sitting Bull. For there is hardly a 'tribe' of which you have heard, which does not present problems of exact definition. Take the Yanomamö case, that I have mentioned:

They are divided into approximately 125 widely scattered villages. Many . . . villages have yet to be seen by outsiders [on] essentially unexplored rivers.

Further, there is 'considerable variation in the tribe, in a cultural linguistic, and biological sense' [19: p. 254]. They number 10 000 to 15 000 we are told—or 12 500 ± 2500, a 20 per cent margin of error either way.

There are hundreds of other units whose definition has not truly been attempted. Even an entity such as the Ibo, a West African 'tribe' of 'national' scale, whose definition was laid down in monographs and by indigenous consensus for generations, suddenly saw its Ikwerri section split off during the Biafran war, to declare itself 'not Ibo'. Some of you will know that in the nineteenth century the term 'Ibo' had been acceptable to only a handful of the many millions who later gladly bore it, even after the Ikwerri secession. Nevertheless, the Ikwerri declaration coming in the 1960s, looked rather like a stretch of southern England declaring itself 'not English'. It is, in fact, this 'arbitrary' feature that is one of the last available minimal criteria of a 'tribe' or 'ethnicity'. Ethnicities demand to be viewed from inside. They have no imperative relationship with particular 'objective' criteria. They have not 'internalized' even such objective criteria as an outsider purports to discover. They are in this sense 'named by the people'. There was much discussion in the Nigerian and even the British press, for example, over whether the Ikwerri 'spoke Ibo'. The very definition of 'speaking Ibo' (which is a continuum of dialects) made this finally a fruitless discussion, but by the Ikwerri criterion even Norway might fall apart tomorrow. It is also of interest that one of the causes of the Biafran war lay in disputations over the Nigerian census. The point is that the pace-setting Western societies denied themselves such easy luxuries many centuries ago. You are supposed to know who you are and what you are—and (exactly) 'stand up and be counted'. On the whole, rational scientists still subscribe to this, despite growing signs of the restoration of the phenomena of ethnicity in those societies themselves (as shown by Cohen [20]).

Misapprehensions of 'Ethnic' population behaviour

Ethnicities generate an apprehension of 'otherness' among non-members, and the lay equation of 'tribes' with animal species is old (far older than Custer). In the past, certain steppe-peoples seemed, to settled observers, to resemble animal populations in their frightening apparent tendency to multiply in numbers and to burst out of their bounds. They appeared to 'swarm'. They swept like a terrible plague, suddenly dwindling as rapidly as they grew. The ancient cases of the Huns, Goths, and other German tribes, and medieval cases such as the Magyars, Mongols, and the like, are deeply ingrained in the historical consciousness of our civilization. The present world-picture does not lack elements that raise these old images to prominence even among members of an audience of this kind. We should take these cases seriously, in order to see how easily alien populations are judged to be out of control. How often have we heard of the desication of the inner Asian steppes driving out virile hordes? Yet if we take the classic case of the Huns, we know that the swollen masses under Attila included almost every people from the Rhine to the Urals. The swarm effect, as it was experienced, was a combination of mobility plus accretion. The mobility may be broken down into a combination of technological factors (such as the horse and the bow) and broadly social ones. Gibbon was well aware of some of these. Among the former factors:

The active cavalry of Scythia is always followed, in their most distant and rapid incursions, by an adequate number of spare horses, who may be occasionally used either to redouble the speed or to satisfy the hunger of the barbarians . . . [27: p. 5]

Among the latter:

The individuals of the same tribe are constantly assembled, but they are assembled in a camp, and the native spirit of these dauntless shepherds is animated by mutual support and emulation. The houses of the Tartars are no more than small tents, of an oval form, which afford a cold and dirty habitation for the promiscuous youth of both sexes. The palaces of the rich consist of wooden huts, of such a size that they may be conveniently fixed on large waggons, and drawn by a team perhaps of twenty or thirty oxen. The flocks and herds, after grazing all day in the adjacent pastures, retire on the approach of night, within the protection of the camp. The necessity of preventing the most mischievous confusion in such a perpetual concourse of men and animals must gradually introduce, in the distribution, the order, and the guard of the encampment, the rudiments of the military art [27: p. 6].

And this anthropological insight:

The connection between the people and their territory is of so frail a texture that it may be broken by the slightest accident. The camp, and not the soil, is the native country of the genuine Tartar. Within the precincts of that camp his family, his companions, his property are always included, and in the most distant marches he is still surrounded by the objects which are dear or valuable or familiar in his eyes. [72: p. 7]

The accretion of subject and allied peoples—even as leaders— derived from certain other peculiarities of an ethnic polity: what I shall be calling its 'recruitment component'. These belong

entirely in the cultural sphere. On one aspect—'fictive' kinship—
Gibbon has an interesting early word:

The custom, which still prevails, of adopting the bravest and most
faithful of the captives, may countenance the very probable suspicion
that this extensive consanguinity is, in a great measure, legal and
fictitious. But the useful prejudice which has obtained the sanction of
time and opinion produces the effects of truth; ... [27: p. 9]

The 'swarming' of the Huns could have occurred without any
significant numerical change in the originating population at all.
We have indeed no certain knowledge of the precise definition of
the originating population. When the Attilan entity collapses in
A.D. 454 we catch glimpses of small remnant groups of successor
'Huns' (Utigurs, Kutrigurs) of very limited significance, incorporated in other rolling, swelling ethnicities. A century later
the Avars 'swarmed' by incorporating a large Slavonic population
[20]. The rapid collapse of their apparent numbers in A.D. 796
was such that a Russian proverb came to say: 'They perished like
the Avars, and there survives of them neither progeny nor heir'
[18: p. 73]. Save, that is, for the Balkan Slavs themselves, whose
own expansion occurred (in the view of many authorities) behind
the 'Avar' screen.

The process I describe has as much in common with the growth
and collapse of a fiduciary phenomenon like the South Sea bubble
as it has with any biological one. The sudden shrinking of such
barbarian enemies is a function of their presupposed size. Conversely, the rapid increase in effectiveness of the Germanic
peoples was certainly connected with the growth of confederacies—
that is, ethnic self-redefinitions—which transformed the ethnic
map from the multitude of peoples given by the ethnographer
Tacitus in the first century to a much more limited number of
polities by the fourth century under names new and old, such as
Franks, Saxons, Burgundians, and the like. Even Custer's fatal
Sioux were themselves 'Dakota', literally 'a confederacy'. Ethnicities, as I said earlier, have this powerful quality of self-definition
and redefinition. It is not (I emphasize strongly) that population
changes played no role at all in any of these matters, but that they
were overlaid, and totally reshaped by changes in the mode of
self-identification of the ethnicities concerned. As we shall see,
this is a little more basic than saying merely that 'the social,
political, military or economic organizations changed', for it gives

us a way of motivating the changes in man-made stuctures of such a kind. In any event, we are presented in all this with something surely that animals do not do.

Present-day ethnicities: some practicalities

Let us return to present-day ethnicities, and think about the numbering question: turning these entities into 'demography', if you like. If we remember that most ethnic groups in the Third World present definitional problems, it will be realized that even the determination of population size, in the quite practical sense of a count of people, is a far from simple task. To go on to discuss numerically the dynamics of the population of such entities can be extremely hazardous.

Documented cases are beginning to emerge of relationships between neighbouring peoples—different 'tribes' if you will—which spread the population dynamic over some aggregate much larger than any one ethnicity. Imagine that if you ran away to sea you became a German, or to become a Londoner you gave up your mother tongue. We should find no doubt that the populations of the resulting individual ethnicities were not demographically stable. Work on some very small Bantu-speaking groups of West Africa suggests a situation something like this over a considerable area [7]. Certain ethnicities wax and wane by accretion and loss, according to their economic or commercial success. Paul Spencer's work on the pastoral Rendille and Samburu of Kenya demonstrates a kind of 'classifying symbiosis' between the two ethnicities of a most interesting kind. Essentially Rendille lose population continually to the Samburu. If you do not make it in the rather close Rendille cattle-breeding economy, you merge with the more open Samburu cattle economy, and you are redefined as Samburu. One lineage, the Ariaal, forms a sort of valve between the two [38a]. We should note that linguistically the two peoples belong to different language families [38]. Conversely Hurault [33] found that the statistics for the *Lamidate* of Banyo bore signs of internal diversities, which suggested that the significant demographic units were certain older ethnicities submerged in the Banyo state. These cases are very important if we are to grasp that a *'population'* as a scientific, demographic bundle of indices need not be the same as an 'ethnicity' or as I shall now sometimes prefer to say: a 'people'.

Suppose we leave aside for the moment the question of the bounds of a given group. We still find the most extraordinary difficulties in getting certain crucial data: for example, the sex of children and the age-structure. Because the demographic survey will usually be the first ever made, the dynamics of the population have to be determined retrospectively, from an accurate construction of the life histories (marital, fertility experience) of the living and (by report) of certain categories of the dead, for example, the deceased children of informants. If the information is properly recorded from a random sample, the treatment of the data can be statistically quite respectable. From this base indeed substantial demographic superstructures can be built effortlessly. The nature of the random sample will of course be affected by the supposed definition of the universe—back to the 'square one' of the definition of the ethnicity. In the end we have to fall back on a kind of compromise with bureaucratic opinion and honest general repute. So we sample supposed settlements and villages, a proportion of which turn out not to be there any more, or to be in the wrong place, or to be misprints of some sort (unnumberable names). In 1963-5 I had the privilege of assisting brilliant French-trained demographers in the devising of a sampling frame for a stretch of Africa containing 80 or more supposed ethnicities [40]. They would agree with me that the actual sample came from a reality different from that of the supposed universe.

The further retreat into practicalities does not solve our problem. We are now face to face with the people. The expectation of candour in reply to questions about 'population' is, when we reflect on it, a surprising one, even if we assume that certain possible fears (about taxation or the like) have been allayed. In an 'ethnic' situation nothing which shakes the self-definition of the group will be easily elicited. An ethnicity is an ideal structure in which hardly any demographic variable is not already prejudged. In the 'folk-demography' the group is (to take one common example) always expanding in numbers, more boys than girls are born, all women are married at puberty, all wives had maximum fertility, all old persons are extremely old, all men have, have had, or will have several wives, and so on. Anthropologists as well as demographers when faced with the challenge of eliciting 'objective' population data from behind this screen of obfuscation, have responded in skilful ways [15]. They have achieved stretches, or short lengths, of accurate data. A lot of labour has been put into the precise determination of the sex and age-structures in populations of this sort. Mortality and fertility rates rest upon them. Yet even the best work relies upon model population tables, standard age-pyramids, and standard approximations to level out supposed irregularities.

In work on ethnic populations certain structural anomalies could never come to unambiguous light. Some extraordinary but limited imbalance in the older ages, for example: an excess of men aged 78 years or a lack of women aged 67. Such immanent 'real' phenomena are inaccessible because they are swamped by the margin of error in the determination of ages above about 50. Either the data would not show the imbalances, or, even if they did, we should not be allowed to believe them. If members of an ethnicity of this type had gone so far as to refrain from sexual intercourse for a year or two in the past, we could not accept the evidence of it in our crudely constructed age-pyramids. Such gross distortions would be smoothed away in our 5-year, even 10-year, age-groupings of the data.

If a so-called 'primitive tribe' has had some interesting mode of adaptation affecting population indices we really have to be specifically told about it. And if we are, what then? I cannot help being reminded of the case of Major Tweedy. He reported of the Ngie people of the Cameroon Highlands in the 1920s that all persons over the age of 40 were killed and eaten by adherents of a certain 'Kwap juju'. Some elderly persons who could not evade Major Tweedy's eye were, he was told, the parents of Kwap juju doctors; the doctors, it was hinted, being naturally loth to despatch their own old people—even in the interests of population control. The officer's successor reported that the story must have resulted from the (by then) late major's unfortunate gullibility [17]. But we cannot ever know the facts on the Kwap juju; by this second visit the Ngie were fully apprised of the bad administrative impression that had been created by an unfortunate (surely satirical?) tendency, and they rectified it to everyone's satisfaction. Nevertheless the very outrageousness of the Kwap juju story made it susceptible to an 'averaging-out' operation. The outrageous does occasionally happen, but if it did happen and we were told about it, we still may not know whether to believe it. By the time anthropologists get to peoples of this sort, the last chance of actually observing something as outrageous as that has usually gone. Anthropologists have not unequivocally determined to this day whether or not certain African divine kings were buried alive or not [25b]. Among one noted people of Africa I lived surrounded by repeated tales of active cannibalism, but I cannot to this day decide whether the events all happened. If the people have deceived *themselves*, by what criterion shall the anthropologist say whether he has been deceived?

The problems of age determination diminish after long personal acquaintance with the demographically surveyed population. But for large-scale statistical surveys one needs 'rule of thumb' methods. In manuals for 'tribal' demography it is suggested that the people should be asked to count certain cycles: of farms cleared, or of age-set membership, for example. Experience shows that these cannot always be related to exact chronologies. Unfortunately even ordered age-set cycles are not found everywhere. So-called 'calendars of events' are set up by the inquirer to help people to pin down birth dates or life histories. To do all this for only 100 people is a task of real complexity, but most anthropologists will achieve this over time. Given enough time they may manage 1000 people or even more. But the greater the accuracy, generally the smaller the scale of the survey, and the less its extrapolative value. Meanwhile the supposed 'calendar of events' method teaches us more about notions of history and time than about ages. Even big 'colonial' events may make patchy impact. In one group among whom I worked, people could remember noting the end of World War II, but not its beginning. The coming of early 'white men' needs an archival knowledge of casual explorations. Really well-remembered local events, of course, are often no more datable than the birth dates they were expected to elucidate. Generally, the more complicated the political structure, and the older and the more violent the contact with the outer world, the better the dating. But of course, this immediately reduces the value of the results as an index of a population system adapting in its own way. Even studies like Turnbull's [41] or Chagnon's on elusive groups cannot be taken as providing data characteristic of a supposed 'Tribal Epoch' [19: p. 252].

If our difficulties with age structure in ethnic populations lead us into such ramifications, it is no wonder that we experience problems with sex ratios at birth. So difficult are our studies that if a somewhat unbalanced ratio of say 109 males per 100 females emerges, it is justly viewed as almost certainly due to survey error. We have to rely on reports by mothers who suppress or wrongly report the sex of their deceased infants, or do not distinguish between early infant deaths, stillbirths, and miscarriages. But as a result of our necessary caution, we may have underestimated certain real variations in non-Western sex ratios. As Teitelbaum shows [39: p. 90], commonly used calculations for the Net Reproduction Rate can vary significantly with quite small differences in the assessments of the female proportion of births. In the midst of all of this a moderate but well-disguised tendency to female infanticide would probably not be detected.

Wherever we look, then, demographic studies make ethnicities look relatively *less* distinctive, for two reasons: When the people are ill documented the material is eked out by model data; when the people are well documented they have by this very fact entered into modern conditions. This very brief survey of some practicalities was therefore necessary to show that as more and more 'good' studies are made, and as Third-World statistics increase in quantity, the further we move from ethnic reality.

Demographic 'consciousness'

Let us now take the provisional position that if a certain 'demographic consciousness' is a feature of modern societies, the relative absence of it would correspondingly be one aspect of societies thought of roughly as 'ethnic' or 'tribal'. It does not take much examination, however, to show that we are not dealing with two clearly differentiated categories. The ideal type of the modern society, documented to the eyebrows, its own adaptations including adaptations to its own statistical data about itself—this must seem easy to visualize. We contrast this with the group lacking knowledge of even its total size, let alone its growth rates and the like. But some demographic consciousness in our sense goes far back in the history of the old civilizations [28]. Enumerations were made for purposes of tribute, tax, and military service. Adaptations of corporate behaviour were attempted in the light of some of these data. Yet, as historical demographers tell us, these data were usually distorted (even 'wrong') by modern statistical standards. Is there then something like a demographic *false* consciousness' that we have to recognize? But the 'wrong' data are not likely to be randomly wrong in such circumstances. The old folk-statistics document deep-seated hypotheses about the social unit. Thus early parish-registered christenings [21] do not yield birth statistics: but were they not, in another sense, the births that counted? Graunt's analyses of the Bills of Mortality gave unbalanced mortality statistics, but the new urban deaths were perhaps the striking social fact [29, 32: pp. 145–9, 8]. To go still further, then, the inadequately or erroneously documented pre-modern polities are not easily distinguished in principle from societies in which no statistics are formally taken, but which nevertheless have elicitable images of how their group is constructed and how situated in time and space. This is the essential 'consciousness' upon which attempts at numeration and mensuration may well ultimately depend, even in our own time.

Let us ask another key question: To what extent and by what processes is it possible for human groups to become aware of their demographic structures? [8: p. 7]. We are not permitted the simple expedient of pressure on food resources. This limitation is too draconian, on the one hand, and uninteresting, on the other. The difficulty is that even a supposedly objective circumstance like pressure on food-supply is experienced through remarkable distortions. Thus, even outright starvation might be attributed to the malice of enemies. It is true that the slaying of these enemies might reduce pressure on food, in some gross sense, but in such conditions by the time we have worked out the permutations we soon tire of a simple pressure-on-food model. At all stages we meet direct intervention by human beings in defining the crisis stage itself—to the extent indeed that pressure-on-food seems like a social rather than a biological concept. For a few weeks in 1973 quite affluent middle-class persons in Great Britain began, as a result of a rise in beef prices, to behave as if meat supplies had totally dried up (many even seemed to take on a hollow-cheeked appearance, when asked by television reporters how they were managing to carry on!).

The Douglas effect

Professor Mary Douglas, in an important paper, had already pointed out that human groups are 'more often inspired by concern for scarce social resources, for objects giving status and prestige, than by concern for dwindling basic resources' [23: p. 268]. By examining the cases of supposed population homeostasis in the anthropological literature, she came to the conclusion that these rested characteristically on a clear-cut evaluation of limited social advantage. As she said, the big question is rather why population homeostatis does not occur. One suggestion she made was that certain kinds of social breakdown change the structural (*not* the biological) limitations and permit population explosion. Whatever the specific arguments for or against in individual cases [38], I would point out the degree of complexity that the possibility of such a conclusion reveals. A common lay view of 'social breakdown' sees it as causing population decline. I will not repeat Professor Douglas's lucid and well-documented arguments. Her 'oysters and champagne' [23: p. 271] view of scarce resources is now widely known. The consideration of certain apparently key economic resources in isolation can certainly mislead us.

An example of the Douglas effect can be given from my own material on the savannah Highlands of Cameroon. Among the Esu people, ordinary farming land is quite plentiful. An upper limit to the growth of settlements is set by the relative shortage of raffia-palms (the latter being used for house-building). These are all restricted to stream-valleys. It is not the case, however, that people wait to move away until building materials have actually run out. Rather, raffia-palms are constantly subject to litigation and the jealous definition of rights. Men brood, and harm each other by witchcraft because of conflicts over such rights. Village and ward headmen tend to be powerfully placed. Political power and witchcraft are frequently joined in them. The weak and the young tend to hive off elsewhere. We may decide to put the ecological limitation at the beginning of the chain, but if we do, we are far removed from the simple world of termites who have eaten up their last tree. The Esu migrate at a very high rate, despite an amplitude of ordinary agricultural resources. But no one can doubt that the raffia-palm thicket situation is already a *socially defined* scarcity. Part of the image of an Esu man is that he is independent enough to go off to a private raffia-palm thicket at will, as if he were a ward head. (Vain dream—like the motorist's image of everyone parking his car outside his city destination.) The Esu are to be contrasted with the case of the Ibo heartland, where a very high out-migration occurs, but with rural densities of over 1000 to the square mile compared with 7 to the square mile among the Esu [9: p. 212]. Later I shall suggest that among the Ibo the Douglas effect has in fact been interestingly overridden, without significant breakdown of the status system.

Even the most deprived human groups are aristocrats in their definitions of scarcity. If animal models are applied, humanity need never feel serious nutritional constraints until the last rat, mouse, cat, dog, and recently deceased comrade is eaten up. Once we come to man, we are in a new topsy-turvy world. He lives in an '*as if*' environment of as yet unexploded hypotheses, of '*as if*' shortages and '*as if*' riches. This is no 'naked ape'; this is the ape wearing emperor's clothes—not quite the same thing! In this sense, perhaps, rather than that of Professors Fox and Tiger, he merits the label 'The Imperial Animal' [26].

Having thus touched glancingly on current 'ethologism' (Callan's term [17a]), I should add that I am aware that even in the animal models resource-pressure is buffered by some intermediate structuring. But Fox and Tiger do recognize, in a way that some other more popular writers do not, that 'territory' is not enough to understand man.

While humans do have fights over territory that are equivalent to animal conflicts, their fights over property and other focuses of symbolic attachment such as nationality or religion are not so readily equatable. [26: p. 227]

There is no time here to examine every way in which even this statement is still inadequate—in particular that fights are 'over' symbolic features. It is sufficient to say that the human being in society simply lives in a different kind of space: what we may call a 'world-structure' [7a]. Crude population density plays different roles in different 'world-structures'. In Hamlet's words: 'I could be bounded in a nutshell and count myself a king of infinite space.'

A cloud of unknowing

In the circumstances, we may have to say that a major determinant of population size is the degree of evolutionary success or failure of that fuzzy cloud of unknowing which is a society's image of its own world-structure. This structure is built up by processes of naming—that is of labelling or categorizing—rather than by numbering. This is the insubstantial front along which the supposed social version of 'adaptation' takes place. When demographic changes occur they are 'apperceived', if I may use that term, through that structure. I am not sure that human beings are always in much better case when aided consciously by demographic data. These may merely give us another mode of expression for changes whose 'causality' lies outside demography. In illustrating the 'unknowing' aspect of world-structures I give examples from very different parts of the world.

The 'lost generation'

Consider first the peculiar case of the 'lost generation' in English society. The nation was believed to be fatally weakened by the losses of World War I. In the words of Mr. Baldwin in 1935:

Have you thought what it has meant to the world to have had that swathe of death cut through the loveliest and best of our contemporaries, how our public life has suffered because those who would have been ready to take over from our tired and disillusioned generation are not there? [11: p. 425]

Mr. Corelli Barnett calls this a 'legend', even a 'myth', thus bringing the topic within our present competence. He notes that proportionately Britain lost fewer men than Germany, but that none thought that Germany's national energy was impaired. On the Western Front itself the 512 564 United Kingdom dead was of the same order as the Italian losses on a single front (460 000). Yet the Italians under Mussolini were not felt in the 1930s to have lost military vigour. Most striking of all:

Even the British losses in officers on all fronts—the true source of the legend of the 'Lost Generation'—was, at 37,452 killed, considerably less than the 55,888 lost by the air crews of Bomber Command during the Second World War, and which led to no comparable legend. [11: p. 426]

Finally, even the massive blood-letting of World War I left 46 per cent of males of military age in the population in 1926, as opposed to 47 per cent in 1911. Mr. Barnett concluded brutally that 'the

truth was that the Great War crippled the British *psychologically*
but in no other way' (*ibid*, his italics). He noted that it was the dis-
proportionate loss of some small number (say 150) of the inner
core of the small British governing class, which led to the legend.
'Unconsciously arrogant', the survivors made the error of thinking
that 'because their own small circle had been decimated, the vitality
of the British nation had been critically impaired' [11: p. 428]. I
do not know that any change in our view of the Lost Generation
has been the result of anything in the figures themselves. Mr.
Barnett talks of 'psychological factors': I have been leading my
argument to face you with the proposition that the primitive cloud
of unknowing, the self-image through which human aggregates
experience the world, is still very much with us—deck it about
with eroded age-pyramids though we may. We may note the further
lesson that not all social experience contributes equally to the
establishment of that self-image; knowledge and the interpretation
of knowledge are already located in segments of the very structure
that it is expected to explain.

'Dying out'

Every so often one meets with a people among whom the opinion
has spread that it is 'dying out'. I have worked among one such
(the Bantu-speaking Bakweri of Mount Cameroon) alone or with
colleagues for many years. This is my second example. Their
numbers were about 16 000 in the 1950s. We found high divorce
rates, venereal disease, prostitution, honky-tonks for male migrant
workers, and low completed family size—we estimated in 1957 a
net reproduction rate hovering around 1·00 (or stable) for the
previous 30 years [4]. All that, and *de facto* population homeostasis
too! It is remarkable what demographic indices will put up with.
But the self-image of the people had been shrinking over the same
period. They saw themselves embattled against zombie foes derived from the ranks of their wickedly murdered children, driven
on by known entrepreneurs who had profited from the new economy by witchcraft. Even our own findings were swept into the
maw. Some of the knowledgeable (teachers and the like) came to
aver that it was the Net Reproduction Rate that witches were
striking at—an accommodation with science worthy of broad-
minded South Bank theologians.

The Bakweri had good grounds for feeling that their population was not expanding, but the experience of rapid *decline* was a complicated one. Houses fell empty. Migrant workers moved into the area in large numbers. Some Bakweri moved out to plantation employment. The relative number of strangers doubled in a generation. Added to which the Bakweri self-definition excluded from the ranks of 'real Bakweri' their members who were living outside the rural areas. The rural population was not demographically stable. By a series of changes more ideological than economic, which are published elsewhere [6], the zombies were defeated. At present the demographic indices are probably not very different from before, but the Bakweri no longer hold as common knowledge the opinion that they are dying out. Many think their numbers are increasing, but they are probably as 'wrong' statistically as before.

The supposed propensity to 'die out' was, of course, one much associated with the Custer view of tribes—especially in situations of continual harassment, in which the last stages are best called 'killing out'. However, when numbers decline below a certain point, ethnicities in contact with others may finally *define* themselves out—by not recognizing the children of unions with people of other tribes, for example. When numbers are small, an ethnicity with a more open definition of itself may increase faster than through the best available fertility rate. It is not always easy to keep track of these processes as 'fictive' kinship blurs the genealogical record, as Gibbon long ago noted. Jacquard's paper [34] on the special effect of sheer smallness on the dynamics of a population does not examine such factors.

The more one documented the Bakweri situation, the more 'wheels within wheels' were to be found. Thus the Bakweri set a very high store upon fertility. Certain fertility medicines that were customarily prescribed for pregnant women were regarded as so important that the failure of a husband to provide them was actually a ground for divorce [4: p. 58]. Yet they consisted of purgatives, administered by crude wooden or gourd enemas—which must have added to, rather than reduced, the obstacles to healthy gestation [9]. In such ways social entities build in 'double-bind' situations. We simple observers would be hard put to decide the determinants of population size among the Bakweri, but the possibility that one of them has been a mildly abortifacient 'fertility' drug cannot be excluded. This situation has more in common with the great thalidomide error than it has with the behaviour of any animal population we know.

Fertility and the 'suckling law'

Of course, human intervention in demography is everywhere great in the field of fertility [31, 22]. There are direct interventions and indirect interventions, intended or unintended in either case, and any of which may be effective or ineffective [35, 14]. All have taken place against a background of some degree of ignorance and disease. It is not surprising that maximum female fertility or something approaching it has rarely been documented. Many African societies, even in healthy modern conditions, have total fertility much reduced by the requirement that a woman should not conceive a second or a subsequent child while her previous one is suckling. This period may last one or two years. It is probably one of the most effective direct interventions on fertility documented in African societies. Yet it is clearly in any overt sense 'unintended'. Women (and men) in such societies, when asked what total family size they would like, characteristically say '100', or 'as many as possible'. Yet a mean total fertility of 6 seems to be that generated by the suckling law—far below the figure for Victorian vicarages. The fixing of a long suckling period may sometimes be directly related to food-types. There may be no suitable alternative to mother's milk. Yet in many of these societies this is not true. Whether or not alternative foods are taken may even be neutral, so long as the child has maternal milk. A woman's last child may, indeed, stand up to the breast as late as the age of 5. The suckling law is often stated to be a powerful support for male polygyny, and this too has been argued to be a net reducer of total fertility, if only on grounds of reduction of average coital frequency per woman. But polygyny does not always lead to sexual exclusiveness. Large harems, in which institutionalized lovers are recognized, may on the contrary provide peculiarly favourable conditions for fertility. The Ibo are such a case. The royal harems of the Cameroon grassfields are relatively barren in contrast [37a].

It is probable that the suckling law is *grosso modo* of 'beneficial' demographic effect, but it cannot be directly linked to basic resources. On the contrary, a food crisis may lead to an uncertainty, even an ambiguity, as to what is the 'proper food' for children. The painful tragedy of the Biafran infants is still fresh in our memories. The collapse of mothers' milk supply and the disruption of root-crop imports—a source of the mashes made up for young children —led to a totally uncontrolled situation. Protein broths were not socially recognized supplements, and eggs were not eaten. So it was that in many households chickens and goats remained alive while infants imperceptibly wasted away. Long-standing ideas on childcare may thus fail to mesh with a new and unprecedented reality.

Gerontocracy

We can sometimes deduce what kind of 'objective' demography a 'folk-demography' would require. Fig. 6 is the notional age-pyramid for gerontocracies of types discussed by Spencer [38].

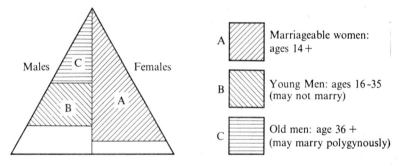

Males   C   Females

B   A

A — Marriageable women: ages 14 +

B — Young Men: ages 16-35 (may not marry)

C — Old men: age 36 + (may marry polygynously)

FIG. 6. An idealized 'gerontocratic' age-pyramid. (Ages only illustrative.)

Essentially the male age tranche (B) is restricted from marriage— say by service in war camps. This leaves the whole marriageable group of women (A) available for polygynous marriage with males (C) over age 35. Dr. Spencer's excellent Samburu analysis is very close to this. Younger males may have adulterous relations with the younger married women, so that actual fertility may not be significantly reduced. But the folk-demographies of human societies do not necessarily always fit what we might see as objective facts. Plenty of societies with a folk-demography of a high rate of male polygyny do not in fact achieve the delayed marriage of males that would make this a possibility. In warlike conditions the model may have grown from a kind of external necessity. Where these do not exist, it is a human artefact embedded now in the world-structure, defining behaviour in its own right.

Many lessons may be drawn from this example. The point I am concerned with here is that folk-demographies outlive or transcend their core of reality. It requires a greater effort to see that the 'lost generation' was a folk-demography of a similar type, and finally that much of the 'demography' of a series of lectures like this (and especially of the more popular manifestations associated with the enterprise) is the sophisticated folk-demography of westerners of our historical period.

How 'adaptive' are societies?

Since we have had to throw doubt on the degree to which crude sociological and demographic restraints can be directly apprehended, it is perhaps useful to point out a neglected area in which something like a direct link between a demographic variable and human world-structures does occur. The accommodation of new generations is an unavoidable feature of even the most technologically simple societies. This particular feature should not be confused with the direct and indirect interventions in fertility that we have discussed. The actual physical arrival of a certain number of new individuals is a reality of a particular unavoidable sort. There has to be an immanent 'recruitment theory' if each newcomer is not to be defined out of the society. A world-structure without an adequate 'recruitment theory' clearly will soon lose its human base. Upon this feature are built the commonest folk-demographies. What are conventionally called kinship systems are for this reason among the finest flowers of human constructions. They ensure that each new person is already a *kind* of person at his birth, and they provide a map of the relationship of kinds to each other (e.g. 'father' to 'son'), and of the transformations of kinds into each other (e.g. 'son' into 'father' through the reproductive cycle). It is a commonplace now to see kinship terminologies as systems that map articulated sets of kinds of person, although differences exist about numerous technicalities.

If we are to relate the 'world-structure' idea of society to conventional evolutionary selection, we see that it is only at this point that failure in a structural component *must* wither the whole structure. As soon as human beings ceased to respond directly to biological constraints, the possibility arose that a group could develop a world-structure which would define babies as alien, or polluting, or as disposable. We may rest assured that none of our ancestors can have belonged to such a group. You may speculate if you wish as to conditions in which a recruitment theory might generate such features over short stretches—but that is not the same as absence of a recruitment theory.

The absolute requirement that there *be* a recruitment component throws some light on the supposed 'fictive' element in kinship systems. The term rests frequently on a misapprehension. The emergence of newcomers to the notice of the world-structure rests upon sets of mainly genealogical categories, which are inevitably homologous in part with the chain of reproduction through which most of the new entrants come; but a recruitment theory that can also recruit and assimilate 'strange' children or active adults is clearly advantageous, since it does not rest exclusively on the chances of biological fertility. We touched on this in connection with 'dying', or very small, ethnicities. There is certainly no reason why a satisfactory theory should have to embody a set of biologically accurate genealogical discovery procedures for who copulated with whom. The fact that this latter distinction has emerged in special historical circumstances underlines the point.

We now see that when Lorimer [35] and others [14] ask whether a segmentary lineage system is expansionary in tendency, the question is more complicated than it seems. Societies with such systems express the recruitment process through the image of a continually branching genealogy. Placed on its side its branches look like those in a model of successive multiple choices. These genealogies have been long known to be ideal only (e.g. [25a, 16, 2]) and the way they are constantly revised in 'fictive, ways, with retrospective effect, is about as well documented as anything in social anthropology. Lorimer's question should perhaps be answered by saying that the expansionism lies essentially in the genealogical image: an open-ended system of nodes of multiple choice. Any real birth is a real addition at one of the nodes. When lines die out they are simply suppressed from the genealogy. All surviving nodes thus imply that additions are possible. In such systems, then, an expansionary self-image may remain in existence, even in conditions of objective stability or decline. The effect is then not to encourage expansion but to neutralize the actual experience of it. If we return to our idea of the space or world-structure in which societies live, we note that the Ibo, a people with an open-genealogy segmentary lineage system, achieved remarkable rural densities of up to 1600 per square mile, which were tolerated with great resilience. At no time could expansion of the lineage be experienced as disadvantageous by Ibo, despite growing evidence of exhaustion of agricultural land [1, 2]. We may note indeed the appearance of ever greater industry, inventiveness, and incentive that the Ibo exhibited through the recent period of growth. The cherished male status crop, the yam, was even abandoned as staple over large areas in favour of the recently introduced cassava. In other words the 'Douglas effect' did not work where we might have expected. Rather it was overridden by an extremely powerful recruitment component, and without any evidence of internal social breakdown of the sort that the Douglas hypothesis needs.

It may be guessed that the adaptation required open migration; another kind of breakdown occurred when this was barred by Northern Nigeria—leading to the Biafran war. Such cases do not refute the Douglas effect—we are even further away from a simple pressure-on-resources model. The Douglas effect is a small-scale and possibly short-term aspect of the more general self-defining phenomenon inherent in the world-structure concept. If you like, the recruitment component itself was paradoxically the point at which the effect occurred. Thus, it could not result in population homeostasis—the 'oysters and champagne' were *people*, which were always, by definition, 'scarce' and always a source of 'prestige'. The Douglas effect, in its proper usage, may then not be expected inevitably to intervene homeostatically. After all, the 'proletariat' was so called because its wealth lay in its offspring (*proles*).

Conclusion

The way in which the adaptations of human beings have been vested in a partly unconscious social system is one of the marvels of evolution. For there is no doubt that this truly blind, because unsuspecting, abrogation of sovereignty by the individual over his own animal survival lies in the form of the human consciousness itself. If a crisis is sufficiently unprecedented, the social forms all too often grind themselves to destruction, because individuals simply do not 'see', that is, grasp or perceive, the nature of the crisis. To ask about the determinants of population size is really to ask about what I have called 'world-structures', about kinds of consciousness, and their accuracy in helping groups to survive. One fears, however, that we cannot assume that they have a 'purpose' or 'function' to help us survive. All human societies existing today may be soberly stated to have survived in spite of the most grotesque misjudgements of events in the past. The fact that they have only a direct relationship with evolutionary pressure through their recruitment component, and that in the direction of more openness, may be a great weakness.

If you are accustomed to say that certain population determinants are 'social', I hope I have shown that we must be very careful to think what we meant by that. It is surprising that many intellectual persons of a scientific bent, whose own minds and lives are a continuum of nuances and subtleties, are often easily satisfied with ideas of social systems made up of simple causal chains, which would not safely guide them through ten minutes of real life. Anthropologists are not able to help out by saying that there are 'simple' societies where life *is* like that, as if we can still return to well-tried mechanisms. The contribution of such peoples is to suggest to us that even major variations in population indices may be affected by minor changes in the 'world-structure' of human groups. Furthermore that, if there are changes in basic resources on a scale much greater than that of a given human group, its world-structure will determine how those changes are apperceived, and indeed decide whether they are apperceived at all. Perhaps our danger today resides in the greater specialization and isolation of those groups in our own culture who shape our view of reality and thus our actions. There may be a crisis ahead, but as usual the one we are living in is mixed up with a crisis of interpretation. That is why I have suggested that demographic studies are not necessarily neutral or objective. They rest on too many quasi-realities, among which the term 'population' is pre-eminent. Our main task, therefore, is to restore 'the people' to their central place in the picture, custodians of the cloud of unknowing that got us into the ambiguous situation we are in today.

REFERENCES

1. ARDENER, E. (1954). Kinship terminology of a group of Southern Ibo, *Africa* **24**, 85–99.
2. ——— (1959). Lineage and locality among the Mba-Ise Ibo, *Africa* **29**, 113–34.
3. ——— (1961). Social and demographic problems of the Southern Cameroons plantation area. In *Social change in modern Africa* (ed. A. Southall). Oxford University Press, London.
4. ——— (1962). *Divorce and fertility—an African study*. Oxford University Press, London.
5. ——— (1967). The nature of the reunification of Cameroon. In *African integration and disintegration* (ed. A. Hazelwood). Oxford University Press, London.
6. ——— (1970). Witchcraft, economics, and the continuity of belief. In *Witchcraft confessions and accusations* (ed. M. Douglas). Tavistock, London.
7. ——— (1972). Language, ethnicity and population, *J. Anthropol. Soc., Oxford*, **3**, No. 3, 125–32.
7a. ——— (1973). *Some outstanding problems in the analysis of events.* Association of Social Anthropologists Conference paper. (To be published.)
8. ———, and ARDENER, S. (1965). A directory study of social anthropologists, *Br. J. Sociol.* **16**, 295–314.
9. ———, ———, and WARMINGTON, W. A. (1960). *Plantation and village in the Cameroons*. Oxford University Press, London.
10. BARNES, J. A. (1949) [1951]. Measures of divorce frequency in simple societies, *J. R. Anthropol. Inst.* **79**, 37–62.
11. BARNETT, C. (1972). *The collapse of British power*. Eyre Methuen, London.
12. BATES, R. H. (1970). Approaches to the study of ethnicity, *Cahiers d'Etudes Africaines* **10**, Pt. 40, 546–61.
13. BARTH, F. (1969). *Ethnic groups and boundaries*. Allen and Unwin, London.
14. BENEDICT, B. (1972). Social regulation of fertility. In [30], pp. 73–89.
15. BLANC, R. (1960). *Manuel de recherche démographique en pays sous-développé*. C.C.T.A., Paris.
16. BOHANNAN, L. (1952). A genealogical charter, *Africa* **22**, 301–15.
17. BUEA MS. (1926). *Assessment and intelligence reports on Ngie, Ngwaw, Mogamaw and Ngemba*. Cameroon Archives, Buea.
17a. CALLAN, H. (1970). *Ethology and society—towards an anthropological view*. Clarendon Press, Oxford.
18. CHADWICK, H. M. (1945). *The nationalities of Europe*. Cambridge University Press.

19. CHAGNON, N. A. (1972). Tribal social organization and genetic microdifferentiation. In [30], pp. 252–82.

20. COHEN, A. (1969). *Custom and politics in urban Africa*. Routledge and Kegan Paul, London.

21. COX, J. C. (1910). *The parish registers of England*. Parish Reg. Soc., Pub. Rec. Off., London.

22. DEVEREUX, G. (1955). *A study of abortion in primitive societies*. Julian Press, New York.

23. DOUGLAS, M. (1966). Population control in primitive groups, *Br. J. Sociol.* **17**, pp. 263–73.

24. DUMOND, D. E. (1965). Population growth and cultural change, *S. W. J. Anthropol.*, **21**, 302–24.

25. EPSTEIN, A. L. (1958). *Politics in an urban African community*. Manchester University Press.

25a. EVANS-PRITCHARD, E. E. (1940). *The Nuer*. Clarendon Press, Oxford.

25b. —— (1962). The divine Kingship of the Shilluk of the Nilotic Sudan. In his *Essays in social anthropology*. Faber, London.

26. FOX, R. and TIGER, L. (1972). *The imperial animal*. Secker and Warburg, London.

27. GIBBON, E. (1787). *The decline and fall of the Roman Empire*, Vol. III (reprinted 1954). Dent, London.

28. GLASS, V. D. and EVERSLEY, D. E. C. (1965). *Population in history*. pp. ix + 692. Arnold, London.

29. GRAUNT. J. (1662). *Natural and political observations upon the Bills of Mortality*. London. Reprinted (1964). *J. Inst. Actuaries* **90**, Pt. 1 (No. 384), 4–61.

30. HARRISON, G. A. and BOYCE, A. J. (eds.) (1972). *The structure of human populations*. pp. xvi + 447. Clarendon Press, Oxford.

31. HAWTHORN, G. (1970). *The sociology of fertility*, pp. 161. Collier-Macmillan, London.

32. HOLLINGSWORTH, T. H. (1969). *Historical demography*. pp. 448. Hodder and Stoughton, London, for Sources of History.

33. HURAULT, J. (1969). Eleveurs et cultivateurs des hauts plateaux du Cameroun: la population du Lamidat de Banyo, *Population* **5**, 963–94.

34. JACQUARD, A. (1968). Evolution des populations d'effectif limité, *Population* **2**, 279–300.

35. LORIMER, F., *et al.* (1954). *Culture and human fertility*. UNESCO, Paris.

36. MITCHELL, J. C. (1967). On quantification in social anthropology. In *The craft of social anthropology* (ed. A. L. Epstein). Tavistock, London.

37. —— (1966). Theoretical orientations in African urban studies. In *The social anthropology of complex societies* (ed. M. Banton). Tavistock, London.

37a. REYHER, R. H. (1952). *The Fon and his hundred wives*. Doubleday, New York.

38. SPENCER, P. (1965). *The Samburu*. Routledge, London.
38a. ——(1972). Social and demographic processes among the Rendille and Sambuuru: a case study of growth and symbiosis between two ethnic groups. (Forthcoming).
39. TEITELBAUM, M. S. (1972). Factors associated with the sex ratio in human populations. In [30], pp. 90–109.
40. TURLOT, F., DURUPT, M. J., and HOLIN, F. (1969). *La population du Cameroun Occidental*. Société d'Etudes pour le Développement Economique et Sociale, Paris.
41. TURNBULL, C. M. (1972). Demography of small-scale societies. In [30], pp. 283–312.
42. WALLERSTEIN, E. (1960). Ethnicity and national integration in West Africa, *Cahiers d'Etudes Africaines* **1**, Pt. 3, 129–39.

I.4. Population size and complex communities, with a consideration of world population

WILLIAM BRASS

Professor of Medical Demography, London University

Introduction

IN conformity with the over-all theme of this volume my purpose is to explore the factors which control the relation of population size and growth to the environment in complex communities. Since all but a tiny proportion of human beings in the world are now a part of such communities in relevant and substantial ways, the subject is therefore the growth of world population and the laws (if any) which it obeys now and may obey in the future. In this exploration it will be necessary to sketch out the basic ideas of population dynamics, the anatomy and physiology, as it were, in order to provide a view of what has to be explained and of the natural constraints which are imposed by the structure of demographic relations. It should, perhaps, be obvious that the account will be about questions rather than answers. If there were answers with a satisfactory claim to scientific validity the scene would be a very different one. I am not concerned here with propaganda in support of action of one kind or another to remedy a situation which many (including myself) believe to be undesirable but with some of the reasonably well-established factors which should be taken into account in the consideration of such action.

World population growth

The history of world population growth is now so well known that only a brief reminder is required to put the discussion in perspective. The basic measures, taken from a previous paper of mine [2] and brought up to date are shown in Tables 1.4.1 and

1.4.2. The total world population at mid-1972 was around 3800
million with about 70 per cent in the poor countries (a simpler and
better term than underdeveloped, developing, and so on) and 30

TABLE 1.4.1

Estimates of the size and growth of world population†

				Year			
	I	1750	1800	1850	1900	1950	1972
				Population size (millions)			
Total	300‡	791	978	1262	1650	2486	3777
Rich countries	‡	201	248	347	573	858	1114
Poor countries	‡	590	730	915	1077	1628	2663
			Per 1000 annual rate of increase from preceding date				
Total		0·5‡	4	5	5	8	19
Rich countries		‡	4	7	10	8	12
Poor countries		‡	4	5	3	8	23
			Percentage division of world population				
Rich countries			26	26	28	35	35	29
Poor countries			74	74	72	65	65	71

† The rich countries are taken to be those of Europe, U.S.S.R., North
America, temperate South America, Australia, New Zealand, and Japan.
‡ Crude estimate for which division by region is not justified.

TABLE 1.4.2

*Estimates of annual crude birth, death, and natural increase rates
(average rates per 1000 in periods)*

	1800–1900			1900–50			1960–70		
	Birth rate	Death rate	Natural increase	Birth rate	Death rate	Natural increase	Birth rate	Death rate	Natural increase
Rich countries	38	30	8	26	18	8	20	9	11
Poor countries	41	37	4	41	32	9	41	17	24

per cent in the rich. If there were sufficiently accurate data for the past, we would probably find that this size had been reached in a series of jerks, possibly even with stagnation, but our knowledge only allows a broad view which evens these out into a progressive acceleration of growth. Prior to the birth of Christ, the annual rate of growth averaged less than 1 per 10 000 per year; from then until 1700 it was about ½ per 1000 per year; the huge leap to 5 per 1000 in 1700–1900 was followed by a relatively modest rise to 8 per 1000 in 1900–50, but the latter average disguises to some extent the sharp upturn towards the end of the period, which has continued to give a current rate of over 20 per 1000 per year. It is interesting to note that the most striking relative transformation of growth rates was in 1700–1900 when the death rates were lowered in the present rich countries, although the upturn of the past 30 years, following the extension of this benefit to the poorer countries, has had a far greater absolute effect in terms of population size.

The fall in death rates in the richer countries was followed by a drop in birth rates also, but the natural increase at 10 per 1000 is still very high by any previous standard; in the poor countries the birth rate at over 40 per 1000 is probably higher than was ever attained before and combines with a still heavy, although much reduced, mortality to give a yearly growth of the order of 24 per 1000. It is essential to bear in mind, as a yardstick but not as a forecast, the implications of continued growth at current rates. With an over-all growth measure of 2 per cent p.a. the population size would multiply seven- to eight-fold in a century, over fifty-fold in two centuries and some 20 000-fold in five centuries. The last multiple is in fact 80 000 if the rich and the poor countries are treated separately, since the numbers in the swifter-growing section swamp those in the slower and push up the over-all rate.

Whatever the arguments about the seriousness of the consequences we can conclude with certainty that the population size is not now in a state of continuous, balanced control. That temporary imbalance is not necessarily a disaster can be seen from the past history of a number of the richest countries. It must be noted, however, both that the present discrepancy between birth and death rates is far larger than has been previously experienced and that the imbalance has been substantial for at least two centuries.

Population control in primitive communities

In order to emphasize more sharply the nature of the factors which influence the control of population size in complex communities, it is convenient to indicate the situation in primitive conditions as a contrast. To bring out the essentials only a schematic, simplified picture is necessary of a small tribal group, subsisting by hunting–gathering or, perhaps, by small-scale, limited agriculture in an environment far from ideally favourable. In demographic terms the key feature would be the high and erratic death rate; this could be regarded, in fact, as the defining characteristic of a primitive population from the present viewpoint. In such an admittedly exemplary case the control of the relation of community size to resources can plausibly be taken to operate in ways for which there is reasonable evidence—although it falls short of being fully convincing and specific investigation is difficult.

The high and fluctuating mortality is a dominating influence, since it limits greatly the extent to which the birth rate can exceed the death rate. Although it is biologically possible for fertility to be so high that growth is substantial even with the level of death rates postulated (say 40 per 1000 per year), a moderate restriction of births by social processes can preserve a rough balance. Perhaps the two most important means are the long duration of breast feeding of children which leads to intervals of post-partum infertility averaging up to 12 months and separation of husband and wife, for example when the former goes on lengthy hunting trips or cultivates an area far removed from his main holding. There are many studies of post-partum infertility but those of Potter and colleagues [23] and of Morley [19] are especially interesting in the present context. Henin's [16] work on the settlement of nomadic tribes of the Sudan is relevant to the separation issue. The point about these two fertility control mechanisms is the immediacy of their impact, since both length of lactation and separation intervals would increase when resources were limited. A picture then emerges of how population size reacts sharply to the relation with the environment. Moderate growth in good times is quickly reversed by a rise in mortality in bad, which would also lower the live birth rate by increasing foetal deaths; and with equal speed and directness the bio-social influences reduce fertility. Good data which have a bearing on this interpretation are hard to find, but there is a series of vital statistics from Iceland which provides accurate fertility and mortality measures from the beginning of the eighteenth century. In the early period, there were several years in which over 10 per cent of the population died, with a reduced birth rate and a sharp population decrease. Hansen [15] is at present studying the vital statistics patterns over time.

Dynamics of population growth

In attempting to understand the factors in the birth–death balance of complex communities, we must be aware of certain demographic relations which regulate population dynamics. These relations are not, of course, different from the ones which operate in primitive communities but their implications are profoundly so because of the changed levels of the vital rates. The most basic is the lowered incidence of mortality and *its relative stability*. The expectation of life at birth (the mean years lived per person born at the current rates of dying) now exceeds 50 years in most of the poor countries and 70 years in the richer ones. Variations from year to year, although significant for, say, the burden on the medical services, are of negligible impact in modifying the growth rate. This compares with life expectancies of around 25 years on average in the primitive community, dropping in severe epidemics to 6 years as, for example, in eighteenth-century Iceland.

Lotka [18] provided the scientific ideas and tools for studying the relation of the long-term growth of a population to its fertility, mortality, and age-distribution. He showed how the Net Reproduction Rate, which can be defined as the expected number of female children born per female child who experiences over her lifetime the prevailing age schedule of mortality and fertility, measures the long-term increase in population per generation, when transient effects of age-distribution become negligible. Thus a Net Reproduction Rate of 2 means a potential doubling of the population size in a generation of some 27 years, equivalent to a $2\frac{1}{2}$ per cent p.a. growth rate. (The generation length varies with the distribution of births by age of mother and the mortality pattern, within modest limits, but this is unimportant for the present purpose.) To a good enough approximation, for bringing out the fertility–mortality–growth relation, the Net Reproduction Rate can be taken as the mean completed family size of women (all children, not just survivors), reduced to slightly less than one half to give the girls and multiplied by the proportion of females who survive from birth to the middle of the reproductive period (say 27 years).

If there was no mortality at all a completed family size of 2·05 children per woman (or about 2·2 per marriage with the nuptiality patterns in Britain and most of Western Europe) would give a Net Reproduction Rate of 1 and imply ultimate zero population growth. In the rich countries about 97 per cent of girls survive from birth to the middle of the reproductive period. This raises the completed family size per woman required for zero growth only to 2·1. The negligible impact of mortality on population increase in developed countries was put in perspective in the 1959 paper of Coale [4] which examined the growth implication of immortality. An increase in mean family size from 2·1 to 2·5 in a country of low death rates gives a Net Reproduction Rate of 1·2, corresponding to a long-term annual growth rate of 7 per 1000; a mean family size of 3·0 implies a natural increase of 15 per 1000 p.a. There are two important conclusions. In the richer countries, population growth is dominated by fertility and it is sensitive to relatively small changes in family size.

In the poorer complex communities of today the order of the measures is different but the consequences not dissimilar. Typically, some 70 per cent of females survive to reproduce with mortality which although extremely high relative to what has been achieved in the most healthy countries (150 of 1000 births dead by age 2 compared with the present minimum of 13 per 1000) is still much reduced from the past. With a norm of about 6 for the completed family size, the Net Reproduction Rate is 2·0, with a potential doubling of the population in a generation or $2\frac{1}{2}$ per cent increase p.a. To reduce the growth rate ultimately to zero would require a halving of family size to 3 children, even in the unlikely event that, meanwhile, mortality remained at the same high level.

In complex communities then, the influence of the moderate to low, relatively stable mortality in the control of population size is slight. Any such mechanism must operate through the birth rate. But the response here must be quite different in kind from that postulated earlier for primitive communities; the long breast-feeding and separation controls, effectively, have disappeared in the rich countries, are being reduced in the poorer ones, and in any case are not set into action in the same way by high, fluctuating mortality. Influences on fertility, then, must be less direct and immediate. In addition, controls through birth rates have a fundamentally different effect than those operating on mortality. Deaths occur at all ages and fluctuations, although to some extent selective, alter the numbers over a broad range of life. The effect on the age-structure of the population, and through this on the relation of fertility to the birth rate, although not neutral, is moderate and regular. The demographic stability of a community is not greatly affected by fluctuating mortality. On the other hand,

TABLE 1.4.3

Projections of the population of England and Wales on different assumptions (size of population in millions)

Year	Mortality of 1970					Falling mortality				
	Total fertility from 1975									
	1·8	1·9	2·0	2·1	2·2	1·8	1·9	2·0	2·1	2·2
1975	49·3	49·3	49·3	49·3	49·3	49·3	49·3	49·3	49·3	49·3
2000	50·1	51·0	52·0	52·9	53·9	51·3	52·3	53·2	54·2	65·1
2025	47·7	50·2	52·7	55·3	58·0	51·7	54·1	56·7	59·4	62·1
2050	41·8	46·0	50·5	55·4	60·5	48·3	52·8	57·5	62·7	68·1
2075	36·0	41·7	48·0	55·1	62·9	43·6	50·0	57·1	65·0	73·7

a change in the birth rate has an immediate effect only on the numbers of young children, and the age-composition consequences take generations to work themselves out. The implications of this will now be examined more specifically.

The relation between the Net Reproduction Rate and the ultimate population growth takes a long time to establish itself when there is a change in fertility from a previously relatively constant level. Thus, if the birth rate falls over a period of say 15 or 20 years, the numbers in the reproductive period who are the product of the higher past measures form a larger proportion of the population; the age-composition then favours comparatively higher birth and lower death rates, and thus slows the decrease of the growth to its new potential level. There is, then, a momentum from the past which slows the process of braking (or indeed acceleration). Tables 1.4.3 and 1.4.4 give examples from different extremes of the range of complex communities. The first shows population projections for England and Wales under several different assumptions, calculated recently by my colleague Dr. V. Beral. Although the mean family size for ultimate zero growth is 2·1, if this measure was maintained from 1975 with the present

TABLE 1.4.4

Projections of the population of Africa on different assumptions (size of population in millions and percentage increase over 1970)

Falling mortality and net reproduction rate reaching 1·0 by:

Year		1970–5	2000–5	2040–5
1970	Number	344	344	344
1980	Number	373	432	442
	% increase	8	26	28
1990	Number	419	530	570
	% increase	22	54	66
2000	Number	464	620	729
	% increase	35	80	112
2050	Number	565	899	1664
	% increase	64	161	383

mortality the population would continue to grow at a fair rate with an addition of 6·0 million (12 per cent) by the year 2025. If mortality fell in accordance with the present trend downwards the growth by A.D. 2025 would be 10·1 millions (20 per cent). Assuming a decrease of the mean family size to 1·9 (10 per cent below the level for ultimate zero natural increase) the maximum population size for current mortality would not be reached until about the year 2000 at 1·7 million (3 per cent) greater, and with projected mortality by A.D. 2025 at 4·8 million (10 per cent) more. These calculations illustrate both the sensitivity of the low fertility/low mortality balance and the long time-scale of adjustment.

Frejka [12], in his studies of the implications of present demographic measures for the future in the different regions of the world, has made some illuminating calculations for Africa. In these he has projected populations on a wide range of different assumptions, not primarily to provide forecasts of what will happen but to examine the implications of different paths. Some relevant values are shown in Table 1.4.4. In all projections the Net Reproduction Rate is assumed to fall to one over different periods of time. Alternative schedules of mortality and fertility change are also considered but the variations from these do not affect the present assessment. The points to note are that differences in the braking speed have relatively little effect on the population size by the end of the century but an enormous impact in the longer term. For example, a fall to a Net Reproduction Rate of 1, in 70 years as compared with 30 years, gives a 112 per cent population increase as against 80 per cent by the year 2000, but the corresponding additions by A.D. 2050 are 383 per cent and 161 per cent. The meaningful time-scale of population growth is generations rather than years.

The consequences of the concentration of number adjustments at an age-point, that is the births, are not confined to the changes in population size. They also affect the relations between the proportions in age-groups. Contrary to intuition the age-composition of a population is mainly determined by the level and trend of fertility and not by mortality. Of course, if the incidence of deaths falls, people live longer and, therefore, contribute to an increase in numbers in the older age-groups: since mortality decreases, however, normally affect all age-groups (at least up to middle years of life) there will also be greater numbers in the reproductive span, giving more births and children at the same level of family fertility. The lower mortality then causes a higher growth rate but little change in age-composition, except perhaps towards the end of life. There is a close correspondence between the proportion of children in a population and the mean completed family size, whatever the mortality. Thus 6 children per woman completed family size equates to about 45 per cent of the population under 15 years and $2\frac{1}{2}$ children per woman to about 22 per cent.

If there is a fairly rapid change in fertility, cyclic movements are induced in the age-structure as the birth cohorts move through the reproductive period. In severe cases the economic consequences could be serious. Over the past few years many computer models of this process have been examined, most extensively by Frejka [11]. He vividly, if extremely, illustrated the phenomenon by calculating the age-composition and birth-rate fluctuations which would occur in the U.S.A. if the annual growth were to drop sharply to zero and fertility adjusted to hold the population size constant. At the point of time of his study this required a fall in the crude birth rate to 8 per 1000 by 1970, but thereafter it had to increase to 16 per 1000 by 60 years later. Over this period the proportion of the population under 20 years of age would have moved from 38 per cent in 1965 to 20 per cent in 1990 and up again to 30 per cent in 2040. This shows another aspect of the uneven and reluctant way in which population size responds to fertility change.

The desirable balance is of low fertility against low mortality, and many of the rich countries are or have been within reach of that position. The low level of fertility required compared with the 'natural' level and the sensitivity of the birth–death equation have been explained. It is useful to consider briefly two questions which are important for the achievement of the aim. The first is the distribution of completed family sizes. Women married in 1959 in England and Wales, at all ages under 45 years, had by marriage duration 12 years given birth on average to 2·22 children. Only 14 per cent of them had 4 or more births and 9 per cent had none. The great majority had 1–3 children, and this will remain true at the end of their reproductive period. Adjustments in family size to control population growth must come, therefore, primarily from shifts in the 1–3 range (although, of course, a complete revolution in attitudes to childlessness in marriage is possible). The significant movements are not from large to small families but within degrees of smallness.

The other issue is the extent to which the present efficiency of contraception makes it possible for a refined control of family size to be possible. Clearly, fertility can be lowered below the level necessary for zero growth even at the low mortality of the richer countries. In a number of cases this has happened, but it is not the same question. Even with low probabilities of contraceptive failure at each act of intercourse the expected conceptions in regular partnerships, over the substantial length of the reproductive period remaining when the desired family size has been achieved, are appreciable (certainly in comparison with the changes in tenths of a child per family which have important population growth consequences). Although there have been excellent studies of this problem, for example by Potter [22], the details are still somewhat doubtful, since with most methods contraceptive efficiency depends in part on the strength of the desire to avoid pregnancy. The general conclusion must be, however, that the precision of control of conception is unsatisfactory and that a refined determination of individual family size must rely fairly heavily on abortion.

Possible population control mechanisms

The factors and constraints which must govern any mechanism for controlling population size in complex communities have been outlined. The conditions in primitive communities were different. Nevertheless, it is still possible to hold that there has been a change in expression of the forces rather than a transformation. On this view the long period of lowered mortality and high growth rate is regarded as merely a greatly extended fluctuation during which it has been possible because of technological advance to cushion the immediate impact of the environment and resources on mortality. The control mechanism is then still the increased death rates which will come in time from famine and pollution, with the secondary reaction of fertility to these. Although there is often some element of belief in authoritative world action also, this assessment reflects a substantial body of opinion, particularly among biologists. Ehrlich [8] is the obvious example. There is certainly an arguable case, but to sustain it the social and economic forces which led to substantial falls in fertility in the rich and some poorer countries have to be dismissed as largely irrelevant.

The socio-economic description which has formed the frame-work within which social scientists have considered the control of population size is the transition theory. Although many demo-graphers (including Notestein [21], its main inventor) are far from happy about its explanatory and regulatory power, it has yet to be replaced by anything with comparable generality. A recent account is given by De Jong [5] following the caution usual nowa-days that the theory is not a law of population growth but an empirical description of the world's demographic history; even this statement is extremely doubtful. Briefly, the theory says that mortality is reduced by socio-economic advances. At some interval of time the same advances lead to a comparable reduction in fertility. Over the period, the transition is from birth and death rates in balance at a high level, through rapid growth as the latter fall earlier than the former to a new balance at low rates. On this basis most of the world is now in the intermediate phase.

There are a variety of difficulties which make this an unconvincing candidate as a model which can guide the understanding of the control of population. The crucial one is simply that size and growth do not appear as forces in the process at all but only as a consequence of other developments. There is no claim that size and growth as such will be critical elements in the promotion of the socio-economic changes and thus, through negative feedback on fertility, correct towards stability. On the contrary, the prevailing view is that very high population growth rates hinder the attainment of the economic levels associated with such factors as urbanization, employment and status of women, and universal and lengthy schooling, which contribute to the restriction of family size. It is, therefore, not immediately clear that there is any necessary relationship between the population size and socio-economic changes rather than a coincidental one.

Some of the complexities of the problem can be illustrated by asking the question, 'Does economic improvement lead to higher or lower fertility?' There is reasonable evidence that peasant farming communities have higher fertility than nomadic groups and that the more assured food-supply, with the associated modifications in social organization that come from the settlement to agriculture, increase the growth rate: see, for example, the paper by Henin [16]. In Europe fertility fell as the standard of living rose, but the sharpest decrease to very low levels in the 1930s came in the economic depression. Up to the 1950s family sizes were larger for the poorer social classes in Europe but in several countries this relationship has now been reversed [26]. The answer can only be that in some circumstances economic improvement can lead to higher fertility and in some to lower fertility. This relativity in the operation of socio-economic factors is reinforced by the results from the Princeton study of the fertility transition in Europe which has been undertaken over the past few years. A massive effort was made to gather together detailed measures of fertility trends, not only for countries but for significant regions within them, and to relate these to social and economic indicators. Although only limited reports [6, 17] have as yet been published, it is clear that there were great variations in the response of fertility to the socio-economic developments both in size and in time. The general trend downwards had multiple causes which did not operate in the same way in different populations.

One directly demographic feature has been postulated as a major determinant in the transition process. When mortality falls, the probability that parents with small families will have no surviving children (particularly sons) to comfort and support them in old age is reduced. It is argued that this removes one strong incentive to a large family norm. Heer and his co-workers [20] have constructed theoretical models of how this process might work. These have been rightly criticized for not taking into account the problems of variations in mortality from family to family as well as the complexity and the lengthy time-scale of the process of realization that conditions have altered. Clearly, however, this feature has a basic importance as the removal of a constraint which would hinder the operation of other influences. It does not automatically ensure that they will have an effect.

Although many accounts of transition theory imply that the richer countries have already passed through the intermediate phase and reached the haven of balance at low fertility and mortality (see Bogue [1] and De Jong [5]), the evidence for such a claim is weak. Many of these countries still have growth rates of the order of 1 per cent p.a., which is too high to be sustained for great lengths of time. It is true that Net Reproduction Rates fell to near 1, implying ultimate zero growth, in most of Europe during the 1930s, but this was a transient phenomenon; more refined cohort analyses, which take into account that families are built over the mating lives of the parents and not established by the rates in a short period of time, demonstrate that reproduction continued on average to be above replacement. Forty years later, the transition is still resolutely avoiding completion [13]. This is not to suggest, of course, that there is anything inherently unlikely in the birth rate falling to equal or indeed descend below the death rate. What is lacking is any convincing explanation of how or why the two should have any close correspondence to each other at all.

It is possible to describe the demographic trends of the past two centuries in terms something like the following. Mortality fell because of technological innovations in food and water supply, housing, social organization, and finally medicine. The improved survivorship of children and the other consequences of the technological advances opened up a number of options for ways of living, some of which could best be pursued if parents had smaller families. It altered their assessment of the value of children as opposed to other good things. The Western countries developed in such a way that these options were taken, and fertility in consequence reduced. It might be argued that there was a high probability that, given a range of attractive options to large families, societies would choose them. That there is no necessity for them to do so is illustrated by religious communities such as the Hutterites of North America, who have successfully combined high fertility and low mortality to the extent of increasing at least twenty-fold in 70 years [7]. There is nothing in this description to suggest that falls in fertility should exactly compensate for the drop in mortality.

The fall in death rates in the poorer countries has been faster than in the West, and the impact of technological innovation, particularly in medicine, has been greater simply because it came at a later and therefore more advanced stage. The equation of other developments, for example, in education, employment of women, and industrialization in the poor countries with the history of change in the rich is more difficult because of doubts about the comparability of what is being measured. Nevertheless, directions are similar. Thus the trends in conditions which can lead to alterations in the relative value given to the production of children are evident. That falls in fertility may follow such movements, in cultures which do not stem directly from those of people of European stock, is shown by the example of Japan [27] and, more recently, Ceylon [9] and Malaya [3] among others. There is no reason to expect that patterns of change in the relation with fertility measures in the Third World will follow closely those of the West (and it has been pointed out above that the latter were far from regular). We may guess that the probability that the options to large families will be accepted in the poor countries is increased by the impact of the preceding choice of the rich, which creates both a norm and an ideology. There is convincing evidence that the adoption of the ideas and practice of family limitation was facilitated, at least, by the existence of an appropriate, geographically near forerunner: see, for example, the discussion by Demeny [6] of the determinants of change in nineteenth-century Austria–Hungary. The present abundance of forerunners and the wider spread of communications are likely also to accelerate the speed of adoption of the new practices once these have been accepted by a significant nucleus. It is then possible to foresee a substantial fall in fertility and reduction of population growth over the next 20 or 30 years in the poorer countries, without holding either that the process could be ascribed to anything which was logically termed a control mechanism or that it solved the problem of keeping a satisfactory balance between population size and resources.

State intervention

The discussion has focused on the response of the individual, potential parent to social and economic forces. The balance of pressure is now complicated by the widespread adoption of government population policies, that is, deliberate measures by the state to influence growth rates and, in the long term therefore, size in the interests of development aims; generally at present the attempt is to reduce birth rates and hence growth, in the belief that economic advantage, in investment allocation and manpower management, can thus be gained. This can certainly be regarded as a concept which is different in kind from the possible control systems previously considered, and one which is specifically and directly concerned with the balance of population against resources and the environment. In theory, at least, it is also a mechanism which can act with foresight, applying correction pressures at the stage when their results can appear in the required time, instead of when the imbalance has already occurred.

The essential argument is whether state policy can be effective, whether it can contribute any extra factor which can outweigh, reinforce, or counteract the powerful social and economic forces which are the prime determinants of family size. If a positive answer is given to the question, the next step is to define the means by which the policy can operate. It is not appropriate to give a detailed assessment of the conflicting viewpoints here (the literature is large and varied). There is, however, much evidence to suggest that the powers of the state to influence fertility or growth, at least to the extent that it has been regarded as practicable to apply them so far, are limited and marginal, whether the measures take the form of service provision, economic incentives or deterrents, legal prohibitions, or otherwise. There are, of course, several countries (Taiwan [10], South Korea, Singapore [30]) in which falls in birth rates coincide with government policies towards such an outcome, but in each case it is arguable that the socio-economic conditions could have caused the fall without state intervention. The reasons why some population scientists doubt the capacity of government measures to modify the existing pressures significantly are nicely illustrated by two recent 'natural' experiments.

Between 1961 and 1968 the birth rate in Hong Kong, standardized for age-composition changes, fell from 35·5 to 25·3 coincidental with a strong government-supported programme to reduce population growth through the use of family planning. Sui-Ying Wat and Hodge [29] have examined the demographic trends in terms of features of social change. They derived an equation expressing the average linear relation of fertility to indices of higher education, women in the labour force, and infant mortality for the period 1952–67, which partly precedes and partly includes the major family-planning effort. When the recorded index values are inserted in the equation the resulting estimated fertilities agree closely with those recorded for each year. The addition of a family-planning utilization measure improves the relationship only slightly. A plausible conclusion is that the fall in births was mainly a consequence of social and economic change; the government family-planning programme altered the expression of the fertility determinants but contributed little, if anything, to the impact of the forces.

A series of events, which leads to the same conclusion, occurred in Romania: see, for example, the studies of Glicklich [14] and Teitelbaum [28]. In that country the crude birth rate had fallen by 1966 to 14·3 per 1000; the major control on fertility was the high incidence of legal abortion for which there are no official statistics, but estimates suggest the numbers per year substantially exceeded the live births. On 1 November 1966, the government amended the abortion law, restricting the application of its provisions to a small group of cases where there were serious health problems, because of fears about the slowing rate of population growth. The action was, therefore, a specific measure of population policy. In the third quarter of 1967 the crude birth rate reached 39 per 1000, an unparalleled level for a developed country, but it immediately began to fall rapidly. By the end of 1971 it was below 20 and still decreasing despite the state's prohibition of aids to contraception. The story is not yet over and the full implications are not assessable, but the resistance of a population to government pressure exerted contrary to the dominant social forces is obvious. The latter were thwarted but mainly, and perhaps entirely, in the short term only, despite the extremity of the action.

These case studies illustrate sufficiently the point that government policy is operating within a context of powerful, fundamental fertility determinants. It is difficult, therefore, to isolate its contributing effects, and the attempt to do so may not even be meaningful for the present purpose if they are small and narrowly specific to the particular situation. Nevertheless, in some circumstances, marginal influences may be important if they stimulate the initiation of desirable trends and accelerate their pace or conversely if they retard or deflect undesirable movements. The examination of certain features of population dynamics in the earlier part of the paper brings out the importance of what might seem small variations in basic demographic measures. There are good, if not conclusive, reasons for believing that government policy can have such modifying effects. A convenient illustration comes from the recent events in Mauritius since in this small and, in social and economic terms, relatively simple and homogeneous country the picture may be sharper and more vivid than elsewhere. The island, of some 720 square miles and, in 1971, about 800 000 population, is mainly dependent for its livelihood on sugar production. About 70 per cent of the inhabitants had their origin in the Indian subcontinent (53 per cent Hindus, 17 per cent Moslems), 3 per cent are of the Chinese ethnic group; most of the remainder are Creoles, largely of African descent and Catholic in religion (as are some of the Chinese). In the late 1940s and early 1950s, the death rate in the country fell with a rapidity unequalled elsewhere, mainly because of public-health measures such as malaria eradication, which could be applied relatively easily because of the island's conditions (compactness, fair prosperity, good communications, a literate population, etc.). The decrease in crude death rate was from 27·5 per 1000 in 1944–8 to 12·9 per 1000 in 1954–8. Population pressures on the limited economy and area soon became evident and a government-supported family-planning programme expanded rapidly from 1964–5. By 1971, the crude birth rate had dropped to 25·1 per 1000 from 40 per 1000 in 1963, with a fascinating and consistent picture of the spread in family-planning acceptance from high-parity women in the late reproductive ages to those newly married with 1 child and even no children [31]. The trend was led by the Chinese, whose fertility fell by 1971 from that of a primitive population to European levels, followed closely by the Indian group and then the Creole group. Over this very short period of time, there were few, if any, signs of improvement in the social and economic indicators which might be regarded as signposts of fertility determinants. Although conditions were such that a drop in the birth rate might have occurred without government support for family planning, it is hard to accept that the effect would have been so rapid and comprehensive. A much more plausible judgement is that the deliberate policy and action triggered and accelerated the movement.

To return to the main theme, it is possible to see population policies operating as a partial control mechanism where the discrepancies between the aims and the constraints (economic, social, political, psychological) are small. On this view government action could adjust small deviations from a desired balance back in the right direction, serving as a guide rather than an authority. Perhaps most of the developed countries of the world have approached sufficiently near to the desired balance for these conditions to be applicable. Such a belief, of course, does not by itself give any grounds for hope that a solution, other than worsening conditions and resource exhaustion with higher mortality, will be found in those countries, for example India, where the discrepancy between policy and constraints is at present large. Equally, the constraints imposed by the social and economic conditions may not be unalterable, but we know little about how desirable changes can be initiated or encouraged within the scope of the measures which are practicable. Optimism that the more severe consequences of unbalanced population growth will be avoided must rely more on a belief in the lucky accident (or perhaps that the history of the developed countries will increase the probability of repeating the earlier accident) than in any deterministic system of nicely adjusted painless control.

Stability of population size in developed countries

With such imbalance and resulting problems in the poorer regions of the world, it may seem academic to give much emphasis to the situation in the richer countries where the trends are relatively so gentle and the changes which would reverse them so small. Nevertheless, the long-term consequences for population size and use of resources in such countries are by no means slight; the strength of the concern is sufficiently well exemplified by the establishment by governments of Population Commissions and similar instruments, as in the U.S.A., the Netherlands, Australia, and the United Kingdom.

We may ask whether, in countries such as these, there is any underlying 'natural' mechanism which could help to reverse sharp fluctuations away from the level of demographic measures which could maintain a relatively constant population size. There is one interesting, but far from established, possibility. Ryder [25] has suggested that in modern times of fairly effective contraception there is a negative correlation between family sizes in successive generations in the U.S.A., that is, a birth cohort which is larger than those for neighbouring periods will tend to produce smaller numbers of children than the average level and vice versa. Study of this phenomenon is extremely difficult because of the limited length of time-series for which low fertility has been established through extensive deliberate planning of families and because of the interference of major disturbances, particularly the World Wars, but there are certainly some indications of its existence in the United Kingdom as well as the U.S.A. The suggested influencing factors are the relative disadvantages which a cohort locally larger in time suffers (in education, careers, etc.) modifying decisions on family size by a reaction against the experience. The presence of such a self-adjusting reaction could be an important factor in preserving an achieved equilibrium, particularly if it was reinforced by deliberate state policy applied through propaganda and economic measures. Because of the long time-scale of demographic effects and the sensitivity of population size to marginal changes some such model of combined intrinsic forces and directed, corporate intervention seems essential if a balance with resources is to be maintained. This is not a foolish vision but we are a long way from having the knowledge to translate model into reality.

REFERENCES

1. Bogue, D. J. (1969). *Principles of demography*, Wiley, New York.
2. Brass, W. (1970). The growth of world population. In *Population control* (ed. A. Allison), pp. 131–51. Penguin Books, Harmondsworth.
3. Caldwell, J. C. (1963). Fertility decline and female chances of marriage in Malaya, *Population Studies* **17**, 20–32.
4. Coale, A. J. (1959). Increases in expectation of life and population growth, *Proceedings of the international population conference, Vienna*. International Union for the Scientific Study of Population.
5. De Jong, G. F. (1972). Patterns of human fertility and mortality. In *The structure of human populations* (ed. G. A. Harrison and A. J. Boyce), pp. 32–56. Clarendon Press, Oxford.
6. Demeny, P. (1972). Early fertility decline in Austria–Hungary: a lesson in demographic transition. In *Population and social change* (ed. D. V. Glass and R. Revelle), pp. 153–72. Edward Arnold, London.
7. Eaton J. W. and Mayer, A. J. (1953). The social biology of very high fertility among the Hutterites, *Hum. Biol.* **25**, 206–64.
8. Ehrlich, P. R. and Ehrlich, A. H. (1970). *Population resources and environment: issues in human ecology*. W. H. Freeman, San Francisco.
9. Fernando, D. F. S. (1972). Recent fertility decline in Ceylon, *Population Studies* **26**, 445–53.
10. Freedman, R. and Takeshita, J. Y. (1969). *Family planning in Taiwan*. Princeton University Press, Princeton, New Jersey.
11. Frejka, T. (1968). Reflections on the demographic conditions needed to establish a U.S. stationary population growth, *Population Studies* **22**, 379–97.
12. —— (1971). Alternative population prospects for Africa, Paper contributed to the African Population Conference, Accra. (To be published in the Conference Proceedings.)
13. Glass, D. V. (1968). Fertility trends in Europe since the Second World War, *Population Studies* **22**, 103–46.
14. Glicklich, M. (1972). *Some demographic effects of Romania's pronatalist population policy*. Dissertation as part requirement for the M.Sc. degree at the London School of Economics.
15. Hansen, H. O. (1972). Data supplied by the author from studies not yet published.
16. Henin, R. A. (1968). Fertility differentials in the Sudan, *Population Studies* **22**, 147–64.
17. Livi-Bacci, M. (1972). Fertility and population growth in Spain in the eighteenth and nineteenth centuries. In *Population and social change* (ed. D. V. Glass and R. Revelle), pp. 173–84. Edward Arnold, London.
18. Lotka, S. J. (1939). *Théorie analytique des Associations Biologique*, Part II. Hermann et Cie, Paris.

19. MARTIN, W. J., MORLEY, D., and WOODLANDS, M. (1964). Intervals between births in a Nigerian village, *J. Paediat. African Child Health* **10**, 82–5.
20. MAY, D. A. and HEER, D. M. (1968). Son survivorship motivation and family size in India: a computer simulation, *Population Studies* **22**, 199–210.
21. NOTESTEIN, F. W. (1952). The economic problems of population change, *Proceedings of the eighth international conference of agricultural economists, East Lansing, Mich.*, pp. 13–31, Oxford University Press, London.
22. POTTER, R. G. (1971). Inadequacy of a one-method family planning programme, *Studies in Family Planning* **2**, 1–6.
23. ——, WYON, J. B., PARKER, M. and GORDON, J. E. (1965). A case study of birth interval dynamics, *Population Studies* **19**, 81–96.
24. REGISTRAR GENERAL FOR ENGLAND AND WALES (1971). *Annual Statistical Review*, Part II. H.M.S.O., London.
25. RYDER, N. B. (1970). Contribution to the third conference on the mathematics of population. University of Chicago, Chicago, Ill.
26. TABAH, L. (1971). *Rapport sur les relations entre le fécondité et la condition sociale et économique de la famille en Europe; leurs répercussions sur la politique sociale. Second European Population Conference.* Council of Europe, Strasbourg.
27. TAEUBER, I. B. (1956). Fertility and research in fertility in Japan, *Milbank memor. Fund Quart.* **34**, 129–49.
28. TEITELBAUM, M. S. (1972). Fertility effects of the abolition of legal abortion in Romania, *Population Studies* **26**, 405–17.
29. WAT, SUI-YING and HODGE, R. W. (1972). Social and economic factors in Hong Kong's fertility decline, *Population Studies* **26**, 455–64.
30. WOLFERS, D. (1970). The Singapore family planning program: further evaluation data, *Am. J. Pub. Health* **60**, 2354–60.
31. XENOS, C. (1973). Data supplied by the author from studies not yet published.

1.5. Population growth in developed countries

D. V. GLASS

Martin White Professor of Sociology, London University

THOUGH there are many common factors in the demographic situation of industrialized countries, there are important differences in the socio-economic context within which those factors operate. In a general lecture not many of those differences can be explored. But I shall try to indicate some of them and also draw attention to developments which appear to me to be especially significant in attempting to assess the present situation and the prospects for the near future.

In order to appreciate what is happening today, it is useful to begin by looking at the general picture in the 1930s. For many industrialized countries that period saw the lowest birth rates and levels of fertility since the initiation of the secular decline in family size—a decline which generally began in the late nineteenth century. There were differences in the extent of the decline as between Western and South and East Europe, partly explained by different marriage patterns. Most of the overseas countries in the industrialized group also showed relatively low levels of fertility— notably Australia, New Zealand, and the U.S.A. Japan was exhibiting the early signs of a demographic transition, but its Gross Reproduction Rate in the early 1930s was still more than as high as that of England and Wales. In much of the Western World there was a feeling of impending depopulation, a feeling added to by the publication of population projections, many of which assumed a further fall in fertility. France intensified its pronatalist measures, leading finally, in 1939, to the comprehensive '*Code de la Famille*'. There were also pronatalist measures in Belgium, Italy, and Germany; and Sweden, too, initiated policies, to counter the threat of falling numbers— though on a very different basis. Concern with prospective depopulation in Britain did not result in pronatalist action. Instead, there was a major improvement in our vital statistics and, later, the appointment of a Royal Commission on Population. Though he no doubt intended it as a joking aside, Sir Dennis Robertson was reflecting a not uncommon view when he said, in 1945, that one of the two entries which every conscientious Englishman made in the Agenda Section of his diary was 'must raise net reproduction rate to at least one' (the other was 'must increase the volume of exports at least 50 per cent above the 1938 level') [17]. Japan, too, in spite of its high Gross Reproduction Rate, included pronatalism in its imperialist policy.

Yet it was also during the 1930s that there was a break in the secular decline of fertility in those countries which had been most affected by it. By the mid-1930s, the beginnings of stabilization had been achieved. That this was not realized at the time is understandable. The available demographic statistics were generally inadequate, even in Europe and the U.S.A., and so were the techniques of analysis. But in addition, even if there had been comprehensive statistics and suitable analyses, it would have taken quite a number of years to be reasonably sure that family size had really ceased to fall, especially when, at the same time, intervals between births had been changing. In demography, as in many other fields, there is often no substitute for waiting. To cite one example: in Britain marital fertility had already begun to rise by the time the Royal Commission on Population began its work, though it was largely through the work of the Commission that this was shown to be happening. The period or conventional Net Reproduction Rate for England and Wales, which had been under 0·8 in the 1930s, was almost 1·2 in 1946-9, appearing to imply a dramatic change from a prospect of an ultimate fall in numbers of 20 per cent per generation to a prospective increase of about the same magnitude [16]. In some other Western countries the change was even more startling. Period reproduction rates exaggerated the quantitative extent of the change. Nevertheless, the demographic situation after World War II was different from that at the beginning of the 1930s.

An important factor in this new situation was the transformation of marriage patterns in many countries. Prior to World War II, Western demographers had paid relatively little attention to the role of marriage in population growth. This is not quite so absurd as it may seem: changes in marriage had been fairly small from the 1850s to the 1930s, and did not account in any major way for the over-all decline in fertility, but from the 1930s onwards both demographic and socio-economic circumstances combined to produce a very different picture. The composition of the population in the marriageable age-range altered, producing a higher ratio of men to women. Several factors were involved: the elimination from the marriageable age-groups of the effect of the losses of men in World War I; return migration in the 1930s and the change in the sex ratio of emigrants after World War II; and also the less sex-selective impact of that war on mortality in many countries. Again, taking England and Wales as an example, in 1931 there were only 835 men aged 25–49 for every 1000 women aged 20–44; by 1961 that ratio had risen to 1020:1000. Increases of this kind occurred in many countries, even in Eastern Europe, and made it possible for a larger proportion of women to marry. But the translation of possibility into reality must have required socio-economic assistance, such as the full employment of the war and immediate postwar years, the higher relative wages of young men and women, and the substantial increases in the employment of married women. It is not unlikely that there was also some epidemic effect, in the sense that when a certain threshold of marriage frequency among one's reference group has been passed, the pressures upon the rest of the group to marry are likely to increase. Such pressures may lead to earlier marriage, young men and women becoming anxious to avoid being 'left out' or 'on the shelf' [5, 6].

In the early 1930s, and probably for the previous two or three centuries, countries in Europe west of a line from Trieste to Leningrad tended to show what John Hajnal [7] has called a 'European' marriage pattern—with a high age at first marriage and under 90 per cent—sometimes under 80 per cent—of women in the age-group 45–9 ever-married. In Eastern Europe, age at marriage was lower and the proportions ever-married were often well above 90 per cent. The demographic and socio-economic factors I have mentioned combined to alter the patterns in many Western countries from the 1930s onwards. To cite England and Wales again, by 1963 proportionately more women had been married by age 30 than was the case by age 50 in 1931. In 1963, in the age-group 20–4, almost 60 per cent of the women had been married, as against only 26 per cent in 1931. If the 1963 marriage rates continued, 96 per cent of women would have been married at least once by their 50th birthday. Nor were such changes limited

to Western Europe. In Eastern Europe, too, age at marriage fell—
quite substantially in several countries. Even the U.S.A., with
traditionally higher female marriage rates and lower ages at
marriage than Western Europe, experienced a marriage boom. In
1960, 72 per cent of women aged 20–4 had been married as compared with 54 per cent in 1930.

Given these increases in the marriage rates, over-all fertility
and replacement rates would have risen even if family size had
remained unchanged. A larger proportion of women in the child-
bearing ages would be married, and especially fairly recently
married, and on both accounts more likely to bear children.
Further, younger marriages generally produce larger families.
But even allowing and standardizing for these factors, many
countries showed additional rises in fertility resulting from the fact
that, at most ages at marriage, women were also having more
children than they had in the past. The increases were modest—a
reduction in childlessness and a shift from 1 to 2 and from 2 to 3
children per family predominated, and there was certainly no
return to large families. But the combination of more and earlier
marriage, moderate increases in family size, and a shortening of
intervals between births—with an increasing proportion of total
fertility being compressed into the first ten years of married life—
gave rise to more abundant annual crops of births. Period replacement rates reflected this fact—in England and Wales they
rose to 1·33 in 1965; in France to 1·34 in 1960–4; in the U.S.A.
to 1·73 in 1955–9; and in Canada to 1·82 in that period, to cite
a few examples. These rates gave the impression of staggeringly
high prospective population growth—though in fact, looked at
more realistically in terms of birth or marriage cohorts, the level
of replacement was considerably lower.

Not all developed countries shared in this upswing. In Eastern
Europe, which prior to World War II was still a region of fairly
high fertility, birth rates and period replacement rates fell fairly
generally after the war, in spite of earlier marriage. This was so in
Czechoslovakia and Hungary as well as in Poland and Romania.
But the greatest fall occurred at the other side of the globe, in
Japan. The period Net Reproduction Rate (over 1·7 in 1947–9,
partly reflecting the immediate post-war baby boom), was only
0·91 in 1960–4. These countervailing tendencies meant a narrowing of the differentials between developed countries.

The postwar movements in fertility which I have attempted to summarize may not seem very remarkable in absolute terms, but they are noteworthy in at least two respects. First, what happened in Western and Central Europe, as well as in the U.S.A., Canada, and Australasia, appeared to represent the exhaustion, and in some cases the apparent reversal, of a trend which had been more or less uninterrupted since the 1870s—indeed, in France and the U.S.A. since the beginning of the nineteenth century—and which had turned even more sharply downward after World War I. Secondly, these changes occurred while at the same time modern techniques for controlling reproduction were becoming more widely accessible and more widely used.

The prolonged decline which reduced fertility by more than 50 per cent between the 1870s and the 1930s is one of the most remarkable features of modern social history. Though there is evidence of effective control of fertility by various groups in earlier periods, the spread of control to an extent which systematically brought down national levels throughout the West was unprecedented. There has been considerable discussion about the causes and also about the nature of the process—whether it was one of innovation or of diffusion. The terms are not exactly free from ambiguity. But in one major sense diffusion rather than innovation was involved—that is, the reduction in fertility was achieved by the wider and more persistent use of old techniques, which owed very little to new technology. Of course, the vulcanization of rubber and, subsequently, the use of liquid latex were important for the development of mechanical contraceptives. However, there is no reason to doubt that the major methods of control applied were coitus interruptus (withdrawal) and abortion. Even in the 1930s this was still the case.

Further, though there were organized movements advocating the use of birth control—they all derived directly or indirectly from the pioneer Malthusian League in this country—such movements received no support from established authority. The churches, both Catholic and Protestant, were opposed to the use of birth control. When, for instance, at the beginning of this century (1908), the Church of England finally decided, with great reluctance, to consider the subject, the committee concerned recommended the 'prohibition of all so-called neo-Malthusian appliances' and 'the prosecution of all who publicly and professionally assist preventive methods'. At almost the same time the Synod of the Netherlands Reformed Church referred to birth control as 'the great sin against the Creator's commandments'. The medical profession was generally hostile; and the state was at best indifferent, but more often antagonistic. Laws were passed, prohibiting, or at least seriously restricting, the sale of contraceptives or the dissemination of birth-control advice—in the Netherlands in 1911, for example, and in Sweden in 1910 [4]. Those countries which adopted pronatalist policies not surprisingly passed similar and even more restrictive legislation; this was especially so in France, Italy, and Germany. Abortion as a means of birth prevention was prohibited everywhere. Even the Soviet Union, which began by legalizing abortion as part of its programme for the socialist emancipation of women, in 1936 retreated to a much less liberal position.

It was not until the 1930s and later that in a very few countries the situation began to improve. In Britain, clinics began to receive some governmental aid, and authoritative opinion, supported by some eminent members of the medical profession, came gradually to recognize the legitimacy of, and the need for a wider provision of, birth-control advice. The birth-control movement as such, greatly strengthened by the formation of the Family Planning Association, broke away from the economic theory of the old Malthusian League and instead campaigned for birth control and family planning as valuable in their own right, regardless of the relevance of the population question. New birth-control clinics were opened, and the numbers of clients increased. Even so, the clinics made only an extremely small direct contribution to the total practice of birth control, and the contraceptive generally recommended by the clinics—the diaphragm—was the least widely used by couples controlling their fertility. In Sweden, it was concern with the threatened depopulation which helped to legitimize birth control, for the basic premise of the new pro-family policy recommended by the Royal Commissions of 1935 and 1941 was 'voluntary parenthood', and the earlier restrictions were removed. Voluntary parenthood was also the basic assumption of the British Royal Commission. Mrs. Margaret Pyke, then Chairman of the Family Planning Association, said of the Commission's Report, 'we could not have written it better ourselves' [10]. But these relaxations occurred at the end of the period. They do not account for the spread of fertility control but were, rather, a recognition and acceptance of the fact that control had so spread as to have become part of customary reproductive behaviour. Using techniques which, at the individual level, were not very efficient and which might, in the case of illegal abortion, be dangerous, populations throughout the West lowered their family-size norms under the pressure of competing alternatives, and succeeded in enforcing those norms. Indeed, as a distinguished American demographer has argued in respect of the U.S.A. in the 1930s, under the impact of economic distress, many couples probably undershot their new norms [18]. This seems to me to be a likely explanation of that fact that, in Britain, uninterrupted marriages taking place in 1925 still showed almost 17 per cent of childlessness after 20 years of married life. No general survey of ideal or desired family sizes has suggested so high proportion of couples wanting to avoid having any children at all.

At the end of World War II, almost throughout the industrial-ized nations, the practice of fertility control had become so wide-spread that it was scarcely possible for established authority to avoid accepting it as a fact. Protestant Churches revised their formal attitudes and the Catholic Church, too, came to accept the principle and to focus the argument upon means rather than ends. In fact, the Catholic Church had authorized the use of the safe-period method in 1930. However, it was not until the 1950s that rapid population growth was conceded to be a problem. In the Soviet Zone, ideology was still anti-Malthusian, but fertility control was accepted on grounds of women's rights and health, no doubt aided by the existence of an acute labour shortage and the need to make full use of the female labour force. Not all the restric-tive legislation was repealed immediately. In West Germany and Italy the Nazi and Fascist laws remained on the statute books for some time. In France, it took a new birth-control movement, divorced from Malthusian theory, to help to generate the pressure which finally led to the repeal of the repressive 1920 legislation. In the U.S.A., it took a Supreme Court decision to give full legal status to birth-control clinics and associated activities. But even before the ending of restrictions, facilities for advice had become more accessible and fertility control more systematic.

In Eastern Europe, access to modern contraceptives was very slow to develop. Instead, following the Soviet Union's reintroduction of a liberal abortion law in 1955, most other countries in the Soviet zone legalized abortion on very wide grounds, and legal abortion became an accepted means of limiting family size. Only the German Democratic Republic, after a trial liberalization in 1947, retreated in 1950. But even there, in 1972 a new law allowed every woman access to abortion on request during the first 12 weeks of pregnancy, the costs being covered by social insurance. In Japan, not as part of deliberate government population policy but in response to public demand, existing legislation was modified shortly after World War II to allow what is virtually abortion on demand—though Japanese officials, who are not especially proud of the development, sometimes deny that this is so. The Japanese population reacted after World War II somewhat as the German population had done after World War I. Highly industrialized and determined to prevent their standard of living from falling, they chose the restriction of their fertility as the most effective form of insurance. In contrast to what had happened in Western Europe, age at marriage rose in Japan. In 1960, 68 per cent of women aged 20–4 years were single; the figure in 1930 had been only 38 per cent.

There are few direct surveys relating to birth-control practice in the 1950s. Nevertheless, there is little reason to doubt that, in a generally more permissive atmosphere in many countries, the proportion of couples controlling their fertility increased and there was some shift from coitus interruptus to more effective techniques, including, in Eastern Europe and Japan, legal abortion. In Britain an estimate based on our 1959–60 sample survey suggests that, for the couples married in 1950–4, the proportion ever-practising birth control was probably around 87 per cent—an estimate fairly closely confirmed by a second survey in 1967–8 [4]. Coitus interruptus was still a widely used technique, but not so widely as was suggested by Lewis-Faning's 1946 survey. Female methods accounted for some 28 per cent of current or most current practice, the condom for an additional 49 per cent, and withdrawal for about 20 per cent. American surveys are not exactly comparable in their form of analysis, but taking the wives aged 30–4 in the 1965 U.S. survey as representing women whose first marriages fell roughly within the period 1950–9, the proportion who had ever-used contraception was 83 per cent for Whites and 69 per cent for Blacks. As to the techniques currently used by birth controllers in that age-group in the U.S.A., coitus interruptus was negligible, female methods accounted for almost 34 per cent, rhythm for 13 per cent, and the condom for 24 per cent, while sterilization (female or male) accounted for 16 per cent [21]. Yet this was the period during which marital fertility was still rising in Britain and the U.S.A., as well as in many other Western countries.

Since the 1950s the availability of fertility control in the West has been affected by rather different circumstances, and the consequences of that control have been different. The mounting concern with rapid population growth in developing countries had at least two results. First, research into contraception became respectable, and Foundations became increasingly involved in supporting it. The manufacture of contraceptives was inevitably affected. But the immediate 'pay-off' of this research went to developed rather than to developing countries. The Pill in its various modifications was more easily afforded and more willingly accepted by women in industrial societies, and soon became one of the more widely used means of birth limitation in those societies. Secondly, once population increase in the Third World had become a cause for international anxiety, that anxiety could scarcely fail to have its repercussions on those developed countries whose crude birth rates continued to be fairly high. Moreover, for some people, a question of ethics appeared to be involved. It did not seem justifiable to advocate birth control for India and Pakistan without attempting to secure tighter control of fertility at home. Very strong support was given to this conclusion by the emergence of the new ecological front. Paul Ehrlich became both a campus hero and a household name in the U.S.A., and had considerable success elsewhere. With population growth being regarded as a major element in pollution and with the world appearing to be caught in the trap of M.I.T. computer simulation programs, pressure groups in many countries advocated wider access to contraception and, if necessary, the implementation of deliberate antinatalist policies. Commissions of inquiry were appointed in the U.S.A. and in Australia. In Britain the Select Committee of the House of Commons took up the subject, and its recommendations led to the appointment of a Governmental Panel on population policy. Demands for women's rights also played a part in pressing for the wider provision of birth-control facilities and for the legalization of abortion. The combination of pressures and concerns led to the extension of birth-control services—in Britain on a national basis and in the U.S.A. for special groups in the population. Abortion was made legally available on wide grounds in Britain in 1967, and over 100 000 British women had legal abortions in 1971 [11]. Perhaps the most striking development has been in the U.S.A., where the Supreme Court recently decided that it is unconstitutional to deny women the right to abortion, and that during the first 3 months of pregnancy the decision and the method should be entirely a matter for women and their doctors [15]. It is unlikely that other Western countries will be able to resist much longer pressures of this kind and strength.

Looking at the situation today against the background of recent changes, it is clear that in the industrialized world as a whole the control of fertility is more widespread than ever before. In Eastern Europe and in Japan the control is largely by means of legal abortion, and not infrequently there are more abortions than live births. In Japan, even though the use of contraception proper has been spreading and abortion rates have begun to fall, it has been estimated that in 1965 there were still 2·96 million abortions as compared with 1·82 million live births [14]. In Hungary, in 1968, abortions exceeded live births by some 50 per cent, and it is believed that in the Soviet Union, too, abortions are in excess of live births by a substantial margin [1, 3, 12].

In the rest of the developed world, abortion—still often illegal—no doubt plays a sizeable part but contraception proper is now also used by the vast majority of married couples, and this is attested to by the results of recent direct-sample investigations. Surveys undertaken for the International Health Foundation in 1970 yielded estimates of the proportions of married women (under 45 years of age) ever-using birth control in several countries. The proportions range from 68 per cent in Italy to 86 per cent in France, with Belgium and West Germany being around 77 per cent and 84 per cent respectively [8, 9]. For Denmark the comparable figure from a national investigation in 1970 is almost 90 per cent [20]. A 1970 inquiry in the U.S.A. reported an over-all figure of 84 per cent—85 per cent among Whites and 75 per cent among Blacks [21]. And our own survey in Britain in 1967–8 showed that among women married in 1961–5 (under 35 years of age at marriage, uninterrupted first marriages), over 91 per cent

had already been using birth control by the time they were interviewed [6]. The birth-control methods involved vary considerably in effectiveness. In Italy, Belgium, and France, coitus interruptus and the safe period were still major techniques in current
use. But the Pill had become very important in several countries.
It accounted for 22 per cent of current use in France and almost
50 per cent in West Germany. For the U.S.A., at the time of the
1970 survey, the comparable figure was 34 per cent, and was substantially higher among younger couples (49 per cent for wives
under 30 years of age). In Britain, among wives married in 1961–5
and currently or recently practising birth control, 21 per cent of
the middle-class and 25 per cent of the working-class women were
using the Pill.

The surveys show that in some countries, even now, significant
proportions of married women have never used contraception.
In addition, statistics of 'ever-use' of birth control hide considerable inequalities in contraceptive practice. There are differences
in such relevant matters as the acquisition of professional advice,
the point in the reproductive history of women at which control is
initiated, the specific techniques adopted, and the persistence and
care with which they are applied. If these inequalities are to be
reduced, far more serious efforts will have to be made in all
countries to provide facilities easily accessible to all women. That,
so to speak, is only the 'mechanical' aspect of the problem; the
question of differences in family-size norms lies deeper in the
social fabric, linked to social class, religion, and education. But
even the 'mechanical' aspect could be manipulated to yield results
of significance. Couples who use birth control to plan or limit
their families still have accidents, by no means all of which are
simply accidents of timing. On the contrary, many conceptions
are definitely unwanted. The more widespread use of contraceptives as effective as the Pill and the provision of facilities for
termination of pregnancy could do much to reduce the frequency
of unwanted pregnancies. Indeed, a study based upon a comparison
of the results of the 1970 and 1965 surveys in the U.S.A. suggests
that this has been happening with the shift from the earlier, conventional methods to the newer and more effective techniques
[21, 2]. The study concludes that this reduction in unwanted
fertility is a major factor in the drop in the U.S. birth rate since
the 1960s, fertility rates having fallen in almost every age group.

Since proportionately more of the higher-parity pregnancies tend to be unwanted or accidental, abortion in Britain and henceforth also in the U.S.A. may still further reduce the incidence of large families; and it may also reverse the post-war upward trend of illegitimate births.

This brings me back to the demographic situation and to the prospects of future growth, and it is necessary to distinguish between Eastern Europe, the Soviet Union, and Japan on the one hand and the remaining industrial societies on the other. In the former group, fertility has generally continued to fall. The period Net Reproduction Rates are almost all barely above unity, and in Czechoslovakia and Hungary they are below unity. In Japan, too, the rates were below unity in 1955–9 and 1960–4 and again in 1968–9. It is most unlikely that those countries will adopt anti-natalist policies. On the contrary, they are concerned about prospective labour shortages, and many of them have been trying to encourage couples to have more children. I doubt whether such policies will be very effective as compared with the pressures which have persuaded couples so greatly to restrict family size. Earlier attempts to raise the birth rate in other countries were scarcely successful. Even the withdrawal of the formerly open abortion law in Romania, followed by a sharp rise in the birth rate, is now showing a smaller effect as couples are no doubt resorting to alternative methods of controlling fertility [19].

However, in the other group of industrial countries, too, the trend of stable, and then rising, fertility appears to have been broken again. Since the 1960s age-specific fertility rates have been falling, quite sharply in some countries. I have already suggested that period reproduction rates are not always good indicators of likely future growth; they are synthetic indices, and they are affected, for example, by the proportions of recently married women and also by changes in birth spacing. A better indication of the level of replacement is given by birth cohort reproduction rates, based upon the mortality and fertility experiences of the actual period through which the women have passed from birth to the end of the child-bearing period. If indices of this kind are used, then for many industrial countries the reproduction rates for women born in the 1920s and early 1930s, and reaching the end of the child-bearing period during the 1970s and 1980s, would be considerably lower than the period rates. For England and Wales, for example, the birth cohort rate would only be around 1·03, implying an ultimate increase in the population of only 3 per cent per generation, if the specified levels of mortality and fertility were to persist. By contrast, the period rate was over 1·10 in 1955–9 and about 1·30 in 1960–4, implying very considerably higher prospective rates of population growth. Birth cohort rates for other industrial nations would also be lower than the period rates. For some time those cohort rates will rise not only because of the relatively high child-bearing levels of the 1950s and early 1960s, but also because of the lighter mortality experienced by later generations of women. Thus if the generation of women born in England and Wales in 1926–35 had experienced current mortality instead of actual mortality, their replacement rate would have been about 1·15 instead of 1·03.

But there is a limit to the extent to which falling mortality can continue to raise the replacement rates of women in industrial countries. If there were no deaths before age 50, an average of 2·06 live births per woman would give a replacement rate of 1·0. At current levels of mortality, with female expectations of life at birth at around 74 and 75 years, it would take just over 2·1 live births per woman to yield a replacement rate of 1·0. The possible contribution of further reductions in mortality is thus very small, and it is future movements in fertility which will be critical. And it is just these movements which are difficult to forecast. In some countries, fertility has been falling sharply in the last few years— in the U.S.A. [13] and Canada, for example, where the current statistics for 1970 and 1971 would imply an average of only about 2·3 live births per woman. We cannot tell as yet how far changes in birth spacing contribute to the fall, and how far ultimate family size itself is being reduced. We may be seeing a pendulum movement in birth spacing as the younger groups of married couples, with wider use of more effective techniques of birth prevention, are responding more quickly to short-term changes in economic and social circumstances. But some genuine fall in ultimate family size is not unlikely, given both the greater capacity to avoid unwanted pregnancies and the wearing-away of the euphoria of the earlier postwar years.

Both the uncertainty of the situation and the possibility of a renewed and genuine reduction in fertility have a direct relevance to discussions of population policy in the developed countries.

Accepting the view that, all things considered, we should aim at near-stationary or fluctuating-stationary populations, the implications of present trends are not such as to justify a population hysteria or the promulgation of measures which aim solely at the further reduction of family size. The prospective rates of growth in the Soviet zone and Japan are minimal and this may come to be the case for many other industrial nations. Even with the current high expectations of life at birth, and an average of 2·4 live births per woman, such as may be the level reached by women born in 1931–40 in England and Wales, the intrinsic ultimate rate of population increase would be less than $\frac{1}{2}$ per cent per year, requiring more than 150 years for a population to double in size. Of the nineteen countries in Europe—outside the Soviet zone—for which I have been able to obtain period total fertility rates for very recent years (1967 or later) nine have a total fertility rate of not more than 2·4; and this is also the case for the U.S.A. and Canada in 1970–1. Another three countries have rates of not more than 2·5—even at that level, with current mortality, the long-term implication would only be a doubling of the population in about 120 years.

I am not arguing against population policy as such. In any case, every country already has some kind of policy, implicit if not explicit. What I am suggesting is that the initial stages of explicit policy should take into account the fact that the demographic situation in industrial nations is very different from that in the Third World. Neither the present age-structure nor the present level of fertility implies rapid population growth. Most couples are already restricting their fertility, and their targets of family size are relatively modest. This being so, I should argue that the measures now justifiable are those which are desirable in their own right on individual and social grounds and which might at the same time result in lower fertility. One such measure would be the full generalization of access to expert advice on, and to the most suitable means of, birth limitation. It cannot be claimed that this has already been achieved. Nor is it likely that it can be achieved simply by legislative changes, or that the fullest use would be made of even comprehensive services unless there were also a wider education in citizenship and a better induction of young people into adult responsibilities. Similarly, more realistic action to promote equality of opportunity for women—in higher education, for example, and in employment—would be socially justifiable in its own right and might also lead to lower levels of fertility. Certainly the evidence strongly suggests that those married women engaged in full-time employment have fewer children on average than women involved exclusively in household responsibilities.

We do not know how far such changes would in fact bring down family size. The effect might be small. But it is also possible that the reduction would be such as to lead to pressures for pronatalist rather than antinatalist demands. Nevertheless whatever the demographic consequences, developments of the kind suggested would be desirable. In my view, not until the results of such developments have been assessed would it be justifiable to envisage other and more single-minded approaches to population policy.

REFERENCES AND NOTES

1. BERENT, J. (1970). Causes of decline in fertility in Eastern Europe and the Soviet Union, Part 2, *Population Studies*, 24, 247–92.
2. COMMISSION ON POPULATION GROWTH AND THE AMERICAN FUTURE (1972). *Population and the American future. U.S. Government Printing Office*, Washington, D.C.
3. DAVID, H. P. (1970). *Family planning and abortion in the socialist countries of Central and Eastern Europe*. The Population Council New York.
4. GLASS, D. V. (1966). Family planning programmes and action in Western Europe, *Population studies*, 19, 221–38.
5. —— (1968). Fertility trends in Europe since the Second World War, *Population Studies*, 22, 103–46.
6. —— (1970). The components of natural increase in England and Wales. IN *Towards a population policy for the United Kingdom* (eds. A. Parkes *et al.*). Suppl. *Population Studies*, May.
7. HAJNAL, J. (1965). European marriage patterns in perspective. In *Population in history*, (ed. D. V. Glass and D. E. C. Eversley), pp. 101–43. Arnold, London.
8. INTERNATIONAL HEALTH FOUNDATION (1971). *Family planning.* Geneva.
9. —— (1972). Personal communication from Mr. P. H. A. M. Neijens, 18 December.
10. FAMILY PLANNING ASSOCIATION (1963). *Family planning in the sixties.* Family Planning Association, London.
11. —— (1973). Abortion in Britain today, *Family Planning*, January 1973.
12. MAGGS, P. B. (1972). *Law and population growth in Eastern Europe.* Tufts University, Melford, Massachusetts.

13. METROPOLITAN LIFE, *Stat. Bull.* September 1972.
14. MURAMATSU, M., Personal communication.
15. *Newsweek*, 5 February 1973.
16. *Population Index*, April–June 1972. Most of the period Gross and Net Reproduction Rates cited in the paper are taken from this collection. Others have been computed from the relevant national statistics.
17. ROBERTSON, D. H. (1945). The problem of exports, *Econ. J.* **55**, 321–25.
18. RYDER, N. B. (1971). The time series of fertility in the United States, I.U.S.S.P., *International Population Conference, London* 1969, Vol. I. Liège.
19. TEITELBAUM, M. S. (1972). Fertility effects of the abolition of legal abortion in Romania, *Population Studies* **26**, 405–17.
20. USSING, J. and BRUNN-SCHMIDT (1972). *Nogle Resultater fra Fertilitetsundersøgelsen.* Copenhagen.
21. WESTOFF, C. F. (1972). The modernization of U.S. contraceptive practice, *Family Planning Perspectives.* July 1972.

1.6. Economic influences and population size in developed countries

GÖRAN OHLIN

Department of Economics, Uppsala University

Present and past population scares

THE fear of over-population which emerged in the 1960s was first inspired by the obstacles which rapid population growth obviously raised to social and economic change in the very poor countries. The issue grew into a global one when recent exponential population growth was found to imply that in 100 years, which to anyone with a modest interest in the lives of his parents or grandparents is not a very long time, the world population might be some ten times larger than it is now.

The implications for the richer, industrialized countries, which are now called 'developed', were at first considered to be merely indirect. Their own population growth was fairly moderate and did not contribute much to the population explosion. Their dwindling role in the world, the prospect of intensified international rivalry over natural resources, and a greater call for international aid seemed to be the principal issues.

Recently, however, population growth has come to be presented as highly alarming for the developed countries as well, especially in the U.S.A., where the rate of growth has been higher than in Europe. However, even in the U.S.A. it is now only about 1 per cent p.a. In the early nineteenth century it was more than three times as high and, except for the 1930s when it dropped to 0·7 per cent, the growth rate of American population has never been lower than at the present time. But a growth of 1 per cent a year will double a population in 70 years, and only last year a commission appointed by the President and Congress solemnly reported its conclusion that 'no substantial benefits will result from further growth of the Nation's population'. It had looked for, but not found 'any convincing economic argument for continued population growth' [6].

In less circumspect words far more alarmist views have been expressed by those who see the growth of population as the principal source of many of the acute problems besetting the rich countries of the world. The Malthusian mood has probably never held such sway in the West as today.

Only a generation ago things were very different. In the 1930s the stagnation of population growth and the prospect of an actual decline preoccupied demographers and economists. They envisaged an attrition of investment opportunities, declining growth of incomes, appalling problems of economic adjustment, a petrification of institutions, and political disintegration. Gunnar Myrdal argued that the issue was fatally important; 'Democracy, not only as a political form but with all its content of civic ideals and human life, must either solve this problem or perish' [15]. The problem in question was the contraction—the failure even to replace itself.

Many of the disastrous consequences which were then predicted as the outcome of stagnation are quite similar to those now attributed to rapid growth. This is not much of a surprise to anyone familiar with the history of population thought. The truth is that people have almost always worried about population, especially since the advent of Malthus and the census. Growth or stagnation, emigration or immigration, the flight from the countryside, the growth of the towns, the ageing of the population, or an alarming increase of the young: any demographic change has excited vivid alarms and speculations about its pernicious consequences. Even the dramatic improvement in health and the fall in mortality, which to most minds represents the most undisputed gain in the record of modernization, gave rise to earnest worries about the eugenic implications of the survival of the unfit.

Against this background it is wise to approach the present population scare with some caution. The subject of population—its determinants, its movements, its consequences—has been investigated, studied, and debated almost as long as men have been aware of society as a phenomenon. It seems self-evident that population must be very important, but how and why is not self-evident.

The economics of fertility

The difference between the developed and the developing countries may seem obvious to the naked eye, but the statistical picture is more equivocal. In terms of income they all fall along a spectrum. The sharpest distinction between two groups of countries in the world is actually drawn by fertility. The great divide that separates the developed from the developing countries is the demographic transition, the shift from a regime of high mortality and fertility to one where they are low. The developing countries are in the first phase of that transition, their mortality has declined quite rapidly and is still falling, but fertility is, with some notable exceptions, responding fairly slowly or not at all, pretty much as in the developed countries 100 years ago.

In the developing countries, the falling trend of mortality is thus the dominant fact behind current growth. In the developed countries, on the other hand, the demographic transition is more or less completed, and mortality is fairly uniform. Further medical progress is likely to have only a marginal demographic impact. On the other hand, fertility is volatile. It differs considerably among developed countries, and its behaviour is so difficult to interpret that many have been inclined to think it a matter of fads and fashions whether people on an average have two or three children.

That the number of children people have must at least be very heavily influenced by economic conditions is such an obvious thought that, in one form or another, it has formed part of all systematic analysis of population problems. Adam Smith and his contemporaries assumed that prosperity would stimulate population growth in two ways—a better life would reduce mortality, and the greater demand for labour would lower the age of marriage and increase the number of children. Malthus was more distrustful and suspected that the poor were not sufficiently induced to a prudential postponement of marriage. As for marital fertility he assumed a 'constancy of passions', and was in any case inclined to regard deliberate birth control as 'vice'.

With the advent of the great fertility decline in the late nineteenth century—outside of France where it started almost a century earlier—the fertility hypothesis was reversed. It was increasingly obvious that fertility was inversely correlated with income and wealth. The rich not only married later but they also showed lower fertility in their marriages. As in developed countries today, it came to be assumed that education, income, and status were associated with low fertility. This is indeed characteristic of the fertility transition. It came as a surprise when a fertility survey from Stockholm in the 1930s revealed a positive correlation between income and fertility. Similar findings have since been made elsewhere on a local scale [4]. In national figures the patterns remain more ambiguous; a U-shaped statistical curve, with large family size for very low and very high incomes is so far the most that the reversal has achieved.

However, during the secular decline fertility also seemed to be correlated with the trade cycle. Marriages and births were both, in the short term, clearly associated with general economic conditions [9, 19, 12]. But the statistical tests could only show that some part of the observed variations in fertility could be attributed to short-term economic fluctuations. It is quite possible to argue that the most striking thing is how little these economic changes actually explain [18].

The inability to pinpoint the determinants of fertility was not just an academic problem. It contributed to the humiliating failure of demographers to forecast the course of fertility and growth after World War II. In all the industrialized countries fertility rose above the pre-war level, and in North America it rose particularly high and continued to rise throughout the 1950s. When in the 1960s American demographers had finally agreed to accept this irregular state of affairs, fertility abruptly and capriciously declined.

This situation has probably had a very healthy influence on demographic research. It has made for greater humility, and it has started a search for a better theory of fertility.

The crudest explanations of why 'the rich got richer and the poor got children' had been that only ignorance of contraception and lack of prudence prevented the poor from limiting their families in a way that was assumed to correspond with their interests. The same assumption is often made today about the developing countries.

Another notion, namely that the cost of raising children, paradoxically, may be a greater deterrent to the rich than to the poor had been intrinsic to the idea of '*capillarité sociale*', the term which Arsène Dumont used in the late nineteenth century to explain why the ambition to rise in society thwarted fertility. As Banks has documented in his study of *Prosperity and parenthood* in Victorian Britain, the competitive spending associated with social standing and the cost of raising middle-class children seemed to have a lot to do with the fact that marriages were increasingly postponed and fertility turned down [1].

On the whole, however, fertility remained a subject for sociologists until the sixties, when Gary Becker suggested that the demand for children could usefully be analysed with the help of regular economic theory [2]. For most parents in developed countries, he argued, children might be regarded as consumer goods yielding psychic satisfactions. As in the case of other such goods, the demand would be a function of people's tastes, the quality and cost of children, and the income of the parents.

Some demographers were inclined to regard this as an economist's prank, but along the lines suggested by Becker a large body of empirical studies have now evolved, and there is little doubt that this represents a major step forward [7, 8, 17]. It is worth noting that, in the cost of children, a very significant item is the income forgone by mothers who might otherwise be working. This means that family income is not such an innocent variable as used to be thought.

Can it be assumed then that people have more or less the number of children they want? Not really—even in developed countries many people obviously do not have much control over this matter. Contraception and abortion remain sensitive and contested areas of public policy. The recent U.S. Commission on population also suggested that people's choices in this regard were not truly free, since they were made in a social context with so-called 'pronatalist pressures'.

However that may be, it stands to reason that, even if people had exactly the number of children they wish to have in their own family, this might not produce the size or growth of population that is in the broad social interest. For one thing, people have no control of the size of other people's families which, nevertheless, may affect them and their own children in a number of ways. For another, modern societies relieve parents of many of the costs of children, which means that the private economic choices underlying fertility are made on assumptions which understate the social cost. This leads to the big and thorny issue of the economic and social implications of population growth.

The cases for and against population growth

A great many consequences of demographic change are of an almost mechanical character. Changes in the age-distribution result from changes in fertility and affect such things as the ratio between the active and the dependent population. The need for schools, hospitals, etc. will fluctuate. I shall regard these as second-order problems, and pass them over. Nor shall I discuss such intriguing questions as whether a high proportion of young people makes for political instability and revolutionary change—which, incidentally, does not seem to be borne out by the facts [20]—or whether the '*générations creuses*', the hollow age brackets due to war losses, have depleted any countries' capacity for political and intellectual leadership.

I shall focus quite narrowly on the economic consequences of the size of population and on the related problem of the consequences of demographic growth, stagnation, or decline.

Ever since Malthus and his eighteenth-century predecessors, it has been assumed by some that the scarcity of resources and the law of diminishing returns must imply that continued population growth leads to immiseration, and eventually has to come to an end. One difficulty about this view is that so far it is in complete contradiction with historical experience. As Simon Kuznets, the indefatigable analyst of economic growth, carefully put it, 'since the end of the 18th century, the available statistical records reveal no cases in which the prevalent substantial rises in population were accompanied by secular declines in *per capita* product' [13]. This is serious, but of course, it is not a decisive objection to modern Malthusianism. In a trivial sense it is obviously true that population cannot grow indefinitely in a finite world. It cannot even grow for very long. The question before us, however, is whether population growth in the developed countries, today or in the foreseeable future, is a good thing or a bad thing or even, as some have insisted, a catastrophe.

One hears little these days about the benefits from population growth, of which so many were so convinced in the 1930s. It is perhaps worth recalling some of the stronger arguments. Keynes and many others stressed the greater mobility of a growing population and labour force. Rapid structural change is the characteristic of modern economic growth, and it is probably facilitated by a high proportion of young entrants to the labour force, the latter forming a mobile group. A growing population also mitigates the problem of declining industries and reduces the risk of failure due to erroneous investment decisions, which stand a better chance of being validated by market expansion.

The French, who have longer experience of slow growth than other countries, have coined the term 'economic Malthusianism' to describe a restrictionist rather than expansive orientation—a mentality formed by static and closed careers with slow advancement opportunities in a stationary population.

Savings and capital formation may be suspected of forming a larger part of the national product in a growing society if people largely save for retirement, simply because those who are using up their savings will be relatively fewer than in a stable population.

Kuznets has emphasized an entirely different argument in favour of a large population—it would produce a larger absolute number of geniuses and talented people and a greater contribution to the stock of useful knowledge [13].

To most people, today, these arguments probably do not add up to a very convincing case for growth on economic grounds, and it may even be difficult to understand why population decline was felt to be so terrible. But let us look at the case against population growth.

The more extreme variants of this argument are primarily concerned with World population, and the shrill and naïve warnings of imminent global famine do not depend on what happens to population in the developed countries.

The shortage of non-renewable resources is another matter. Here the developed countries dominate the scene. The supply of energy is a particularly serious problem. It seems likely that between 1960 and 1990 the world will consume more than 80 per cent of the world's oil supplies. Oil simply will not last very long into the next century. As we have all heard, much will then depend on whether and when nuclear fusion will become a controllable source of energy. This is a question entirely beyond my field, and I only want to make some general observations about it.

In the first place, population growth has contributed and will contribute very little to the rapid increase in energy consumption and the depletion of mineral resources. When energy consumption increases at something like 7 per cent p.a. and population at 1 per cent or less, it is not from that 1 per cent that the explosive effects of compound interest derive. Secondly, resource pessimism seems to me, as to most economists, to neglect the fact that resources are economically and not physically defined. Oil just was not a resource until 100 years ago. When resources become scarce and rise in price a great number of substitutions and economies take place. Thirdly, there is a consistent bias, as Kuznets has put it, in that 'the clearly observable limits of *existing* resources tend to over-shadow completely the dimly discernible potentials of the new discoveries, inventions, and innovations that the future may bring' [13].

Besides the dearth of resources there is a whole list of problems of the modern world which are being laid at the door of population growth. The ecologists are, without compare, the greatest population haters and the ones who most often suggest that population should not only be stopped from growing but that it would be a far better thing if it were much smaller than it is. It is difficult to resist the impression that to many ecologists the optimal situation would be one without any people at all.

Obviously, ecological problems must be taken very seriously indeed. The problems of water and air pollution are already being coped with in a tentative manner in some countries. They are not very difficult problems, in principle, and where the political will exists to pay for a better environment, progress will probably be rapid, although the need for international agreement and co-operation is a delaying factor.

Here too, the main point is simply that neither the size nor the growth of population is consequential. Sparsely populated countries like Australia or Sweden have the same environmental problems as others—partly because no matter how large the country, people will cluster in metropolitan agglomerations of very similar character, but also because modern industry is capable of miraculous feats of pollution if the rules of the game are foolish enough to permit it. I even suspect that linking population growth to pollution does harm to the serious approach to either problem. As Frank Notestein, the grand old man of American population studies, has remarked, 'it is a distraction from an immediate attack on pollution to concentrate attention on the importance of stopping population growth in, say, 20, 30 or 50 years' [16].

Urbanization is another prominent item in the list of modern discontents. It is only too easy to blame traffic congestion, rising rents, and urban decay on population growth, but this is obviously wrong. The principal reason for urban growth and congestion is the relative superiority and attractiveness of urban life, and the reason for urban decline lies in inadequate planning and other local policies. The forces making for concentration and agglomeration are fairly overwhelming in modern society, so much so that it makes little or no difference whether population as a whole is growing a little or not.

From time to time serious worries are expressed about the psychic effects of crowdedness and density. One of the most suggestive pieces of research on this subject is that of Calhoun, who conducted a series of experiments on the effects of density on a certain strain of rats, with very spectacular findings [5]. As the density was increased in his colonies, the evidence of social pathology multiplied in uncanny analogy to developments in metropolitan cities. But the hypothesis that density as such is a major source of strain and stress in human societies does not stand up to tests very well [10]. Without detracting from the urgency of urban problems, I would suggest that current anti-urbanists are remarkably unappreciative of the civilizing influence of the civitas. Creativity and intellectual and artistic progress is, as a matter of historical fact, associated with the cities and not with the bucolic countryside.

Above all, however, urban density bears little or no relation to the size or growth of the over-all population.

My conclusion is that the case against current population growth in developed countries is not very much stronger than the case for it. The U.S. Commission, to which I have already referred, seems to have been aware of this when it chose the restrained formulation that it could see no benefits from further growth. There is an echo in this statement of a passage from John Stuart Mill, who said:

There is room in this world, no doubt, and even in old countries, for a great increase of population, supposing the arts of life to go on improving, and capital to increase. But even if innocuous, I confess I see very little reason for desiring it. [14]

This, I suggest, is the mood in which the population problem of developed countries may well be viewed, and is being viewed today.

There is simply no convincing reason to believe that the economic situation in North America or Europe would be different if population on either continent were, say, 50 million smaller or larger. Most of the worries about growth turn out on inspection to concern the social consequences of economic and technological growth rather than the economic consequences of demographic growth. The only objection to population growth around which it would be easy to rally most students of the matter would be the aesthetic one.

Zero population growth

Nevertheless, it is a fervent belief in some quarters that the growth of population, even in developed countries, must be checked so as to achieve zero population growth (ZPG) in the very near future.

Looking at current trends of fertility one wonders whether the excitement is necessary. The Net Reproduction Rate, which is an indication of the direction of growth if present patterns of fertility remain constant, is already less than unity in Denmark, Germany, and Sweden, which points to a decline. Switzerland, Canada, and Belgium are very close to this. In view of what we know about social and political responses to demographic change, it would not be surprising, if in a few years, we shall again hear more about the dangers of depopulation than about the perils of population growth, although it should be remembered that the inertia of growth is considerable.

The vital issue, however, is whether our present knowledge about the consequences of population change is such as to warrant intensified government policies, in the limiting case coercive ones, to ration the right to have children or, alternatively, to impose it as a social duty. It is a widespread impression among demographers that population policies in the past have been remarkably ineffective [3]. This impression was formed during the fertility transition, when pronatalist policies ranging from family allowances to prohibitions on contraceptive information failed to stem a decline in the birth rate which was primarily determined by the drop in mortality. It is by no means certain that incentive policies do not work today, and coercion seems to me to have no place in this singularly touchy area.

But the real problem is that we do not really know what the social interest dictates. We can see the inconveniences of a declining population and also those of a growing one, but it is only by exclusion that we arrive at a half-hearted preference for stabilization, and for those ills we have rather than others of which we know not. This is not the best point of departure for a deliberate policy. The fact of the matter is that we do not know enough about the fine tuning of population growth to justify major restrictions or interventions in the presumed and overriding interest of society.

It is possible that our political process will evolve towards a firmer planning of the kind of society we wish to see a generation from now and that this will include a conception of the desirable numbers. I have no illusions as to the intellectual consistency of such an exercise. Whose welfare is to be considered—that of the living or of the next generation? There are possibilities of serious conflicts of interest even if we do not at all consider the interest of the unborn, which would create a totally insoluble problem.

With some other students of population I share the sneaking suspicion that we are actually guilty of the renowned fallacy of misplaced concreteness when we seek to make population a pivot of analysis and separate the causes and effects of population movements. We would never try to discuss the causes of industrial production in one chapter and its effects in another. This is what we do with population, but the result suggests that we have not yet succeeded in disentangling it from the web in which it is enmeshed. It should be self-evident that we cannot seriously discuss the consequences of population growth without considering its origin. There is not only a quantitative difference between the population explosion in developing countries, where the rapid mortality decline is to a large extent an extraneous force upsetting the demographic equilibrium, and the situation in developed countries, where the causes of growth, ill-understood as they remain, do seem to relate largely to prosperity.

At any rate, there is no warrant for the fear that population movements in developed countries are on a disaster course, and it would be a serious mistake to let the concern over population deflect attention from far more urgent issues in post-industrial societies.

REFERENCES

1. BANKS, J. A. (1954). *Prosperity and parenthood*. Routledge, London.
2. BECKER, G. S. (1960). An economic analysis of fertility. In National Bureau of Economic Research, *Demographic and economic change in developed countries* pp. 209–40. Princeton University Press.
3. BERELSON, B. (1971). Population policy: personal notes, *Population Studies* **25**, 173–82.
4. BERNHARDT, E. M. (1972). Fertility and economic status—some recent findings on differentials in Sweden, *Population Studies* **26**, 175–84.
5. CALHOUN, J. B. (1962). Population density and social pathology, *Scien. Am.* **206** (Feb.), 130–46; (1970). Population. In *Population control* (ed. A. Allison), pp. 110–30. Penguin Books, Harmondsworth, U.K.
6. COMMISSION ON POPULATION GROWTH AND THE AMERICAN FUTURE (1972). *Population and the American future*, U.S. Government Printing Office, Washington, D.C.
7. EASTERLIN, R. A. (1969). Toward a socio-economic theory of fertility. In *Fertility and family planning: a world view* (ed. S. J. Behrman *et al.*), pp. 127–56, University of Michigan Press, Ann Arbor, Mich.
8. —— (1972). The economics and sociology of fertility: a synthesis. Paper prepared for the *Seminar on early industrialization, Institute for Advanced Study, Princeton University, June 18–July 9, 1972*.
9. GALBRAITH, V. L. and THOMAS, D. S. (1941). Birth rates and the interwar business cycles, *J. Am. stat. Assoc.* **36**, 457–76.
10. HEER, D. M. (1968), *Society and population*. Prentice-Hall, Englewood Cliffs, N.J.
11. KEYNES, J. M. (1937). Some economic consequences of a declining population, *Eugen. Rev.* **29**, 13–17.
12. KIRK D. (1960). The influence of business cycles on marriage and birth rates. In National Bureau of Economic Research, *Demographic and economic change in developed countries*, pp. 241–60. Princeton University Press, Princeton, New Jersey.
13. KUZNETS, S. (1960). Population change and aggregate output. In National Bureau of Economic Research, *Demographic and economic change in developed countries*, pp. 324–51. Princeton University Press, Princeton, New Jersey.
14. MILL, J. S. (1848). *Principles of political economy*, Bk. iv, Chap. 6.
15. MYRDAL, G. (1940). *Population: a problem for democracy*. Harvard University Press, Cambridge, Mass.
16. NOTESTEIN, F. W. (1970). Zero population growth, *Population Index* **36**, 444–52.
17. SCHULTZ, P. (1969). An economic model of family planning and fertility, *J. pol. Econ.* **77**, 153–80.
18. SWEEZY, A. (1971). The economic explanation of fertility changes in the United States, *Population Studies* **25**, 255–68.

19. THOMAS, D. S. (1941). *Social and economic aspects of Swedish population movements, 1730–1933.* Macmillan, New York.
20. WEINER, M. (1971). Political demography: an inquiry into the political consequences of population change. In *Rapid population growth: consequences and policy implications* (ed. R. Revelle), Vol. I, pp. 567–617. The Johns Hopkins Press, Baltimore, Md.

I.7. Development and population growth in poor countries

DUDLEY SEERS

Fellow of the Institute of Development Studies, Sussex University

THIS paper will deal with the population pressures, and with some of their implications, in the 'developing' countries. But the context will be international and the treatment in part, political. The 'developing' countries account between them for the majority of mankind. Besides which, questions about the adequacy of fuel, food, and metals are ultimately questions about the world as a whole. This is implicitly recognized in the sudden rush of aid offers to these countries to support policies of family planning and in the speeches of rich-country political leaders—though I shall argue that both of these are ineffective and immoral, and that our example would carry much more weight than our advice.

The population upsurge in poor countries

I am unable to provide as precise an analysis as Professor Glass has done for the 'developed' countries. One reason is that Professor Glass is a demographer, whereas I am not. In addition, the data are simply not available. Registers of births and deaths are rarely comprehensive, if they exist at all; there are far fewer special surveys and analyses; even census material is much less reliable. And I am talking about many more countries at very different levels of economic and social progress.

Yet the general picture is clear enough. The pace of population growth has accelerated in the Third World, from a slow growth in the nineteenth century to $2\frac{1}{2}$ per cent a year in the 1960s—even faster in Latin America—due primarily to the decline in mortality (especially infant mortality) and reflecting the growing control over diseases such as smallpox, malaria, and typhoid. As a result, population profiles with a very broad base have been created, half the population, or nearly half, typically being less than 15 years old.

Population growth is viewed with some complacency in Africa and much of Latin America. Indeed there is an evident relation between size of population on the one hand and political power and independence on the other. Nevertheless, whatever the merits of a large population *per se*, there are great strains involved in rapid population growth.

Consequences

One consequence of rapid population expansion has been a chronic food problem. It would be quite incorrect to assume (as is often done, at least tacitly, by neo-Malthusians) that a population increase has no effect on the output of food (and other products), but in rural areas which are already crowded the effect is limited. While during the early years of the 1950s, [1] food output rose at a faster rate than population, *per capita* production in the Third World was about constant over the 1960s as a whole, despite some acceleration in the Far East in the second half of the decade [2].

Secondly, the pressure of population growth is making it difficult for governments to keep pace with the growing social needs— for water supplies and sewerage, for housing and education. Not merely undernourishment but also slum conditions and illiteracy remain chronic, even in countries with rapidly rising national products. It is hard, therefore, to spare capital for purposes economically more productive. Private savings may also be reduced by the difficulty of providing for the consumption needs of large families.

Thirdly, the decline in mortality in the 1950s, especially in infant mortality and child mortality, led to a particularly sharp acceleration in the growth of the population of working age (i.e. 15–64), from less than 2 per cent in 1950–5 to more than $2\frac{1}{2}$ per cent in 1965–70, taking the Third World as a whole [3]. This contributed to high levels of unemployment, which has reached around 10 per cent in many countries (as high as 25 per cent in Jamaica in 1972), and is higher still for young people.

A more widespread effect (but a less measurable one) is that people have been crowded into low income work. Sometimes this takes the form of additional adults working on family farms which can barely support the present number. But often it involves large numbers flocking into the cities (city populations in much of Latin

America and Africa are growing at 6–7 per cent a year, which means they almost double in a decade), adding to the proliferation of badly paid jobs. Moreover, the surplus labour depresses wages, so that a further consequence is a continued, perhaps even growing, concentration of incomes [4].

Population growth is, of course, by no means the only explanation of unemployment and underemployment, and still less of inequality. One other reason is that organized employment in the cities has failed to increase fast enough, despite rates of economic growth which have been high by British standards—often 5 per cent or more over more than a decade. To attempt an explanation would take us too far afield, But the heart of the matter seems to be that the process of economic growth was distorted by the uncritical transfer of production technique and styles of consumption from the industrial countries.

Demographic prospects

There are indications that the demographic pressure may slacken. In Hong Kong, Singapore, Puerto Rico, Trinidad, and Mauritius, birth rates have already fallen from over 34 (per 1000) at the beginning of the 1950s to under 27 at the present time, with most of the decline in the rate occurring in the 1960s [5]. This is a spectacular decline, much faster than that which happened earlier, in the industrial countries. Substantial declines have also taken place in a number of other countries, e.g. Costs Rica and Taiwan (see Table 1.7.1), where the rates still were fairly high in recent years.

All these countries have certain features in common. Their governments have backed family-planning agencies. But this support did not start until after the birth rates started to fall. (Moreover, Jamaica with a strong population policy did not show an especially fast decline.) What may be more to the point is that the countries involved are all relatively prosperous, industrialized, and urbanized; women enjoy both educational opportunities and access to paid employment in many sectors and not just in domestic service [6]. They have all (except Mauritius) enjoyed fast rates of export growth.

Thus one might conclude that, as economic and social advances take place in other countries, especially the provision of more

TABLE I.7.I

Birth rates for selected countries 1950–72†

	(1) 1950–4	(4) 1955–9	(3) 1960–4	(4) 1965–9	(5) 1970–2 (provisional)
LATIN AMERICAN AND CARIBBEAN					
Chile	33·7	35·9	34·8	29·5	—
Costa Rica	49·1	49·1	44·8	39·6	32·3
El Salvador	49·0	49·3	48·6	44·5	41·4
Guatemala	51·3	48·7	47·7	43·6	(40·3)‡
Jamaica	34·8	39·0	40·3	36·6	34·6
Mexico	44·9	45·9	46·0	43·9	43·5
Panama	37·5	39·8	40·6	38·9	36·6
Puerto Rico	36·6	33·7	31·2	27·3	(26·4)‡
Trinidad	37·7	38·3	36·9	27·4§	(24·1)‡
ASIA					
Hong Kong	34·2	36·2	32·8	25·0	19·7
Malaya	44·1	44·4	40·3	35·5	—
Singapore	45·5	42·8	35·6	26·9	23·0
Sri Lanka	38·5	36·6	34·9	32·1	(29·6)‡
Taiwan	45·9	42·8	37·1	30·2	—
OTHER 'DEVELOPING' COUNTRIES					
Fiji	40·4	40·7	39·2	32·9	(30·1)‡
Israel	32·5	27·9	25·5	25·4	27·4
Mauritius	46·2	41·0	38·9	31·8	25·3
Tunisia	30·8	39·9	42·8	43·2*	—
'DEVELOPED' COUNTRIES					
Australia	23·0	22·6	21·9	19·7	21·1
France	19·5	18·4	18·0	17·2	16·9
Hungary	21·1	17·8	13·6	14·3	14·7
Japan	23·7	18·2	17·2	17·8	(19·0)‡
Sweden	15·5	14·5	14·5	15·0	13·9
U.S.S.R.	26·4	25·3	22·4	17·6	(17·6)‡
United Kingdom	15·9	16·4	18·2	17·5	15·8
U.S.A.	24·5	24·6	22·4	18·1	(17·7)‡

† Those with over 500 000 people designated by U.N. as having 'virtually complete' registration statistics. Some 'developed' countries have been omitted.

‡ 1970–1   * 1965–70

§ This figure is based on 32·8 for 1965, the rate given in Government of Trinidad and Tobago, Central Statistical Office *Annual Statistical Digest* (1968), Table 23, and previously quoted in *U.N. Monthly Bulletin of Statistics. U.N. Demographic Yearbook* (1969) gives 37–9 (estimated by E.C.L.A.), which would imply an average of 28·8 for the period. The source points out that these are registered births.

Sources: (1)–(3), developing' countries: KIRK, D. A New Demographic Transition? In National Academy of Sciences, *Rapid Population Growth*, **2**, p. 128. Johns Hopkins Press, Baltimore, Md.

(1)–(3), 'developed' countries: *U.N. Demographic Yearbook* (1969) and earlier issues.

(4)–(6), all countries: *U.N. op. cit.*; *U.N. Monthly Bulletin of Statistics* (1973) or *U.N. Population and Vital Statistics Report*, Apr. 1973.

education for women, this, in due course, will also induce declines in birth rates—as happened earlier in Western Europe and even in Argentina. However, the process is a slow one in countries where the population is large and mainly rural. In Mexico, for example, the decline in birth rate has been from about 46 in 1960 to 43 in 1972. Preliminary indications from the recent round of censuses suggest that the birth rate in India has fallen somewhat, but it is not yet much below 40 [7], and in Indonesia it still hovers above this level. In parts of Africa it is 40 to 50 and, moreover, the rate may still be rising as health conditions improve. There are signs that in China, on the other hand, a significant decline may be beginning in fertility [8].

Certainly the route to higher living standards followed by small islands concentrating on exports of manufactures or petroleum is not open to many countries. In those with large rural populations there is a vicious circle: population growth prevents the alleviation of poverty, which prevents the moderation of population growth.

TABLE 1.7.2

Total population in major areas and regions of the world: 1930 and 1960, 1970–2000 (projected)

	Millions					
	1930	1960	1970	1980	1990	2000
World	2070	2986	3632	4457	5438	6494
Developing countries†	1328	2040	2580	3299	4168	5115
Africa	164	270	344	457	616	818
Asia‡	1056	1557	1953	2465	3052	3645
Latin America§	108	213	283	377	500	652
Developed countries‖	742	947	1055	1169	1289	1399
Europe	355	425	462	497	533	568
Japan	64	93	103	116	125	133
North America	134	199	228	261	299	333
Soviet Union	179	214	243	271	302	330

† Not quite identical with 'less developed regions' as defined in *The world population situation in 1970*.
‡ Excluding Japan.
§ Including Caribbean.
‖ Including Oceania.

Sources: for 1930, *U.N. Demographic Yearbook* (1969); for other years, U.N. *The world population situation in 1970*, Population Studies No. 49 (1971), Table 15 (medium variant).

A factor that will check the fall in the birth rate, even if age-specific fertility rates decline, is the large number of girls reaching child-bearing age. Thus it has been estimated that, even if the fertility of women aged 15–45 in Kenya fell immediately to mere reproduction levels, which is, of course, unthinkable (and mortality continued to decline at a moderate pace), the population would still increase from 11·3 million in 1970 to 17·4 million by the end of the century [9]. Above all, in the big countries of Asia, little improvement is taking place in the economic or educational levels of the rural masses.

As Professor Glass has emphasized, in the field of demography we need to wait and see. But perhaps it is safe to conclude that there will only be a mild slackening of the rate of population growth in the Third World as a whole, in the next decade or so. Since the majority of the total human population lives in the Third World, this is also true of the world as a whole. The projections in Table 1.7.2. are more or less compatible with this analysis.

Prospective consequences

Moreover, the population of working age in the Third World will (barring war or some other gigantic catastrophe) continue to grow at a pace becoming, if anything, faster in the 1980s [10]. We can be much more certain about this; nearly all the working-age population of 1990 has already been born. The problem of providing enough employment, especially of a kind which will be considered satisfactory, will become even more formidable. It will test the political structure of even the strongest countries of the Third World, and, although this is why population policies are opposed by revolutionaries, it is far from certain that revolutionary regimes would be able to tackle the basic social problems effectively. If they did so, then indeed birth rates might fall.

This demographic outlook also raises prospects of continued food shortages and of strains on world resources of materials and (especially) fuel.

There is plenty of scope for further increases in agricultural yields in the Third World, although the task will not be easy. Already the high-yielding varieties of cereals have been introduced by a large proportion of the farmers who have access to the irrigation and credit required to take advantage of them. Moreover, while general supplies, apart from foodstuffs, have not been conspicuously short so far, the whole picture is now changing. Without endorsing all the conclusions on resource constraints of the Club of Rome (or the M.I.T. group) [11], there are certainly grounds for concern. Yet their projections made no allowance for closing the gap between 'rich' and 'poor' countries. To put this point another way, in as far as the public of the rich, industrial countries manage to maintain high, let alone rising, consumption levels in the future, this can only be achieved at the expense of others, who will grow increasingly restive under great demographic and political pressures. What is in prospect, in fact, is competition of growing ferocity for the use of certain resources [12].

Purely as a hypothetical calculation, if in 1985 the whole world had the same ratio of cars to people of working age as applies *today* in the U.S.A. (1·4 : 1), the total world car ownership would be more than 2000 million cars (or ten times as many as today). On energy, the Meadows–Forrester study assumes a growth rate of 3·4 per cent p.a. [10]. If worldwide energy consumption in 1985 is calculated on the hypothesis that the whole world would, by 1985, enjoy today's U.S. standards, the growth rate would be 14·6 per cent a year, and consumption would then be more than four times as large as they estimate [13].

The adjustment of demand to supply could take place by 'automatic' means as material and fuel prices rise. There will be some shift to types of production which do not require scarce resources. But to economize on fuel will be difficult, especially in cold climates. Military conflicts could arise in the Middle East, where countries like Saudi Arabia, Kuwait, and Abu Dhabi have a very much greater share of the world's fuel reserves than of the world's military power, and where there is an additional source of tension over Israel.

An international population policy?

The resource problem underlines the need for a worldwide population policy. But on what grounds are the countries of the Third World to be urged to limit their population growth? Our credibility as advisers is undermined by the racial prejudice which is still evidently a strong force in Europe and North America. The suspicion cannot be avoided that what the spokesmen of the leading industrial countries are talking about is control of the world's *non-white* population. Stressing the population theme in public statements and aid policies, therefore, may well have the opposite effect from what is intended.

Most of the environmental school tacitly assume that an appeal can be made on the basis of the interest of the human species as a whole. But such an argument can hardly be put forward by the representatives of countries which turn a deaf ear to proposals for opening their markets to competition from the Third World, which devote virtually the whole of their R and D capacity to their own problems, which insist that most aid loans be spent in the lender's country (often on inappropriate and expensive equipment) and which reject many requests for aid—while offering to increase aid to family planning. An appeal to a superior international order can hardly be made by governments which exert commercial, political, and at times military power to support their own economic and strategic interests (especially access to petroleum and mineral resources), and which indeed even occasionally try to overthrow foreign political leaders who are uncooperative (Arbenz in Guatemala and Allende in Chile are merely two examples) [14]. Yet such leaders may be precisely the ones most likely to bring about the improvements in the living conditions of the mass of the population which seem to be ultimately the necessary, perhaps also sufficient, condition for a slackening in the pace of the world's population growth.

If rich countries really want to ease the world population problem, the way to do this is not primarily by promoting the distribution of contraceptives but adopting policies that help to raise incomes and employment overseas policies in fields such as trade, research and aid. Even more important would be backing (instead of trying to undermine) governments which are genuinely trying to improve socio-economic conditions, especially in rural areas—whatever the attitudes of these governments to foreign investments.

Thus the deep tensions in the international politico-economic system are aggravated by the world-population pressure and at the same time prevent its cure. Moreover, the industrial countries clearly have little enthusiasm for population policies themselves. It may be argued that their need to adopt these is less urgent, but here we are looking at the matter as a world problem. One must allow for the relatively high resource needs of each citizen in an industrial country. We should also bear in mind that example is infinitely more persuasive than aid or rhetoric.

TABLE 1.7.3

Crude death rates for selected countries† 1950–71
(deaths per 1000 population)

	1950–4	1955–9	1960–4	1965–9	1970–2
LATIN AMERICA AND CARRIBBEAN					
Chile	14	13	12	10	—
Costa Rica	12	10	9	7	6
El Salvador	15	14	11	10	(15)‡
Guatemala	22	20	17	16	7
Jamaica	12	9	9	8	9
Mexico	15	12	10	10	(7)‡
Puerto Rico	9	7	7	7	(7)‡
Trinidad and Tobago	11	10	7	7‡	—
ASIA					
Hong Kong	9‡	7	6	5	5
Malaya§	14	11	9	8	—
Singapore	10	7	6	5	5
Taiwan	10	8	6	5	8
OTHERS					
Mauritius	15	12	10	9	8
DEVELOPED COUNTRIES					
Australia	9·4	8·8	8·7	8·9	8·8
France	12·7	11·8	11·2	11·1	10·7
Hungary	11·4	10·3	10·1	10·8	11·7
Japan	9·4	7·8	7·3	6·9	(6·7)‡
Sweden	9·7	9·6	10·0	10·2	10·2
U.S.S.R.	9·4	7·7	7·2	7·6	(8·2)‡
United Kingdom	11·7	11·6	11·8	11·7	11·7
U.S.A.	9·5	9·4	9·5	9·5	(9·3)‡

† Those over 0·5 million population designated by *U.N.* as having 'virtually complete' registration statistics. For 'developing' countries, rates given in source have here been rounded to nearest whole number.

‡1970–1.

§ i.e. West Malaysia.

— Data not available.

Sources: *U.N. Demographic Yearbooks* (1966, 1969, 1970), *U.N. Monthly Bulletin of Statistics* (1973), and *U.N. Population and Vital Statistics Report* (Apr. 1973).

The birth rates in only two industrial countries, the U.S.A. and the Soviet Union, show a big decline in recent years, despite the appearance of the Pill as a method of birth control, and even in these cases there has been no official population limitation policy. These are both countries in which the rate was relatively high a decade ago. In some others, the tendency has been upward, notably in Japan. Yet the death rate stays persistently below 12 throughout the developed countries, despite their high average age, and all the time medical progress is extending the life-span (see Table 1.7.3).

There is some danger that in reaction against recent Malthusian exaggerations, professional opinion in the developed countries will swing too far in the direction of complacency—at least from a global viewpoint. (Can one perhaps sense this in the papers of Professors Glass and Ohlin?)

More could certainly be done to help women avoid unwanted births, and policies in taxation and other fields could influence attitudes to family size. Probably by these means one could bring about zero population growth in the industrial countries, within the coming century, with birth and death rates balancing at about 10 per 1000. But this implies a large proportion of the population (and a larger proportion of the electorate) aged over 70. Would this be in any sense a desirable sort of society? And what are the ethics of our hanging on to life whilst in effect denying it to those who would have been born—especially those in the poorer countries with lower resource needs? Perhaps we should, in the developed countries at least, be contemplating shorter lives.

The study of population is always an interesting subject because it is apparently both technical and statistical, yet the great issues of the meaning of life itself and the significance of different lives are never buried very deeply under the figures.

REFERENCES AND NOTES

1. *The state of food and agriculture* (1971), Table I–2, pp. 2–3. F.A.O., Rome.
2. Monthly Bulletin of Agricultural Economics and Statistics (Apr. 1973), pp. 3–5. F.A.O., Rome.
3. *Labour force projections*, Part V (1971), Tables 2 and 5. I.L.O., Geneva.
4. *Towards full employment*. A report by the inter-agency mission to Colombia (1970), Chapters 2 and 3. I.L.O., Geneva.

5. The birth rate is, of course, an unsatisfactory indicator of long-run fertility trends, but it is the only measure widely available. Besides, the size of the addition to the population does have intrinsic meaning in the short term.

6. For evidence on the corelation between fertility and education, female participation, etc. see KASARDA, J. D. *Demography* (Aug. 1971), GREGORY, P. *et al.* J.D.S. (Jan. 1973), VALLIN, J. *Population, Paris* (Juillet–Oct. 1973).

7. Sample Registration System, *Bulletin*, Government of India, Office of the Registrar General, New Delhi. (July–Dec. 1972) shows rates of 39 for the rural population, 30 for the urban, in both 1970 and 1971. Note that fertility has remained high despite a strong population policy.

8. PRESSAT, R. La conjoncture démographique: L'Asie, *Population, Paris* (Mars–Avril 1973).

9. CRAMER, J. (1971). Staff paper No. 109. University of Nairobi, Kenya.

10. I.L.O. [4] It can be calculated from the figures shown there that the population of working age in the Third World will grow, in the period 1980–5, slightly faster than the current rate of 2·6 per cent.

11. MEADOWS, D. H., MEADOWS, D. L., RANDERS, J., and BEHRENS, W. W. (1972). *The limits to growth.* A report for the Club of Rome's Project on the Predicament of Mankind. Earth Island Publications, London.

12. One might add that this prospect is full of menace to Britain (a chronic importer of food, fuel, and materials, thus chronically vulnerable to pressures on world supplies).

13. CHAUNCEY STARR (1971). Energy and power. *Scient. Am.* **225**, No. 3 (Sept.), 37–49, makes the following calculations:

> At present the U.S. consumes about 35% of the world's energy· By the year 2000 the U.S. share will probably drop to around 25% due chiefly to the relative population increase of the rest of the world. The *per capita* increase in energy consumption in the U.S. is now about 1% per year. Starting from a much lower base, the average *per capita* energy consumption throughout the world is increasing at a rate of 1·3% per year. . . . By 2000 (it) . . . will have moved only from the present one-fifth of the U.S. average to about one-third of the present U.S. average. . . . If the underdeveloped parts of the world were conceivably able to reach by the year 2000 the standard of living of Americans today, the worldwide level of energy consumption would be roughly 100 times the recent figure.

14. Demographic strains may be one factor weakening the capacity to resist such foreign pressures.

1.8. Fertility control and individual behaviour

RAYMOND ILLSLEY

Professor of Sociology and Director, M.R.C. Medical Sociology Unit, Aberdeen University

DEMOGRAPHERS are, justifiably, chary about predicting the future course of fertility. Death rates are relatively predictable; migration outwards exerts a generally predicatable influence on population changes in Britain; migration inwards, though subject to periodic political pressures, is nevertheless ultimately subject to control through legislation. Fertility remains the great unknown which has falsified estimates of growth over the past 50 years. The uncertainty relates not merely to ultimate family size, although this is the major variable of concern in current debates about population policy. It applies to age at marriage—our theories did not permit us to predict the sharp fall in age at marriage in the 1950s and 1960s. Indeed the increasing volume of further education, particularly for women, suggested the possibility of even later marriage. Decreasing intervals between births, after early marriage, in a society making fuller use of contraceptive techniques, emerged as a historical, statistical fact rather than as an expectation based upon the application of demographic theory. The sharp rise in illegitimacy rates and in pre-nuptial conception from the mid 1950s to the present day, following a long-term decrease over the preceding century, appeared as a paradox in the age of birth control and the Pill. Even more paradoxical was the fact that the highest increase occurred in the more educated sections of the population and in the urban areas where illegitimacy ratios had previously been comparatively low [14]. Experienced demographers could point ruefully to other unanticipated movements which have confounded prediction and led to methods of population projection based on alternative assumptions about future fertility, where the consumers of such projections are left to make their own best guess between equally probable, but widely different, possibilities.

Not only were such developments not anticipated; even now, *post hoc*, we cannot firmly interpret such changes in a causal fashion except at high levels of generality. The occurrence of a wave of sexual liberation, illegitimacy, and abortion and its timing in an era of increasing control over natural phenomena will doubtless be explained historically, but in the meantime we wait, year by year, to see whether rates and referrals have in fact gone up or down, without any conviction that we can forecast the amount of change or even its direction.

I do not advance these statements in any destructive sense. Like official demographers, I feel chary of prediction and theoretically and empirically ill-equipped to interpret the recent past. My concern is best expressed in three questions:

Is the nature of the problem so intractable that prediction must always be meaningless?
Alternatively, does our inability to predict stem from inadequate data?
Or again, are we collecting the wrong kind of data, so that even its refinement must add little to our understanding?

Such questions are important because, in the absence of such understanding, we may adopt measures which yield negative results or which, because of their intrusion into the private world of the individual, may restrict rather than extend freedom.

In one sense of the term 'data' we have more 'data' about fertility than about most areas of human activity. It is not, at face value, a highly complex activity resulting, like economic production, from the coordinated organization of huge enterprises in which each person sees only a tiny fraction of the chain of events and interrelationships which produce the ultimate product. It is a routine everyday activity, experienced during part of their lives by all members of society, and conducted in enterprises which in terms of formal organization are as simple as the family farm. The mechanics of fertility and the logical dimensions of its control are easily comprehended. Davis and Blake [9] produced a logical schema which set out in eleven simple categories the cultural conditions through which fertility might be influenced. I shall nevertheless argue that the activity only appears simple and comprehensible because our knowledge is limited and because it is so common that we take it for granted.

Existing 'data' are adequate, or even voluminous, in a further sense. For more than 100 years the events of fertility have been recorded, for the whole country, as they occur. We know the identity of those who marry, their previous marital state, their ages, and their place of marriage. With less accuracy, and for a shorter period of history, we know the occupations of the spouses and their parents. Each birth is recorded, the number of previous children, the duration of marriage, the marital status, and the occupation and ages of the parents. If children die, the death is registered, if adopted this too is recorded, and if the parents are divorced, this too is publicly available knowledge. Such information is supplemented every 10 years by detailed census information on the fertility of marriage, and from time to time by large-scale *ad hoc* studies. It is available for the nation as a whole, for subgroups such as counties, cities, and urban or rural districts and for various socio-economic groupings. Each annual volume is formidable in its array of cross-tabulated material.

Similar material emerges from other societies experiencing different stimuli, or similar stimuli at different periods of time, thus permitting cross-cultural study and giving opportunities to examine natural experiments.

More recently, we have become aware of opportunities from the more distant past, and the literature is beginning to abound with elegant analyses of fertility behaviour in French, Bavarian, Italian, British, and American villages of the seventeenth and eighteenth centuries. It is from such data, i.e. recorded material from historical periods of varying distance from everyday contemporary life— either French village, nineteenth-century Scandinavia, or the last decades of the Registrar General's statistics—that much of our population theory derives. I wish to consider its advantages and its limitations for understanding the decisions on individual fertility made by contemporary men and women. The historical material is gathered together with extreme ingenuity and painstaking accuracy from sources so piecemeal that, for many decades, they appeared unpromising starting-points for demographic science. Their reconstruction is therefore a feat of some magnitude. They possess features which make them appropriate for model-building. These features, however, may be, at the same time, their greatest limitation for application to contemporary problems.

First, the antecedents of the behaviour studied are already

known, at least in broad historical, social, economic, and techno-logical terms.

Second, they relate to relatively simple units of sparsely populated areas, in which communication was difficult and the rate of change comparatively slow—if not in population terms, at least in terms of social, economic, religious, or cultural change.

Third, the outcomes of behaviour are known. The studies themselves provide the fertility behaviour of the population in question, and we can trace the long-term historical repercussions and adjustments. With hindsight we can concentrate selectively upon the major determinants of change in that period, and by a process of inference can identify the salient processes by which stimuli give rise to particular forms of behaviour. Knowing ante-cedents, context, events, and outcomes, explanations can be offered and theories evolved, which, although at a high level of generality, cannot be contradicted by next year's unanticipated statistical returns, but only by newly discovered data. Fertility behaviour in eighteenth- and nineteenth-century Ireland has received consider-able attention, and has affected historical, demographic, and sociological theory. In the events leading up to and following the Irish potato famines of the 1840s we can see, dramatically, the interplay of land tenure systems, farm inheritance, and agricultural innovation [7]. We can trace the mechanisms whereby pressures on individuals modified personal behaviour, social institutions, and the machinery which had hitherto operated to ensure at least a crude control over population growth. We are thus able (although admittedly the data are inadequate) to identify:

1. The agricultural/economic background prior to change.
2. The institutional means whereby age at marriage, fertility within marriage, and the proportions of persons marrying were regulated.
3. We can infer the combination of stimuli which led to modifi-cations of behaviour and the meaning of these stimuli to the individuals involved.
4. We can further trace how the altered perceptions of individ-uals concerning expected yields and the availability of land for tillage led to the sub-division of holdings.
5. A direct link can be established between these changes and

age at marriage, proportions marrying, and the number of children within marriage.

6. We can trace population growth, its end-point in 1840s famines, and the consequent reversal of behaviour and return to previous institutional measures of control.

The facts may be incorrect, but that is irrelevant—sufficient building blocks exist to construct a plausible theory linking events occurring at the societal level with marital and reproductive institutions, their meaning to the individual, and his subsequent response.

With deepening research the number of such intellectually elegant examples multiplies. Perhaps the best documented and satisfying example is that put forward by Banks [2], demonstrating the steps whereby political and economic change, leading to higher education costs, motivated the Victorian middle-class to adopt methods of family spacing and limitation. Again the crucial step in this argument is not merely the demonstration of general pressures upon the Victorian bourgeoisie but the articulation of developments at the societal level with motivations of individuals to behave in a specified way.

I turn now to another body of information potentially capable of theory building and of prediction—i.e. recorded data of recent origin arising out of official returns or *ad hoc* population surveys. It differs considerably from historical material in that the outcome, which was a 'given' in historical examples, is now the unknown. Where therefore we had been able to infer motivations and meanings from a chain of events and responses such inference is no longer possible. Not only is the outcome not known, we cannot tell whether we are at the beginning, the middle, or the end of trends in behaviour or whether indeed absence of overt trend is produced by counteracting forces. The wave of illegitimate pregnancy which, starting in London in the early 1950s, followed the mini-skirt up the motorway, did not hit the North of Scotland until the end of the decade, for we were still completing the long secular decline [14]. Indeed, frequently in the statistics of that time one can see the illegitimacy ratio beginning to climb in the cities and burghs whilst outside, in the traditionally more illegitimate countryside, the ratio was reaching its all-time low point.

A further difference arises between recent and historical examples in the difficulty of identifying a stimulus. Neither geographically nor socially do there exist within modern society the simple village units which are the favoured subjects of historical demography; instead a multiplicity of heterogeneous groups, linked by complex relationships and communication systems, are bombarded with quickly changing stimuli, all potentially relevant not only to fertility but to many aspects of individual and group behaviour. We therefore lack knowledge of trends, outcomes, and stimuli, all of which are 'givens' within the historical situation.

Finally, because of rapid changes in technology we are faced with situations without precedent, in which potential responses are themselves unknown. Thus, what were 'givens', or at least plausible hypotheses, in past circumstances, whose combination allowed us to infer the nature and strength of pressures and motivations upon fertility behaviour, become themselves problematic.

This does not invalidate the body of techniques or of theory evolved from the study of past periods or different societies. Some general theories produced at an earlier period begin to look a little naïve. For example, Carr-Saunders's [6] generalization that 'the evolution of human culture brought a universal tendency toward the maintenance of an optimum population appropriate to the resources of each area and the economic technology of its occupants' would need considerable re-interpretation to fit the contemporary scene. It may have long-term validity, but only in the sense that each population may constantly redefine its notion of the 'optimum' to fit its own circumstances. Theories relating to the effect of lowered death rates on fertility behaviour are clearly inappropriate to the modern industrial world, where almost all live births result in adults. At another level of generality, however, it may still have validity in suggesting how individuals experiencing particular needs or holding certain ideologies adjust their reproductive behaviour to offset costs and maximize benefits. There is no reason to doubt Kingsley Davis's theory of the multiphasic response, i.e. that

the process of demographic change and response is not only continuous but also reflexive and behavioural—reflexive in the sense that a change in one component is eventually altered by the change it has induced in other components; behavioural in the sense that the process involves human decisions in the pursuit of goals with varying means and conditions. [8]

Davis illustrates, from postwar Japan, nineteenth-century Scandinavia, and eighteenth- and nineteenth-century Ireland, the stimuli to marital and reproductive change, and the massive multiphasic responses—that is, in its extreme form, the response by all available means. Correctly, in my opinion, he interprets these responses 'in terms of behaviour prompted by personal rather than national goals'. How otherwise can we interpret the common phenomenon of a fall in fertility coinciding with an increase in national economic prosperity? Davis makes the important distinction between individual and collective levels of living as motives for what are ultimately individual decisions.

The answer to the central question about modern demographic history cannot be posed, then, in the framework of ordinary population theory which assumes the sole 'population factor' to be some relation between the population–resources ratio and the collective level of living. It is doubtful that any question about demographic behaviour can be satisfactorily posed in such terms, because human beings are not motivated by the population–resources ratio even when they know about it (which is seldom).

This is certainly my reaction when visited in Aberdeen by journalists and T.V. producers who ask whether Aberdeen's attainment of zero population growth reflects the city's realization that the world is over-populated. Our experience in talking to young people and couples suggest that a sizeable proportion are not even aware that Aberdeen had long been noted for its liberal abortion practice. This emphasis upon the individual's perception of the world from his own small corner and his reaction to events in terms of his personal goals points fertility theory in the right direction. Its difficulty of application as a tool for the analysis of current and future behaviour is well illustrated, however, in Davis's own formulation

that the explanation of as fundamental a feature of society as its demographic changes is not to be found in some inflexible biological or economic law, or in some particularistic cultural idiosyncrasy but, rather, in the main features of the operating social organisation, on the one hand, and, on the other, in the changing conditions which arise from past performances and the altering international politico-economic environment.

That certainly leaves a wide enough field in which to search for relevant influences.

The theory of multiphasic response and its emphasis upon individuals' perceptions of their own needs as stimuli to action is compatible with a further and relevant model drawn from economic theory—the utility model. Essentially the model assumes that individuals behave in such a way as to maximize utility by a balancing of costs and benefits. In its baldest form the theory is a truism for the only measure of what people want is what they do— unless we adopt an older explanatory view that they know not what they do but that we, from outside, can interpret their true wishes—a dangerous pathway into population psychiatry. The concept of utility begins to have relevance if costs and benefits are identified and defined, and if we move beyond the economic model of cost and benefit, for, as noted above, rising prosperity may itself bring greater costs and, conversely, the obvious 'costs' of parenthood may be perceived as benefits. This model, too, there-fore can only become applicable if we enter into the social world of the individual and understand the meaning, to that individual, of the consequences of decisions or non-decisions.

Any comprehensive theory of fertility behaviour must contain within its formulation:

(1) means of identifying 'objective' components in economic, social, cultural, and technological situations deriving from changes in any sector of society which may have repercussions on individual behaviour;

(2) a knowledge of the subjective meanings attached by individuals to the phenomena and events associated with sexual and reproductive activity; and

(3) it must also comprehend the processes through which objective-type influences impinge on everyday decisions and influence their conduct.

Decision-making

I now turn to some of these processes and subjective meanings, and first to the process of decision-making itself. Decision-making may be a grandiose term to employ to describe actions which very frequently bear the obvious hallmark of unpremeditation. It is used here to mean the process by which action or non-action emerge out of the interaction of sexual partners and their joint interaction with their social environment.

The most extreme and simple model of decision-making makes the assumption that individuals take decisions, consciously or tacitly, after reviewing the full range of alternatives and their implications for the short- and long-term future. Even on the assumption that this rational-comprehensive method of decision-making [4] has relevance to more than a handful of individuals and couples, it must nevertheless be heavily qualified.

By their nature many of the factors in decisions relating to fertility are unpredictable. This applies, for example, to the timing of conception, the degree of fecundity, the outcome of pregnancy, the experience of pregnancy and labour, the sex of children, the future occupational careers of the partners, and the national economic situation throughout the period of parenthood. Since each stage of the life-cycle is itself a new experience, decisions must be taken on the basis of personal perceptions and predictions. The information at the disposal of decision-makers therefore is not the 'objective' future situation but perceptions at the point of decision itself.

Moreover, not all alternatives are open for consideration. Decisions do not emerge from a *tabula rasa* but from the range of possible alternatives available at a given time. I shall deal later with some of the constraints arising out of ideologies, powerlessness, life-styles, and status.

Finally, decisions taken at the beginning of a 20-year cycle must inevitably be affected by later experience and by supervening events, developments, and attitudes deriving from the external world.

The rational-comprehensive model of decision-making is therefore, in the circumstances of marital fertility, intrinsically impossible to apply. We all recognize its invalidity yet nevertheless it is often implicitly assumed in health and sex education and in the provision of services.

A more widely applicable model is variously known as successive limited comparisons, incrementalism, or the art of muddling through [4]. The essential features of the model are that, for each individual, standing on his own personal space and in a unique relationship to his perceived environment, the decisions are not, and cannot be, taken between the full range of possible alternatives. Perspectives on choice are limited by past socialization experiences, by existing aspirations and expectations, by biological, economic, and social constraints, and by the cultural norms prevailing and perceived. Decisions therefore relate to choices between limited alternatives, and the eventual long-term pattern of behaviour is built up out of a series of successive decisions, each of which has a unique quality because of intervening events and prior decisions. The ultimate pattern therefore results from a series of incremental steps. To explain marital and fertility behaviour we must therefore understand not merely the objective external world, including the world of ideas which may to each individual have an intrinsic objectivity, but also their perception of alternatives at each point in the cycle, their aspirations and expectations at each stage, and the feedback from prior experience. Hence the inherent inadequacy of projections of future activity from past behaviour, except in highly structured and stable circumstances. Few studies have concentrated on this process and our understanding is extremely limited. Yet, without such understanding, major population theories derived (validly) from historical study cannot be applied to current situations. In discussing some of the parameters of decision-making below I am conscious of the dictum used by Deusenberry [10] and amplified by Hawthorn [11] in discussing the utility model that 'Economics is all about how people make choices. Sociology is about why they don't have choices to make.'

Ideologies

The flood of intervention programmes in under-developed societies, and of associated sociological, anthropological, and evaluation studies, as well as sharp changes in our own society in recent years, have emphasized the importance of ideologies concerning marriage and parenthood. By ideologies I mean a loosely connected system of ideas about what is socially acceptable. Such ideologies, differing from society to society and group to group within societies, apply to sexual relationships, marriage, parenthood, and family size. They relate not only to behaviour itself but to goals and attitudes and are variously enforceable by law, religion, childhood socialization, education, and social interaction. Their prime significance for our purpose is the constraint they impose upon the range of choice.

We know that not all individuals marry, wish to marry, or can marry, but the underlying assumption in our own and most contemporary cultures is that when children become adults they *will* marry. The costs in terms of money, personal freedom of movement and emotion are clearly enormous and the benefits incalculable. Reasons for this near-universal assumption have been advanced from many disciplines—subjective biological or psychological urges, objective economic reasons relating to the organization of production, consumption, and the division of labour, societal reasons relating to the need to maintain the existence of a social group and its culture, to prevent conflict over inheritance or sexual possession, and to ensure stable conditions for the upbringing of children. Whatever the reasons advanced at the macro or societal level, if we accept Davis's arguments quoted earlier, it seems unlikely that the personal decisions of individuals are based on an understanding and acceptance of sociological-type reasoning about the need to transmit culture to later generations or to ensure the continued existence of social institutions. It seems more probable that, from the individual's viewpoint, the basis for the assumption is its universality. The pressures to conformity and the attribution of a generalized deviancy to individuals who may deviate in one fundamental respect from accepted norms are now being documented by sociologists in numerous settings. In certain societies the norm is so strong and universal that women must be married from menarche to the grave, however nominal the marriage. In our own pluralistic society where freedom of choice is theoretically available, unmarried persons still tend to be defined as deviant and reasons are sought for non-compliance. The male suffers from lack of sexual potency (a highly regarded attribute in males); there may be *a priori* assumptions about homosexual inclinations, selfishness, or physical unattractiveness. Such arguments, though easily refutable by looking at these same characteristics in males who do marry, are likely to be raised, at least at the gossip level (and sometimes more formally, in bureaucratic institutions), about any male who persistently refrains from marriage. In the female, suggested comparable reasons are lack of attractiveness, lack of emotional warmth, unspecified unnatural feelings, and psychological disturbance. Whatever the reasons attached as a label to particular individuals, being a bachelor or a spinster tends to signify a disability and to attract disapproval, stigma, or pity. Whilst this universal assumption is held, reasons are sought for non-marriage—yet in the present climate of opinion concerning population we should perhaps be promoting research into the reasons why people *do* marry: what pressures they perceive from their social interaction, what cues are dropped and picked up, what compromises are reached, and what alternatives are open in other forms of living or other occupational or affectional outlets. Such studies seem particularly pertinent at the present time, when evidence begins to accumulate that the younger generation is experimenting with alternatives and feels freer than hitherto to discuss marriage with some cynicism.

A further, near-universal assumption is that marriage means parenthood [5]. This too is enshrined not only in popular thought and literature but in the religious doctrine that marriage is divinely intended for the procreation of children. The childless couple, like the bachelor and spinster, attract a variety of stigmatizing speculation. Questions are raised about potency, sterility, selfishness, or lack of natural feelings; and the conversation and social habits of peers who have become parents creates a social isolation and division of interests. From our point of view the problem goes much further—repeated studies in Western industrial society produce findings that the one-child family falls outside the range of family size regarded as ideal. The latest large-scale study in Britain, *Family Intentions*, conducted by the Social Survey Division of O.P.C.S. [19], showed that the number of married women under 45 who considered no children, or one child, as ideal 'for families with no particular worries about money' as less than 1 per cent, whilst only 2 per cent considered one or fewer children as ideal for people like themselves. Ideal family sizes for those without particular worries about money were 2, 3, and 4—with 4 the most popular single size. For people like themselves 2, 3, and 4 were still the most ideal sizes, although 2 now became the preferred ideal. For population conservationists such findings could have gloomy implications. It could be argued that, with increasing prosperity, couples might increase their family size towards the ideal of 3·5 or at least towards the mean of 2·5 considered ideal for people like themselves. We have already seen, however, that collective prosperity cannot be equated with individual prosperity and that 'prosperity' or 'monetary worries' are relative concepts. Worries are the result not of income alone but of perceived future income, and rising income must be balanced against the perception of future needs, aspirations, costs, status, etc.

Do the answers to survey questionnaires of this kind have any practical meaning? Leaving aside semantic questions such as interpretation of 'ideal', 'preferred', 'wanted', or 'likely' and the technical question as to how far answers may reflect what the respondent thinks is expected of her, the processes of decision-making outlined earlier suggest that women (rarely their husbands) are being asked to adopt a mode of decision-making quite contrary to actuality. Their answers are therefore more likely to reflect their perception of ideologies than to have practical bearing upon their own behaviour.

The lack of predictive ability of survey questionnaires for the future behaviour of the respondent is borne out by other findings, for example those of the *Growth of American Families* study [18], which suggest that intentions correlate extremely poorly with performance at the level of the individual, although, through counterbalancing errors, the number wanted and the number achieved for the population as a whole are virtually identical. Clearly much depends on the stage of family building at which questions are asked. Most studies show some tendency for a convergence between preferences and achievement as families build up, the changes in preference reflecting an accommodation to reality.

Similar findings emerged from a study conducted in Aberdeen city over the period 1951–64. Part of these findings have already been published [17], and I will not give details of the sample and research design at this stage. Women having their first pregnancy in the years 1951–3 were sampled, and during the sixth month of pregnancy were asked how many children they wanted to have. Those remaining in the city (and this introduces a bias) were re-interviewed, and again asked the same question, 5 years later. After 10 years their responses were compared with the number of children they had. Not all, of course, had completed their child-bearing span. The average number wanted at first pregnancy was 2·34. After 5 years, the mean number wanted was 2·2, and the number achieved was 2·0. After 10 years, they had a mean family size of 2·34, exactly the number wanted 10 years earlier. The means therefore showed close correspondence. The correlations, however, were low; only 43 per cent had achieved the number of children that they wanted initially, and this necessarily includes some benefit of the doubt because, for example, a woman who had 2 children was classified as achieving her preferred family size if she had originally stated 1 or 2, 2, or 2 or 3. Twenty-six per cent had more than they wanted, and 31 per cent had less than they wanted. Within these groups, the divergences were occasionally extreme, and particularly for those who had produced more children than they wanted initially. Consequently the number of births resulting from excess over preferences considerably outweighed the shortfall in those who had not achieved the number they originally wanted.

Several points emerge from this analysis. First, we should be paying particular attention to the parental experiences and marital decision-making processes in family formation as each of these affect three groups—those who achieve, under-achieve, and over-achieve in relation to initial preferences. If such processes can be understood, at the individual level, we may receive some guidance for the framing of population policy and the provision of services which will be acceptable because they are perceived as relevant. Policies and services which proceed out of recognized need and are focused on appreciation of how pressures are felt and decisions made are more likely to be politically acceptable, and more likely to be used, than those based on abstract notions of national or international welfare.

Secondly, at the individual level, the correspondence between what people regard as ideal, what they want for themselves, and what they achieve is extremely low. We should not therefore place much reliance on survey results of this kind as indicators of future action. The fortuitous correspondence between preferences and achievement at the group or national level may be highly susceptible to change. Examination of our own discursive interview data over a period of time suggests that in a sizeable proportion of the population the realities of biological, medical, emotional, and economic life within marriage will continue to ensure a shortfall between initial expectations and ultimate family size. On the other hand, excess of births over initial preferences represents involuntary child-birth rather than the scaling-up of preferences, and might be reduced or eliminated if our policies and services reacted with a multiphasic programme which enhanced the personal power of individuals.

Thirdly, we should attempt to understand how present ideologies of the ideal family emerge and become fixed. Again questionnaire answers about ideal family size are unrealistic guides to
individual action, but if ideologies act as constraints on the perceived range of alternative choices and if they are, as it firmly
appears, always in excess of what people regard as applicable to
themselves, secular movements in ideal family size may be
important indicators of the pressures upon individuals. Provided,
therefore, that we recognize them for what they are—reflections of
popular ideology—responses to such questions may have a useful
predictive function.

We know extraordinarily little about the origins of these popular
ideologies. We can, of course, speculate. Identification with their
own family of origin (generally speaking larger than today's
family size) appears to have some influence [19]. Past and present
literature, from the Bible, through Shakespeare, to modern
women's magazines may transmit a continuous stream glorifying
marriage, motherhood, and the family man. Many similar streams
of communication are identifiable. Perhaps most important is the
fact that the full range of means for limitation of families—
contraceptives, abortion, and sterilization—has been controlled,
debated, stigmatized, and upheld at times as destructive of fundamental institutions and accepted morality. Babies can be produced
at will, but prevented most effectively only on medical prescription
or with the active approval of the gynaecologist. I am not suggesting that literature should be censored or that conception should
require prescription, but, if population control is necessary,
popular ideology might change rapidly if governmental, religious,
educational, and industrial policies were clearly seen to support
innovations in services at all levels. The attempts of our local
public health and maternity services in Aberdeen over 25 years to
introduce such innovations have been carried out against external
governmental, professional, and religious opposition. The City
Council's Family Planning Clinic established in the 1940s had to
be quietly hidden under the title of the Gynaecological Advisory
Clinic, so that its true purpose would not be evident. Abortion and
sterilization had to be introduced slowly and cautiously against
external disapproval: the city's decision some years ago to provide
the Pill free of charge to married and single women is now itself
endangered by governmental policy. Whilst this is a somewhat

bitter local side-comment, its intention is to emphasize the room for action still available to us, in the removal of restrictions on individual choice, without the need to take action restricting existing freedoms.

Constraints on power

Ideologies provide a framework and a constraint on decisions. Equally important, however, are those constraints which prevent the implementation of individual preferences. I mentioned earlier that, in our longitudinal study of Aberdeen couples, 26 per cent had more children than they originally wanted. This occurred despite some termination of pregnancy and the sterilization of 10 per cent of the sample of women during the 10-year period of the study. Most of this excess of births over preferences was involuntary, reflecting the limited power of this group to match ends and means. If this group had had the power to achieve their preferences or, like the opposite group, to scale down their reproduction to meet their developing needs and experiences, zero growth would have been reached at an earlier point. Several components of power are relevant. The first relates to the individual's perception of himself, or herself, as having power to control events. A salient feature of the educated middle-class is their assumption that every event has a cause, that causes can be found, and that once found, remedial action becomes possible. Events can therefore be controlled and manipulated, and long-range coordination of ends and means becomes a perceived possibility. For the educated middle-class this is, in fact, a realistic assumption based on personal experience and the observation of their peers. Frequently, however, in studying family formation we meet the opposite, fatalistic assumption that events control the individual, that things happen to people by chance or fate, and that consequently planning for distant goals is irrelevant because it is inherently doomed to failure. The origins of this value-orientation are ill-understood. Like the educated middle-class I take the view that events have causes and that for a sizeable proportion of the population the fatalistic assumption is validly drawn from their experiences—whether these experiences represent the culture of their group or their personal knowledge of the unpredictability of the events which have impinged upon their education, upbringing, housing, occupation, and their contacts with the external world of institutions and bureaucracies [15, 16]. It is true that couples can, today, plan their family spacing and size with extreme accuracy. It is also arguable that, if in the limited area of family planning this goal could be achieved, it might break the cycle of powerlessness on other fronts. These, however, are irrelevant truths if they are not perceived as truths, for action follows upon the perception of possibilities not upon external truth.

In a recently completed study of skilled and unskilled occupational groups each of which 10 years after marriage had achieved family sizes of either 2 or of 4 or more, the fatalistic attitude summed up in such phrases as 'I'll have my number whatever I do' or 'My sister went to the Clinic and babies came even faster' occurred very frequently among those who had 4 or more children, and particularly among the unskilled group. Janet Askham [1] explored the women's attitudes towards planning and its relevance to other areas of behaviour, including several dimensions of housing, employment, unemployment, job satisfaction, financial saving, as well as reproductive habits. In each area she identified fatalistic and non-fatalistic behaviour patterns. Among the skilled group with 2 children, the average number of fatalistic behaviour patterns across all activities was 1·9 per family. Among the unskilled group with 4 or more children the average number was 6·3 per family. The other two groups had intermediate means. Whilst this is a highly summarized statement of a complex analysis, it indicates that a planning orientation in relation to family size is closely associated with a more generalized life-style. The breaking of the cycle may therefore be dependent upon efforts to increase the individual's perception of his power on a wide front—possibly a fruitless exercise unless it is accompanied by actual increase in power. Again our knowledge is limited, although experience in programmes of social intervention suggest that attempts to advance along a single front are not demonstrably effective. Certain couples drawn from powerless groups can be identified as biologically sub-fecund, and it might be worth investigating how far such involuntary control of fertility has repercussions on other aspects of their life-style.

Power has many components, of which self-perception and motivation may be the most important, but they carry the necessary corollary that, through information and access to means, there should be an ability to exercise power. Public and professional attitudes to the provision of information and access to available techniques of birth control and family limitation remain ambivalent. Sex education, for example, is superficial, sporadic, and often self-contradictory, accepting the need for education but afraid that, once gained, it will be used by young people. Interviews with single girls requesting abortion suggest that, however impeccable the scientific or diagrammatic quality of the biological information imparted at earlier ages, its absorption has been limited and possibly seen as irrelevant to the sexual scene of everyday teenage life [13].

Superior technology has potentially changed the nature and the frequency of the decisions which must be made in sexual interaction and the power of the participants. Earlier methods of birth control, for example, involved constant negative decision-making, at every act of intercourse, under the pressure of emotion, involving active joint cooperation to prevent the natural consequences of behaviour. With the I.U.D. and, to a lesser extent, the Pill, the decision is made infrequently, not under emotional stress, involves active effort on the part of one member, and is a positive decision for conception. We know lamentably little at the level of the individual about the use of birth control, its discontinuance, the changes in marital decision-making involved, or in the relative power of man and wife in sexual relations. Ease of access varies greatly between areas of the country, and difficulty of access usually means most difficulty for those with the lowest motivation and power. This has been well illustrated in the use made of freer abortion laws. The rate of referral in Aberdeen for termination of unmarried women was low in the years before the approach of the Abortion Act. As the rate of illegitimacy began to rise sharply, particularly in young middle-class women, and as the rate of termination also increased, the proportion of both referrals and terminations mounted most quickly among students, nurses, and professional and semi-professional women. Among the least-skilled groups the rate of referral and termination, and the rate of increase of illegitimacy, was much slower and has never reached parity with the middle-class group. The reasons are complex. They involve not only the attitudes, motivation, and life-styles of the woman and her family but also the untutored sociological preconceptions and the personal values of the medical

decision-makers. The success of the middle-class group in present-
ing and maintaining their request undoubtedly occurred largely
through confidence, aggressive persistence against professional
reluctance, knowledge acquired from a network of relevant
contacts, and the ability to understand and penetrate the complex
referral and decision-making machinery, to interpret the cues
dropped by doctors, and to adapt their case to the criteria known
to be employed by general practitioners and gynaecologists [12,
13].

In an ambiguous situation, therefore (such as prevails still in
relation to contraception, abortion, and sterilization), information
access and self-perceptions derived from general life-styles and
situations are important determinants of action. If the situation
were less ambiguous, if the pathways were less tortuous, the services would appear more available to the powerless. To achieve
these goals we require much deeper and widespread study of the
world as it appears to them, the definitions which they hold
regarding the medical, professional, and bureaucratic systems,
their information base, and their sub-cultural modes of reaching
decisions.

Finally, and briefly, I turn to changes occurring in the status
of women. Traditionally, the roles of women have been defined
in terms of marriage and motherhood, of affect and caring, of
acceptance and submission. The changes in birth control and
family planning in this century have been associated with a
change and an upgrading in the status of women. Changes in the
law and the activities of women's pressure groups have made
these movements in status highly visible in recent years. Their
visibility, however, may give a misleading impression of the speed,
strength, and coverage of change. Increasing participation in further
education and in the work force, as argued for example by Blake [3],
might substantially change ideologies, and the attribution of roles
and of power and indirectly, by providing other opportunities,
reduce the pressure on women either to marry, to have children,
or to have many children. Some groups however are virtually
untouched by these changes, and the range of alternatives is still
sharply constrained. If, therefore, as seems likely, a higher and
different status for women is an important component of stimulus
and response in fertility behaviour, this, too, is an area for deeper
study—not only at the survey-statistical level but by observation

and understanding of the influences and pressures experienced by women in their everyday activity and their interaction with the diverse aspects of their social, economic, and cultural environment.

In general, I have argued that the anticipation of future trends in fertility cannot be derived from retrospective data and that large-scale theory drawn from classical demography cannot be applied to our present needs without its supplementation by observational data and theories based on the full range of techniques and perspectives possessed by the social sciences. Otherwise, projections become meaningless mathematical exercises, since the assumptions built into projection and simulation studies are, and must be, as naïve as the social science from which they are drawn. Explanatory theories must be able to identify and articulate the major movements occurring in our social and economic structure with the everyday world of men, women, and families, not as perceived by administrators but by the individuals themselves. It is the everyday world as seen by actors within it, as opposed to the constructed world of the historian, economist, demographer, or biologist, about which we know so little scientifically. The cheaper or simpler device of using animal populations, historical situations, or pre-literature societies as substitutes will add hardly a comma to the type of information we need. I have suggested areas of potential interest—decision-making processes, the formation and maintenance of ideologies of family life, problems of power and status, and the impact on decision-making, ideology, and power of the ambivalent attitudes implicit in social policy, the professions, and social services. Clearly they are only examples drawn from a vast range of choice. Underlying these suggestions is the implication that changes which have already occurred in these phenomena and have led to reductions in fertility have not yet penetrated fully into our social structure. Perhaps the most significant feature of these changes is the population-control movement itself, and its deliberate attempt to substitute a new ideology for the old. Historically, the movement may be seen as an agent for change, but more probably it will be a piece of data in a theory of multiphasic response showing how ideologies eventually catch up on earlier developments in practice.

REFERENCES

1. ASKHAM, J. (1973). Personal communication.
2. BANKS, J. A. (1954), *Prosperity and parenthood*, pp. vi + 240. Routledge and Kegan Paul, London.
3. BLAKE, J. (1965). Demographic science and the redirection of population policy. *J. chron. Diseases* **18**, 1181–200.
4. BRAYBROOKE, D. and LINDBLOM, C. E. (1963). *A strategy of decision*, pp. ix + 268. Free Press, New York.
5. BUSFIELD, J. (1973). Ideologies of reproduction. In *The integration of a child into a social world* (ed. M. Richards). Cambridge University Press, London.
6. CARR-SAUNDERS, A. M. (1922). *The population problem*, pp 516. Clarendon Press, Oxford.
7. CONNELL, K. H. (1950). *The population of Ireland 1750–1845*, pp. ix+293. Clarendon Press, Oxford.
8. DAVIS, K. (1963). The Theory of change and response in modern demographic history. *Population Index* **29**, 345–66.
9. —— and BLAKE, J. (1956). Social structure and fertility: an analytic framework. *Econ. devel. cult. Change* **4**, 211–35.
10. DUESENBERRY, J.S. (1960). In *Demographic and economic changes in developed countries*, Universities-National Bureau Committee for Economic Research. Princeton University Press, Princeton, New Jersey.
11. HAWTHORN, G. (1970). *The sociology of fertility.* pp. 161. Collier–Macmillan, London.
12. HOROBIN, G. (ed.) (1971). Therapeutic abortion in north east Scotland, *J. biosoc. Sci.* **3**, 87–131.
13. —— (ed). (1973). *Experience with abortion: 'a case-study of North East Scotland.* Cambridge University Press, London.
14. ILLSLEY, R. and GILL, D. (1968), Changing trends in illegitimacy, *Soc. Sci. Med.* **2**, 415.
15. RAINWATER, L. (1960). *And the poor get children.* Quadrangle Books, Chicago, Ill.
16. —— (1965). *Family design: marital sexuality, family size and contraception.* Aldine Publishing Company, Chicago, Ill.
17. THOMPSON, B. and ILLSLEY, R. (1969). Family growth in Aberdeen, *J. biosoc. Sci.* **1**, 23–38.
18. WHELPTON, P. K., CAMPBELL, A. A., and PATTERSON, J. E. (1966). *Fertility and family planning in the United States*, pp. xxxiv + 443. Princeton University Press, Princeton, New Jersey.
19. WOOLF, M. (1971). *Family intentions*, Office of Population Censuses and Surveys. Social Survey Division Report, SS408, pp. x + 153. H.M.S.O., London.

1.9. An evaluation of the effects of population control programmes

BERNARD BERELSON

President, The Population Council, New York

THIS series of papers began with a study of animal populations and their biological constraints. We have dealt with tribal and complex communities, rich and poor countries, the individual and the world. You have thus had a thorough analysis of population problems in both their magnitude and their complexity. Now it is my task to close the circle, to conclude on human populations and their constraints, biological and otherwise—and mainly otherwise.

To that end, I shall not speak of the present demographic condition in which the world finds itself nor of its causes and its consequences; you have already heard those from my betters. In my remarks I shall take it for granted that population size and population growth have become problematic not only to some demographers but also to ecologists and environmentalists, economists, public-health administrators, politicians and statesmen, and informed citizens. Population, in short, is now defined as a problem, though not always the same one, by any means. In earlier times, problems of this character were not so readily identified and, when they were, not so readily addressed. These days the very recognition of a public problem means that something must be done about it. I am here to evaluate that something.

Before evaluating the situation, let us be reasonably clear about what that something is. For my purposes here, it is the (more or less) deliberate effort by governments to affect the rates of population growth in their countries—not the incidental demographic effect but the intended one. I limit myself to governmental actions and to population growth; there are non-governmental efforts at 'population control' as well as governmental policies to affect population distribution, but those are other stories. I address myself to the current situation, not the historical one. So the question becomes: What have governments done recently to affect population growth, and how have those efforts worked out?

What *can* governments do? Broadly speaking, there are only five things they can do. They can (1) communicate with people in order to influence their demographic behaviour in the desired manner, (2) provide services to effect the desired behaviour, (3) manipulate the balance of incentives and disincentives to achieve the desired regulation, (4) shift the weight of social institutions and opportunities in the desired direction, and (5) coerce the desired behaviour through the power of the state.

As framework to what follows, let me elaborate that classification somewhat.

With regard to *communication*, we can distinguish three things governments can do, in principle. First, they can provide, or encourage others to provide, factual information about population- and fertility-related matters—for example, that a particular growth rate appears to have specified collective effects on the economy or the environment, or that children born to older mothers have a specified higher risk of certain abnormalities, or indeed that birth control is possible, practised, effective, safe, and available, with the appropriate specifications. Second, they can provide what might be called education or enlightenment—a blend of the (alleged) facts and the values to which they relate, with analysis and 'soft' recommendations as to the path of wisdom, individual or collective. Such programmes can be carried out within formal school systems, through systems of adult education, through the mass media, or through such institutions of government as Presidential or Royal Commissions. Third, they can directly persuade people, or try to, by means of 'hard-sell' argumentation and exhortation—for example, by dire predictions of what will happen if the desired behaviour is not adapted, by calls to patriotic obligation, and by demands that individual preference be subordinated to the national need, whatever that is perceived to be.

With regard to *services*, governments can do two things: (1) they can legislate or decree what is medically and morally acceptable as means to demographic control in their societies (and make their use easier or harder through tax, tariff, regulatory, or police powers); and (2) they can provide and/or support the related services alongside the private sector, typically through the public-health network. As examples, governments can say that the Pill or sterilization or abortion is, or is not, legitimate within the country, and specify conditions; and they can take the initiative in making available the actual services, including supplies, to the entire population at risk or to that segment deprived of such services under current circumstances—that is, they can establish family planning programmes, as they are now called.

With regard to *incentives*, governments can raise or lower the costs of having children through such measures as maternity leaves and benefits, family and children allowances, tax benefits or penalties, social security provisions, educational fees, child labour legislation, and money payments for the *n*th birth, periods of non-birth, or for the initiation or continuation of the practice of fertility control. Money is clearly a powerful motivator of human beings, and it can be applied in this case as in any other.

With regard to *social institutions and opportunities*, governments can influence the social situation in a variety of ways, that in turn influence the demographic outcome, or at least have the potential of doing so: they can regulate marital status, and particularly the age of marriage; invest in nutrition and sanitation and health sufficiently to affect the mortality rate, especially the infant or child mortality rate; determine the extent to which popular education will be available, especially for girls; control the extent to which subsistence agriculture is replaced by modernized agriculture on the one hand and industrialization on the other; affect the distribution of income with a view to raising the poor; determine how much housing of what kinds will be available to whom, with particular reference to family size; encourage or discourage certain religious observance; and affect the status of women within a society, especially with regard to their employment outside the home. According to the received wisdom, such institutional factors largely determine human fertility, up or down, at least on the historical scene.

Finally, with regard to *coercion*, governments can seek to achieve the desired rates or numbers through the power of law and its penalties: for example, as has been suggested, by declaring the *n*th birth illegal and making it punishable in some way or through forced sterilization of the undesirable.

Those are the things that governments *can* do, by way of formal policy, to affect population growth. Let me now inquire into what is actually being done in the world today and what difference such policies and programmes seem to make.

Before proceeding, however, I need to specify the territory to be addressed. The topic assigned to me in this series is broader than most people think in three respects. Most people think of 'population control programmes' as referring to efforts to decrease the birth rate in India and the rest of the 'Indias' of the world. Yet they can, in fact, deal with efforts to *increase* fertility as well as to decrease it (and until World War II that was the main object of formal policy), with programmes in *developed* countries as well as developing, and with policies on *mortality* and *international migration* as well as on fertility. All of these are efforts at population control and all need to be evaluated together for a comprehensive view.

Coercion

I start with coercion and work backwards up the list of possible policies. First, note that coercion is generally accepted for two of the three factors that affect population growth, but not the third— accepted, that is, for mortality and migration but not for fertility (with an important exception to which I shall return). We give the state the right to compel vaccination or sanitation practices or the use of insecticides to control disease, all for the common good; and similarly we acknowledge that the state has the legitimate power to decide how many foreigners may enter the country and how many citizens may leave, and under what conditions. But we do not give the state the right to determine that one must have at least X children or cannot have more than Y children— even though that determination may not be much different, in logic or in philosophy, from the accepted analogue that one must not have more than one spouse at a time.

Second, where applied, governmental controls can be demographically significant: the declines in mortality consequent upon the compulsory introduction of public-health measures made a difference, and among other things contributed to the population problem of the developing world; the control of migration makes a major difference in such countries as Australia and Israel on the receiving end (and for that matter still the U.S.A.), as well as Greece and Turkey, at least for a time, on the sending end.

But direct coercion with regard to fertility level is still objectionable in the modern world, though both proposed and predicted by the doom-sayers in the population community: in response to their perceived crisis, they consider that child-bearing is not a right but a privilege to be conferred or not by the state—to be managed, like death control, for the good of all [1].

Social institutions

Now let us move to that set of factors that is simultaneously the most powerful in affecting natural growth rates and perhaps the least used to that end as a matter of deliberate governmental policy. Fertility and mortality respond to those fundamental changes in the organization of human society that characterize the shift from traditional to modern status—urbanization and industrialization and their attendant impact on kinship and belief systems, popular education, nutrition and sanitation, and the liberation of women. These are the elements of social change that presumably manufacture the motivation for smaller families by increasing the economic cost of children, by undermining the sense of fatalism, and by providing the parents, and particularly the mother, with alternate opportunities in what is now called life-style.

As is well known, the world is demographically polarized: if one ranks countries by their birth rates, from the high of Nigeria and Iraq at 50 or more down to the low of Germany or Hungary at 15 or less, and then draws a line at 30, there will hardly be a developed country above the line or a developing country below it (see Table 1.9.1). Moreover, the two sets of countries, above crude birth rate (CBR) 40 and below CBR 25, are quite different: the countries with high birth rates have low values on the modernization scale, and the countries with low birth rates have high values (see Table 1.9.2). There is only slight overlap in these large institutional factors, reflecting the demographic importance of standard of living, health, and education.

Two observations about the massive building blocks of modern-

TABLE 1.9.1

Birth rates (approximate, circa 1970); countries with populations of 10 million or more

CBR†	
55	Nigeria
50	Algeria, Afghanistan, Ethiopia, Iraq, Kenya, Morocco, Sudan
	Bangladesh, Pakistan, Tanzania, Iran
45	Zaire, Colombia, Nepal, Philippines Mexico, Peru
	Brazil, Indonesia, Venezuela Thailand, India
40	Egypt, Turkey, South Africa
	South Vietnam
	North Vietnam
35	West Malaysia, Chile
	Ceylon, South Korea
30	
	Taiwan
25	
	Argentina Romania
20	Spain, Australia Japan, Netherlands Canada, U.S.S.R., Yugoslavia U.S.A., France, Italy, Poland United Kingdom, Czechoslovakia
15	Hungary East Germany, West Germany

† Sources of data for Tables 1.9.1. and 1.9.2:
Crude birth rates, *Vital Statistics Report*, Series A, Vol. XXIV, No. 1, 1 January 1972; Life expectancy at birth, *Demographic Yearbook* (1970), Table 20; Gross domestic product, *Yearbook of National Accounts Statistics* (1969), Table 1B; School enrolment, UNESCO *Yearbook(s)* (1969, 1970). Data not available in these sources are estimates based on various sources available at the Population Council.

TABLE 1.9.2(a)

Per capita *gross domestic product* (*circa 1970*), *in high- and low-fertility countries with populations of 10 million or more* (*in U.S.* $)

GDP†	High-fertility countries (CBR = 40+)	Low-fertility countries (CBR = 25−)
		U.S.A. ($3955) Canada ($2621) France ($2400) Australia ($2300) West Germany ($2178)
$2000		Netherlands
		United Kingdom
$1500		Japan
		Italy
$1000	Venezuela	
		Spain
	South Africa	Argentina
	Mexico	

GDP†	High-fertility countries (CBR = 40−)	Low-fertility countries (CBR = 25+)
$500		
$100	Colombia, Turkey Philippines Iraq, Iran Brazil, Peru Algeria, Morocco, Egypt Thailand, Kenya Sudan Indonesia Nigeria, India Afghanistan Zaire, Nepal, Tanzania Ethiopia	

TABLE 1.9.2(b)

Life expectancy at birth (circa 1970), in high- and low-fertility countries with populations of 10 million or more

Life expectancy†	High-fertility countries (CBR = 40+)	Low-fertility countries (CBR = 25−)
80		Netherlands
		United Kingdom Poland Italy U.S.A., France, East Germany, West Germany Japan, Hungary, Canada Australia, Czechoslovakia
70		Romania, U.S.S.R. Yugoslavia
	Venezuela	
	Mexico Brazil	

† See footnote to Table 1.9.1 on p. 138.

Life expectancy†	High-fertility countries (CBR = 40+)	Low-fertility countries (CBR = 25−)
60		
	Peru, Turkey	
50	Iraq Algeria, Morocco, Pakistan Iran South Africa Sudan	
40	Nepal, Tanzania	
	Afghanistan Nigeria	

TABLE 1.9.2(c)

Female enrolment in elementary school (circa 1970), in high- and low-fertility countries with populations of 10 million or more

Percentage†	High-fertility countries (CBR = 40+)	Low-fertility countries (CBR = 25−)
100	Mexico, Peru	Argentina, Australia, Japan, U.S.A., Canada, France, Italy, East Germany, West Germany, Hungary, Poland Netherlands, Romania, United Kingdom, U.S.S.R.
	Colombia, Venezuela	Czechoslovakia
90		Yugoslavia
	Philippines	
80		Spain
	Thailand	
70		
	Indonesia Turkey	

† See footnote to Table 1.9.1 on p. 138.

Percentage†	High-fertility countries (CBR = 40+)	Low-fertility countries (CBR = 25−)
60	Egypt	
	Algeria	
50		
	Kenya	
	Iran	
40	Iraq India	
30	Tanzania Nigeria	
20	Sudan	
10		
	Ethiopia, Nepal	
	Afghanistan	

ization. First, they are so central to the human endeavour that
they are typically sought in their own right rather than for demographic ends: whatever impact they have on fertility and mortality,
and hence on rates of population growth, is incidental to their
intrinsic value. So they have large demographic consequences with
small demographic intent, without being 'population policy' if
that requires a conscious attempt to influence population variables.
Increasingly, however, planning officials in the developing world
are coming to appreciate the demographic benefit of such social
changes and the reciprocal influences involved. They are now more
likely to consider that the demography matters, and that adds
another reason for their modernizing plans, if one were needed.

Second, the institutional factors are so 'large' that they are not
moved quickly or easily. There is no particular trick to telling
how to lower fertility in India, as I noted on another occasion
recently:

How, in theory, can India cut its birth rate in half? — get a major proportion of the labor force into industry and thus sharply raise the
standard of living and promote urbanization, give every Indian including the girls at least 6–8 years of schooling, forbid child labor, cut
infant mortality to below 25, raise the female age at marriage to 25 or
so, establish the nuclear family with separate residence, get 35–40% of
the women of reproductive age into the labor force, set up a functioning
system of social security. . . . The point is less that such measures are
uncertain of success, than that they cannot be achieved: the policies
are reasonably clear, their early implementation is impossible. [2]

Thus it is relatively easy to prescribe for a lower birth rate in
India and inordinately hard to achieve it in that way. Most of the
poor countries are seeking 'development', and when it comes, at
least in the current definition, it will also hasten the realization
of 'population control'.

Third, how a country moves through the developmental transition is a complicated matter, and there must be some flexibility
in the mix of social policy measures in which demographic considerations can be taken into account—What can be done to
discourage undue fertility, consistent with other objectives?—
that important query we have insufficiently addressed.

Incentives

The manipulation of incentives to the end of *higher* fertility
has long been practised in a number of developed countries, with
uncertain results. The manipulation of incentives to the end of
lower fertility is just now being tried in a few developing countries,
with as yet uncertain results. As I said, money is a profound
motivator but, as someone has observed, countries have historically tried to buy babies at bargain prices and that may not work.

Several countries, mainly in Europe, have sought a somewhat
higher birth rate mainly through children's allowances tied progressively to birth order, and partly through income-tax exemp-
tions and maternity benefits. The picture is externally complicated
and far from clear. To some extent, such an allowance may itself
work in the opposite direction: it is additional income, regardless
of its source, and hence may have a (small) downward effect on
fertility at the margin; and if the typically small changes in income
do make for change in fertility, the allowance system re-distributes
income up and down for different people, and hence may balance
out [3]. Beyond that, the intended effect of such child subsidies
is to raise desired family size, but if that is already below actual
fertility, as it often is in the (poorer) populations most likely to be
affected, the subsidy will go to quality not quantity. The latest
analysis of this intricate subject, in all developed countries with
comparable data, carefully concludes:

No pro-natalist effect of family allowances was observed; however,
several problems with the particular data used precluded any firm
conclusion on the underlying effects. Further empirical investigation
into the determinants of the size of family allowances in different
countries revealed that relatively low birth rates were more likely to be
the cause of than the result of relatively generous child subsidies because of the implicit population concerns of many of the countries
investigated. [4]

More intensive research on the Scandinavian countries, where
better data were available, found that

when some measure of average child subsidies was included among
other variables explaining changes in fertility rates over time in these
four countries (Denmark, Finland, Norway, and Sweden), the effect of
child subsidies on fertility was positive although not always statistically
significant. [5]

All the same, there are new and serious efforts in Eastern Europe to increase birth rates through child subsidies that sharply increase the allowance for the crucial parities, notably, for example, in Bulgaria where the programme concentrates on bringing into existence the third child by providing a monthly increment of nearly 45 per cent of the average salary for the third child as compared with 16 per cent for the second and 4 per cent for the first and the fourth or higher [6].

Over all, however, one is left with the fact that the continent where child allowances have been most fully developed is also the continent with the lowest birth rates, so they cannot have been overwhelmingly successful. Still, the question remains: What would European birth rates be without such allowances? The birth rate is now about 16; with a completed family size of only 1·5 child per family it would be 12, so there is room for a theoretical effect, though in all likelihood not a very large one.

In the developing world, incentives for lower fertility are emerging these very years in special forms. Here are the major examples:

The Ernakulam vasectomy camp in India, July 1971: a week's ration for the family, a sari and a dhoti, some household utensils, 3 kg of rice, special leaves with pay for 6 days for employees, and Rs. 45 and a special lottery ticket for a first prize of Rs. 10 000 (to men whose average annual income was not over Rs. 100). A similar effort was later held in an entire state in Gujarat.

The Taiwan educational bond scheme, September 1971–: a pilot project in one rural township, for couples with 0–2 children and the wife 30 or under; annual savings deposits towards later educational fees which, with interest, would send 2 children through high school; the account cut in half on birth of third child, cancelled on birth of fourth.

Tamil Nadu tea estate programme, May 1971–: monthly deposits of Rs. 5 into a savings account for non-pregnancy, for women aged 17–40 with 4 or fewer children; account paid out at age 45, minus amounts tied to parity, with entire account forfeited with fifth child.

Singapore programme, 1967–: assignment of public housing regardless of family size (earlier preference to larger families), paid maternity leave limited to 3 children, and delivery fees scaled by parity from S$10 to S$100 (U.S.$4–36) for the third child or more; later, reduction of income-tax relief from 5 to 3 children, further reduction of paid maternity leave to 2 children, and a further increase in delivery charges, from S$50 to S$250 for the lower income groups.

Do such measures work to dampen fertility? Here again we cannot be sure, partly because of technical difficulties in disentangling the effect of this particular input among all the others and partly because of the recency of the effort. In Singapore an analyst concluded that no effect was observable from the earlier measures, given the available data [7]. But in the tea estate and Taiwan experiments, 90 per cent and 75 per cent of the eligible women enrolled, respectively, with very few subsequent drop-outs; contraceptive practice rose from 19 per cent to 31 per cent in the Taiwan population, and there were only two pregnancies reported in the first 10 months in Tamil Nadu [8]. In the Indian vasectomy camps, that attracted 5–10 per cent of the total eligible population or tens of thousands of cases in a few weeks time [9], most observers believe that the incentive system was not without influence; and in the earlier system of finder's fees in Madras it was found that numbers markedly declined when the fees were markedly reduced [10].

Services

That brings us to governmental policies with regard to the services of fertility control. Such policies can either facilitate or retard, and probably at present do both.

In this connection one typically thinks of the national family-planning programmes and their success or failure in lowering birth rates in the developing countries. But it is worth noting first that governments can and do affect demographic rates by their decisions as to what means of fertility control shall be available within the country. Tariffs and taxes on contraceptive supplies are probably a minor instance, but the legal availability of sterilization or induced abortion can be major. Just to mention the two most dramatic cases—one up and one down: the legal termination of pregnancy under appropriate medical conditions was probably a key element in the dramatic postwar decline in Japanese fertility; and the withdrawal of that opportunity surely had a dramatic impact on Romanian fertility after 1966, with the story not yet over. In the U.S.A., where governmental inhibitions on abortion practice have recently been removed by judicial action, it has been estimated that such availability might subtract about 1·5 points from the birth rate [11] or, say, around 8 per cent—which may sound slight but is substantial when measured against other single impacts in a short period of time. The practice probably has other effects which are more substantial—for example, the health consequences of turning dirty abortions into clean ones—but the demographic impact is by no means trivial. India and South Korea have recently legalized the medical termination of pregnancy, and some countries of Eastern Europe may now be looking to its restriction as a means to relieve their perceived demographic distress.

Indeed, making induced abortions legal or illegal may be one of the most effective single ways the modern state has of changing birth rates up and down, although the Romanian case shows that its effect upward is not lasting; as one observer concludes, 'once a motivated population has had access to effective means of fertility control, even strong measures to raise fertility by withdrawing the means may have only temporary success' [12]. Finally, the legalized restriction of abortion is itself a kind of negative coercion—this is the exception I noted earlier—since people are prohibited by the state from the free use of medically acceptable means: a coercion as to fertility means though not, at least directly, as to fertility level.

Now to family-planning programmes in the developing world: what of them? Finally we have reached this key point, but now in context.

In recent years many of the governments in the developing world have adopted policies to provide, or help provide, family-planning services, often for the purpose of reducing population growth. Quite aside from any outcome, the line-up is impressive testimony to the rational determination of governmental policy, regardless of size and geography and culture and religion and political ideology (Table 1.9.3). Among the larger countries, only Brazil, Burma, and Ethiopia have not joined the trend of policy. Thus, in less than a decade, a broad consensus has grown up in the developing

TABLE 1.9.3.

Government positions on family-planning policies, for developing countries, by size

Size of population (millions)	Type of family-planning programme†		
	Official policy to reduce population growth rate	Official support of family-planning activities for other reasons	Neither policy nor support
400 and more	China (1962) India (1952)		
100–400	Indonesia (1968)		
50–100	Bangladesh (1960) Pakistan (1960)	Nigeria (1970) Mexico (1972)	Brazil
25–50	Egypt (1965) South Korea (1961) Iran (1967) Philippines (1970) Thailand (1970) Turkey (1965)		Ethiopia Burma
15–25	Morocco (1965) Colombia (1970)	South Africa (1966) Sudan (1970) Afghanistan (1971) North Vietnam (1962) South Vietnam (1968)	Zaire
10–15	Kenya (1966) Taiwan (1964) Ceylon (1965) Nepal (1966)	Tanzania (1970) Uganda (1972) Chile (1965) Venezuela (1968)	Algeria North Korea Peru Iraq
<10	10 countries	15 countries	55 countries

† Source: NORTMAN, D. (1972. 'Population and family planning programs: a factbook'; *Reports on population/family planning*, (September 1972). The Population Council, New York.

world to support the provision of some modern means of fertility control. In itself, this is something of an historic achievement.

But a policy is not a programme, and in several of these countries the word has not yet been replaced by the deed. Two colleagues of mine recently analysed the status of programmes in twenty developing countries prominently involved in this effort, to see which of fifteen implementing measures had actually been put into practice—measures such as favourable public statements by political leaders, availability of commercial contraception, absence of customs regulations on contraceptive supplies, training facilities, field workers in place, and use of mass media. Of the fifteen measures, the median number present in these twenty countries is 4, and only five countries have as many as 8 or more—India, Hong Kong, Singapore, South Korea, and Taiwan [13]. It is unlikely that a policy to provide voluntary fertility control, or for that matter anything else, will succeed in the absence of genuine programmatic effort.

So programmes range in quality of effort. What can they do by way of outcome? A few years ago, in appraising the state of family-planning programmes, I concluded that they were 'simultaneously impressive, frustrating, uneven, inadequate, promising, and doubtful' [14]. In my judgement, that is roughly the situation today.

As anyone knows who has looked at the matter, the causal analysis of fertility changes is extremely difficult to carry out with definitive results. Even the generally accepted propositions of the historical demographic transition are today being challenged and qualified, and the detailed evaluation of today's programmes in lowering birth rates, after 3, 5, or 8 years of operation, is full of technical problems: how to collect good data to start with, how to disentangle this effect from everything else that is going on, how to identify the precise conditions under which it occurs, and how to handle the indirect and the substitution effects. It is hard enough in some settings simply to gather good data on initiation of contraceptive practice in response to programmatic effort, and moving from that to continuation rates and then to averted births and effect on age-specific marital fertility rates becomes progressively harder, not to mention the difficulty in assigning the cause.

I thus pay my respects to the technical problems of measurement, and at the same time alert you to the provisional character

of our knowledge. On the whole, I believe that this social movement has been about as well studied in recent years, at the going
level of scientific sophistication, as any effort comparable in
complexity and magnitude, but that is not to say that all the
technical problems have been solved. However, this is not a
technical session and, as one of your distinguished economists
once said: having looked that awkward question squarely in the
face I quickly pass on. For something of substance can still be said.

Let us begin with the key controversy in this field. Can current
programmes do very much, can they 'succeed', in the absence of
those large changes in social institutions that we earlier reviewed?
For the moment, let me defer the question of what is to be considered 'success', for obviously a 'yes' or 'no' answer depends
upon that definition, and simply try to indicate the upper and
lower limits of programme effect, based on our current experience.
How much can a service programme do in different institutional
settings? How do supply and demand interact in the case of
fertility control?

As a measure of demand, of interest and motivation on the part
of the individual, verbal expressions are somewhat suspect as a
guide to behaviour, and in any case run the danger of tautology—
motivation is 'high enough' when it works to the requisite degree
of fertility control and otherwise not. Instead, let us deal with the
socio-economic character of the society that presumably creates
the demand in the first place—the large building blocks of social
change. As we have seen, in this respect the developing world is
certainly not of a piece. Similarly, there is a range in programmatic
effort among countries, from strong to weak.

The controversy over the social-setting versus family-planning
approach to fertility decline in the developing world is usually
formulated in a way that heightens the controversy more than it
does our understanding or our ability to cope through policy
intervention. Let us now examine the situation in twenty-six
developing countries with national family-planning programmes.
First, I classify the countries by their relative development on
three major indicators presumably associated with motivation for
a small family: *per capita* Gross Domestic Product as an indicator
of standard of living, infant mortality as an indicator of health, and
female enrolment in formal schooling as an indicator of popular
education. I divide each ranking into thirds, and then construct a

An evaluation of the effects of

composite index so that each country can be categorized over all as high, middle, or low [15]. As examples, Taiwan and Singapore are high, Iran and Colombia are middle, and India and Indonesia are low. That classification represents the institutional setting, motivational to the extent that these factors of modernization reflect motivation for fertility control.

Then, independently, I classify the family-planning programmes of these twenty-six countries as strong-, moderate-, or weak-based on their coverage, their continuity and duration of effort, the vigour with which the programme is actually pursued, and so on

TABLE 1.9.4

1971 programme acceptors, as percentage of M.W.R.A. non-users†

Programme strength	Institutional setting		
	High	Middle	Low
Strong	Taiwan 18·7 South Korea 14·3 Hong Kong 11·4 Singapore 8·6 13		
Moderate	Jamaica 13 — Chile 9 — 11	Mauritius 10·0 Thailand 9·1 Colombia 7·6 Iran 6·4 Costa Rica 6 — Ceylon 5 — West Malaysia 3·6 Tunisia 3·4 6	India 3·7 Pakistan 3 — 3
Weak	Philippines 6·2 6	Honduras 6 — Egypt 4·6 Guatemala 3 — Ghana 2 — Turkey 1·0 3	Indonesia 2 — Nepal 2 — Kenya 2 — Morocco 1·0 2

† Source: Numerator from national service statistics; denominator from Population Council estimate of M.W.R.A. using contraception (public and private sectors) in 1971.
M.W.R.A. = married woman of reproductive age.

[15]. As examples, South Korea is strong, Iran is moderate, and Kenya is weak.

Thus each country has been classified simultaneously on both setting and programme, and contraceptive use can be measured accordingly. The results are not without interest (Table 1.9.4).

Both factors are important. At each level of programme the developmental setting makes about a three-fold difference in annual acceptances and at each level of development the programmatic effort makes a two-fold difference. Taken together, they define the range of programmatic effect, *given* the present tech-

TABLE 1.9.5

Programme users as of about 1970, as percentage of M.W.R.A.†

Programme strength	Institutional setting					
	High		Middle		Low	
Strong	South Korea	28				
	Taiwan	25				
	Singapore	25				
	Hong Kong	17				
		24				
Moderate	Chile	15	Mauritius	18	Pakistan	9
	Jamaica	10−	Ceylon	7	India	8
			West Malaysia	6+		
			Thailand	6+		
			Tunisia	6+		
			Colombia	6+		
			Costa Rica	6		
			Iran	3		
		12		8		8
Weak	Philippines	8	Egypt	6	Nepal	2+
			Honduras	5−	Kenya	2+
			Turkey	3	Morocco	1
			Guatemala	2	Indonesia	1−
			Ghana	1−		
		8		2		2

† Source: Data from LAPHAM and MAULDIN [13], Table 2, line 5a, supplemented by NORTMAN (see Table 1.9.3, footnote), Table 16, col. 4, and similar estimates for Ghana, Honduras, Jamaica, Chile, Costa Rica, and Pakistan.

nology of fertility control—from, say, 10–15 per cent of the married women of reproductive age (M.W.R.A.) non-users annually with a good programme in a favourable setting down to 2 per cent or less with a weak programme in an unfavourable setting [16]. Programme effort makes more of a difference where the setting is at least moderately encouraging.

So both readiness and effort matter, as is also demonstrated by the cumulative proportion of M.W.R.A. using contraception provided by the programmes, as of about 1970 (Table 1.9.5). Here programme duration is involved. The countries in the upper left box have been at this effort for about 10 years, on average; but even here, as another indicator of the importance of the setting, the Philippine programme has achieved in about 2 years what it took the middle countries about 5 years and India about 7 years (of the expanded programme) to do. If anything, programme effort seems somewhat more powerful in cumulation.

The regular progression from left to right and from top to bottom in these tabulations suggests that we should guard against the unqualified either/or: that family planning is either impossible in the absence of modernization or unnecessary in its presence. We do not really know what the threshold is, or indeed if there is one, but as someone has observed, the modernizing variables may not all 'go over the dam together'. In fact, they do not, as the decline of mortality itself demonstrates, and with regard to fertility control it may be a key factor indeed [17]. It now occurs in the absence of full or even moderate modernization, and it is presumably connected with fertility rather intimately.

So there appears to be room in the transition for earlier rather than later intervention, and on this kind of problem the thin edge of the wedge can lead to a big difference over time. After all, modernization is not instantaneous, and neither need be the fertility response; whatever can shorten the lag is of historic value. Thus a service programme, even if not 'population control' in itself, can be ready for whatever motivation is produced by general development, and thus the inevitable can be helped along. As Justice Holmes once said, 'the way in which the inevitable comes to pass is through effort'.

Moreover, as a constant fact of life in this field, and of considerable importance, there is an implicit relationship between setting and programme themselves: the more modernized countries can carry on stronger programmes, and the less modernized can build up even a moderate programme only with considerable effort (India and Pakistan). In other words, development extends to administrative capacity as to other matters, and the setting conditions not only response but programmatic effort itself. In this sense, if family-planning programmes have failed, it is an administrative failure by the managers as well as a behavioural failure by the people.

As for declines in birth rates attributable to the programme, they are now claimed only for countries in the upper left box of our table, and perhaps for Mauritius and Tunisia [18]. Otherwise, they are not there on a national basis, they are too small to show themselves, or they cannot be ascribed to the programme on technical grounds. But note that all these countries tend to have

TABLE 1.9.6.

1971 programme acceptors (I.U.D. and sterilization) in Indian states, as percentage of M.W.R.A.

Programme strength	Institutional setting		
	High	Middle	Low
Strong	Gujarat 6·5 Maharashtra 4.3 5·4	Andhra Pradesh 3·5 Orissa 3.3 Mysore 1·4 2·7	
Moderate	Kerala 5·5 Punjab 4·0 Tamil Nadu 3·9 4·5		Madhya Pradesh 1·8 Jammu and Kashmir 1·3 1·6
Weak		Assam 2·0 West Bengal 1·0 1·5	Bihar 1·6 Uttar Pradesh 1·5 Rajasthan 1·1 1·4

† Source: Adapted from Table 13 Supplement and Table 16 Supplement, in NORTMAN (see footnote to Table 1.9.3).

low death rates, most of them at Western standards (below 10). That is apparently a threshold factor of central importance.

What could a strong programme do among a disadvantaged population? Here we have a few experimental tests in India that have yielded substantial results, well above the country average, in the Ernakulam and Gujarat vasectomy camps and the Gandhigram demonstration [19]. But in this context let us take note of the demographic giants—India and China. After all, they account for over half the population of the developing world, so that they are at least half the story of population control in that sector.

First, *India*: There is a range in developmental progress among the Indian states too, and a classification similar to the earlier one shows the same relationship between modernized status and programmatic effort, even within a single country (Table 1.9.6 and 1.9.7) [20]. Again, the relationship is both direct and indirect; that is, the more advanced states not only respond better in contraceptive uptake but are better able to administer such programmes —and in this case both Tamil Nadu and Kerala are aided by a more effective infrastructure that contributes to programme strength. These results show a far smaller range in performance among Indian states than earlier among countries but there is far less variability in both setting and programme. Moreover, they provide an indication of what a strong programme in a disadvantaged setting might do; that is, Gujarat and Maharashtra average about 5·4 per cent as compared with the 13 per cent of the upper left group in Table 1.9.4, or roughly where the middle–moderate countries fall [21]. Over all, given the difficulties on both sides, the Indian programme is of course not 'solving the problem' in that country.

But let us keep some perspective on the matter. As it happens, India's population is about equal to the population of all the other developing countries with family-planning programmes put together, omitting China. Instead of asking how India compares with Taiwan or Korea, then, it might be more appropriate to ask how India compares with the rest of the developing countries put together. That comparison cannot be carried out in a comprehensive manner due to lack of data on both sides but, for example, the programme in Bombay may compare favourably with that in Hong Kong or Singapore, the experimental efforts in Ernakulam and Gandhigram with those in Isfahan (Iran) and Photharam

TABLE 1.9.7

Births averted by Indian programme
(estimate, per 1000 married couples, to 1969–70)†

Programme strength	Institutional setting		
	High	Middle	Low
Strong	Maharashtra 454 Gujarat 323 388	Orissa 353 Mysore 263 Andhra Pradesh 302 306	
Moderate	Tamil Nadu 439 Kerala 403 Punjab 258 366		Madhya Pradesh 272 Jammu and Kashmir 164 218
Weak		West Bengal 269 Assam 75 182	Uttar Pradesh 135 Bihar 127 Rajasthan 126 129

† Source: The figures for births averted per 1000 married couples were calculated by the following formula:

Births saved (2·4689 × number of sterilizations) + 0·9808 × number of I.U.D.s accepted). In all cases the denominator was the number of married females aged 15–44 in 1969–70 (estimated from census 1971 population and proportion married in 1961). Data for I.U.D. and sterilization have been taken from AGARWALA, S.N. (1971). *A study of factors explaining variability in family planning performance in different states of India, June 1971.* International Institute of Population Studies, Bombay (mimeo). The relative weights of 2·4689 and 0·9808 for sterilization and I.U.D. were taken from KURUP, R. S. *et al.* (1970). *Estimates of the reduction in birth rate from the given family planning targets.* Department of Family Planning, New Delhi (mimeo). This method of calculation probably yields an estimate on the high side but the relative position may still be valid.

(Thailand), or the Tamil Nadu incentive plan with Taiwan's. Over all, however, India does less well than 'the other half' in annual acceptances (Table 1.9.8)—though the programme mix is quite different and that works somewhat to India's disadvantage in this comparison. In any case, the other large countries in this comparison do not do any better.

TABLE 1.9.8

Comparison of India and 'The other half' in annual acceptance rate
(1971)

Acceptance rate 1971	India		'The other half'	
	Percentage of population	States	Percentage of population	Countries
Over 5 per cent of M.W.R.A.	9·2	Gujarat, Kerala	31·9	Taiwan, South Korea, Jamaica, Hong Kong, Mauritius, Chile, Thailand, Singapore, Colombia, Iran, Philippines
2 per cent–5 per cent of M.W.R.A.	32·5	Maharashtra, Punjab, Tamil, Nadu, Andhra, Pradesh, Orissa	32·8	Costa Rica, Honduras, Ceylon, Egypt, West Malaysia, Tunisia, Pakistan
Below 2 per cent of M.W.R.A.	58·3	Assam, Madhya Pradesh, Bihar, Mysore, Uttar, Pradesh, Jammu, and Kashmir, Rajasthan, West Bengal	35·3	Guatemala, Ghana, Indonesia, Nepal, Kenya, Morocco, Turkey

That leaves us with *China*. For the time being, it is difficult to say what is the position in China. There are encouraging reports about both the birth rate and the programmatic effort [22], but it is probably well to reserve final judgement until the picture becomes clearer. Certainly an effort is being made to promote lower fertility not only through family planning (including abortion) but through a higher age at marriage and a greater participation of women in the labour force. And while such efforts appear to be moderately successful in the cities, the scientific documentation is sparse—and even more so in the countryside.

But in this context, China is of special interest: more than most countries, it has pursued fertility control in all five ways, if community pressure, heavy propaganda in the name of the revered leader, and the forced intermingling of urban and rural populations for homogenization of viewpoint add up to 'coercion'. Notably, the rural commune may be an apt institution to internalize fertility burdens close to home. What is needed is, first, more facts on the Chinese situation and, second, more scientific analysis of the relations between the social-medical inputs and the demographic outcomes. But it is probably no accident that many of the developing countries with documented declines in fertility are Chinese or Chinese-related, and China may be the great exception to the Western view of the demographic transition.

Communications

Finally, we have worked our way back to the top of our list, namely, information–education–persuasion. All have been tried, with varying success. In the developing countries there have been several studies of communication effect on the acceptance of family planning, through both personal and mass media [23], and a quick summary would be that they have shown positive results of small to moderate size. In any case, there are logistical difficulties of getting any message through the thin infrastructure.

In both the developing and the developed world, population education in the schools is only now beginning to be institutionalized. As for 'heavy' persuasion, that has been tried by means of exhortations to higher fertility—'heroine mothers', awards, and prizes—with no measurable effect; and occasionally to lower fertility where, for example, the downward intent of the younger cohorts in the U.S.A. these years may be attributed in some part to exhortations to fertility control on behalf of environmental cleanliness and ecological balance. The apparently low fertility in Chinese cities may be attributed in some part to the leaders' exhortations to one's demographic duty.

The communication effort can probably have its major effect, in the developing world, by speeding up the individual response to changed social conditions, through information. That is not unimportant, in view of the time factor involved in the problem. It may be a fair summary of the matter to say that information or 'propaganda' is not very effective alone if life conditions are not changing, so in that fundamental sense the creation of demand for fertility control leads back to square one, namely, basic social change.

Conclusion

This evaluation of the effects of population control programmes does not carry us the full distance to the necessary answers, but in my view they are not available at this juncture. By way of conclusion, I offer the following as some summarizing guide-posts that may be helpful along the way.

1. There are only a limited number of things that governments can do to control population growth, and still fewer that will work. Coercion as to fertility is morally repugnant and politically unacceptable, and virtually impossible anyway for administration. Incentives in either direction may be slightly or even moderately effective but become rather expensive as a mass remedy. General development is certainly effective in driving down fertility, but that is already being pursued with all vigour on other grounds and is difficult and slow to achieve even at costs that dwarf such other efforts as service programmes, which now use up only 1–2 per cent of developmental expenditures. Communication campaigns are useful but apparently not crucial in themselves. What else can be done?

2. The current controversy in the field tends to centre on social change (or development) *versus* family planning. But the current discussions are cast too much in that either/or frame—people are either motivated or not, programmes either succeed or fail, the contraceptive technology is either adequate or not—instead of along the continua where they properly belong. For one side, the criterion is a severe definition of 'solution' or 'success'; for the other, it is a timely and incremental contribution to a complicated problem. In the one case, family-planning programmes fail; in the other they have a contribution to make at relatively small cost. The difference may come down to a profound issue indeed: cure as against relief, social revolution or 'band-aid reform'. The issue raises large questions about the politics of development strategy, the possible *vis-à-vis* the necessary, the best as the enemy of the good, the realizable part or the unrealizable whole.

But 'what controls fertility?' is not so much the question as 'what is the next available step to take towards lowering fertility?' where that is desired. We need not agree on ultimate explanations or goals to take that step, we need not do everything at once in order to do something, especially where 'everything' is not feasible anyway. In short, there is no single or simple solution here, or in any similarly complex problem in any behavioural domain. If early stabilization of population is the goal, the present type of family-planning programme will not reach that goal, but if actuated it will move in that direction and reinforce and expedite an inevitable process of fertility control. By the severe definition, what will succeed within the same band of time, resources, and feasibility? As usual, the short- and long-run approaches can help each other: family planning and associated efforts on the one hand, development and modernization on the other.

3. Differing standards are applied to different demographic situations. Incentives are questioned as anti-fertility measures—'bribes' not to have babies—whereas they are considered as desirable contributions to family welfare in the form of child-assistance payments. Governmental imposition is acceptable in the case of migration and death control though not for birth control, except in the reverse case of restrictions on certain anti-fertility means like abortion and sometimes sterilization. In the developed world, incidentally, it may well be that the valves on migration and abortion, open or closed, have been the most effective direct governmental measures affecting population growth in recent decades.

4. Accepting the lowest possible mortality as the desirable state of affairs to which all societies aspire and recognizing that international migration patterns will in the nature of the case apply only in a few special situations, we are left with fertility. How much have governmental efforts focused on fertility actually affected fertility rates? We do not know for sure, but it appears doubtful that governments can increase their countries' birth rates very much in the short term, except for the manipulation of legal abortion (and that may be short-lived in itself, as the Romanian case seems to show) and perhaps the provision of heavy subsidies for the third child as in the current effort in Bulgaria. We do not know for sure, but in certain favoured situations fertility declined in the 1960s by 10–17 points, from a starting-point around 36–40, and the family-planning programmes appear to have contributed

measurably, but of course not solely, to the decline. At least the programme expedited the going trend (as, indeed, it did in the form of legalized abortion to the historic case of Japan, with a 17-point decline in a decade). As the abortion cases themselves suggest, an improved technology will make a difference, and if one prediction is more likely than another in this field, it is that the technology will improve.

5. Once more we cannot know for sure, but it is not at all unlikely that in today's world governmental policies to reduce fertility rates are being more effective than governmental policies to increase fertility rates. As I have suggested, the evidence is not firm either way, but encouraging people to produce more children than they otherwise would is probably harder than encouraging them to produce fewer, and partly because the former requires a major impact on motivation whereas the latter, as a starter, requires only the means to prevent the unwanted pregnancy [24]. The pro-fertility effort does not appear to be notably more successful despite a much longer try.

6. In any case, few governments are pursuing demographic ends in a single-minded, direct manner; such ends are wrapped up in other efforts. Much of what government does demographically is unintended. Directly, governments do what they can: they provide child subsidies as good in themselves, and hope for a demographic effect; they provide family-planning services as good in themselves, and hope for a demographic effect. The one is good for the child and the family; the other is good on medical and humanitarian grounds. Neither does any apparent harm, both foster individual choice, and both distribute a little income towards the bottom of the pyramid. All in all, considering what else they might do, that is not a bad general policy for governments—no harm, some social and economic benefits, and probably a net demographic contribution.

7. That leaves a last question: What *should* governments do to 'control' population growth through fertility? In the best of all possible worlds it would be enough for them, I think, to do three things: maximize the flow of full information about the consequences of fertility behaviour, both individual and collective; maximize the capacity of people to regulate their fertility by medically approved means, in accordance with individual conscience; and minimize undue pressures on fertility behaviour either

way. Those conditions are met today for a small fraction of the world's population—and that fraction, incidentally, has very low fertility. If those conditions were met, then let the demographic chips fall where they may—the trade-offs between child-bearing and other ends in life would then have found their free and rational level.

In that context, I cannot close this appraisal of programme effects without the reminder that I have been speaking only of means, and rather administrative ones at that. What we seek is human welfare, personal freedom, the quality of life, and demographic trends and changes take on meaning only in so far as they contribute to such ends. Any evaluation should keep that closely in mind—that is, what we are really after. In short, some costs are too high, for population control is not the final value.

REFERENCES AND NOTES

1. I do not speak here of what might be termed the informal coercion of social norms and social pressures—which may be equally efficient and powerful with the formal requirements of the state. It is probably fair to say, for example, that throughout human history most societies have exercised a kind of informal coercion towards child-bearing within marriage, and a highly effective one at that.

2. BERELSON, B. (1973). *Formulation of population policy*. In *Perspectives in biology and medicine*. University of Chicago Press, Chicago.

3. LLOYD, C. B. (1972). (a) *Some aspects of developed countries that encourage fertility*. Paper presented to Interregional Workshop on Population Action Programmes, Manila, November 1962, United Nations, unpublished. (b) Her dissertation *The effect of child subsidies on fertility; An international study*. Faculty of Political Science, Columbia University, New York. Available on demand from University Microfilms Limited, High Wycombe, Bucks, England.

4. ——, see [3(a)], p. 10.

5. ——, see [3(a)].

6. And a one-time payment similarly tied to birth order: $\frac{1}{6}$ the average monthly salary for the first child, $1\frac{1}{2}$ times for the second, and 4 times for the third, and then back to $\frac{1}{6}$.

7. SMITH, D. (1972). *Report on the feasibility of a study of Singapore's anti-fertility policies*. Memorandum (April 1972). The Population Council, New York.

8. For Taiwan, see FINNIGAN, O. D. and SUN, T. H. (1972). Planning, starting, and operating an education incentives project, *Studies in family planning* (The Population Council, New York) **3,**

No. 1, January 1972; LEE, T. Y. (1972). Taiwan, *Studies in family planning* 3, No. 7, July 1972. On the tea estate programme, see RIDKER, R. (1971). Savings accounts for family planning, *Studies in family planning*, 2, No. 7, July 1971; latest results from Ridker in personal communication.

9. KRISHNAKUMAR, S. (1972). Kerala's pioneering experiment in massive vasectomy camps, and THAKOR, V. H., and PATEL, V. M., The Gujarat State massive vasectomy camp. In *Studies in family planning* 3, No. 8, August 1972.

10. REPETTO, R. (1968). India: A case study of the Madras vasectomy program, *Studies in family planning*, 1, No. 31, May 1968.

11. TIETZE, C. (1973). The potential impact of legal abortion on population growth in the United States, *Commission on population growth and the American future*, 1973. The U.S. Government Printing Office, Washington, D.C.

12. TEITELBAUM, M. S. (1973). Personal communication, February 1973. Also see his Fertility effects of the abolition of legal abortion in Romania, *Population studies* 27, November 1972, pp. 405–17.

13. LAPHAM, R. J. and MAULDIN, W. P. (1972). National family planning programs: review and evaluation, *Studies in family planning* 3, No. 3, March 1972.

14. For the elaboration, see BERELSON, B. (1970). The present state of family planning programs, *Studies in family planning* 1, No. 57, September 1970. Also in *Are our descendants doomed? Technological change and population growth* (eds. H. Brown and E. Hutchings, Jr.). The Viking Press, New York (1972).

15. With regard to institutional setting, the countries were classified on a composite index of *per capita* Gross Domestic Product, infant mortality, and female enrolment in primary and secondary schools. Each ranking was divided into thirds. Any country that scored in the top third on all three measures or on two with the third in the middle range appears as high on the composite index; those countries that scored in the bottom third on all three or on two with the third in the middle are ranked here as low; and the remainder are middle. The basic data are from Lapham and Mauldin [13], Table 4, lines 2, 6, and 12. With regard to programme strength, the countries are ranked on the basis of their Y and Q scores in Lapham and Mauldin [13], Table 2, Section B. For those countries not included in these listings, the ranking was done similarly by Council staff.

Since 'readiness' or 'demand' is measured only indirectly in the setting variables, their effect may be somewhat underestimated. It is difficult to get a comparable measure for 'motivation' across these countries but a rough measure (want-no-more-children) from non-similar samples yields Table 1.9.N1.

The same picture emerges, with only the Philippines seriously 'out of line'.

TABLE 1.9.N1

Programme strength	'Motivation'†		
	High	Middle	Low
Strong	Taiwan 18·7 Hong Kong 11·4 15	South Korea 14.3 14	
Moderate	Thailand 9·1 Colombia 7·6 8	Costa Rica 6— Ceylon 5— Tunisia 3·4 Pakistan 3— 4	India 3·7 West Malaysia 3·6 4
Weak	Guatemala 3— Turkey 1·0 2	Philippines 6·2 6	Ghana 2— Indonesia 2— Kenya 2— Morocco 1·0 2—

†Source: Want-no-more-children from NORTMAN (see footnote, Table 1.9.3), Tables 15A and B.

16. Those figures may seem small as an annual return but if the non-fecund, the currently pregnant, the postpartum amenorrheas, and the separated-from-husband are removed from the denominator (a total of around one-third in the typical developing country), then they accordingly increase—and if those actively seeking to become pregnant (another 20–25 per cent) are also removed, then the proportions rise to over 25 per cent and 5 per cent respectively.

17. For example, see DAVIS, K. (1963). The theory of change and response in modern demographic history, *Population Index* **29**, October, 1963, pp. 345–66.

18. As in Table 2, Section C, of LAPHAM and MAULDIN [13]. However, in our tabulation of setting-by-programme the same relationship emerges for the changes in the crude birth rate for the decade 1960–70 (approximately, in points) (Table 1.9.N2).

The data themselves are not firm in several cases, except perhaps as orders of magnitude, but the effect of both factors may be reflected even though the programme existed for only part of the decade in most of the countries (and although not all the apparent decline is attributable to fertility as against shifts in age-distribution or marital status).

TABLE 1.9.N2

Programme strength	Institutional setting†					
	High		Middle		Low	
Strong	Hong Kong	−16				
	Singapore	−16				
	Taiwan	−12				
	South Korea	−10				
		−14				
Moderate	Jamaica	−9	Costa Rica	−15	India	−3
	Chile	−8	Mauritius	−12	Pakistan	−2
			Ceylon	−8		
			West Malaysia	−8		
			Tunisia	−7		
			Thailand	−3		
			Colombia	−3		
			Iran	+3		
		−9		−6		−2
Weak	Philippines	−2	Egypt	−9	Indonesia	−4
			Guatemala	−6	Morocco	−1
			Turkey	−3	Nepal	−1
			Ghana	−1	Kenya	0
			Honduras	0		
		−2		−4		−1·5

† Source: Estimates of 1960 and 1970 birth rates prepared by International Demographic Statistics Center, Bureau of the Census, for Office of Population, Agency for International Development, and presented to the Population Association of America, Toronto, Canada, 13 April, 1972, by R. T. Ravenholt, J. W. Brackett, and J. Chao in *World Fertility Trends during the 1960's.*

19. For documentation, see the Ernakulam and Gujarat citations above [9]. *The Athoor experience*, May 1970, Gandhigram Institute of Rural Health and Family Planning, Gandhigram Post, Madurai District Tamil Nadu, India; and SRINIVASAN, K. *et al.*, Analyses of the declining fertility in Athoor block, *Institute Bulletin*, **4**, No. 3, June 1969.
20. The Indian states were classified with regard to institutional setting on the basis of *per capita* income, female literacy (in lieu of school enrolment), and infant mortality (sample registration system estimates for 1969), with supplementary estimations where necessary

They were classified with regard to programme strength by medical and paramedical personnel and social workers in position, and by urban family-planning centres, primary health centres, and main rural family-planning centres and sub-centres in actual functioning.

21. With the Indian states considered as individual units—they certainly qualify on size grounds—Table 1.9.4, then takes on the appearance of Table 1.9.N3, which provides a useful perspective on the total effort.

TABLE 1.9.N3

1971 Programme Acceptors, as Percentage of M.W.R.A. Non-Users.

Programme strength	Institutional setting					
	High		Middle		Low	
Strong	Taiwan	18·7			Gujarat	6·5
	South				Maharashtra	4·3
	Korea	14·3			Andhra Pradesh	3·5
	Hong Kong	11·4			Orissa	3·3
	Singapore	8·6			Mysore	1·4
		13				3·8
Moderate	Jamaica	13—	Mauritius	10·0	Kerala	5·5
	Chile	9—	Thailand	9·1	Punjab	4·0
			Colombia	7·6	Tamil Nadu	3·9
			Iran	6·4	Pakistan	3—
			Costa Rica	6—	Madhya Pradesh	1·8
			Ceylon	5—	Jammu and	
			West		Kashmir	1·3
			Malaysia	3·6		
			Tunisia	3·4		
		11		6		3·3
Weak	Philippines	6·2	Honduras	6—	Assam	2·0
			Egypt	4·6	Indonesia	2—
			Guatemala	3—	Nepal	2—
			Ghana	2—	Kenya	2—
			Turkey	1·0	Bihar	1·6
					Uttar Pradesh	1·5
					Rajasthan	1·1
					West Bengal	1·0
					Morocco	1·0
		6		3		1·6

22. FAUNDES, A. and LUUKKAINEN, T. (1972). Health and family planning services in the Chinese People's Republic, *Studies in Family Planning* 3, No. 7, Suppl., July, 1972.

23. For examples, see SCHRAMM, W. (1971). Communication in family planning, *Reports on Population/Family Planning* No. 7, April, The Population Council, New York.

24. For example, see FREEDMAN, R., *et al.*, (1972). Frends in family size preferences and practice of family planning: Taiwan, 1965–1970, *Studies in Family Planning* **3,** No. 12, December, 1972, 'fertility continued to decline . . . because more people were using contraception to restrict the number of unwanted children rather than because of changes in the number of children they wanted'. (p. 281)

PART II

Some aspects of population size
in the United Kingdom
and elsewhere to A.D. 2001

(Papers presented at the Workshop
Weekend, 17–18 March 1973)

2.1. Introduction

H. B. PARRY

Fellow of Wolfson College and the Nuffield Institute for Medical Research, Oxford University

AT the time of planning the Workshop, it was thought that the Report of the Population Panel (the Ross Committee) [1] would be available, but, in fact, it was not published until after the Workshop. The scope of the Workshop was therefore deliberately restricted to topics which seemed likely to emerge from the lectures as important issues and upon which the views of people from a wider range of academic disciplines might provide new and stimulating insights. As most of the participants at the Workshop had no opportunity of hearing or reading the manuscripts of the lectures, no attempt was made to provide an integrated study, nor to consider projections beyond the turn of the century.

This decision inevitably ruled out consideration of a number of ecological and resource problems likely to be especially important in the twenty-first century, adequate discussion of which would have been protracted. The programme was therefore purposively restricted to the narrower field covered by five working parties, each of about 20 persons, in Biomathematics, Economics, Biology, Medicine, and Sociology, with a final plenary session.

REFERENCE

1. *Report of the Population Panel* (1973), Cmnd 5258. pp. xi + 135. H.M.S.O., London.

2.2. The biomathematical base for demographic data

2.2.1. The collection and handling of demographic data now and in the future

BERNARD BENJAMIN

Director of Studies in Statistics, Civil Service College

The scope of demographic data

THE scope of demographic data can be very wide indeed. Those data may cover many aspects of population growth and change, extending beyond the pace and direction of population growth itself to means of describing changes in the sex, age, occupational, educational, cultural, ethnic, and even health characteristics of the population.

Population statistics can be separated into measures of stock and measures of flow. Measures of stock describe the population as it exists at a particular point of time, the main source of data being the population census (whether this be a count on the ground or the standing contents of a total population register) or its sample-survey analogue. Measures of flow describe the movements in to or out of specific groups within the population (changes of status), including movements in to or out of the population (births, deaths, international migration). Flow measures derive from registration systems—arrangements for recording vital events or changes in the status of individual persons. These systems may be formal, compulsory, and total as for the registration of births, deaths, marriages in most countries; they may be counterparts of essentially administrative procedures, e.g. the creation or termination of social security records, but still total and obligatory though not subject to penalty on failure to record; they may be compulsory but not total, e.g. the sample counts of immigrants and emigrants in the United Kingdom; they may be intended to be total but nevertheless are not compulsory, e.g. the various registers of chronic disease or local authority housing waiting lists; or they may be neither total nor compulsory, e.g. a sample of births, as in the British Birth Surveys of 1958 and 1970.

Economic development and data accessibility

It has to be borne in mind that a vital statistics system only becomes possible at a time when it becomes necessary. It is not possible to sustain a system of vital registration and census enumeration until the economy of the country becomes sufficiently developed to provide the skilled manpower and the requisite organization; but it is also not until this stage of economic development is reached, at which it becomes useful, indeed necessary, for a birth, death, or marriage to be registered (e.g. the appearance of the joint stock company and the separation of the owner from the asset owned and the need for property transference, to establish identity), that the population is ready to accept and cooperate with a vital registration system.

We have only to think of the number of different reasons for needing a birth certificate today to understand why birth registration is so complete in Britain. Yet before 1836, when the system was introduced, these needs, if existing, were not pressing and, equally, it would probably have been difficult to find the resources to man a widespread network of local register offices.

It is now recognized that, in order to administer the affairs of the country in such a way as to satisfy the social and economic aspirations of the electorate, the United Kingdom Government requires a great deal of information about the size and structure of the population and that the population census is the only reliable source of this information. But in 1753 the first Bill to authorize a census was passed by the Commons against stiff opposition, only to be thrown out by the Lords; the need for the information had not then become sufficiently demonstrable to gain public acceptance. It was to take another 50 years before the pressure had mounted to the point of overcoming resistance.

A corollary of this interaction between economic development and both the need for, and the feasibility of, population data collection is the constraint imposed upon the sophistication of the recording and collection of data, by the level of education of the population. Education is part of economic development. The Office of Population Censuses and Surveys (formerly the General Register Office) has always been extremely careful to ensure, in the interest of effective and reliable response, that the sophistication of records is not extended beyond the capacity of the lesser educated members of the public to comply with data requirements.

The world situation

In the light of these considerations it is not surprising that, at present, only for one-third of the world's population—in the more developed countries—is there a satisfactory system of registration. Where registration is lacking, survey methods have been used but not on a sufficiently extensive scale to make any real inroad to the deficiency of data. The problem of deficient recording is particularly acute for infant deaths; it has been estimated that only 2 per cent of such deaths are registered with reliability.

The situation is more satisfactory in relation to population census data, mainly as a result of the World Census Programme sponsored by the U.N. Statistical Office. In the first programme an attempt was made to encourage as many countries as possible to carry out a census between 1955 and 1964. Some 200 countries complied though this still left 35 countries which had never had a nationwide census and another 11 where the last census was more than 10 years old. The second programme is related to the period 1965–74, and, as yet, very little data are available. Nevertheless, while it is true that the proportion of the U.N. estimates for the total mid-year population of all countries in 1969 which could be regarded as census based was 95 per cent., the remainder being based on partial census, sample survey, or conjecture, some of these census data were old and some were subject to substantial errors in the sex and age-distribution if not in the total populations.

On the vital registration side the improvement is very slow. (The pace of economic development is slow, inhibited as it is by the pressure of population growth.) For the present there is heavy dependence on non-traditional methods, i.e. surveys. The U.N. is encouraging development by continuously reviewing the stages reached by different countries, holding regional seminars, promoting experiments in which registration is initiated in sample areas and checked by periodic surveys, supporting the establishment of associations of civil registration officers, and highlighting deficiencies by the publication of statistical series in the *Demographic Yearbook*.

The available survey methods of obtaining demographic data

are well developed both in relation to their physical execution and in relation to the techniques of analysis and interpretation. Much of this work is associated with the name of Professor Brass, who is also taking part in the Workshop. But these methods require skilled manpower and money. In countries where *per capita* income is wretchedly low, progress is dependent on the provision of foreign aid for which there are many competing needs even within the general population field.

The picture is not a very encouraging one. Nevertheless, the pressure for improvement continues. The next World Population Conference in 1974 will probably report an increase in the number of countries taking positive action to control population growth and will stimulate others to follow. This activity itself improves the climate for the collection of demographic data. Such data are essential to the monitoring of family-planning programmes and to the appraisal of health-service programmes, of which family planning may be a part. This year will see the second conference of National Committees for Health and Vital Statistics to be held under the auspices of the WHO in Copenhagen. The first was held in 1956 in London. The Conference will aim to demonstrate to the less-developed countries the value of health and population statistics in the management of health programmes.

If we are now looking ahead to the end of the century, then it is likely that we can expect a significant degree of catching up in demographic recording by the less-developed countries. It would be surprising if there were not, by the year 2000, vital registration systems covering the greater part if not the whole of the world's population.

Vital registration in Britain

After nearly 140 years of vital registration in Britain there is no detectable shortfall from completeness in recording. The current problems are of scope and technique in relation to both input (the registration of the event) and output (information stocks and flows).

One general point that must be interpolated here is that most demographic measures are in the form of rates. The denominator of the rate—the population at risk—normally comes from the census, at which a relatively large battery of questions is acceptable. However, there is little point in obtaining sub-division of the denominator if the numerator cannot equally be sub-divided. But the numerator comes from civil registration at which it has not been usual to have an extensive battery of questions. There is therefore pressure to increase the scope of registration data. Let us consider some of the data needs.

For prediction purposes we need fertility and mortality rates of high specificity. This means that for every birth or death we need to obtain a great deal of social, economic, and demographic information about the parents. Some of this information is already collected—sex, age, date of marriage, occupation, cause of death—but it would be desirable also to have some information about educational background, housing conditions, industrial dependency, and urban/rural location. It is also important to know the date of any previous maternity and its outcome so as to be able to determine birth spacing trends.

This implies a formidable registration inquiry which may not be socially acceptable. Moreover, resentment would be increased by the knowledge that much of this information is constant from one registration to another; for example, the sex and age of the parent, the citizenship and country of origin, the educational background, and possibly also the usual occupation. Much other information is recorded at the periodic population census.

If therefore new information (census-type or registration) were to be recorded only *once* and at the same time became automatically deposited in a national computer-based data bank (as currently used in Norway) and with sufficient identification, it would be possible quickly to retrieve a consolidated record of all the information needed for particular statistical purposes. The actual amount of the information surrounding any event which is new would be relatively small and the proportion of the whole record which at any one time is dependent on interrogation and at risk of error from carelessness or memory failure would be greatly reduced.

This goes far beyond record linkage in the sense in which this term is normally used. Record linkage normally refers to a system in which a new consolidated record is laboriously built up by the linkage (matching) of abstractions from separately compiled and separately located files. The actual matching is relatively simple (though not, at a remove in time, foolproof) but the document handling and computer input represents an inordinate work load. Record linkage is an old idea and an old-fashioned idea in the present state of computer technology. What is needed is a system of consolidation of personal records at the instant of their inception. Every new addition from whatever source is deposited in the central personal record at the time of first recording the information.

While it would be possible to feed census information into such a data bank there would have to be fairly frequent censuses if the information were to be sufficiently updated at any one time. We are led inevitably therefore to the idea of a continuous population register such as already exists in Scandinavia, the Netherlands, Israel, and several Eastern European countries.

There are two main problems: invasion of privacy and costs and benefits. The solutions to these two problems are mutually conflicting. Data banks are costly to install and even more costly to update. It follows that one should maximize the benefits by extending the data bank to serve as many administrative and statistical purposes as possible. There is a temptation to extend the civil record to cover defence purposes, education programming, taxation, pension and sickness insurance, and medical records. But this greatly increases the number of government officials who would have access to the register and, because of the enormously increased content of the personal record, greatly increases the personal damage resulting from any breach of confidentiality.

However, the temptation to be all embracing is very real. In 1963, attempts to secure a common personal numbering as between social insurance and birth registration, i.e. as between D.H.S.S. and O.P.C.S., were rendered abortive because several other government departments insisted that they too should come within the same system.

In the United Kingdom public apprehension about the confidentiality of personal data banks is acute. This is despite the fact that personal data banks do operate successfully in many other countries and even on a limited scale in this country (the National Health Service central register, the National Insurance register) without anyone being harmed. There were, 200 years ago, exactly the same fears about the census itself, and in 1971 these fears were revived by a number of opportunist politicians on the false premise that, because private credit registers did invade privacy, government registers must also do so. The record of O.P.C.S., however, has always been impeccable. Furthermore, security techniques for computer banks are infinitely more effective than any of those which have operated for paper records.

It seems likely, however, that the British public are going to have to live with this idea for a lot longer before they accept it. I believe they will accept it eventually.

The future of the registration service

Whether or not information collected at registration is instantly fed in to a data bank, extension of the scope of data and increasing concern for the quality of data are compelling the introduction of better skilled manpower into the registration service. Because the registrar was originally appointed to his office on the grounds of his being the only person who could write, O.P.C.S. seemed to have formed the view that anyone who can write can be a registrar.

Vital registration and the population census taken together can be regarded as a gigantic intelligence system of a degree of complexity calling for a high level of technical skill at all levels even at the very lowest. The registrar, who in addition to being entirely responsible for the accuracy of registration data is also a key official in the conduct of the field work of the census, ought to be regarded as the local population intelligence officer; in place of the blind application of the quill pen there should be substituted a real insight into objectives of the system and a proper professional approach. The registrars want this badly enough and have set up an Institute of Population Registration to provide a training and examination system. They have been encouraged by the Registrar General of Scotland, but not in England and Wales, where the George Graham view of a registrar as a mere scribe still persists.

The population census

What developments are likely to take place in the population census? I have written fairly extensively elsewhere about the basic principles of census taking and the problems of current interest [1, 2]. I propose therefore to confine myself here to a brief review of the possibilities for change.

Statistically, in this crowded island, there is little or no justification for carrying out 100 per cent censuses. Sampling in the field reduces the burden upon the public and officials and is highly desirable for that reason. Fewer, but better identified, households and fewer, but more carefully supervised, interrogations means better quality of response. It is true that there is some bias in the sample component but the amount of the bias is not great; it causes more damage to the census through the delay in assessing (some would say 'fussing' about) its extent than by the actual effect on the census statistics. Had a pilot census been allowed prior to 1961 both bias and delay might have been avoided. There were also faults, not in the design, but in the identification of the 1966 sample but these might have been rectified by better (if more expensive) field organization. I would hope that we have seen the last 100 per cent census.

However, we still need considerable effort to be invested in the development of reliable methods of sampling in the peculiar conditions of the population census, namely, as at present, the lack of an adequate pre-existing sample frame. If we had a continuous population register this, as in some other countries, would provide the frame. Could we take only a small step and ask people to register for a forthcoming census just as they register for a forthcoming election? Very little information would need to be recorded.

Extension of scope

Pressure to increase the scope of questions asked at the census grows with the increased complexity of the social and economic system within which we live. The British census is run 'on the cheap' and is based on self-enumeration. Field workers do very little more than deliver and collect the schedules (questionnaires); the schedule is completed by the householder. This method has advantages of speed and therefore of simultaneity as well as cost. Given such a method there is a limit to the number of questions (around 30) to which a householder will address himself before either from tiredness or irritation his response becomes unreliable, if not entirely lacking.

The effective number of questions can be increased in the following ways.

1. Apart from a common core of questions present on all sample schedules, use a variable further list of questions—a different set in each of a number of sub-samples. This idea though seemingly

attractive has a big snag. The essence of the population census is that the questions are interrelated—you want to cross-classify, sex, with age, with occupation, with education. If questions stand on their own the census is not the right vehicle—an *ad hoc* survey is to be preferred. So if occupation is on one sub-sample schedule and education is on another, you cannot cross-classify the two characteristics. The method could work for sets of characteristics that are interrelated only within the set. In practice this is a very severe limitation.

2. Hold more frequent censuses with varying scope so that over a period of years all questions get asked. In essence this is the same as the previous method (1), and is subject to the same disadvantage, but to a much less degree since there would be a much greater proportion of questions common to successive censuses. Expressed in annual terms expenditure on censuses would have to be much increased above the present level.

3. Abandon self-enumeration and adopt a canvass method with an extended questionnaire. This would not only greatly increase the cost of the census but it would increase the time taken to complete the enumeration—from days to weeks. In turn, this would mean greatly increased opportunities for both double enumeration and omission. Such a method, however, would have the advantage of compelling O.P.C.S. to improve, indeed to transform, the quality of its field staff. The probability of this method being adopted is indeed a further reinforcement of the case for according an enhanced role to the local registrar. This method would also have the advantage of providing interviewers capable of marking schedules effectively for automatic document reading thus eliminating much manual coding and punching, and very much reducing the time taken to complete the input stages of data-processing.

New questions

As to new questions that may appear, the following seem to be some of the likely candidates:

1. *Income.* The main argument for an income question is the need to understand the relationship between income and housing, family size, education, occupation, and other characteristics as a basis for projecting the demand for services and forecasting the

likely social effects of changes in the relative affluence of different strata of the population in different localities. Public resentment of questions about income is much less than it was since statements of income are required for so many purposes (education grants, house mortgages, etc., as well as income tax). It would be necessary, of course, to be even more careful about confidentiality. It will probably always be necessary, and sufficient, to ask the respondent to place himself in an income bracket rather than to state precise details of income.

2. *Motivation for migration.* In recent censuses in this country there has been a question about any change of address in the previous year. This has helped to fill a long-felt gap in knowledge about internal migration in the country; the main streams of movement and the demographic characteristics of the movers (e.g. types of household, ages, occupations). Whether the migration rates derived from these data can be applied to make predictions about the future is a vital question for urban planners. It cannot be answered without some knowledge of the reasons for movement. Is the movement from large towns owing to lack of employment opportunities or to lack of housing or to revulsion from the concrete facelessness of the new inner-town development? It might be argued that this is a matter which should be handled on an *ad hoc* basis by the Social Survey, which is now joined to O.P.C.S. (though not as well assimilated as some of us would like). However, catching all types of move clearly requires a national sample and the questions on motivation would have to be related to many other characteristics that are normally inquired about in a population census and these would have to be repeated in any survey. Moreover, an *ad hoc* survey would have difficulty in identifying movers among other members in a household-sampling frame. It would be necessary to make an initial trawl of large dimensions. It seems desirable, if the census can be so extended, to add to the normal census migration questions.

3. *Condition of housing.* Urban authorities need to know a great deal more about housing than the number of rooms in the dwelling, the tenure (rented or owned, etc.), availability of certain facilities (inside toilets, hot water, etc.), and garage accommodation—the items at present accommodated in the census. They want to know the age of the dwelling, its rateable value or rent, the possi-

bilities for conversion to increase the number of persons accommodated or to improve the amenities, and whether or not the building is entirely obsolescent. If the census does not encompass these matters, the urban authorities will have to conduct their own individual surveys (incidentally repeating much of the census inquiry on other related topics). If 250 planning authorities conduct surveys at an average cost as low as £10 000 (and this is a very conservative figure), this costs the nation £2·5 millions—much more than the cost of adding questions to the census. It might be argued that some of these questions are matters of expert opinion; I would think that if the questions are properly designed (and there *is* a need for improved methodology) they are within the capacity of most householders.

4. *Neighbourhood activities.* The urban planning authorities would also like to know something of shopping and institutionalized leisure activities of the population, partly out of interest in the land use and transportation problems which these many activities generate but partly also out of interest in identifying natural neighbourhood foci, if any, around which to structure their plans. Once again, these activities are very much linked to social, economic, and demographic characteristics.

5. *Health and welfare.* Most health surveys (actually ill-health surveys) are local not general and begin expensively by recapitulating much of the normal population census inquiry. Instead of tagging on a census to a question on sickness how much easier to tag on a question about sickness to the census. There might be a question asking about general practitioner consultation or a question about disablement. There are a number of difficulties. For example, if you shorten the period of recall in order to reduce errors of memory failure, you introduce seasonal bias. There are also problems of definition in disablement, and there is the need to accept answers in language of low diagnostic value. In my view the usefulness of fairly simple information acquired in this way has been consistently underestimated.

Output improvements

The non-specific extraction of piles of computer output based on a cross-tabulation of every combination of census characteristics would be a negation of design. Given the flexibility and the compact data-storage facility of the computer it is no longer necessary for a census authority to plan almost wholly in terms of a publication programme or to regard *ad hoc* tabulations as exceptional and a matter for a deferred programme of post-censal analysis. This was the pre-computer tradition. In this era the publication programme represented an enforced 'package' for all consumers, thoughtfully and painstakingly designed to meet most requirements, but not in fact tailored to any individual customer. It is now possible for O.P.C.S. to supply statistical information on a wide range of topics and based on small areal units (as small as enumeration districts) in any desired format—printout, punched cards, computer tapes—at a very modest cost to the customer. The customer can then use his own data-processing equipment to store this information and to compile statistical summaries for any desired combination of the chosen areal units, e.g. for special development.

In this way there has been a transition from the once-for-all analysis of the census records in terms of a rigidly predetermined printed store to the establishment of the census as a more dynamic data bank that may be drawn upon continuously at comparatively short notice and in any desired format within the restraint only of the scope and continuity of the data-processing resources available to O.P.C.S. The next step will be to provide for instant recall of data from O.P.C.S. files on to visual display units in customer offices.

All users, however, do not possess computers with which to conduct their own rearrangement of summary data; in any case the summary data do not provide for cross-classifications, i.e. for the study of relationships. For many of its customers O.P.C.S. still has a large publication programme, and it ought to be put in a position where it can provide a really good 'on-demand' service. Moreover, there is the overriding problem of speedily producing the basic data tapes from which the total output (summary computer files or published tabulations) emerges. O.P.C.S. must be allowed to take a leap ahead computer-wise (as the Meteorological Office has done), and gear itself for the census after the next one instead of, as hitherto, for the census before last.

Coordinate or grid referencing

As an alternative to tabular presentation census statistics can be represented pictorially by mapping enumeration districts and inserting census indices or colouring the districts to indicate the distribution interval within which the index for a particular district lies. However, the enumeration district has no natural shape. It represents a parcel of land chosen for the convenience of enumeration and it rarely conforms to a functional concept or to a socio-economic entity; moreover, its size and shape change from one census to another so that inter-censal demographic changes are difficult to perceive. Since the basis of the enumeration district is census administration it is difficult to attain any functional or social conformity though an approach to this ideal has been made in the U.S.A. with its defined census tracts which are deliberately kept stable from one census to another.

An obvious alternative, to which the advent of the digital computer has lent impetus, is to assign parts of the enumeration district, even individual buildings, to the standard grid of the Ordnance Survey. One can go even further with the grid system and actually assign a coordinate fix to dwellings. Grid references or coordinates are digits. These digits can be stored with the associated census information. This makes possible the use of computer technology to produce an automatic computer output in map form. It is not, however, for automatic mapping alone that grid references are essential since it is possible to analyse any irregular area (e.g. an enumeration district) in terms of linear segments the terminal coordinates of which can be handled by the computer and so used to produce a map of the area; the process extends to effectively shading the area according to the associated demographic index. The main virtue of the grid is its immutability and its use therefore as a base for inter-censal comparisons. It is likely that grid referencing will become a standard census procedure.

Speed

The above is not an exhaustive account of matters relating to the census, but I would like to make one last remark before turning briefly to some non-census matters. It is this; we must bring to an end the recurring frustration of the census statisticians who plan on each occasion to produce the results very quickly only to find themselves inevitably, in the second year after the census, explaining why there will be delays. Though the reasons proffered are usually technical (e.g. computer breakdowns, underestimation of response errors), I am convinced that the real cause lies in a lack of understanding of the need to make firm decisions on scope, content, and analysis well before census day and to stick to those decisions 'come hell and high water'. Administrators must not be allowed to dither about decisions until the complicated network of procedures has been strained beyond critical path methods of recovery. Ministers must resist attempts to load last-minute questions on to the census, however important to current political issues they may appear. The present method of census taking involves a fairly long cycle of preparation and organization and very early decision-taking; it is not geared to second thoughts (beyond the normal implementation of the lessons drawn from pilot inquiries). If the government wants more flexibility, it must either reserve as much as it can for *ad hoc* survey or accept more frequent censuses of the 'rolling' type, to which I have already referred. I am sure that these difficulties will be solved and that we shall see very great improvements in the speed with which census results are produced.

Social surveys

The population census is a large social survey. Smaller *ad hoc* sample surveys too have their place in demographic data gathering. Now that the techniques are well proven we ought to be doing much more about the monitoring of fertility trends. We need an annual survey of the attitudes of married couples towards family size (their own family size that is). We have had a Family Intention Survey in 1967, but it was made a matter of such intensive analysis (unnecessarily so) that the results were not published until 4 years later [3]. I understand that the subject has since been taken on board by the General Household Survey (GHS), which O.P.C.S. are now conducting on a quarterly basis, but nothing has yet been published. The GHS was started in the autumn of 1970, so that it looks as though there is a problem of speed here too.

It has been assumed by those of us who had recommended the

transfer of the Social Survey to the General Register Office [1] that it would add a further dimension to the population census. Here would be an organization that could get quickly into and out of the field without waiting for the necessarily longer process of the population census. It does not seem to be working out that way, though in the longer term I am sure it must and can be made to fulfil this role.

The sample survey could contribute to immediate knowledge on almost every topic normally covered in the population census. Apart from fertility trends to which I have already referred, it could help particularly to extend knowledge on migration and on morbidity where in both cases serial statistics are particularly desirable.

REFERENCES

1. BENJAMIN, B. (1970). *The population census*. S.S.R.C., Heinemann Education Books, London.
2. —— (1970). The 1971 Population census and after, *J. R. stat. Soc. A*, **133**, 240–56.
3. WOOLF, M. (1971). *Family intentions*, Office of Population Censuses and Surveys. Social Survey Division Report, SS408, pp. x + 153. H.M.S.O., London.

2.2.2. Demographic data and predictions of national and regional population trends

WILLIAM BRASS
Professor of Medical Demography, London University

Estimates of future populations by countries, regions, and smaller sub-divisions are an important basis of planning for a wide variety of economic and social purposes. There is no other topic where the science of demography has so clear an applied function as a service and a guide. Yet the subject has been relatively neglected over the past 30 years or so. Any forecasting of the future is troublesome and uncertain. In demography there is a history of notable failures which, with hindsight, have been criticized perhaps more harshly than they deserved [6]; it is far from difficult to see what has gone wrong with a population forecast once the specified date is past. The odds against even modest success from the development of a systematic, scientific approach to demographic prediction has clearly inhibited the attempt. The essential future estimates are made, therefore, by a combination of inspired guesswork and judgement informed by experience.

It is often argued that the gain from the use of scientific methods of prediction, as compared with subjective ones, would be zero or negligible. The two main strands in this argument are, first, that the future is inherently uncertain and, secondly, that the subjective judgements are sensible ones. Put in another way, the uncontrollable error is so large that the moderate deviations arising from variations in judgement are irrelevant. Against this a good case can be made that the subjective methods have not always shown a sufficiently sharp reaction to the evidence of change, with consequent unnecessary biases, at least for short-term forecasts [14]. But even more fundamental is the proposition that only by the application of systematic procedures on clearly stated assumptions will it be possible to explore forecasting errors in a defined way, and thus improve assessments of reliability. This point of view has stimulated the present paper.

The aim is not to give a comprehensive or balanced review but an intentionally dogmatic outline of an approach which could establish demographic prediction on a more rigorous basis. For a combination of reasons of usefulness, practicality, and exposition, fairly severe limitations are imposed on the situation considered, as discussed below.

1. The population is taken to be that of a developed country like the United Kingdom with low mortality, relatively low and controlled fertility, and statistics of fair detail. In the less-developed countries with higher mortality and high fertility, a large element of guessing is usually imposed by the lack of adequate data on trends. Improved methods for these conditions would seem to depend on advances made with better data.

2. The predictions considered are medium-term ones for some 20–30 years ahead, such as are required for the moderately long-term planning of, for example, trained manpower, higher education, new towns, transport, and water supplies. Short-term forecasts of, say, 5–10 years ahead raise interesting but rather different problems. Although these have been studied just as little as the corresponding medium-term exercises, the problems are more

technical and essentially less intractable; probably effort expended on them would be of less applied value. In contrast, the estimation of populations in the distant future (say a century or more ahead) depends on such tenuous indications and experience that the attempt, although fascinating, falls within the category of speculative exploration rather than scientific extrapolation. In some 20–30 years' time almost all in the population will either be the survivors of those alive now or their children; in 100 years most will be the children of parents whose births are a generation or two in the future. The length of experience of population development with fertility under good control is well short of a century. It is also worth noting that the best methods for short-, medium-, and long-term predictions are not necessarily the same. For example, the direct extrapolation of a trend of falling fertility for the next 5 years may be quite successful but, over 100 years, is nonsense.

3. Migration is not considered. In most countries its effects on the total population are relatively small and specific. It is not easy to devise any firmly based general approach. Internal migration is of major importance for the estimation of regional populations. At present this is a subject which is being actively studied in Britain, as elsewhere. The problems are complex and as yet, poorly illuminated by empirical observations, but they are problems of a substantially different kind from the main theme of this discussion.

4. Population prediction is treated as a 'closed' operation, i.e. dependent only on the information contained in demographic measures and not incorporating external variables (economic, social, and political) as such. No one doubts that fertility and mortality, the components of population change, are influenced by such factors. Equally, the attempts to quantify the relations for the past have been uniformly unconvincing [8]. There is overwhelming evidence that the impact of socio-economic change on fertility and mortality has varied greatly with place and time. Again, for short-term forecasts, a reasonable case can be made that social and economic features which can be measured now will be reflected in the demographic rates of the next few years (although this has not been demonstrated convincingly except for falls in fertility and mortality from high levels). In the medium term, predictions of social and economic change would be required to relate to the

population measures. The piling of speculation upon speculation does not seem a promising path, when knowledge of even the simplest determinants is so doubtful. The investigation of 'closed' systems is based on the belief that the best indicators of the possible future effects of external determinants are the observed 'determined' demographic measures of the recent past.

Before the formal processes of calculating population changes over time are discussed, attention should be drawn to some other considerations which are not always given sufficient weight. The first is that population size is not the only measure of interest and, for many purposes, it is relatively unimportant. The proportional distributions by categories such as age-group, marriage status, family size, and composition are basic for particular forms of planning; the detailed time paths of development of these proportions are also often required for sophisticated exercises, e.g., in manpower or housing management. A consequence of this is the need to bring the composition by groups explicitly into the prediction process. The simple idea of first deciding on total population and then distributing it over the categories of interest does not work satisfactorily because the population growth itself is a function of the substructure (numbers in reproductive age-groups, marriage, family size division, etc.). Although in theory it might be possible to devise a consistent system of aggregate estimation followed by sub-division, no one has yet done so.

Another general point concerns the balance between the effects of changing levels and of changing patterns. It seems intuitively obvious that what determines population growth and structure are the general levels of mortality, fertility, marriage, etc. and this is true in the long term. In the short and medium term, however, pattern alterations can cause substantial deviations. For example, a shift in the timing of marriage (say to younger ages), without any change in the mean family size, will cause a birth 'bulge' with important consequences, at least over the 20–30 years period at issue, even if the change in birth rate is ultimately transient. The asymptotic theory of population growth due to Lotka is sometimes misinterpreted because of the exclusion of such 'transient' effects. In particular, it would appear from Lotka's results that further mortality falls in countries with low death rates could have little influence on population development, because already over 95 per cent of births survive into the reproductive period. In fact, the effects over a limited period, with certain types of age-distribution and mortality change, can be considerable [2].

In the light of these ideas (the need for detailed sub-division, consistent with aggregate change, over time paths and the relevance of 'transient' effects) a natural approach to population prediction is to proceed by sequential steps over short time-intervals, moving from the structure at one point to that at the next. Attention is focused on the changes from time t to $(t + 1)$, where t starts at zero and increases by unit intervals. This approach is usually called by demographers 'projection by components', although the name is not particularly helpful in indicating the essential features of the method. In practical applications the time-interval of projection is normally constant at 1 year or 5 years. Since the interval is also the increase in age of a person in the population the age-grouping is taken to be of the same width. Thus a surviving person moves up one age-group over one interval. Although 5-year steps are adequate for projections where demographic measures are changing relatively slowly and family size distributions are not estimated, the 1-year unit is required for any refined application. For example, it is difficult to handle additions of children by number already born to the mother with any wider interval.

The component method of projection can be described elegantly and efficiently in the notation of matrix algebra [4]. The population total at time t is expressed as a vector of the numbers in the sub-divisions of interest, e.g. by age-group, marital status, previous births of women. Of course, all the relevant cross-classifications must be counted separately such as 'females, aged 35, widowed, two children'. A similar vector gives the numbers at $(t + 1)$. To project the vector at t to that at $(t + 1)$, measures are needed of the contribution that each category at t makes to each at $(t + 1)$ (based on specific probabilities of dying, of marriage, and of births). These measures can be arranged as a matrix with columns for the contributing groups and rows for the receiving ones. The organization of the procedure this way serves as a basis for theoretical development (largely by keeping proportional contributions constant over time and obtaining long-term mathematical results), but also has the practical ends of describing the necessary measures and calculations tidily and compactly. It soon becomes clear with such a presentation that the measures of change or transition have to be available in great detail.

The basic idea of this system is simple. In practice there are many difficulties, mainly arising from two factors. The first is the missing transition measures; for example it is unlikely that death rates *specific* for 35-year-old widows with two children will be known. The second is the inconsistencies which can arise, most obviously in the projections for the two sexes. Thus in monogamous societies the numbers of female and male marriages in an interval must agree, and the newly widowed women must accord with the deaths of married men. A good deal of effort has recently been devoted to these issues [16]. To someone interested in techniques their study can be absorbing, but it seems doubtful whether refinements in this area will appreciably improve the accuracy of future estimates.

A projection does not become a prediction until there is a plausible specification of how measures will change with time (or specifications, for it is as important to give some guidance on orders of uncertaintly as on preferred estimates). On the present formulation the specifications are to be derived from trends in the past. Here there are several distinct, although related issues. One set of questions is concerned with the choice of the best measures, or parameters which describe the measures, for the prediction and with their likely paths of movement over time. The other set is concerned with the choice *among* paths for a particular population at a given moment and the determination of rates of movement along the specified tracks. There has been remarkably little research in any of these topics until quite recently, and what has been done is as yet only tentative and preliminary. In particular, the large amount of materials on demographic measures over time in a range of populations has hardly been examined in the light of developing ideas about the significant parameters of change.

The measures needed for projection are sets of values related by some form of structure, for example probabilities of dying by age, rates of child-bearing by duration of marriage, proportions of women of a given age with *n* children who will give birth to another within a year. Age is a critical variable since it marks the changing characteristics of the individual over time. Clearly the values in any particular set follow interlinked paths; probabilities of death, or marriage, or of giving birth at one age are not independent of the measures at other ages. But most of the older methods of prediction treat the problem as if the values were unrelated. Thus the future death rates at a given age may be estimated by fitting a trend line to a series of the same measures in the past and extrapolating. Commonly this has been done by a least-squares fitting of a linear or quadratic function of time to the logarithms of the rates. This approach is unsatisfactory since it does not take advantage of the measure linkages or ensure their preservation.

What is required is the quantitative description of each set of values (a 'model' is the usual term in demography, although not always in other sciences) in terms of a few parameters which contain the total useful information that can be extracted from the past trends. It is clear that such parameters do exist because of the regularities in populations over space and time in, for example, the pattern of survival to different ages. Biological and social effects are sufficiently consistent to impose recognizable structures. Several such models have been proposed recently in the context of population projection. Coale [5] has devised a three-parameter double-exponential function for describing first-marriage rates by age; the parameters reflect essentially the proportion ultimately marrying, the 'location' of the common ages of marriage, and the dispersion of the ages, respectively. Romaniuk [10] has been using a five-parameter Beta distribution of the specific fertility rates by age of woman in applications to the population of Canada; in particular cases the parameter estimates required may be reduced. Farid [7], following others, explored the possibility of fitting fertility by duration of marriage in England and Wales by a three-parameter Gompertz curve. Although reasonably good descriptions of observed rates were achieved with all of these models, their value for population prediction is open to criticism (more cogent for practical than theoretical uses). The functions are fairly complex, which makes the interpretation of the way the rates change with the parameters far from obvious and the empirical examination of paths over time from observations difficult. In fact, little has yet been done on this. The number of parameters, particularly in the Romaniuk model, is larger than seems reasonable for describing the *significant and predictable trends*. The emphasized phrase, perhaps more precise than is justified, serves to convey two linked ideas; that only a major directional change in pattern, for example earlier age at marriage, is likely to have effects on the future population estimates which are appreciable, relative to the

range of uncertainties; and that trends fitted to subsidiary movements in pattern are unlikely to be extrapolated with any success.

The criticism implies that useful, simpler functions for describing the measures are possible, either explicitly or implicitly,
in a predictive procedure. In fact, a rather different approach has
already been used for mortality and can be extended to other components. This is the construction of relational models, which
directly express measures at one time in terms of those at another
without the intermediary and unnecessary search for description
as functions of the age (duration) scale. Put in another way, the
method assumes that there is some transformation of the scale,
particular to the population but constant over time, which leads
to a simple description of the measures. It has been used in statistical analysis for a number of purposes other than prediction but
essentially with the same aim of assessing changes [9]. The
possibility of absorbing into the transformation peculiarities in the
relation between measure and natural scale leads to the simplifi-
cations in the expressions of such models.

The most obvious application is to mortality, because the relation between death rates and age over the whole span of life is
a complex one, which requires functions with many parameters for
description. Such functions have been the subject of investigation
for some three centuries. Nevertheless, a relational model system,
with only two parameters, has now been extensively studied and
applied to various graduation, estimation, and projection problems
[1]. In the projection context, the model can be described in the
following way. If $q(x, t)$ is the probability at time t of death by age
x in a population (or a relevant sub-group), there is a transformation of the age scale x such that $\log [q(x, t)/\{(1 - q(x, t)/\}]$ is
linear on the new scale for each value of t. Since one half the natural
logarithm, of a proportion divided by one minus the proportion,
is a transformation called the logit (used in statistics in analogous
ways) the relation can be written as $Y(x, t) = a(t) + \beta(t) Y(x, 0)$
where $Y(x, t)$, the logit of the probability of dying by age x at
time t, is expressed in terms of the corresponding value at time
zero and two parameters $\alpha(t)$ and $\beta(t)$, which vary with time.
In projection, $Y(x, 0)$ is provided by the current life-table; the
specification of $\alpha(t)$ and $\beta(t)$ over time then gives estimates of the
future mortality at all ages.

The justification of the model is empirical. Not only has it been shown to fit the observed data well but the parameters are readily interpretable. When $t = 0$, $\alpha(0)$ is zero and $\beta(0)$ is one. As $\alpha(t)$ becomes smaller (that is moves towards negative values) the death rates fall at all ages in a plausible pattern even if $\beta(t)$ remains fixed at its initial level of unity. Changes in $\beta(t)$ alter the relation between early and late mortality (i.e. allow steeper trends, compared to averages over populations, for younger persons or vice versa.) Of course, such a system cannot allow for all the particular and transient fluctuations in the trends of death rates for every age; it can describe the broad paths which determine the main features of population growth and structure.

Although the procedure outlined works well if the initial mortality pattern is typical, it is less satisfactory for deviant sets of death rates, since the abnormalities are unlikely to be retained for a lengthy period. There is good evidence for the transience of such deviations [13]. A useful modification is then the introduction of a limiting pattern towards which, over time, the mortality is expected to tend. This is constructed from the experience of populations of extremely low death rates; in fact even lower incidences can be reached by the choice of sub-populations with particularly favourable health conditions. If $Y(x, T)$ is written for the logit of probabilities of dying by age x in the limiting pattern, then $Y(x, t) = \{1 - W(t)/\} Y(x, 0) + W(t) Y(x, T)$, where $W(0) = 0$ and $W(T) = 1$, serves as a projection formula in which mortality moves smoothly along a path which is empirically established as plausible from the initial rates to those postulated at time T. This modification is particularly appropriate when the current death rates are moderate to high, and data for measuring past trends is incomplete.

There has also been some investigation, although not as much as there should be, of how $\alpha(t)$ and $\beta(t)$ have moved with time in populations with a long record of accurate death statistics. The indications are that $\alpha(t)$ is a convenient measure of comparative levels of mortality, because its rate of change with time has remained roughly constant over a wide range of expectations of life. In fact the nature of the model is such that fixed changes in $\alpha(t)$ have less and less effect on the expectation of life as it increases. This progressive decrease in the rate of change of life expectancies at lower mortality levels is, of course, a fact of experience; rather awkward and arbitrary decisions have been made in projections based on expectation of life (e.g. those of the U.N. Population Division [15]) to allow for this. In Sweden and in England and Wales over the past century $\alpha(t)$ has changed at a rate of about 0·012 a year, corresponding to an increase in life expectancy at birth of 4 years in every decade at high mortalities (expectancies of about 40–50 years), but only an increase of 2 years per decade at the mortality levels of the Western world [1]. In developing countries in the recent past somewhat faster changes have been common, of the order of 0·020 per year in $\alpha(t)$ and an increase of 6–7 years per decade in life expectancy.

The path of $\beta(t)$ has been much more complex. In both Sweden and England and Wales it has moved in a cyclic manner around the central value of one as the incidences of deaths at younger and older ages were reduced unevenly or out of phase. Since these cycles have lasted a considerable period, however, with movements in the one direction continuing for more than 50 years, the prospects of using trends in $\beta(t)$ for *medium-term* predictions are not based only on unsubstantiated optimism.

The relational model for mortality has been discussed at some length primarily as an illustration of how the approach could be used more generally for other demographic measures, such as those of fertility and marriage, to define significant parameters, examine their trends, and thus improve projections. Despite the initial problem of the complexity of the variation in death rates with age, once this has been overcome by the use of relational models, the difficulties of mortality projection are perhaps less than those of the other measures, since everyone dies only once, and while a constraint is imposed the historical experience is of steady falls in mortality lasting over long periods. These simplifying regularities do not hold for the other components. Nevertheless there are consistencies which can be illuminated by similar means.

Relational models of fertility by age of woman or by duration of marriage and of marriage rates by age can be devised by investigating simple, appropriate functions which give good time comparisons on transformed scales. There are several such functions which can be considered. In fact a number of them give results which are by no means unreasonable. To distinguish between their advantages and limitations extensive empirical studies are required but have not yet been undertaken. The logit function as used for the mortality model in fact, can also be applied to fertility and marriage in the form $Y(x, t) = \text{logit} \{F(x, t)/F(t),\}$ where $F(x, t)$ is the cumulated rates to age (or duration) x at time t and $F(t)$ is the value of $F(x, t)$ at the end of reproduction (total fertility, mean family size of marriage, or proportions married). This leads to linear relations exactly the same in form as for mortality but in addition to the two parameters for defining these, there is the third parameter $F(t)$. Other analogous three-parameter models are obtained by taking $Y(x, t)$ as $\log [-\log \{F(x, t)/F(t)\}]$ or alternatively

$$\log \left[-\log \left\{ 1 - \frac{F(x, t)}{F(t)} \right\} \right].$$

The indications are that these may perform rather better than the logit function. In fact, the first of these can be derived from the Gompertz curve used by Farid [7], by replacing the natural marriage duration scale with an arbitrarily transformed one. If the parameters in these relational models display regularities over time for empirical data (and there are good reasons for believing they should), the projection methods described for mortality in terms of $Y(x, t)$ apply directly with the appropriate changes in definition for the other demographic measures.

So far the discussion of the exact meaning of 'measures for the current period' implied by the t has been deliberately avoided. In fact, the examination of relational models is valid whether the rates by age (duration) are for cohorts actually experiencing them over their lifetime or for a cross-section of the population in a given period. For cohorts the t will represent a convenient distinguishing marker, such as year of birth or of marriage, and for cross-sectional measures it represents the time of occurrence. The value of cohort indices for analysis and projection (particularly for fertility and marriage) is well established [11]. Period measures are subject to much wider fluctuations owing to temporal and transient effects which tend to average out in the cumulated experience of cohorts. This is especially important for the fitting of trends and prediction of $F(t)$, the cumulated measure of fertility or proportion married at the end of reproduction. On the other hand if attention is confined to cohorts of completed fertility the evidence from movements in rates for the younger women still in the reproductive period is ignored. To allow for this some form of two-dimensional analysis, taking into account trends over both cohorts and time, is required. Attempts of this kind have been made, particularly by Ryder [12]. He has devised methods for estimating completed cohort fertilities beyond those yet calculable (and hence predicting) in terms of levels and rates of change of *period* measures. Although they are not formulated explicitly in terms of models, these techniques depend on the use of characteristic parameters and hence imply models. The characteristic parameters, in fact, are easily interpretable; in addition to the total fertility they are the mean age of the women at the birth of the children and the dispersion about this age. For example, alterations in the mean age of the women at the events acts as a measure of the extent to which cumulated fertilities for incomplete cohorts are being influenced by changes in the timing of births. In principle, if this approach is translated into the language of the relational models, the period parameters $F(t)$, $\alpha(t)$, and $\beta(t)$, say, are used to provide predictions of the cohort $F(c)$ completed fertility measures.

Coale and Farid [5, 7] advocated the use of their models of marriage rates by age and fertility by duration of marriage respectively for the prediction of completed cohort measures. The procedure suggested was the fitting of the model to the lower tail of known rates for cohorts of incomplete experience; the parameters thus estimated allow extrapolation of the curve to rates at all ages. In practice, however, this technique is generally far from satisfactory if as many as three parameters are required. When a relatively small part of the tail is known, small fluctuations in the rates can lead to large implausible variations in the estimated completed $F(c)$. If a large part is known the prediction is only of a small amount of additional fertility over the next few years. Unlike the Ryder procedure this one does not incorporate the evidence of trends over time; it is one-dimensional. The proposal is made below that the most fruitful technique would combine the cohort model fitting and the time trend approaches.

The major question not yet considered is the determination and extrapolation of trends. It is arguable that, given good relational models and a thorough investigation of the behaviour of the parameters in observed time-series, simple and obvious procedures, modified by judgement, will be sufficient and that more elaborate methods would be of negligible benefit in reducing uncertainty. This can best be illustrated from the applications of the logit mortality model. Thus for England and Wales, the continuation of the average rate of change in the $\alpha(t)$ parameter of about 0·012 per year with a constant $\beta(t)$ (since at present the trend in the latter is small and doubtful) may be all that can be justified. It seems worthwhile, however, to consider the means by which such 'commonsense' assessments can be put on a more systematic basis. The kinds of judgement required are of the weight to be given to recent speeding or slowing of change compared to the longer-term movement.

There is a well-developed theory for doing this in industrial and commercial forecasting by 'adaptive prediction' [3]. The future estimates are expressed as weighted sums of the known values for the past with weights which reduce to zero as time recedes, that is the most recent values have the largest effect. The weights can be arranged to accord with different assumptions about the nature of the underlying trends and the persistence of transient effects. The exercise is ultimately, however, an empirical one in which the prediction procedure used is that which has done well over the past for the same population or in similar conditions for other populations. A few years ago Kpedekpo, in an unpublished Ph.D. thesis, explored the application of these prediction techniques to series of broad demographic measures of fertility and mortality. The results were promising but the trial has not so far been extended to the more refined indices considered here and to a wider range of populations.

The adaptive prediction scheme can be modified simply and neatly to incorporate both the estimation of measures from in-complete cohorts, by fitting models to the rates for the lower tails, as advocated by Coale and Farid [5, 7] in their specifications, and the idea of Ryder [12] that the 'timing' alterations must be allowed for to achieve reasonable results. This can be done if the parameters of the appropriate relational model are calculated for completed cohorts and also, provisionally, for incomplete cohorts. The latter are then re-estimated as adaptive prediction weighted sums of the series of values, including the provisional measures. The weights of the latter, however, would have to be reduced to allow for the increasing error in values deriving from a short cohort experience. A further separate weighting to predict for cohorts of the future which had not yet provided any measures would be required, although this could be combined in one operation with the previous one. Whether this more cumbersome procedure which tries to make use of the greater stability of cohort measures would be appreciably better than a straightforward adaptive prediction from series of period parameters could only be examined by trial.

What has been presented above is a plan for a systematic attack on the problems of scientific prediction of population size and structure. It requires a re-analysis of recorded experience in terms of measures which are significant for change. All of the proposed techniques have, in some sense, been applied already in this context if not necessarily in the way suggested. None has yet been adequately investigated. Perhaps the most important element in the paper is the point of view that systematic methods of prediction are, in fact, worth trying.

REFERENCES

1. BRASS, W. (1971). On the scale of mortality. In *Biological aspects of demography* (ed. W. Brass), pp. 69–110. Taylor and Francis, London.
2. —— (1974). Population size and complex communities and a consideration of world population. In present volume, pp. 51–71.
3. BROWN, R. G. (1963). *Smoothing, forecasting, and prediction of discrete time series.* Prentice-Hall, New York.
4. CARRIER, N. (1969). Calculation of family structure as a demographic example of the organizational power of matrix notation in mass arithmetical operations. In *Population growth and the brain drain* (ed. F. Bechhofer), pp. 92–105. University Press, Edinburgh.
5. COALE, A. J. (1971). Age patterns of marriage, *Population Studies* 25, 193–214.
6. DORN, H. F. (1950). Pitfalls in population forecasts and projections, *J. Am. stat. Assoc.* 45, 311–34.
7. FARID, S. M. (1973). On the pattern of cohort fertility, *Population Studies* 27, 159–68.
8. MEADOWS, D. H., MEADOWS, D. L., RANDERS, J., and BEHRENS, W. W. (1972). *The limits to growth.* Universe Books, New York.
9. PETO, R. and PETO, J. (1972). Asymptotically efficient rank invariant test procedures, *J. R. stat. Soc.* A, 135, 185–206.
10. ROMANIUK, A. (1973). A three parameter model for birth projections, *Population Studies.* (In press.)
11. RYDER, N. B. (1959). Fertility. In *The study of population: an inventory and appraisal* (eds. P. M. Hauser and O. D. Duncan), pp. 400–36. University of Chicago Press, Chicago, Ill.
12. —— (1971). Notes on fertility measurement, *Milbank memor. Fund quart. J.* 49, 109–31.

13. SULLIVAN, J. M. (1973). The influence of cause-specific mortality conditions on the age pattern of mortality with special reference to Taiwan, *Population Studies* **27**, 135–58.
14. THOMPSON, J. (1970). The growth of population to the end of the century, *Social Trends*, No. 1, 21–32. H.M.S.O., London.
15. UNITED NATIONS POPULATION DIVISION (1970). *World population prospects, 1965–2000, as assessed in 1968*. Working Paper 37, United Nations, New York.
16. WIDEN, L. (1969). *Methodology in population projections*, Urval, No. 2. National Central Bureau of Statistics, Stockholm.

2.3. The economics of population changes in the United Kingdom and elsewhere

2.3.1. Economic implications of population growth in the United Kingdom†

B. C. BROWN AND G. B. RICHARDSON

Department of the Environment, London: Reader in Economics, Oxford University

THIS paper will consider the likely effect of population growth on our material welfare as conceived, rather narrowly, in terms of the consumption of goods and services that form part of the national product. In that we are interested in the growth of consumption potential we shall for the most part take no view about the likely future balance between government and personal consumption or about the kinds of goods that may compose these. Of course, population growth influences welfare, in ways not registered in figures for consumption, through its effect on the general amenities of life; we have chosen to limit our analysis by leaving this out of account. We shall be concerned, moreover, with average standards of material welfare, but it would not be absurd to hold the view that, in judging whether population growth is desirable, one should give weight not only to the standards reached but also the number of people alive and enjoying them; Bentham's celebrated (but strictly meaningless) reference to 'the greatest happiness of the greatest number' evades the issue. Certainly there are parents who deliberately choose to have larger families knowing that their material standards will thereby suffer. Any balancing of standards and numbers involves a value-judgement which we do not make; at the same time, however, it

† Both the authors of this article were members of the Population Panel the Report of which was published in March 1973 (Cmnd. 5258). Although the views expressed here are our own, use has been made of the work done in the preparation of the Report. In particular we have examined the economic implications of population growth at the rates envisaged in the Report. The reader wishing to study the detailed calculations that can be made in relation to some of the consequences of population growth will be referred to appropriate parts of the Report; we have chosen here to concentrate on discussing the assumptions, arguments, and procedures associated with the analysis.

would require some estimate—such as we try to reach—about the likely relation or 'trade-off' between the two.

The effect of population on living standards

Population affects living standards in three ways. First, both the size and rate of growth of population may influence labour productivity, i.e. output per worker. Secondly, population growth affects the relationship between output per worker and output per head in that this will depend upon the ratio of workers to non-workers and therefore upon the age-structure. And, thirdly, by influencing investment requirements, population growth affects the relationship between output per head and consumption per head.

Probably the most important of these causal connections is that between population and productivity. At the same time, however, it is the most difficult to predict. Thinking first in terms of a closed economy—the world as a whole—we can identify two opposing influences. To the extent that natural resource endowments are fixed, then a larger population (other things being equal) will be poorer than a smaller one. This was the basis of the pessimistic prognostications of Malthus and Ricardo; rising numbers pressing on scarce land were in the long run to reduce standards to subsistence level. But Adam Smith on the other hand had pointed out that the wealth of nations depended on the division of labour, the extent of which was limited by the size of the market. Population growth, by enlarging the market and permitting a finer degree of specialization, might for this reason raise the level of productivity. On the face of it, however, the economies of scale and specialization may not be inexhaustible, so that, once population has increased sufficiently to create a market large enough to secure their full exploitation, this beneficent effect would be spent. Only technical progress could then postpone the evil day, and it is therefore interesting to inquire whether such progress might itself depend upon population growth.

Smith's own line of argument implies that it does. Technical progress is largely (though not wholly) endogenous to his system; an increase in the demand for particular goods or services, brought about by an increase in the size of the market, makes it more profitable to find better ways of supplying them. Economic growth, in other words, is both the cause and the effect of economic advance. But there is a relationship between population and technical progress that is yet simpler and more direct. Some of us are always adding to useful knowledge, and the more of us there are the more rapid (other things being equal) the growth in knowledge is likely to be. There is no reason to expect a larger population to have less talent among its members than does a smaller one, whereas there is reason to expect a larger population to be able to support more people whose specific job it is to secure technological advance. The point can be seen most clearly if we imagine that all technical progress results from the efforts of a special knowledge-producing class. The cost to society of maintaining such an establishment will depend on its size relative to the total population but the benefit obtained from it will depend upon its absolute size. In this respect the gains from knowledge differ from the gains from machines. In order to obtain the same labour productivity, a larger population will need an absolutely larger number of machines and machine makers than a small one; but it need not have more knowledge producers in order to secure the same flow of new ideas. The cost of creating new knowledge, in other words, is a fixed overhead so that the burden imposed per head is the less the larger the population. Of course, this is not the case in relation to the transmission of knowledge; the capacity of a teacher, like that of a machine, is limited, and the larger the population the larger the number of teachers that have to be supported. We have supposed for simplicity a single knowledge-producing class, but it is of course a commonplace that people learn by doing and that new knowledge may be augmented in this way. The larger the population, it would therefore seem, the greater will be the flow of new knowledge thus produced.

Other things being equal, therefore, technical progress will be more rapid the larger the population; and perhaps it is the very simplicity of the argument leading to this conclusion that has led to its relative neglect. Of course the *ceteris paribus* clause is very important; rising numbers might so burden the economy with the need to provide additional equipment and education that the resources available for discovering new knowledge might be reduced. Here we have one reason why productivity may be affected by the rate of growth of population as well as by its size. Put more generally, it implies that an increased need for extensive investment may reduce the level of that intensive investment on which productivity growth depends. But there are circumstances that work the other way. A rising population will be younger and perhaps more energetic and adaptable, though less experienced, and the machines that its members use will on average be more up to date. If the labour force is expanding, moreover, it may be possible to channel the new workers into the right jobs rather than transfer older workers (with presumably greater difficulty) from what they have been doing. Rising population, it has also been suggested, is a stimulus to investment, and therefore more likely to ensure full employment; this may be so, but it should not be difficult to find other ways of stimulating demand. It may not be fanciful to believe, however, that rising numbers may be associated with a general buoyancy and faith in the future such as would raise those animal spirits often considered to be the basis of adventurous investment behaviour.

These then seem to us to be the main features affecting the relationship between population and productivity in a closed economy. Over the last two centuries population has probably expanded about four-fold, and total output has risen far more than in proportion. But this does not entitle us to assume either that population growth has always and everywhere favoured living standards in the past or that it will do so in the future. The effect of population growth will depend upon its rapidity and upon the circumstances of the countries in which it occurs.

Population and the economy in a small country

We have been discussing the relationship between population and productivity in a closed economy. The analysis was therefore more relevant to the world as a whole rather than to any particular part of it. Let us now consider the relationship as modified when we take the case of a country, such as Great Britain, which is small in terms of both population and output with respect to the rest of the world.

We can begin by observing that one country can escape, through international trade, from the restraints imposed by the scarcity of domestic resources and that, provided the country's share of world trade is small, its terms of trade will be independent of the extent to which it does so. In the same way, it should be possible to enjoy whatever economies of scale are available despite the small size of the home market. Having said this, it is necessary to make several reservations. World trade is by no means free, and a country seeking to expand its share of it may encounter increasingly serious obstacles. It will, moreover, take time to build up exports and, if the rate of growth of population requires this to be done rapidly, the terms of trade may suffer.

It should also be noted that, even although a country's terms of trade remain unchanged, it may suffer a reduction in real incomes as a result of having to import more. This might prove to be the case, for example, in relation to food. Under free trade a country will start to import food when the cost of doing so comes to equal the marginal cost of home food production. But the average cost of this production will be less than its marginal cost. As an increasingly large share of food comes to be imported, the average cost of all the food consumed will rise. And the same principle will apply to any other imported food which is also produced at home under conditions of rising marginal cost.

We endeavoured to assess the relevance of these several factors to the situation of the United Kingdom. The larger our population, the greater will be our imports of food and raw materials. But by 1970 our population was only $1\frac{1}{2}$ per cent of the total and its percentage rate of increase is likely, on current estimates, to be only a quarter of that for the world as a whole. Our foreign trade represents only about $6\frac{1}{2}$ percent of the total value of world trade and our imports of food and raw materials a much smaller proportion. Provided world trade continues to expand, this country ought therefore to be able to increase the volume of its own trade even although its share in the total should fall. There therefore seems little reason to expect the future prices of our exports and imports to be very different according to whether our population should increase by the end of the century to, say, 60, 70, or even 80 millions.

We mentioned above that under free trade the average cost of certain commodities—such as food—would be the greater, the larger the proportion imported. This would be the case when the average unit cost of home production is less than the unit cost of imports. Here we have a circumstance, which, considered by itself, gives an advantage to a smaller population. Although trade makes it possible to escape from the limitations set by the scarcity of natural resources, countries still gain from possessing them. Of course, it is possible (and for the E.E.C. it is currently the case) that subsidies and tariffs cause the marginal cost of home production to exceed that of imports so that a greater reliance on the latter could in fact reduce the average cost of consumption. In any event, in the British situation, the effect we are considering is likely to be small. The reader may here be referred to Appendix 3 of the Report of the Population Panel which considers the result of a very drastic—five-fold—increase in imported food prices. The gain from having a population some 20 per cent smaller would probably then be about 4 per cent of income per head. Of course, there are commodities other than food our demand for which is met partly from imports and partly from domestic production at rising marginal cost; and if the prices of all of these were to rise, the advantage from having a smaller population— other things being equal—would be greater. Nevertheless the advantage is likely to be substantial only for fairly large changes in population in the context of very marked increases in the prices of imported food and materials.

In discussing the relation between population and productivity for the world as a whole we contrasted the tendency towards diminishing returns, occasioned by pressure on scarce resources, with the tendency towards increasing returns deriving from the existence of scale economies and the smaller cost per head, for larger numbers, of obtaining a given rate of increase in knowledge. When we turned to consider the case of one country, small with respect to the world as a whole, it appeared that diminishing returns could be set aside through trade. Let us now inquire whether the gains from increasing returns would still be enjoyed. In so far as scale economies in manufacture and distribution are concerned, specialization and trade may make it possible for a small country to obtain the same benefits as a large one. But for it to do so fully, trade must be free and confidently expected to remain free. And as neither the international market, nor indeed the E.E.C., fully meets these requirements, there would be some advantage on this score from an enlarged home market. The size of the British market, measured in terms of total output, will increase in any case, but it will increase more if population grows at a faster rate than a slower rate. We find it impossible to estimate the magnitude of this benefit from rising numbers; one cannot measure the extent to which the present size of our home market prevents the full exploitation of scale economies, far less the differential effects in this respect of having populations of say 60 or 70 millions in the United Kingdom by the end of the century in the technological and trading conditions of that time. However, it seems safe to assume that if the West-European market does become more fully integrated, as it is reasonable to expect, these differential effects would be likely to be very small.

We observed earlier that, for the world as a whole, the achievement of a given rate of technical advance would impose a greater burden per head on a small population than on a large one; and this should be true to some extent also for one particular country. But in this particular context, it is exceedingly difficult to estimate how great the gain might be. For knowledge originating in one country can usually be taken over before long by other countries either as a free good or at a cost, in terms of licence fees, that is less than the cost of producing it. It is widely appreciated that investment in fundamental research is likely to yield a return which is greater for society as a whole than for a private firm that makes it, and this is why governments commonly subsidize (or themselves undertake) the activity. In the same way the benefit to the world as a whole from a particular investment in research will generally exceed the benefit to the country that makes it. Therefore, although larger countries will be able to undertake more research for any given burden per head than do smaller ones, it is not clear that it will always be in their interest to do so. Investment in research, or at least in fundamental research, may therefore be pushed further in some countries than purely national self-interest would justify. Nevertheless, it would seem that large countries do have a potential advantage over small ones in this respect even although we are unable to estimate how great it might be.

It is likewise very difficult to estimate the likely effect on productivity, within the United Kingdom, from having a growing and therefore younger labour force. The general arguments bearing on the issue have already been mentioned. Let us observe here that the magnitudes involved, in so far as this country is concerned, are very small. In the Report of the Population Panel (Table 17, p. 51) figures are given of the age-distribution associated with the three models of population growth that were there examined.† In the low-growth case, those between 15 and 44 years of age would form some 64·4 per cent of the population of working age in the year 2011; the corresponding figures for medium-and high-growth are 66·6 per cent and 69·2 per cent. Whatever one's relative valuation of youth and experience, structural variations of this order are hardly likely to make much difference.

Much the same can probably be said about the gain, enjoyed by a rising population, of having a more modern stock of capital equipment. The faster the rate of growth in a country's population, moreover, the greater will have to be the provision it makes for the education, housing, and equipment of additional workers. This is a matter we shall examine below.

Let us now take stock. Our analysis was to be divided into three parts. First we were to consider the effect of population growth on output per worker; secondly, its effect—through differing dependency ratios—on output per head; and thirdly—through differing investment requirements and other prior calls—on consumption per head. We have now just completed the first part. Population growth, at the rate at which it can be envisaged in this country, seems unlikely to have any very significant effect on productivity. But this conclusion is uncertain; it is possible, for example, that rising numbers, associated with a marginally younger work force, might stimulate productivity growth by a more than negligible extent; and it is similarly possible that the world terms of trade might move against manufactures so very strongly that any increased reliance on imports of food and materials (which population growth would entail) would significantly disadvantage us. In these and other respects we simply do not know with certainty what the future may hold in store and there seems to be no way in which the magnitudes of the possible effects examined can reliably be estimated. When we now turn to the consequences of different population structures and investment requirements, the scope for quantitative estimation is much greater, and there is a danger that when, in the final summing up, we try to couple the preceding conclusions with those that are to follow, we shall lose sight of the imponderables. This is a matter to which

† We shall refer to these as 'low-growth', 'medium-growth', or 'high-growth' models. They correspond to projected populations, for the year 2011, of 60·7, 66·1 and 74·3 millions.

we shall revert again later, but it is sufficiently important to warrant prior mention at this stage.

Population and investment

We shall not set out the detailed calculations relating to population structure and investment requirements; these are given in the Report of the Population Panel, and it is more appropriate here to concentrate on the underlying principles. In order to make the calculations, the Panel assumed that output per man hour would grow, up to 2011, at 3 per cent p.a. (a figure which corresponds to $2\frac{1}{3}$ per cent growth in output per head if we allow for reduced hours and longer holidays). In fact the differences in material welfare between the three population models examined were much the same proportionately for productivity growth rates of 2 per cent or 4 per cent; differences in the rates become crucial to the comparison only if themselves associated with differences in rates of population growth.

The size of the labour force, for any given population, will depend both on age-structure and activity rates. If activity rates are the same for different population growth rates, then the proportion of the population available for work in 2011 will be smaller, the higher the rate of population growth, so that total output per head will be 8 per cent less in the high-growth model than in the low-growth model. Activity rates, however, may not remain the same, in that if there are more children more mothers are likely to be at home looking after them. The Population Panel Report (§ 219) estimates that in this case, the difference between total output and employment in the high- and low-population growth models might narrow (in 2011) from 13 per cent to 8 per cent. And it is perhaps worth noting that this effect of a lower activity rate would appear before faster population growth began to add to the labour force; thus in 1986 the larger and faster growing population would have a labour force and a total output some 5 per cent *less* than the slow growing population.

Part of current output does not contribute directly to current living standards but is used either to protect us individually or as a nation or to maintain output growth. And the amount of output required for these purposes varies both with the size of the population and its rate of growth.

The largest element in output thus used is investment. The faster the rate of population growth, the larger will be the expenditure on industrial equipment needed to maintain a given rate of increase in labour productivity; and the larger similarly will be the expenditure required on new houses, schools, hospitals, roads, airports, etc. Thus although it is estimated that by 2011 total output might be some £20 billion greater in the faster than in the slower growth case, nearly half of this would be needed for additional investment in capital equipment, stocks, and work in progress. The relationship between investment, technical progress, and output growth is complex and subtle, whereas our methods of estimation were simple and crude. Separate estimates were made for the replacement of old equipment and the provision of additional new equipment, it being assumed that the latter requirement would be determined by the rate of output growth as projected independently. It does in fact seem reasonable to assume that an increase of £1 million a year in output would require the same additional capital at a given date (and hence technology) whatever the size and rate of growth of total output. We made in effect a similar assumption with regard to the *labour* input per unit of output. It may be observed moreover that whereas varying the ratio of additional capital to additional output made a substantial difference to estimated investment requirements, it had very little effect on the differences between the three models in the proportion of output required for investment.

The other prior calls on output are mainly in the field of public consumption. Some public expenditure, although treated as current consumption, is of the nature of investment—education or research spending being an example; some of it is to protect us against evils arising out of our own activities—pollution, congestion, crime—against natural hazards, or against foreign attack; and some of it represents social consumption expenditure both on things that we (or some of us) might buy individually if they were not provided socially, and on things that we can only obtain acting together. But the lines between these three categories of public expenditure are not clearly drawn and they do not correspond with the major conventional divisions. Thus the health services are in part investment, in part protection, and in part consumption. There is little point in trying to decide firmly how much of public consumption contributes to current welfare and how much does not;

it is more helpful to make estimates of expenditure on health and education for each of the three growth models, and then show the effect on welfare calculations of including and excluding each of them. In this way one obtains a variety of estimates of the effect of population growth on welfare. Expenditure on education is the item the exclusion or inclusion of which makes the greatest difference; it is likely to be 50 per cent greater in the high-growth case than in the low-growth case.

Population age-structure and standards of living

The standard of material welfare depends not only on the total resources available for consumption, but on the size and (a little less obviously) the age-structure of the population. There is no uniquely correct way of comparing living standards for populations of different age structures. Clearly dividing by the number of heads is wrong; we should generally regard a man with a wife and two children and £5000 to spend as financially better off than a married couple with £2500, but it would be hard to say by how much. It is also relevant that working people may have higher expenses than retired people in that they may need to spend more on housing and travel to work. Because of these circumstances we chose to consider a variety of measures of the relevant consuming population, these varying from a simple count of heads to giving children weights equal to one half, and persons of retirement age two-thirds, of those given to adult workers. In this way one can obtain a range of figures for the comparative living standards associated with the three population projections made for the year 2011. All of these indicate higher standards for slower population growth, the difference between the fast- and slow-growth models varying between 6 per cent and 14 per cent, this latter figure being that given by a simple head count. This difference is small compared with the expected increase between 1971 and 2011 in material welfare, this being 150 per cent even in the fast population growth case. As we get richer, moreover, it is possible that the relative importance we give to increased wealth—as contrasted with non-material benefits—may itself decline.

These calculations do not touch on the question of income distribution. Some people have maintained that slower population growth, being associated with smaller families, would tend to increase the concentration of inherited wealth, and thus reduce the welfare advantages of higher average real income. But this effect could presumably be offset by fiscal measures. Neither did we consider it necessary to discuss in any detail the effects of changing preferences between income and leisure. In order to obtain figures for the effect of population growth on material standards, we did make particular assumptions about activity rates. If people chose to work shorter hours or to take longer holidays than we allowed for, then output would increase less rapidly, but, if the choice were made with knowledge of the consequences, welfare would be greater and comparisons between the three population models would not be affected.

It is important that the calculations are seen in proper perspective. They indicate the magnitude of the effect of population growth on living standards attributable to the influence of this growth on the age-composition of the population, the size of the labour force, and the need for investment and other expenditure which does not directly contribute to welfare. They take no account of any effect population growth may have on productivity growth; there is no firm evidence regarding this relationship, but it is worth bearing in mind that if productivity were to grow by just $\frac{1}{4}$ per cent p.a. faster in the high-growth case than in the low-growth case, then the latter's advantage (as we have calculated it) quite disappears. All that we considered ourselves able to say about the effect of population growth on productivity was that, in the context of our models, with average rates of population growth differing by about $\frac{1}{2}$ per cent, it would be likely to be small in whichever direction it operated. In these circumstances, the reader may wonder why we troubled to make detailed calculations of the effect of differences in age-composition, and in investment and other prior calls on resources. Our view was that our inability to quantify some things did not absolve us from the obligation to try to put figures, or limits, on such magnitudes as were more amenable to calculation. The upshot, however, is that our final conclusion has to be qualified and tentative. We think it likely, but by no means certain, that a low rate of population growth would be more favourable to material welfare than a fast one. In any event, the difference is most unlikely to be large, so that one can at least say, negatively but with some confidence, that a strong case for either low or high rates of population growth cannot be grounded solely on their predicted effects on our material standard of living, narrowly conceived.

2.3.2. The economy of poor countries and their population stabilization: an introduction

I. M. D. LITTLE

Professor of Economics of Underdeveloped Countries, Nuffield College, Oxford.

Introduction

As an introduction to Mr. Robert Cassen's paper, which will be concerned with the Indian problem, I would like to make a few points concerning population growth in developing countries as a whole.

The population explosion in developing countries since 1950 has been entirely the result of a reduction in death rates, largely infant mortality rates; this reduction in turn has been very largely the result of the spread of preventive medicine, especially the control of malaria, and owes little or nothing to any improvement in general living standards or diet. It has thus been a technological revolution, and not a cultural or economic one.

In Western countries, death rates fell far more slowly, and there was thus much more time for societies to adapt; so the present phenomenon in developing countries has no historical precedent.

Of course, there is a population problem. The rate of population growth cannot be doubled in a decade without tremendous stresses, especially if the doubling was unforeseen—which it was. But it does not follow from this that the ultimate size of the population, which promises or threatens, is the problem. In recent years, economists have moved from discussing the optimum size of populations to discussing the rate of growth; but the second derivative, that is, the acceleration of the population size, is also important.

The population size

One may ask whether there is an optimum population density for a country, and further ask whether any developing country exceeds this density, or threatens to exceed it. For a small country, population density seems to be virtually limitless without threatening Gross National Product per head. Such a country can import food, and industry has economies of scale. Hong Kong has 10 000 per square mile, and Botswana has half a person per square mile. Looking at the matter country by country, the room for growth seems vast; indeed only sheer congestion would seem to provide an incentive to limiting population. In the case of large countries, the influence of their own size on their terms of trade may provide a restraint. So probably only countries like China, India, Pakistan, Bangladesh, Indonesia, and ultimately Brazil, need feel any restraint in the next century so far as population size goes. Even in these cases it may be difficult to show that there would be a gain in income per head in the long run from a smaller population.

But what about the world? Can it contain 10 billion people at a high standard of living? This may well be a problem, though possibly more because of a lack of fossil fuels than because of food. I do not pretend to know how serious the problem is. But if it is serious, then there is a divergence of country interest and world interest, especially in the countries that lack natural resources, and are not themselves very large like India. It is the resource-poor countries which have the greatest interest in limiting world population. If they are also small, then their interest lies in increasing their own population, while limiting that of the world.

Countries like India and Bangladesh have an interest in limiting world population as well as their own. We have to recognize that there is a risk that the Indian subcontinent can never attain a reasonable standard of living because sufficient industrialization will become too expensive in view of the increasing relative cost of fuel and raw materials. The upshot is that I do not see any very general developing country interest in limiting the absolute size of the population. There is likely to be a divergence of interest between the resource-rich and the resource-poor.

The growth rate of population

If a country is below its optimum population size, which is probably true of the great majority of developing countries, then there must be an optimum growth rate of population. Economists have done little to define this. They have done little more than argue that present growth rates are too high. I think more should be done to try to define optimum growth rates. This is because merely preaching that growth rates are too high tends to make the audience suspect that a zero population growth rate is being advocated. This is naturally resented by many of the developing countries which see their populations as being too small, and do not want to encourage large-scale immigration.

What are the reasons for thinking that an optimum growth rate exists? The first is that it is harder for a family with many dependents to save. This argument has been challenged on the reasonable grounds that most savings are not provided by poor families anyway. A stronger argument seems to be that much more investment has to go into such things as education and housing when the population growth rate is rapid, and that there is therefore less left for improving the standard of living per head. This latter argument seems to me to be quite convincing. But the most convincing is that from employment, combined with the fact that there is a limitation on the speed with which people can learn new tricks. Thus no amount of investible resources would enable industry to grow (in any less-developed country, with few exceptions) fast enough to absorb the extra working force which is becoming available at present growth rates. This is likely to be true for the rest of this century; it may be a transitional problem, but the transition is going to be a very long one. Equally, raising the marginal product in agriculture takes time as well as money, and in some areas it may be very difficult and indeed almost impossible. This means that the increasing number of people will not be able to find a reasonable standard of living by working in agriculture. It is this latter sort of reason which convinces me that population growth is far too fast in most developing countries. I think also that it is the reason which now is convincing a great many developing countries that there is a strong social need for them to reduce their birth rates.

The acceleration of growth rates of population

I think that the problems have been aggravated because ideas, especially concerning industrialization and education, were conceived for a population growth rate of, say, around $1\frac{1}{2}$ per cent p.a. in developing countries. With rates of growth of 3 per cent p.a.,

radical re-thinking is necessary. But it has taken many governments 15 years to start re-thinking. Of course, any change in the
rate of growth of population results in changes in the age-structure,
which give rise to problems for health services and education. A
certain waste of resources is almost inevitable, if population growth
rates change at all suddenly.

Conclusion

The long-term outlook for those poor countries which are also
poor in mineral resources does not seem very bright. Unfortunately, however, only the absolutely large developing countries are
likely to be able to improve their lot by reducing their *own* ultimate target population size. But even the small and less densely
populated countries can greatly reduce their problems in the next
30 years or so, if they can reduce birth rates. Many other speakers
have dealt, and will deal, with the problems of achieving this.

2.3.3. Economic–demographic interrelationships in developing countries†

R. H. CASSEN

Institute of Development Studies, University of Sussex

The general case

The process by which the developed countries reached their
present low levels of population growth has acquired the title of
the 'demographic transition'. Very roughly, the transition was from
high to low levels of both birth and death rates, with an intervening
period of relatively rapid population growth while death rates
declined before the birth rate followed. No two countries followed
quite the same pattern; in two in particular (France and Ireland)
the process was radically different in nature and timing from the
rest. Even in the countries which approximated to some similarity
of pattern, no regular relationships can be established between
alterations in birth and death rates and any quantitative indicators
of social and economic change [22, 27].

At the same time, the factors commonly adduced in explanation

† The present paper is intended to be read in conjunction with the references:
many conclusions are stated rather than argued.

of the changes in vital rates are mainly of the kind which accompany industrial development and rising standards of living. Death rates responded to improvements in nutrition, sanitation, education, living and working conditions, public-health measures, and preventive and curative medicine—though in, say, nineteenth-century Europe, there is considerable controversy over the weight of the contribution of each of these factors. Changes in fertility have been ascribed to an enormous range of factors—among them health and nutrition, education and literacy, urbanization, alterations in the economic usefulness of children, in female participation in the labour force, in religious beliefs, the improved survival of children, and the availability of contraception [26].

Because so many of these factors are the concomitants of economic and social development, it is quite reasonable to expect that the developing countries will themselves pass through a process of demographic transition as and when development takes place. Unfortunately this expectation is not too significant, since the important question is the speed with which the transition is likely to occur. (The suggestion that population growth will prevent development altogether has not been much in evidence lately, and will be discounted here.) Scholars have recently begun to look at those developing countries where fertility appears to have been declining: the verdict seems to be that major declines in the birth rate have occurred only where levels of education, nutrition, *per capita* income, and so forth are rather higher than the developing country average. Nevertheless, a number of developing countries have experienced significant declines in birth rate. Fertility does seem to show some negative association with indicators of development, though only when countries are grouped in areas of cultural similarity [38].

There is not much dispute about the sources of reductions in death rates in developing countries in the last 50 years—they have mainly been due, at least in the poorer among the developing countries, to the reduction of famine deaths by the improved distribution of food, and the control of communicable diseases. A topic of major concern in developing country demography today is the relation between birth and death rates. It is argued that parents are interested not so much in having babies as in having surviving children, and therefore that a decline in mortality is a necessary, though not a sufficient, condition for declining fertility.

The insufficiency of the condition may be seen from the fact that many countries have had 50 years or more of significant mortality decline, with little change in fertility; though one reason for its insufficiency may be that infant and child mortality, though reduced, is still at high levels in many developing countries—and it is infant and child mortality which most affect the psychology of child-bearing.

Another complex issue is the role of family-planning programmes; according to some, a large share of births in developing countries are unwanted, and the provision of family-planning services will have a swift impact on the birth rate; according to others, birth rates are what they are for reasons inextricably connected with social and economic circumstances, and only changes in those circumstances will produce reductions in fertility. The weight of the evidence seems to be that family planning can accelerate fertility decline where other conditions favour smaller families, but cannot initiate it among poor, ill-nourished, illiterate, rural populations subject to high mortality [2, 17, 47]. In several countries there is 'political' opposition to family planning—usually the result of groups in the population wishing to maintain their numerical size relative to other groups—in some cases, the sentiment may be national, *vis-à-vis* other nations; whether such attitudes are themselves likely to diminish as development takes place is not clear [59].

The prognosis for the developing world is therefore a likely continuation of rapid population growth for at least the next two decades; even with very swift adoption of small family norms (which is in itself implausible), the existing age-distribution guarantees considerable future growth in numbers [37].

Economists and other social scientists have devoted considerable efforts to analysing the consequences of this growth. The most common method has been to compare two (or more) alternative paths for a given economy assuming different rates of population growth. Several mathematical models have been elaborated to demonstrate the effects of slowing population growth. They are fairly similar in structure and in results. Typically, the high fertility (H.F.) variant shows lower growth of Gross National Product (G.N.P.) *per head* than the low fertility (L.F.) case; in some models, even total G.N.P. is lower under H.F. than under L.F. The main source of difference between outcomes in these models lies in equations relating population growth to savings and to the composition of investment. The H.F. variant will show lower savings (per head or in total) than L.F.; under H.F. investment is diverted to providing social capital (schools, hospitals, etc.) for growing numbers, whereas under L.F. this investment would go to raising the productivity of smaller numbers of people (e.g. [11, 29, 52, 58]). Although these relationships capture certain truths of the situation, they have been too crudely expressed in these models, and are currently coming under critical fire (e.g. [1] and other papers in the collection cited).

Less mathematical treatments of the problem refer to these relationships, and also to others. Under L.F., there may be increased female participation in the labour force; increases in consumption may have positive effects on labour productivity; unemployment will be reduced both by lower labour force growth and by higher and more directly productive levels of investment. These arguments are supported by two empirical considerations: where unemployment is widespread, additional labour is unlikely to be an asset to the economy; and the proportion in the population of the numbers in working-age groups relative to those of non-working age is higher under L.F. than H.F. A reduction in this 'burden of dependency', and all its consequences, is one of the 'benefits' of L.F.

In addition to the analytical literature along these lines, there is a body of studies of the cost-benefit analysis of birth prevention, mostly showing enormous putative gains from prevented births. These studies are reviewed in [50], and will not be discussed here. But as long as there remain major difficulties in attracting clients to family-planning programmes, such studies, even if their methodology is accepted, can do no more than give one confidence that money invested in *successful* programmes is well spent. In many developing countries, there is far from being any automatic connection between expenditure on family planning and prevented births. Unlike the cynic in Oscar Wilde's epigram, the authors of these studies claim to know the value of something whose price is largely unknown.

The above-mentioned statements of the relations between population and economic growth reflect a highly oversimplified view of the process of development, where the main source of growth is capital accumulation, and the main impact of population growth is assumed to be its influence on the volume and nature of capital formation. Most of the studies examine 'dynamic' efficiency, the allocation of resources over time, and neglect 'static' efficiency, the question of the consequences of past population growth for resource allocation at a given time. Some of these other aspects of the effects of population growth on development will be referred to in the discussion of India below—they do not, it should be said here, alter the conclusions reached in previous work.

Examination of the relations between population and development has also proceeded hitherto without reference to the considerable changes in emphasis which have occurred recently in approaches to the theory of economic development. The last few years have seen a major alteration of emphasis in development studies, giving greater centrality to the issues of employment and income distribution. (See, e.g. [30–2].) It would be crude, but not wholly unjust, to say that previously economists put growth to the forefront, in the expectation that unemployment and poverty would thereby be reduced; conscious measures of income redistribution were regarded as inimical to growth, because of a supposed adverse effect on savings. The combination of the actual experience of growth, which in many developing countries has failed to make much difference to the lot of the poor, and a number of theoretical observations suggesting that re-distributive policies may not hinder growth has led to the view that active measures to create employment and alleviate poverty have a much more important place in the strategy of development.

So far, these shifts of thinking have not penetrated the literature on population and development to any great extent. In fact the arguments for re-distributive policies are greatly strengthened by consideration of their relation to the population question. For if the accepted explanations of fertility decline are valid, the demographic transition will accompany economic development the more rapidly, the more development reaches down to the poor. This is particularly true for the poorer among the developing countries.

The possible connections between poverty and high fertility are numerous. One has only to think of the role of education, which is commonly found inversely correlated with fertility. It would be quite mistaken to believe that the low levels of education prevailing in many developing countries are due simply to the inability of governments to provide school places—the low rates of enrolment, and high drop-out rates, are also functions of poverty, even where schooling is free. If mortality is related to fertility, education is important for this reason too—hygiene, health care, and nutrition are education-related. They are also, of course, directly connected with poverty, since adequate housing and sanitation, medical care, and food are not available to the poor. The nexus of poor education, poor nutrition and health, high infant and child mortality, and high fertility is held together by poverty. The need for children as economic assets, which has not been mentioned so far, is also part of this nexus.

If these arguments have any weight, they provide additional grounds for doubting the wisdom of the strategy of 'growth first, distribution later'. They also cast doubt on the more simple-minded cost–benefit analyses, in so far as these rest on the assumption that prevented births can be easily purchased by family-planning expenditures; if birth rates are to be greatly reduced by deliberate policies, it may require an entire change in socio-economic strategy, and one which lasts for decades—a strategy which focuses not only on unemployment and poverty, but also on the development of health services and education which will benefit the poor, together with investments in improved water supplies and sanitation, especially in rural areas.

To say all this is not to cast doubt on the virtue of family-planning programmes, which can and do produce worthwhile results. It is only to caution against expecting too much from them. But such programmes are justified on many grounds. In the first place their absence can cause distress—deaths from illegal abortions are a major health hazard in some countries where family-planning services are not available [1]. In the second place, a well-run—and well-documented—family-planning programme is probably the most practical instrument of research into the prospects for fertility reduction; discovering whether and in what circumstances people adopt contraception when offered is often a better guide to behaviour than the questionnaire surveys (K.A.P. studies) that abound in the family-planning literature [62]. Thirdly, even if not immediately 'successful', these programmes diffuse information which can ultimately prove valuable. And finally, they often can and do, in fact, prevent births at reasonable cost, even if they do not by themselves cause major changes in the birth rate. In all countries there are regions or sections of the population whose circumstances incline them to family limitation; few would argue that those who are so inclined are necessarily capable of efficient attainment of their ambitions—though there is, of course, much evidence that people who wish to limit their families are able to do so without benefit of modern techniques of contraception.

One last feature of the economic–demographic interrelationship deserves mention here, and that is the effect of population growth on income distribution—another subject which has received little attention. We have hitherto been discussing the relationship in the reverse direction of causation. But there is a simple argument suggesting that population growth in developing countries has been partly responsible for the intractable problem of maldistribution of income. If the poverty of a person's domestic background is the major determinant of his earning potential, and if the poor have more children than the rich, it will follow that population growth will tend to work against improving distribution of income. (The second of these assumptions is in fact open to doubt—the poor may have higher fertility than the rich, but end up with smaller families because of much higher mortality.)

So far we have treated mainly the inner components of the interaction process between population and development. There are of course important consequences of population growth which have not been considered—in particular, the difficulties created by this growth for the provision of services. These are the subject of much public discussion, and are not referred to here—the works cited in the bibliography contain innumerable references on such topics. The conclusions most commonly accepted among economists are that none of these difficulties is insuperable, but that each of them requires major efforts of investment and expenditure—they reflect on the speed with which society must run simply in order to stand still.

One cannot discuss the problem of population in developing countries without reference to the fact that many in those countries, and many also (particularly on the radical left) in the rich countries, are suspicious of the expressions of concern and the specific analyses of the problem which are to be found in Western academic literature, and in statements emanating from aid agencies and the like. Some have gone so far as to accuse the protagonists of active population policies of racism and other objectionable traits. Of course, it would not follow, even if people's motives in discussing the population problem were wholly bad, that what they said about the effects of population on development was wrong. Nevertheless, the premise is often believed, justly or unjustly, and the illicit inference frequently drawn [54].

There is another class of objections common (though not universal) among the radical left in both rich and poor countries, namely that rapid population growth will favour revolutionary tendencies, and that this is why non-radical opinion favours population control, and also why population control should be opposed. Possibly now that China has joined the ranks of countries with active population policies [45], less will be heard of this argument. In Brazil, the left is opposed to family planning on such grounds, while the right, also opposed, believes that rapid population growth will help to maintain the political *status quo* and to fulfil the 'national destiny'. (For a good discussion of the debate, accompanied by some curious economics, see [12].) Both sides cannot be right—but they can both be wrong. Indeed, one could with at least equal plausibility make out just the opposite case: that rapid population growth means cheap labour, weakens the labour movement, and raises capitalist profits, and population policy should therefore be supported by the left.

A more substantial aspect of the politics of the population question lies in the legacy of Marx's attack on Malthus. This has led some observers to argue that rapid population growth is only a problem under capitalism; such arguments used to be common in Soviet literature on the problem, though other views are beginning to be heard [6]. A more acceptable version of such views is that the population problem is a function of social organization. It is undeniable that, the better a society is able to mobilize its labour force, the more easily it can adapt to rapidly growing numbers. Once again, though, the fact that China, the society apparently best able to mobilize labour, is actively engaged in limiting its population, ought to reduce the frequency with which this position is adopted in opposition to population control.

One might summarize the most important question raised by our analysis as follows: the demographic transition in the rich countries followed, with varying time-intervals, the process of urban and industrial development. Given that the number of people participating in urban industrial life is likely to grow very slowly in many countries, is it possible nevertheless to bring to the mass of people in such countries major improvements in nutrition, health, education, and living conditions, and will such improvements lead to rapid reductions in fertility?

India

Much of this discussion can be illustrated by the case of India. Whatever arguments may have been advanced elsewhere to the contrary, for countries in different circumstances—and the arguments are not very impressive [5, 8]—hardly anyone has ever claimed that India has benefited economically from the growth in its numbers in recent times, or is likely to benefit from such growth in the future. At the same time dire predictions have been made of India's future—more dire in the non-expert than the expert literature.

Up till the last 50 years, India's population grew very slowly, with high birth rates, and high average death rates, punctuated by periods of extremely high mortality from famine or epidemic disease. Kingsley Davis's classic work on India's population [16] gives a very thorough account of the historical pattern, and more recent research has altered the historical picture only a little. (See, e.g. [14].) With the exception of the Bengal famine of 1943—due to a combination of crop failure, wartime conditions, and maladministration by the British authorities—the last famines which resulted in heavy mortality occurred in the first decade of this century. Plague struck India in 1896, and remained a threat in limited parts of the country up till 1923. But the rapid upward course of the population really dates from the end of the influenza epidemic in 1918, which took an enormous toll of lives in countries of Asia, the Middle East, and North Africa, and in India resulted in an actual decline of numbers between the censuses of 1911 and 1921.

Since Kingsley Davis wrote, progress in public-health measures has reduced mortality still further. Typhus and typhoid, smallpox, cholera, and malaria have all been controlled, and though the diseases still persist, deaths due to them are at a low level. Of the major communicable diseases of the past, only tuberculosis continues to result in a significant number of fatalities [63]. Such changes in birth rates as have occurred have been in the downward direction, but deaths have fallen much faster. Thus the population, which passed the 200 million (m) mark in the 1860s, and 300m in the 1930s, has since been growing at an accelerating rate to reach 548m by the 1971 census.

TABLE 2.3.1†

Year	India (present boundaries): Population in millions	Total growth from previous date (%)	Annual compound growth from previous date (%)
1800	154	—	—
1850	189	22·7	0·4
1871	209·1	10·6	0·45
1881	210·9	0·9	0·1
1891	231·4	9·7	0·9
1901	238·4	3·0	0·3
1911	252·1	5·7	0·5
1921	251·3	−0·4	—
1931	278·9	10·9	0·9
1941	318·7	14·3	1·3
1951	361·1	13·3	1·2
1961	439·2	21·6	2·0
1971	547·9	24·7	2·2

† Sources: [14, 16]; Census reports.

The birth rate in India today is estimated to be of the order of 38–39 (per 1000), the death rate about 17, giving an annual rate of growth of 2·2 per cent (*S.R.S. Bulletin*, April–June 1972). The prospects for the death rate are for a further decline, though perhaps a rather slow one. The decline up to the present has been purchased relatively inexpensively, as described above; significant further decline depends on alteration of the basic conditions of nutrition and sanitation, which imply fundamental re-distribution of income and social change. Seventeen does not seem like a high death rate, given that rich countries have rates of 8–10. It should be remembered, though, that India's pattern of mortality is quite different. In particular, infant mortality is of the order of 140 per 1000 live births (S.R.S., op. cit.); and above 40 per cent of all deaths occur before the age of 5.

If one asks whether the demographic transition is beginning to affect the birth rate in India, the answer must be that, on average, there is as yet little evidence of it. At least up to the early 1960s, the rate of marital fertility (births per thousand married women of reproductive age) differed very little as between urban and rural [64]. On the other hand, urban fertility surveys of Calcutta and Delhi currently being conducted by the Indian Statistical Institute and the Institute of Economic Growth are finding high rates of ever-use of contraceptives; the age of marriage is rising very slowly; and the birth rate has undoubtedly fallen in the last decade, perhaps by as much as 5 (per 1000), and a part of that fall is attributable to lower marital fertility.

Another way to look at the changes is to examine state vital rates. The states for which not-too-untrustworthy data are available are listed in order of birth rates.

TABLE 2.3.2

Rural birth and death rates; selected Indian states, average 1970 and 1971†

	Birth rate	Death rate	1971 population (millions)
Kerala	30·7	9·0	21·3
Tamil Nadu	32·6	17·2	41·2
Maharashtra	33·1	13·3	50·4
Punjab	34·7	11·4	13·6
Mysore	34·7	14·2	29·3
Andhra Pradesh	35·1	16·2	43·5
Jammu and Kashmir	35·6	12·7	4·6
Himachal Pradesh	35·8	16·2	3·5
Orissa	38·5‡	16·8‡	21·9
Assam	39·0	17·5	15·0
Madhya Pradesh	40·3	17·0	41·7
Haryana	41·2	10·2	10·0
Rajasthan	42·0	17·9	25·8
Gujarat	42·4	18·2	26·7
Uttar Pradesh	46·6	21·9	88·3

† Source: *S.R.S. Bulletin*, April–June 1972; Census 1971.
‡ 1970 only.

As can be seen, the order for birth rates corresponds quite well with that for death rates. Indeed, if one were to plot the birth and death rates on a graph, the points would lie not too far from a sloping line showing a positive relationship between birth and deaths. Caution, however, is in order in assessing the data. First, although they are the best figures available, they are by no means immune to error. Secondly, the quality of reporting of the figures probably affects both birth and death rates in the same direction. Thirdly, the most importantly, since so many deaths occur in the early age-groups, there is bound to be a correlation between birth rates and death rates.

Nevertheless the data correspond with other observations: on the whole the states with low birth and death rates are the ones in which social and economic conditions—incomes, education, nutrition—are better than average. The birth rate for Haryana and both birth and death rates for Gujarat are unexpectedly high. All that can properly be inferred is that the figures are, on the whole, not inconsistent with the view of low mortality as a necessary condition for fertility decline. Birth rates are lower where conditions are better. But of the seven largest and most populous states (Bihar, 56·3m and West Bengal, 44·3m are omitted from Table 2.3.2. for lack of data), only Maharashtra, Tamil Nadu, and to a very modest degree Andrha show any sign of a nascent 'transition'.

If the process of development in India is affecting fertility only very slowly, it is natural that the Government of India should try to limit population growth by means of a family-planning programme. There has been quite an extensive programme in operation since 1965. By the end of 1972–3, more than 11m male sterilizations had been performed, 3m of them in that year alone; nearly 5m I.U.D.s inserted (about 0·5m in 1972–3); female sterilizations, which started relatively slowly, have reached about 0·5m in one year; and condom distribution was of the order of 75m pieces in 1972–3, 42 per cent of them through commercial outlets— i.e. bought by the users. All this is evidence of considerable demand for family-planning services. However, compared with the population 'at risk'—the number of couples of reproductive age is more than 100m—the programme cannot yet have made much of an impact on the birth rate [65].

In view of the general discussion in the previous section (*The general case*), it will come as no surprise to learn that the programme has, broadly speaking, worked best in the states where social and economic conditions are somewhat more advanced—largely (if one includes Gujarat, where performance has also been relatively good) the states at the top of Table 2.3.2. It cannot conceivably be argued that the direction of causation may go the other way, that birth rates are low in these states simply because of the success of the family-planning programme, although undoubtedly the programme has made a contribution.

In discussing India's programme, it is worth trying to keep clear two somewhat separate issues—the general low level of acceptance of family planning and the actual reverses of performance suffered by the programme in the late 1960s. To take the latter first, it is well known that both the I.U.D. and vasectomy campaigns got off to a good start, but later the number of clients fell off sharply. Numerous reasons have been advanced for this. In both cases, but particularly with the I.U.D., there have been physiological problems which have created adverse opinion against these particular methods—though the degree of adversity of opinion seems out of proportion to the actual number of cases of bad side-effects [13, 23]. It is perhaps inevitable that a programme in India when put on a mass basis should experience more problems than are observed in preliminary field trials. One must also reckon with the low levels of education and medical sophistication in the country—the tendency to infer *post hoc ergo propter hoc* is common enough in medical matters in all countries; certainly in India, ailments occurring after some experience of family planning have commonly been attributed to the method adopted, whether truly caused by it or not, and the programme suffered to a degree from such behaviour.

The day-to-day running of the programme is so poorly documented that it is very difficult to be sure of explanations [3]. If even a sample of sections of the programme were monitored by well-maintained case-cards, so that one knew something of the characteristics of acceptors in earlier years and today, and of the performance of various parts of the programme's facilities, one would be somewhat better off. These defects of information flow in the programme are only now beginning to be corrected. Nevertheless, the explanation of reverses in the previous paragraph—real or alleged side-effects and adverse reaction to them—must be supplemented by others.

For I.U.D.s and vasectomies, the main outlets of the programme were, until recently, health clinics in urban and rural areas; there were also programmes in all hospitals and *ad hoc* facilities at railway stations, fairgrounds, and the like. Where these clinics offered services to an unchanging population, it may be that only a fraction of this population was interested in the services, and once they had had them, the number of clients was bound to decline—this may be particularly true for the basic unit of the programme in rural areas, the Primary Health Centre which, while ostensibly catering for a large area and population, may have an effective outreach of only a few square miles.

Numerous other purported reasons for the decline in I.U.D.s and vasectomies can be found in the literature. The problem is compounded by the fact that in 1971–3 both parts of the programme began to recover, in the case of vasectomies quite spectacularly, as a result of vasectomy 'camps' [39]. At the same time, the regular clinic-based programme has for several years been operating at a very low level. Apart from the vasectomy camps, the most rapidly improving facet of the programme has been the distribution of condoms. This brings us to the more general question of the low average acceptance of family planning.

Much can be made, in explaining the more general situation, of factors in the programme itself. If the ideal contraceptive technique is effective, simple to use, inexpensive, reversible, without side-effects, and without impairment of sexual pleasure, such a technique clearly does not yet exist [66]. The ideal technique for India would also require no medical supervision, since the day when every Indian will be within reach of skilled medical care is far off. Thus a second general factor is the staffing of the programme. It has not proved possible to staff all the clinics as required by the programme with qualified male and female doctors (especially in rural areas). In the case of non-medical staff, not only has the programme found it difficult to train adequate numbers; it has also employed large numbers with inadequate training, in many cases to the detriment of the programme. The programme has been criticized for ineffective administration, lack of support by the political leadership [18], and a variety of other faults, including insufficient urgency and excessive haste. Undoubtedly much of this criticism is justified; much of it has emanated from official sources. It must also be said, though, that the critics have been more vociferous *ex post facto*, and many of the programme's ills have been the result of trying to do difficult things on a large scale with little previous experience as a guide—and that in a country where it is not easy to achieve success in any field.

Besides, all this is on the side of 'supply'. While there are those who argue that there is sufficient evidence of 'demand' for family planning, and the main necessity is to improve the supply, few would deny that the major problem in India is on the demand side [67]. There is a widespread consensus that birth rates in India are high because Indian parents want large families, rather than because parents do not know how to, or do not have the means to, prevent births which are unwanted. There is also a fairly widespread consensus about why this is so. Parents, it is believed, have a particular desire for male children; under existing conditions of mortality, they may need five or six children to ensure one or two surviving males. Children (especially male children) are economic assets from quite an early age; they are a substitute for social security in the parents' old age; the Hindu religion emphasizes the importance of having a male child to light the parent's funeral pyre. Children are a major source of pleasure to parents, in a society where other such sources are few and far between. There is also evidence of communal and political opposition to family limitation. This is not the place for an extended discussion of the determinants of fertility in India. The above are simply the most commonly held views, with which the author broadly agrees. (A good discussion and bibliography of many of these topics can be found in [43].)

(A note about the economics of families is in order. Family-planning propaganda emphasizes that families will be better off with fewer children; and yet many parents state that they are better off with more. Little is known of the actual costs of raising a child in poor Indian families, of the age at which he or she may become useful, or the contribution the child makes to family income. But it may well be that the initial costs are very low, and that the child's usefulness outweights the costs very early on—perhaps as soon as age 5 or 6; the marginal cost of an additional child may also be quite low—there are some scale economies in family-size. Little effort has been made to reconcile such issues with the cost–benefit analysis of birth prevention, which has often found enormous positive returns to investment in family planning. The cost–benefit studies refer typically to social costs and benefits; but the logic of the relationship between social and private costs and benefits has been little explored.)

All things considered, even a greatly improved family-planning programme—though well worth striving for—is not going to make any rapid alteration in the pattern of India's population growth. Looking towards the future, therefore, one can see population levels ranging only between very high and even higher. It can be calculated that with fertility declining rapidly from present levels, and mortality slowly, the population of India in the year 2000 will be of the order of 950m; with fertility unchanging, the total would reach 1250m [68]. These are but fallible projections; it must be emphasized, though, that a number such as 950m is a fairly *optimistic* projection. Given what is said above about the relationships between fertility and mortality, let alone other considerations, there is no comfort to be derived from speculations about mortality failing to decline.

It is barely possible to confront such figures for India's future population without experiencing a sense of grave concern for what the country is going to be like in 30 years time. And yet this concern has only rarely been pursued with dispassionate inquiry; more often observers move directly from large numbers to despair. To the present author, the tragedy of these large numbers lies not in any premonition of catastrophe so much as in the apprehension that India in 30 years time will be very much as it is now—that huge investment programmes and a great absorption of human energy and skill will go simply into preventing the situation from deteriorating, while the margin for improving the condition of the majority of men will be very small. Population is not so much a time-bomb as a treadmill.

Such a view can be illustrated by the most critical of the relationships between population and resources: the question of the food-supply. The National Commission on Agriculture is currently assessing the long-term food situation, and its results are not yet available; but a preview of some of its likely results is available [55]. The estimates of demand for foodgrains are obviously extremely sensitive to changes in the relevant parameters—the population growth rate, the rise in personal incomes, and the income-elasticity of demand for food. The highest of the various estimates puts foodgrain demand in the year 2000 at 238m tonnes, compared with 108m in 1970–1, or 104m in the drought year of 1971–2. This represents a rate of increase of 2·7–2·8 per cent annually—rather less than the average growth attained in the previous 20 years. It is also higher than the current rate of population growth and, one may hope, considerably higher than the rate which will prevail as the century draws to a close [69].

It thus allows not only for feeding the growing population at the existing *per capita* level but for making up some of the present backlog of foodgrain shortage and lack of purchasing power which manifests itself in malnutrition. At the same time, on a pure extrapolation basis, the rate of foodgrain output growth does not appear unmanageable. Nevertheless, one should not underrate the problem of achieving a doubling and more of foodgrain production in the next 27 years. The growth of the last 10 years has been achieved by dint of extraordinary efforts, and a large share of it has been due to the development and diffusion of new wheat varieties. Up to the present, the 'green revolution' has been almost entirely a wheat revolution. Yet the low productivity of crops other than wheat gives some grounds for hope: if productivity were at a universally high level, the prospects for increasing output would be dimmer [20].

Indian yields, for crops other than wheat, are quite low by international standards, so that production is nowhere near the technical frontier. Yet achieving continued growth at 2·7 per cent annually will require major efforts. Only a quarter of India's cultivated land is irrigated or subject to reliable rainfall—75 per cent of Indian farming is dry farming. The future of India's agriculture depends on extending irrigation—but also on constantly improving plant varieties, on extending the use of fertilizers and pesticides, on the provision of power for pump sets, the improvement of farm management by extension education, and the provision of credit; not to speak of land reform and tenancy regulation. The list is incomplete, but very obviously entails the expenditure of major resources. And as the frontiers of productive efficiency are approached, the marginal cost of increasing the level of output rises, as do the environmental costs of increasing use of modern inputs [70]. Yet so much of this expenditure of resources is simply to extend food supplies to growing numbers—resources some of which could, if numbers were constant, be used for raising individual standards. (One says '*some* of which'—obviously a large share of the additional resources required in agriculture will be contributed by the growing labour force itself. But some of the capital costs—such as that needed for fertilizer plants—could make valuable contributions elsewhere if population were stationary.)

The conclusion is that, while it appears quite feasible to match the food-supply to the growing population, it is far from being a situation which will take care of itself. If the energetic programme required in research and investment should falter, food scarcity will threaten. And, on the demand side, it must be remembered that 'solving' the food problem is not simply a question of matching supplies to the numbers of people; there is also the at least equally important question of ensuring that those who lack food acquire the necessary incomes to buy it. (For a valuable statement of this aspect of the problem, see [36]).

As with the food-supply, so with social services. The difficulty of providing adequate services for a whole population is obvious enough even in rich countries, where populations are growing extremely slowly. In Britain today there is a percentage of people who lack the basic necessities of life. Even if India's population remained unchanged for the next 30 years, it would be a major achievement if by the end of that time adequate education, housing, health, and other facilities were available to all. With the population growing by 350 m or more, it is hard to imagine that either universality or adequacy will prevail. There is first a question of whether public expenditure on these services will be permitted to grow at a sufficient rate—a rate not only sufficient for the growth in numbers, but to make up the backlog for those at present without such services, and the deficiencies in quality of many of the services already provided [71].

The problem for the Indian Government is whether it can afford to provide facilities for all, or whether other demands of the economy must take priority. The models of economic–demographic interaction discussed in *The general case* above assume that provision for the growing population will mechanically absorb capital which might otherwise be devoted to alternative, economically beneficial purposes. They do not allow for the possibility that, while such an effect is partially in evidence, the gap between the requirements of the population and the provision of services may simply not be closed. In Indian education, for example, great strides have been made in extending school and university places; but quality of education has been a casualty, and will long remain so. The Government's choice is a painful one—either important areas of the economy are denied adequate investment, or sections of the population are left without satisfactory social services. In neither case can society or the economy benefit.

It should not be thought that levels of welfare in health, education, housing, or other social provision is simply a function of the services made available by the Government. The economic circumstances of the family affect the ability to profit from services: if the child's labour is needed on the farm or in the home, the fact that a school place is offered free of charge is not enough. Less than 70 per cent of Indian children are ever enrolled in primary schools; of those, a large proportion stay less than 2 years [56]. The poor family will not be able to afford the journey to a health centre more than a few miles away; and so forth. As was suggested in the discussion of the food situation, raising the income levels of the poor is important for achieving objectives; it is not just a question of making the investments which increase supply.

A final subject which should be discussed in this context is that of urbanization. One of the fears often encountered in the population literature is that of unmanageable urban growth. In both Africa and Latin America cities have been growing at rates of 6 or 7 per cent annually. In India, however, such rates have not been observed in recent times; net rural–urban migration is quite small. The most rapidly growing cities are Delhi and Bombay, at rates somewhat above 4 per cent a year. Here economic opportunities have been expanding considerably. Calcutta, however, has slowed down its growth. The 1971 census, when details are published, will even show declining densities for some parts of the city. The notion that urban population densities will increase indefinitely until, on dubious analogies with laboratory studies of animals, they 'explode' in terrible violence and 'disintegrate' is not borne out by Calcutta's history—nor is it very plausible as a prediction. (For a recent general work on urban problems, see [4].) A more likely future for India's cities is a shift in the size-classes of urban increase, as major cities approach the limits of expansion and their growth begins to slow down, while that of smaller cities accelerates.

To say this is only to oppose the worst fears about urban development; it is not to welcome the likely future of India's cities. Even if Calcutta's population density does not increase, the agglomeration continues and will continue to spread. If none of

India's cities were to expand at all, it would be the work of decades to give them adequate housing, sanitation and transport, let alone less basic urban amenities. Anyone who has observed the lamentable conditions of life in contemporary cities of India can hardly regard their future with equanimity. But analysis here as elsewhere suggests that the result of population growth is not catastrophe, in the literal sense of some sudden reversal of experience. It is rather the more slow-moving difficulty of making progress. The growing economy and modernizing society could make swift improvements in urban conditions; instead, the growth of population will neutralize the value of a large share of urban investment.

Turning to the economy in general, one finds the impact of population growth (though not the result of population growth alone) in the widespread incidence of unemployment, or underemployment, and acute poverty. The Western concept of unemployment is unsatisfactory for India; owing to the social character of many work relationships, the frequency of multiple occupations, seasonality of work, job sharing, and so forth, it is difficult both to define the employed state, departure from which would characterize someone as unemployed, or to have any useful notion of labour-force participation rates. Certainly one would be ignoring much of India's employment problem if one attempted to measure solely the number of people entirely without paid employment and actively seeking it. For these reasons, attention has turned, in recent years, to income levels. On the basis of a definition of poverty as an income just sufficient to purchase an adequate diet, it is commonly quoted that 40 per cent of the population lives at or below the poverty line. It should be added that the vast majority of those above that line are quite poor by Western standards. A man earning £15 a month would be in the top 30 per cent of incomes. The number of people in India who lead a material life comparable to that even of a well-off working family in Britain is quite tiny.

Much interest centres on the question of whether the level of living has deteriorated in India in the last two decades. Average income per head has been rising, of course, since the average rate of growth of G.N.P. has surpassed the population growth rate. But what of the 40 per cent in poverty? At a conference in New Delhi 2 years ago, some of the papers maintained that the proportion below the poverty line had increased, or that the poorest deciles had suffered reductions in incomes [33]. The data on which such conclusions are based are, however, not really adequate to measure small changes. Perhaps all that can be said is that, if one looks only at wages, or incomes in kind, and prices, there is nothing to suggest any significant decline in the proportions of the poor to the total population or any significant improvement in the incomes of the lowest deciles. There are, however, other things which should be put in the balance. The average villager is more likely to go to school than he or she used to be; he will be closer to a good road, and therefore have easier access to a nearby town; the town is more likely to have a cinema; the village—if not the villager—will possess a radio; if disaster strikes, in the shape of drought or floods, the village is more likely to receive assistance; it is more likely to be within reach of a modern health centre; and villagers are living longer. It is this last fact which makes one sceptical of any claims that the lowest deciles have become substantially worse off; one might argue that they were previously so close to the margin of survival that any worsening ought to result in traversal of the margin [72].

Nevertheless, poverty and malnutrition are the lot of a huge share of the Indian people. It must be asked to what extent population growth is the cause of this. At such a point in the argument, many would point to China as a vast country with an enormous and, at least until recently, rapidly growing population, where the kind of destitution common in India seems to have been abolished. It cannot be denied, as was said in *The general case*, that if India's socio-economic structure were better adapted to the absorption of labour, its rapid population growth would pose smaller problems. The alternatives, however, would still be a rapidly growing population and slowly improving living standards, or a more slowly growing population with material conditions improving faster. But India has not had a Maoist revolution, and many would believe that it is unlikely to have one. Even within its present economic and political framework, however, poverty and under-utilization of labour cannot be blamed by any means entirely on population growth. Had employment-oriented strategies prevailed earlier (it is understandable why they did not), or had the strategies which were adopted been pursued with greater efficiency and purpose, much of the abject poverty prevailing today might have been reduced, if not eliminated.

But the relative magnitudes must be borne in mind; however much additional employment might have been created with feasible policies, it has to be set against a growth in the labour force of more than 50 per cent in the space of the last 20 years. Whatever could have been done for these growing numbers, much more could have been done for a more slowly growing labour force. There are few (if any) arguments which show that 50 per cent to have added to the economic surplus available for development; there are many arguments suggesting they have reduced it. In fact the two most common arguments are not very forceful for the Indian case: although a large proportion of total savings are domestic savings these have continued to grow in recent years [73], and it is mainly public and corporate savings that have failed to expand sufficiently, in no way due directly to the growth of population; and while there has been some diversion of public investment into less productive uses as a result of population growth, this has, as the author has argued elsewhere [7], not been *pari passu* with that growth. Influences other than population growth on savings and the composition of investment have had considerably more importance [74].

Fundamentally, however, the path to the elimination of poverty in a mixed economy is the development of labour shortage, and with a labour force growing at such rates in a very poor country, conditions of labour scarcity are unlikely to materialize. It is in a way remarkable that the addition to India's numbers of 250m people in the last 30 years has occurred without dramatic deterioration. That should be remembered when the future is being examined. The next 30 years may add something like 400m; but the economy is that much more advanced. It is becoming more adaptable, and wealthier. It is also becoming in certain ways more vulnerable; as economic sophistication grows, so does economic interdependence: the failure of a part may become more expensive to the whole. Thus droughts now hurt industry by reducing the supply of water to hydro-electric plants. And one thing population growth does do is to magnify the impact of natural disasters—the greater the density of settlement in an area, the greater the destruction of personal livelihoods by droughts or floods. In general, one can only speculate as to the relative balance of growing vulnerability, and growing capacity to cope with adversity. The task of analysing the future is to identify potential discontinuities. Will the next 30 years bring simply more of the same, or is there some threshold for particular facets of the economy and society beyond which additional population growth will produce intolerable strains? The evidence so far seems to suggest the former.

Summary and conclusions

India's population is unlikely to cease to grow before the early decades of the next century, by which time it will be more than double its present size. Family planning plays a limited but important part in reducing fertility; it can succeed when other conditions favour it. These other conditions appear to be reduced infant and child mortality, improved education and living standards, and higher employment rates, especially for women. The interrelationships between these factors and the economy and society at large are such that they cannot be thought of as some sort of 'package programme', with costed inputs that can be compared with other programmes. The raising of the incomes of the poor is fundamental to all the important factors; and raising their incomes entails generating employment, which in turn requires a shift in the structure of demand and of the output of wage goods.

This paper therefore really amounts to a suggestion about development planning, that it should be thought of from a population point of view. In particular, planning should focus on the diffusion of the material conditions of socio-economic change which accompany the demographic transition. If the poorer developing countries have to wait for industrialization and urbanization to bring those conditions into existence, they may have to wait an extremely long time.

These arguments reinforce the claims for the superiority of employment-oriented strategies which have been made elsewhere on other grounds. Indeed they go beyond them, in suggesting that other strategies are likely to be neutralized, at least in part, by excessive growth of population.

REFERENCES AND NOTES

The readings which follow are far from exhaustive. They have been chosen in part because they contain good, recent bibliographies themselves or good collections of papers on a variety of topics. Some items are marked *, indicating the present author considers them particularly valuable in this or other respects. Items marked † are those which deserve attention but for various reasons are not cited in the text above.

1. BEHM, H., GUTIERREZ, H., and REQUERA, M. (1972). Demographic trends, health, and medical care in Latin America, *International Journal of Health Services*

2. BERELSON, B., *et al.* (1966). *Family planning and population programs*, University of Chicago Press, Chicago, Ill.

3. BLAIKIE, P. M. (1972). Implications of selective feedback in aspects of family planning research for policy makers in India, *Population Studies*, **26**, November.

4. BOSE, A. (1973). *Studies in India's urbanization 1901–1971*. Tata–McGraw-Hill, New Delhi.

5. BOSERUP, E. (1965). *The conditions of agricultural growth*. Allen and Unwin, London.

6. BRACKETT, J. W. (1968). The evolution of Marxist theories of population, *Demography* **5**, No. 1.

7. CASSEN, R. H. (1973). Population growth and public expenditure in developing countries, *Invited Papers, I.U.S.S.P. Liège Conference, 1973.*

8. CLARK, C. (1967). *Population growth and land use*. Macmillan, London.

9. CLARKE, J. I. and FISHER, W. B. (1972). *Populations of the middle east and North Africa*. University of London Press, London.

10. CLINTON, R., *et al.* (eds.) (1972). *Political science in population studies*, D. C. Heath, Lexington Books, Lexington, Mass.†

11. COALE, A. J. and HOOVER, E. M. (1958). *Population growth and economic development in low income countries.* pp. xxi + 389, Princeton University Press, Princeton, New Jersey.*

12. DALY, H. E. (1970). *The population question in Northeast Brazil: its economic and ideological dimensions.* Yale Economic Growth Center, Center Papers No. 157. Yale University, New Haven, Conn.

13. DANDEKAR, K. and NIKAM, S. (1971). The loop—what did fail? *Economic and Political Weekly*, Bombay. 27 November.

14. DAS GUPTA, A. (1972). Study of the historical demography of India. In [22].

15. DAS GUPTA, P. (1971). Estimation of demographic measures for India 1881–1961 based on Census age distributions, *Population Studies*, November 1971.

16. DAVIS, K. (1951). *The Population of India and Pakistan*. Princeton University Press, Princeton, New Jersey.

17. —— (1967). Population policy: will current programs succeed?, *Science* **158**, 10 November 1967.

18. FINKLE, J. L. (1972). The political environment of population control in India and Pakistan. In [10].

19. FOSTER, P. and YOST, L. (1965). *Population growth and rural development in Buganda*, University of Maryland, Agricultural Experiment Station, Misc. Pub. No. 621.†

20. FRANKEL, F. R. (1971). *India's green revolution.* Princeton University Press, Princeton, New Jersey.

21. GLASS, D. V. and EVERSLEY, D. (eds.) (1965). *Population in history.* pp. ix + 692. Arnold, London.*†

22. —— and REVELLE, R. (eds.) (1972). *Population and social change.* pp. viii + 520. Arnold, London.*

23. G.O.I. (1970). *Family planning programme: an evaluation,* Government of India, Planning Commission, Programme Evaluation Organisation, New Delhi.

24. —— (1972). *Family planning in India—Programme information 1971–2,* Government of India, Ministry of Health and Family Planning, New Delhi.

25. —— (1973), *Economic Survey 1972–3,* Government of India, Ministry of Finance, Department of Economic Affairs, New Delhi.

26. HABAKKUK, H. J. (1971). *Economic development and population growth since 1750,* pp. 110. Leicester University Press, Leicester.

27. HEER, D. (1966). Economic development and fertility, *Demography* **3**, *No. 2.*

28. HERZOG, J. R. (1972). *Investment in social development: some implications of demographic conditions,* O.E.C.D., Development Centre, Paris.†

29. HOOVER, E. M. and PERLMAN, M. (1966). Measuring the effects of population control on economic development, *Pakistan Development Review.*

30. I.L.O. (1970). *Towards full employment.* A programme for Colombia. International Labour Office, Geneva.

31. —— (1971). *Matching employment opportunities and expectations.* A programme of action for Ceylon, International Labour Office, Geneva.

32. —— (1972). *Employment, incomes and equality.* A strategy for increasing productive employment in Kenya, International Labour Office, Geneva.

33. I.S.I. (1971). Papers presented to the Conference on Income Distribution, Indian Statistical Institute, New Delhi.

34. JAIN, S. C. (1971). *Comparative study of effective and non-effective family planning programmes in India,* North Carolina Population Center.

35. JONES, G. W. and SELVARATNAM, S. (1972). *Population growth and economic development in Ceylon.* Hansa Colombo.†

36. JOY, J. L. (1973). Food and nutrition planning, *Journal of Agricultural Economics,* January 1973.*

37. KEYFITZ, N. (1971). On the momentum of population growth, *Demography* **8**, No. 1.

38. KIRK, D. (1971). A new demographic transition? In [57: **2**].

39. KRISHNAKUMAR, S. (1972), Kerala's pioneering experiment in massive vasectomy camps. [47].

40. KUZNETS, S. (1971). *Economic growth of nations.* Harvard University Press.

41. KUZNETS, S. (1972). *Rural-urban differences in fertility: an international comparison.* Yale University, Economic Growth Center. Discussion paper No. 166, November 1972.

42. MAMDANI, M. (1973). *The myth of population control: family caste and class in an Indian village.* Monthly Review Press, New York.†

43. MANDELBAUM, D. (1973). Social components of Indian fertility, *Economic and Political Weekly.* Annual Number, Bombay.*

44. OMINDE, S. H. and EJIOGU, C. N. (eds.) (1972). *Population growth and economic development in Africa.* Heinemann, London.†

45. ORLEANS, L. A. (1972). *Every fifth child: a study of China's population.* Eyre Methuen, London.

46. POPULATION COUNCIL. *Reports on Population/Family Planning.* The Population Council, New York, irregular.*

47. —— *Studies in Family Planning.* The Population Council, New York, monthly.*

48. —— (1967). *Selected questionnaire on knowledge attitudes and practice of family planning,* 2 Vols., The Population Council, New York.

49. RIDKER, R. G. and MUSCAT, R. J. (1973). Incentives for family welfare and fertility reduction. In [47], January 1973.

50. ROBINSON, W. and HORLACHER, D. (1971). Population growth and economic welfare. In [46], February 1971.*

51. S.R.S. (1972). Sample Registration System, *Bulletin,* Government of India, Office of the Registrar General, New Delhi, April–June 1972.

52. RUPRECHT, T. K. (1967). Fertility control, investment and *per capita* output: a demographic–econometric model of the Philippines, *Contributed Papers, I.U.S.S.P. Sydney Conference, 1967.*

53. SMITH, T. E. (1973). *The politics of family planning.* Allen and Unwin, London.†

54. STYCOS, J. M. (1971). Opinion, ideology and population problems . . . In [57: 2].

55. SWAMINATHAN, M. S. (1973). Population and food supply, *Yojana,* New Delhi. 26 January.

56. SEN, A. K. (1970). *The crisis in Indian education,* Shastri Memorial Lecture, New Delhi.*

57. U.S. NATIONAL ACADEMY OF SCIENCES (1971). *Rapid population growth,* 2 Vols. Johns Hopkins Press, Baltimore, Md.*

58. WALSH, B. T. (1971). *Economic development and population control: A fifty year projection of Jamaica.* Praeger, New York.

59. WEINER, M. (1970). Perceptions of population change in India: a field report. Center for International Studies, Mass. Inst. Tech., Cambridge, Mass.

60. WRIGLEY, E. A. (1969). *Population and history.* Weidenfeld and Nicolson, London.*†

61. WYON, J. B. and GORDON, J. E. (1971). *The Khanna study: population problems in the rural Punjab.* Harvard University Press, Cambridge, Mass.*

62. Studies of 'knowledge, attitude, and practice' related to Family Planning (cf. e.g. [48]).

63. Information on these matters is available in medical journals and the like. These changes in mortality will be covered in detail in a book on population and development in India currently under preparation by the author of the present paper.

64. Urban crude birth rates (births per 1000 *people*) are lower than rural, in India as in most developing countries, but this is mainly explained by the high ratio of men to women which results from migration patterns.

65. The Government of India calculated 7·4m births prevented by the programme cumulatively up to the 1971 census. But these results are obtained simply by multiplying the number of operations performed by a variety of uncertain coefficients. Allowing for the fact that many of the programme's male clients have sterile wives, are sterile or even unmarried themselves, and so forth, and also that the programme substitutes, to some degree, for methods of family limitation already in use, a figure closer to 4–5m is more plausible, though possibly 7m had been achieved by 1973. This figure for the cumulative effect of the programme should be compared with an *annual* number of births of the order of 20m (see [24]). If the programme results in 1m prevented births a year, and these births would otherwise not have been prevented, the programme can claim credit for a 2-point reduction in the birth rate.

66. Possibly the list of characteristics of an ideal method should include its ability to be used by one partner without the knowledge of the other.

67. Studies have been made showing that family-planning acceptance is higher where services are better [34]; quite apart from the methodological difficulties involved, such findings do not contradict this view. (See [61] on this view and many other matters; though also see the present author's review of the work in *South Asian Review*, October 1972.)

68. Given an annual decline of fertility of 1 per cent, 2 per cent, or 3 per cent while the Gross Reproduction Rate is 3·0, 2·5–2·0, or 2·0–1·5 respectively, and the expectation of life rising 0·6 years p.a., while the average expectation is less than 60, and by 0·4 years thereafter, the population reaches 956·5m by the year 2000; or 1249·2m with constant fertility and the same rise in expectation of life. (These calculations are taken from *Population projections for bank member countries*. Int. Bk. rur. Devel., Washington, D.C., 1973.)

69. Swaminathan [55] does not make exactly clear in the paper cited what population levels his study assumes; but he is obviously not using the upper limit of 1250m which we referred to earlier. This is quite justifiable—it is unlikely that fertility will not decline at all.

70. Because of the low levels of use of agricultural chemicals, these have not yet become major hazards in India.

71. Details of the current and prospective situation in India are discussed in [7].

72. Of course, much of the improved chance of survival is due to achievements in public health, and it is possible that other aspects of living conditions have deteriorated while death rates have declined. This quite possibly was the case for the period up to 1950, though it seems improbable for the more recent past.

73. Perhaps more slowly than they would have done with lower population growth; but since most private domestic saving is done by the rich, population growth does not much affect it.

74. For a general account of recent trends in the Indian economy, see [25].

2.4. Some biological and psychological considerations operating on populations

2.4.1. Genetic aspects of social structure

JOHN B. GIBSON

Department of Genetics, Cambridge University

IN discussing genetic aspects of human populations it must be emphasized that the term population is difficult to define except in theoretical models and in experiments with laboratory organisms. Individuals of the human species are not distributed evenly in space but occur in clusters, between which there is migration, although marriages tend to occur less frequently between, rather than within, the clusters. Thus the genetic structure is a series of overlapping but partially isolated groups, viewed as a series of neighbourhoods that do not necessarily correspond to the demographic population [3]. Indeed, to some extent, each pair of individuals can be considered to belong to a slightly different sub-group. There is ample evidence for geographic heterogeneity in the British Isles in the distribution of major genetic markers [21] and for continuous characters whose variance has a significant genetic component.

In addition to this horizontal spatial heterogeneity in the human species there is also vertical differentiation arising from social stratification based on various parameters. Both the horizontally and vertically differentiated groups are subject to factors promoting genetic change which are intrinsic to the organism, such as random genetic drift, random or selective migration, inbreeding, and assortative mating. Similarly all of these differentiated groups are subject to the extrinsic forces of natural selection, imposed by the local environments.

It seems unlikely that the present population of the British Isles is in an equilibrium state. The complex patterns of both long- and short-range migration, together with the changes in the environment brought about by the spread of urbanization, will have effects on the genetic structure. One of man's most active pursuits is the alteration in the balance of forces affecting any equilibrium state. As Mather [25] has succinctly pointed out;

'Sometimes our action is deliberate and sometimes unwitting. Sometimes it is directed and sometimes incidental. But conscious or not, directed or not, it must be expected ultimately to have its genetical consequences in the population'.

Social stratification

The vertical differentiation in the demographic population based on social factors is particularly interesting, although it has often been neglected by biologists. I want to consider here its possible effects on the genetic structure, rather than discuss the evidence for geographical heterogeneity. One of the social factors which has received considerable attention from social scientists [26] is the sub-division of the adult working population into a number of occupational or socio-economic classes, and recently biologists also have considered the effects of these parameters on the genetic structure of populations.

The occupational sub-divisions are related to qualification and skills and hence to level of education; thus it is not surprising that school attainment and I.Q. are correlated with the occupational classes of adults. The socio-economic classes reflect many environmental influences which are known to affect the physical and psychological development of children brought up in families in different socio-economic backgrounds. Some of these environmental variables are economic; for example, family incomes will have marked effects on the home environment. Others are more subtle, for example, as Davie, Butler, and Goldstein [9] have recently shown, the percentage of children who are deprived of the protection afforded by immunization against polio and diphtheria increased from 1 per cent of the children in the homes of professional people to 10 per cent of the children of manual unskilled workers.

The extensive data reported on by Davie *et al.*, derived from studies on a large representative sample of 7-year-old children in England, Scotland, and Wales, demonstrate quite clearly social class differences amongst the children in both behavioural and physical characters. Children in social classes I and II were on average 3·3 cm taller than those in social class V. Teachers' ratings of the children's creativity and oral and reading abilities were more often below average or markedly poor for children in manual than in non-manual social classes. Both maternal and paternal interest in the child's educational progress, again as assessed by the teachers declined from social class I to V.

Social mobility and selective migration

Some of the variance in some of these continuous characters, particularly I.Q. [11], is known to have a genetic component, although they are all incompletely inherited. Thus in each social class there will be differences between the I.Q.s of children and their parents. If the relationship between I.Q. and socio-economic class is maintained over generations, then a proportion of children in each generation must move from the social class in which they were born into a different occupational group to reconstitute the adult distribution.

Burt [5], Gibson and Young [16], Gibson [14], and Waller [31, 32] have tested this hypothesis by comparing the I.Q.s of fathers and sons and relating the differences to both upward and downward intergenerational social mobility. All of these studies showed that a large proportion of social mobility was indeed related to I.Q. and that both verbal and performance components of the I.Q. were implicated [15]. In one of these studies, where families in which the I.Q. of the father and two male sibs were known, it was found that the upwardly mobile sibs tended to have higher I.Q.s than the non-mobile or downwardly mobile sibs.

It is also relevant that Tanner [28] has shown height is related to social mobility, women who marry into a higher socio-economic class are taller on average than those who marry in the same or lower social class. As both I.Q. and height have significant heritabilities the observations that they are correlated with social mobility suggest on theoretical grounds that social mobility will give rise to a non-random transfer of genetic material from class to class. This argument, of course, depends on the assumption that the relationship between, for example, I.Q. phenotypes and social mobility implies some significant relationship between I.Q. genotype and social mobility.

Given this assumption the classes will be expected to become, to some extent, genetically differentiated. In addition the classes will also differ for immediate environmental reasons due to differences in educational opportunities, nutrition and home backgrounds, etc. However, Cavalli-Sforza and Bodmer [7], Jinks and Fulker [19], and Thoday and Gibson [30] have pointed out that at the present time it is impossible to decide whether, and to what quantitative extent, environmental factors directly affecting contemporary individuals cause the observed class differences in continuous variables and to what extent the differences are caused by genetic differences that have arisen because differing genotypes have in the past moved into different classes.

The theoretical argument discussed above has been tested in model experiments [30]. The results confirm the hypothesis that social mobility dependent to some extent on a variable with significant heritability does lead to genetic differences between groups.

Inbreeding and assortative marriage

There is considerable evidence for high rates of endogamy in both geographic areas [22] and in socio-economic classes [17]. Indeed, where people live or work or play is so often related to their social class that the effects of propinquity and social-class endogamy are confounded [10].

Marriages between people who happen to live near each other can give rise to inbreeding if the propinquity partly reflects a genetic relationship in the past [23]. Inbreeding, which is not character-specific, does not involve changes in gene frequencies in large populations, but it does lead to an increase in the average homozygosity per genetic locus. Its effects may be particularly relevant in our society in relation to minority groups based on religion, or race, but there is little data on inbreeding coefficients in the United Kingdom population. Assortative marriage can be both negative and positive and is character-specific, but when positive it tends to maintain genetic variance in the population, again without changing gene frequencies [1, 8].

The genetic effects of assortative marriages are particularly important at the present time when differential fertility based on socio-economic variables is declining. There is also evidence, at least for the white population in the U.S.A. [2, 18, 32] and in England [14], that there is now little differential fertility associated with I.Q. differences (see [12], for review). However, social mobility related to I.Q. will give rise to a measure of assortative mating for I.Q. that will contribute to the maintenance of the I.Q. genotypic variance [29]. There is evidence that marriages are positively assortative for age, level of education, and many physical and behavioural characteristics including I.Q. [4, 33] (see also [13, 20, 27] for reviews).

Cattel and Nesselroade [6] have shown that stable marriages are more positively assortative for I.Q. than are unstable marriages, and it has often been demonstrated that the negatively assortative marriages have a lower reproduction rate than the positively assortative marriages, in white populations. Thus an element of differential fertility seems to be present in relation to marriage patterns although it must be stressed that there is a paucity of data for the population of the United Kingdom.

Conclusions

The evidence discussed above serves to emphasize that both genetic and environmental factors, including cultural effects, must be considered in any explanations of social class phenomena.

It is more than a pity that when one delves into the literature concerned with the effects of social structure on the genetic aspects of human populations, data for the British population is notable by its absence. Many writers have cogently argued the need for research into genetic aspects of behavioural variation in human populations but as yet the necessary interdisciplinary response has not been very obvious.

Discussion of the genetic effects of any but the most extreme population policies must suffer immeasurably from this lack of information about the present population structure and the distribution of genetic variability. Perhaps all we can say from a consideration of the points briefly made above (but nevertheless it needs repeating again and again such is its importance) is best summarized by a further quotation from Mather [24]:

The adjustment of the genetic constitution of the population by deliberate intervention . . . is generally regarded as something that we can choose either to undertake or to leave alone; but in truth we must already be in the business of altering our genetical structure. What we are doing to it we cannot as yet see clearly.

REFERENCES

1. ADAMS, M. S. (1969). Genetic consequences of cultural adaptation, *Med. Clin. N. Am.* **53**, 977.
2. BAJEMA, C. J. (1963). Estimation of the direction and intensity of natural selection in relation to human intelligence by means of the intrinsic rate of natural increase, *Eugen. Quart.* **10**, 175.
3. BOYCE, A. J., KÜCHAMANN, C. F. and HARRISON, G. A. (1967). Neighbourhood knowledge and the distribution of marriage distances, *Ann. hum. Genet.* **30**, 335.
4. BURGESS, E. W., and WALLIN, P. (1943). Homogamy in social characteristics, *Am. J. Sociol.* **49**, 109.
5. BURT, C. (1961). Intelligence and social mobility, *Br. J. stat. Psychol.* **14**, 1.
6. CATTELL, R. B. and NESSELROADE, J. R. (1967). *'Likeness' and 'completeness' theories examined by 16 personality factor measures on stably and unstably married couples.* Advanced Publication No. 7, University of Illinois, Urbana.
7. CAVALLI-SFORZA, L. L. and BODMER, W. F. (1971). *The genetics of human populations.* W. H. Freeman and Company, San Francisco.
8. CROW, J. F. and FELSTENSTEIN, J. (1968). The effect of assortative mating on the genetic constitution of a population, *Eugen. Quart.* **15**, 83.
9. DAVIE, R., BUTLER, M. and GOLDSTEIN, R. (1972). *From birth to seven.* Longman, London.
10. ECKLAND, B. K. (1968). Theories of mate selection, *Eugen. Quart.* **15**, 71.
11. ERLENMEYER-KIMLING, L. and JARVIK, L. F. (1963). Genetics and intelligence: a review, *Science* **142**, 1477.
12. FALEK, A. (1971). Differential fertility and intelligence: current status of the problem, *Soc. Biol.* **18**, 550.
13. GARRISON, R. J., ANDERSON, V. E. and. REED, S. C. (1968). Assortative marriage, *Eugen. Quart.* **15**, 113
14. GIBSON, J. B. (1970). Biological aspects of a high-socio-economic group. I. *J. biosoc. Sci.* **2**, 1.
15. —— and MASCIE-TAYLOR, C. G. N. (1973). Biological aspects of a high-socio-economic group. II, *J. biosoc. Sci.* **5**, 17.
16. —— and YOUNG, M. (1965). Social mobility and fertility. In *Biological aspects of social problems* (ed. J. E. Meade and A. S. Parkes). Oliver and Boyd, Edinburgh.
17. HARRISON, G. A., HIORNS, R. W. and KÜCHEMANN, C. F. (1970). Social class relatedness in some Oxfordshire parishes, *J. bio. Sci.* **2**, 71.
18. HIGGINS, J. V., REED, E. W. and REED, S. C. (1962). Intelligence and family size: a paradox resolved, *Eugen. Quart.* **9**, 84.
19. JINKS, J. L. and FULKER, D. W. (1970). Comparison of the biometrical, genetical, M.A.V.A. and classical approaches to the analysis of human behaviour, *Psychol. Bull.* **5**, 311.

20. KISER, C. V. (1968). Assortative mating by educational attainment in relation to fertility, *Eugen. Quart.* **15**, 98.
21. KOPEC, A. C. (1970). *The distribution of the blood groups in the United Kingdom.* Blackwells, Oxford.
22. KÜCHEMANN, C. F., BOYCE, A. J. and HARRISON, G. A. (1967). A demographic and genetic study of a group of Oxford villages, *Hum. Biol.* **39**, 251.
23. LEWONTIN, R., KIRK, D. and CROW, J. (1968). Selective mating, assortative mating and inbreeding; definitions and implications, *Eugen. Quart.* **15**, 141.
24. MATHER, K. (1964). *Human diversity.* Oliver and Boyd, Edinburgh.
25. —— (1965). Medicine and natural selection in man. In *Biological aspects of social problems* (ed. J. E. Meade and A. S. Parkes). Oliver and Boyd, Edinburgh.
26. MATRAS, J. (1967). Social mobility and social structure: some insights from the linear model, *Am. sociol. Rev.* **32**, 608.
27. SPUHLER, J. N. (1968). Assortative mating with respect to physical characteristics, *Eugen. Quart.* **15**, 128.
28. TANNER, J. M. (1966). Galtonian Eugenics and the Study of Growth: the relationship of body size, intelligence test score and social circumstances in children and adults, *Eugen. Rev.* **58**, 122.
29. THODAY, J. M. (1967). Selection and genetic heterogeneity. In *Genetic diversity and human behaviour* (ed. J. N. Spuhler). Aldine Publishing Company, Chicago.
30. —— and GIBSON, J. B. (1970). Environmental and genetical contributions to class difference: a model experiment, *Science* **167**, 990.
31. WALLER, J. H. (1971). Achievement and social mobility: relationships among IQ score, education and occupation in two generations, *Soc. Biol.* **18**, 252.
32. —— (1971). Differential reproduction: its relation to IQ test score, education and occupation, *Soc. Biol.* **18**, 122.
33. WARREN, B. L. (1966). A multiple variable approach to the assortative mating phenomenon, *Eugen. Quart.* **13**, 285.

2.4.2. Family planning and population quality

CEDRIC O. CARTER

Director, M.R.C. Clinical Genetics Unit, Institute of Child Health, London

It is a truism that genetic change and evolution in human as well as animal populations comes about by selection for 'biological fitness'. Biological fitness of an individual may be defined as the number of surviving offspring an individual produces in comparison with the average number of the population. Such fitness should however be assessed over many generations. A group of individuals may be temporarily fit at the cost of the over-all fitness of the population of which they are part.

Genetic evolution in man is not replaced by cultural evolution, the two continously interact. Genetic evolution may facilitate or may limit cultural evolution; conversely cultural evolution may markedly influence the direction and extent of genetic change.

The palaeontological record of our own species shows some of the most rapid genetic changes in mammalian evolution. Mean human stature changed rapidly and increased by perhaps 50 per cent over the period of about 2 million years ago to about half a million years ago. Stature has remained constant, with local exceptions, since then at between 60 and 72 in. with a sex difference of 4–5 in. Average human brain size also increased by some 50 per cent over the same period, and since then has increased by a further 50 per cent while stature remained constant. Mean brain size appears to have become static, again with regional variation, at about 1400 cm^3 in males and a little less in females at about 50 000 years ago. The size of man's jaws and teeth has decreased by at least 100 per cent over the past million years and is probably still decreasing. If selection for any human characteristic is fully relaxed then it will retrogress as a result of the accumulation of disadvantageous mutant genes.

It is also a truism that until very recently most human evolution occurred through selection by premature death; though there are instances of relatively healthy nomadic and simple agricultural populations adopting effective methods of family planning. When man congregated in towns and cities most of the selection was for resistance to infectious disease, but also no doubt the over-all capabilities of couples as parents, psychological as well as intellectual, influenced the survival rate of their offspring.

The recent change of the planned small family does not necessarily alter the opportunity for selection, but it will alter the nature of the selection. An index of the opportunity for selection from variation in fertility is given by the expression: (variance of family size)/(mean family size)^2 [8]. A drop in mean number of live births per family from, say, 6 to 2 children involves no loss in the opportunity for selection, provided that the variance in live births per couple does not decline by more than nine-fold. The genetic change now occurring, however, in countries with Western European culture with low mortality will be for characteristics which influence couples in deciding whether to plan more or less than the average number of children. Anyone interested in the future of our species will be interested in trying to detect what is occurring and what might occur.

In the field of genetically determined gross physical or mental handicap, most of those of us who are directly concerned are reasonably confident that sensible family planning by informed parents will do better than natural selection [6]. A combination of genetic counselling, that is detecting and informing parents of special risk of producing handicapped children, and selective termination of foetuses following early prenatal diagnosis will increasingly offer the opportunity of reducing the birth frequency of such children well below that maintained by the balance between mutation and the most rigorous natural selection. However, to bring this about considerable further technical development and the enlargement of resources to exploit techniques already developed are required. Even more important is the education both of the medical profession and the general public. The more parents ask the right questions about the genetics of handicap, and the more accurate the information they are given by the medical profession, the greater will be the reduction in the birth frequency of genetically determined disease.

In the field of normal variation for qualities of social value the situation is much less clear cut. There will be disagreement as to which qualities are socially valuable, the genetic contribution to the normal variation is usually complex, and selective pressures are not easily measured. Some would maintain, though others would dispute, that the characteristics that make for upward social mobility are also, on the whole, socially valuable. The change to the planned small family in technically advanced countries began among the upper socio-economic classes, so that in Western Europe and the U.S.A. for perhaps 100 years there was a negative correlation between a man's socio-economic status and the number of surviving children he had. However dysgenic the genetic consequences of this might have been it now appears likely that it was a temporary phenomena and that the differential is disappearing or even being replaced by a small positive differential. There were indications of this in the 1951 census of England and

Wales for marriages of up to 10 years duration, and this was more marked in the 1961 census Fertility Tables where it may be seen from Table 2.4.1 that the small group of self-employed professionals had had more children after 15–19 years of marriage than any socio-economic group except the two bottom groups— the semi-skilled and unskilled manual worker groups. The latter two groups will include a proportion of unplanned children. It will be most interesting to see what the 1971 census shows when

TABLE 2.4.1

Average family size of women married once and enumerated by their husband's socio-economic group, England and Wales 1961 census (10 per cent sample)

Socio-economic group	Approximate percentage in group	Family size marriage duration 15–19 years
Professional—self-employed	0·89	2·18
Professional—employed	2·92	1·90
Employers and managers—large units	4·55	1·85
Employers and managers—small units	6·98	1·83
Intermediate non-manual	4·20	1·80
Junior non-manual	12·21	1·76
Self-employed—not professional	3·93	1·92
Foremen and supervisors—manual	4·27	1·99
Skilled manual	30·56	2·11
Semi-skilled manual	14·72	2·15
Unskilled manual	6·88	2·34

the fertility table becomes available. Similar trends are seen in Sweden [4], France [12], and the census data from the U.S.A.

There was also anxiety in the 1950s in Britain and the U.S.A. because of an apparent negative correlation between intelligence, as measured by intelligence tests, and fertility. The negative correlation was between a child's test score, say, at age 11 and the number of his sibs; the usual correlation being of the order of −025. [5, 7, 11]. Further these negative correlations applied within socio-economic group except perhaps in social class I. It was not realized at that time that there are two factors which would mitigate any dysgenic effect with respect to intelligence of such a negative correlation. The first factor is that part of the relationship is due to the fact that mere membership of a large fraternity tends to depress intelligence-test score—an entirely non-genetic relationship. The second that this method of studying the relationship provided no information on those individuals who had no children and so were not ascertained in a survey whose index patients were children.

What is needed are direct studies relating a child's intelligence-test score to his subsequent completed fertility. There are few such studies, three American [9, 1, 2] and one Scottish [10]. All four showed the usual negative correlation of the child's score and the number of sibs, but in contrast a small positive correlation between a child's score and the number of children he or she achieves by age 45 years. The findings in two American studies [1, 2] are shown in Table 2.4.2. It may be seen that the highest fertility is achieved

TABLE 2.4.2

Completed family size by I.Q.
(numbers of individuals in brackets)

I.Q.	Kalamazoo (1963)	Harvard (1971)
⩾120	2·60 (82)	2·14 (206)
105–119	2·24 (282)	2·24 (421)
95–104	2·02 (318)	2·14 (392)
80–94	2·46 (267)	2·08 (420)
⩽79	1·50 (30)	1·87 (94)
	Mean 2·24	Mean 2·14

by those who score highest, there is a rise in fertility among the dull average and it falls again among the mentally retarded. The rise for the dull average may be attributed to unplanned children, and it is noteworthy that in the most recent American study [2] it has disappeared. Both in the Scottish data and that from Michigan there is evidence of interaction between fertility, I.Q., and achievement. It may be inferred from the data presented that it is men with high intelligence who enter occupations in social class I (Scotland) [10], or who achieve 16 or more years of education (Michigan) [3], who have the highest fertility.

In summary, fully efficient family planning by the parents offers the opportunity of a reduction in the birth frequency of severe physical and mental disease. The limited information available also indicates that it will result in positive selection for the genetic element in qualities that make for upward social mobility and, more specifically, as measured by I.Q. score, for intelligence. It is, however, desirable that opportunity for selection should continue, to be provided by substantial variation in family size from, say zero to four children. A policy based on the slogan 'two is enough' could lead to an undesirable reduction in the variation as well as, because of involuntary sterility and some parents who choose to have no children, a mean family size well below replacement rate. A policy based on the slogan 'every child a wanted child', or perhaps better 'every child a planned child', leaves parents a free (and one hopes informed) choice of family size. This, in my opinion, is in Britain likely to lead to a distribution of family size of the type shown in Table 2.4.3, giving a mean family size at replacement rate and substantial opportunity for selection.

TABLE 2. 4. 3.

Possible distribution of family size in Britain with fully efficient family planning

Family size	0	1	2	3	4	Mean size
Distribution (per cent)	10	10	50	20	10	2·10

REFERENCES

1. BAJEMA, C. J. (1963). Estimation of the direction and intensity of natural selection in relation to human intelligence by means of the intrinsic rate of natural increase, *Eugen. Quart.* **10,** 175.
2. —— (1971). Natural selection and intelligence. In *Abstracts of papers presented at the Fourth International Congress of Human Genetics*, p. 20. Excerpta Medica, Amsterdam.
3. —— (1966). Relation of fertility to education attainment in a Kalamazoo public school population, *Eugen. Quart.* **13,** 306.
4. BERNHARDT, E. (1971). Trends in variations in Swedish fertility: A cohort study. Allmana Forgalet, Sweden. *Urval Skriftserie Urgiven av Statistika Centralbyrån*, No. 5.
5. BURT, C. (1946). *Intelligence and fertility.* Hamilton, London.
6. CARTER, C. O. (1972). In *Population and pollution* (eds. P. R. Cox and J. Peel), p. 107. Academic Press, London.
7. CATTELL, R. (1937). *Intelligence and fertility.* King, London.

8. Crow, J. F. (1959). Some possibilities for measuring selection intensities in man, *Hum. Biol.* **30**, 1.

9. Higgins, J., Reed, E. and Reed, S. (1962). Intelligence and family size: a paradox resolved, *Eugen. Quart.* **9**, 84.

10. Maxwell, J. (1972). A follow-up of the 1932 Scottish survey. (Personal communication.); (1961). *The level and trend of national intelligence: the contribution of the Scottish mental surveys.* pp. 77. University of London Press, London.

11. Roberts, J. (1941). The negative association between intelligence and fertility, *Hum. Biol.* **13**, 410.

12. Tabah, L. (1971). Rapport sur les relations entre la fécondité et la condition sociale et économique de la famille en Europe: leur répercussions sur la politique sociale. Paper presented at *Second European Population Conference, Strasbourg, France, Aug. 31–Sept. 7.*

2.4.3. Mental health and population change

DENNIS GATH

Department of Psychiatry, Oxford University

The Humour of living in great, populous and consequently unhealthy Towns, have brought forth a Class and Set of Distempers, with atrocious and frightful symptoms, scarce known to our Ancestors, and never rising to such fatal heights, nor affecting such Numbers in any other known Nation. These Nervous Disorders being computed to make almost one third of the complaints of the People of Condition in England.

(George Cheyne: The English malady)

What would be the consequences, for mental health, of a continuing massive increase in human populations? How far does living in big cities conduce to mental illness? As yet the science of human behaviour is not sufficiently developed to be able to answer these questions with any confidence. We can only make guesses from fragmentary evidence. Lest we jump to unwarranted conclusions, we should bear in mind the passage from Cheyne, expressing as it does some of the notions about mental illness that are current today—that these conditions are on the increase and more severe and widespread among our generation than any in the past, and that they are associated with urban life. Cheyne's treatise was written in 1733, when the population of England and Wales was only 6 million, and the Industrial Revolution was still to come.

The concept of mental health

It is convenient to talk about mental health, although the term cannot be given a precise meaning. According to the charter of the World Health Organisation, 'health is a state of complete physical, mental, and social well-being and not merely the absence of disease or infirmity'. Whatever meaning one may attach to that definition, in practice it is the presence of illness that can be recognized, not the presence of health.

Some writers dispute the validity of the notion of mental illness. Szasz [113] regards mental illness as a myth based on faulty definitions, and Adams [3] maintains, 'there is no such thing as mental illness in any significantly meaningful sense'. Such extreme views are not generally accepted, but it must be recognized [69, 125] that many attempted definitions are unsatisfactory in so far as they denote little more than deviations from standards of conduct valued by society. Other definitions reflect a narrow theoretical standpoint; the psychoanalyst Jones [60] refers to the impairment of happiness by the triad of fear, hate, and guilt arising from the Oedipal situation, whilst the organicist Schneider [101] asserts 'psychic anomaly only comes into the illness category when it can be attributed to some organic disease process'. Several other 'models' of mental illness have been described [106] and not surprisingly it is difficult to find a suitable definition for research purposes [102].

These semantic problems are not just academic but are of practical importance in psychiatric epidemiology, which is concerned with the frequency with which definable forms of psychiatric disorder occur in carefully delineated populations. Clearly any attempt at enumeration depends on how 'cases' of mental illness are defined.

For the purpose of this paper, I shall not restrict the scope to mental illness in the formal sense of disorders such as organic dementia, schizophrenia, or manic-depressive psychosis. Rather I will encompass a wide range of maladaptive conditions, including 'functional psychoses, character disorders, destructive deviance from the societal norm, psychological malaise, and neurotic disturbances which may sap the purposes of men and make their lives an abomination' [66].

Crowded animals

Why study crowded animals? For practical and ethical reasons, only limited observations can be made of human behaviour under conditions of overcrowding. Studies of animals, both in their natural surroundings and under experimental conditions, are less restricted, and offer the advantage that variables can be systematically controlled. The drawback is that it may be hazardous to extrapolate from animal to human behaviour.

The behaviour of crowded animals. Animals crowded together in a limited space may develop striking anomalies of behaviour, particularly in their customary interrelationships. For example, extreme overcrowding of colonies of rats was found to interfere with the satisfaction of basic biological needs such as feeding, nest building, and the care of their young. Some of the male rats showed gross aberrations of social and sexual behaviour, and some even became cannibal towards their young [15].

The commonest behavioural change described amongst crowded animals is increased aggression. When animals such as domestic cats are crowded in a limited space, they 'seldom relax, they never look at ease, and there is continuous hissing, growling and even fighting' [71]. Amongst baboons, inter-group aggession was found to be low when population density was low, and much more prominent when density was high [30].

Hamburg [53] finds that three conditions are particularly associated with aggressive behaviour: overcrowding, meeting strangers, and the presence of valued resources such as food, sex, or nesting places. That threat and attack responses are more evident under these three conditions has been shown in field studies of many species of birds and rodents [76].

Studies of primates have also supported this view. In India, Lindburg [73] found that city-dwelling monkeys were far more aggressive than those living deep in the forest. The explanation was thought to be that city dwellers were crowded and competing fiercely with human beings for food, whilst forest dwellers had plentiful supplies. The effects of stranger contacts amongst rhesus monkeys in India were shown in a series of experiments by Southwick [110]. Amongst confined monkeys, aggressive interactions were much more frequent when strange animals were introduced into established groups. When the space in the compound was reduced by half, aggressive interactions again increased, but to a less extent than when strangers were introduced. In Tanzania, Goodall [50] found that the provision of bananas in a cleared area of forest led to a high frequency of aggressive interactions among chimpanzees and baboons. Here again, as in Southwick's study, it was found that high population density accentuated patterns of interaction that occurred to a less extent at lower densities [110, Chap. 1.1].

Similar findings have been reported by numerous other writers, including Kofford [63], Singh [107, 108], and Vandenbergh [118].

The biochemical and physiological reactions of crowded animals. Hamburg [53] suggests that the behavioural changes of crowded animals may be accompanied by 'physiological and biochemical concomitants that might, when repeated daily over years of the life-span, be injurious to health'.

In both the field and the laboratory, studies of small mammalian species have shown relationships between population density, behaviour, and endocrine function [22, 115]. It appears that, as population density increases to high levels, there is a considerable increase in the function of the adrenal glands, which play an essential role in an animal's response to stress, whether by fighting or taking flight. In several species this is associated with a remarkable increase in aggressive behaviour.

Some studies have been concerned with the toxicity of amphetamine, whose action is similar to that of adrenaline, the secretion of the medulla of the adrenal gland. A relatively small dose of amphetamine will prove fatal to rats or mice confined in a cage with many others, whereas an animal kept in isolation can survive much greater doses. It is presumed that repeated stressful interactions with other animals enhance the effect of the drug. Rodents can be protected against the effects of crowding by means of sedative drugs; on the other hand, under crowded situations, vulnerability to amphetamine may be increased by drugs that increase the excitability of the brain, such as mono-amine oxidase inhibitors.

Axlerod *et al.* [8] have studied the effects of population density on the enzymes involved in the biosynthesis of adrenaline and noradrenaline. The greater the degree of crowding, the greater the elevation of these enzymes found in the adrenal gland. According to Bliss and Ailion [12] crowding and stranger contact increase the turnover of the amines noradrenaline and serotonin in the brain of the rat.

In Hamburg's view [53] the experimental model that emerges is one bearing upon disorders of overstimulation characterized by a high sensory input, frequent agonistic encounters, and the use of drugs that stimulate the brain and sympathetic nervous system. He speculates, 'a conjunction of such conditions may, in the long term, increase susceptibility to various diseases'.

Relevance to man. Hamburg acknowledges that the present evidence does not permit us to answer directly whether the behavioural tendencies described above are present in our own species. However, he tentatively likens the situation of crowded animals to that of human beings in densely populated cities. He points out that big cities involve (1) vast numbers of persons, (2) mobility which relentlessly brings strangers into the city, and (3) the complexity of living which almost daily brings the individual into contact with many strangers, most of whom he will never meet again. Moreover, all this occurs in the presence of valued resources —places, activities, persons, everything from parking spaces to sexual partners.

But are the situations really comparable? The observations on animals confined in cages or compounds were instances of extreme conditions akin to those experienced by prisoners of war. A number of scientists [10, 25, 46] have reported hyper-irritability and anti-social behaviour in men penned up together in prison camps. In theory, people dwelling in crowded cities are free to escape from their surroundings, although it can be argued that in practice the 'culture of poverty' can induce a sense of despair of ever being able to escape [70].

The human situation, as I hope to show later, is complicated by many other social and cultural factors not found amongst lower animals. And it is worth noting that many species of birds and animals have evolved self-protective patterns of social behaviour whereby extremes of overstimulation are avoided, such as the 'peck order' or status hierarchy [72, 126].

It should be emphasized that the aberrant behaviour described in animals is not really the analogue of human mental illness, but rather of irritability or aggressiveness. There are frequent journalistic reports, but not much scientific evidence, that city life is characterized by high levels of irritability and frustration. Experiments by social psychologists have shown that, compared with people living in small and less densely populated towns, the inhabitants of large, densely populated cities are more likely to destroy other people's property in public [127] and less likely to oblige themselves to strangers [5, 74]. Such anti-social proclivities can scarcely be equated with mental illness.

The physiological and biochemical studies on animals are of theoretical interest in so far as similar changes may occur in human beings during agonistic encounters. For example, with human subjects taking part in stressful interviews, the degree of anger elicited was directly related to plasma cortisol concentrations [90]. But it has not been established that urban life is made up of a series of agonistic encounters associated with chronic suprarenal stimulation. Even if such overstimulation does occur, there is no evidence that it has anything to do with mental illness.

Observations of crowded animals are interesting and important, but it is a far cry from the behaviour of crowded animals to the mental illnesses of crowded men.

The historical perspective

The Industrial Revolution occurred in a moment of evolutionary time. In industrialized countries, human populations rapidly became urbanized; over a few generations, the proportion of people living in urban settlements rose from a tiny fraction to a very large one [29]. Drastic changes occurred in man's environment, with little time for changes in his customs or his biological equipment. It is sometimes said that man, hard pressed to adapt effectively to these new conditions, has become more and more vulnerable to mental illness.

In the nineteenth century, a few psychiatrists endeavoured, with the help of institutional statistics, to examine the vexed question of the alleged increase in mental disorder, and its supposed connection with the artificial life of urbanized society. Esquirol [39] compared the numbers of the insane in Paris in 1786 and 1836, and Maudsley [78] studied the apparent increase in England between 1840 and 1870, concluding that it did not correspond to a real trend.

These early psychiatrists realized that mental-hospital admission rates reflect not only the true prevalence of mental illness in a geographical area but also a wide variety of social factors which influence referral and admission to hospital. This is equally true today, when mental-hospital admission rates are influenced by a network of factors such as the availability of inpatient beds, out-patient facilities, and alternative services; the geographical situation of the hospital; the reputation of the hospital; the legal code relating to insanity and commitment; community attitudes towards mental illness and care; and the attitudes of doctors. Clearly, when the basic data are contaminated by so many uncontrolled variables, any attempt to chart rates of mental illness over time must be of low scientific validity. Yet all the available evidence points in the same direction.

If we take first the major psychoses, severe mental illnesses such as schizophrenia, we find that their incidence has remained constant over the past century. Goldhammer and Marshall [49] attempted to establish 'acceptable estimates of age-specific first admission rates to institutions caring for the mentally ill in Massachusetts for the years 1840–1855', in order to compare them with contemporary rates. The records available were reasonably good, and it was possible to enumerate cases which seemed to represent definite psychoses, even though the nomenclature has since changed. The authors concluded, 'there has been no long term increase during the past century in the incidence of the psychoses of early and middle life'...

Pugh and McMahon [92], drawing information from all areas of the U.S.A., confirmed that there was little long-term change in admission rates for psychoses during the first half of this century. Klaf and Hamilton [62] compared schizophrenia 100 years ago and today, and concluded that social change was more likely to modify the clinical manifestations than the frequency of psychosis. Wing [122, 123] found that rates of hospitalized psychosis were relatively similar among Western nations and did not appear to vary greatly from one period to another. In the armed forces, there is impressive consistency in the rates of psychoses requiring hospital care [51]. The rates have not varied much from peace to war, nor during the two World Wars. There is no evidence that psychosis rates significantly increase in civilian populations exposed to bombing attacks or to other major stresses [59]. Indeed, there is no evidence that urban life and the accelerated pace of modern life affect rates of psychotic breakdown [44, 84].

It is often said that the minor forms of mental illness, such as the neuroses, are the hallmark of the twentieth century. In recent years there have been surveys designed to measure as far as possible total mental illness, treated and untreated, in the community. Most of the surveys which have made a serious attempt to include the neuroses in case-enumeration have yielded high rates of psychiatric disorder though varying widely according to the population surveyed and the technique employed [67, 68, 89, 105]. When these various surveys are pooled, 'the evidence points to the presence in all communities of a large group of mentally sick or emotionally disturbed persons, amounting to between a tenth and a fifth of the total population' [105].

Yet there is no evidence of any increase in the prevalence of neuroses over the past century. It may be that these minor forms of psychiatric illness have changed, not in their true prevalence, but only in their 'visibility'. Such a change in the conspicuousness of neuroses could be associated with various factors, particularly the vast reduction in infectious diseases calling for medical attention. 'Once the killing diseases and the threat of starvation have been averted, people become increasingly aware of, and discontented with, minor forms of unhappiness' [19].

In short, there is no evidence of increasing frequency of major or minor mental illnesses concomitant with the increasing complexity of twentieth-century life. Safe in this knowledge, it is intriguing to ask what would be the significance if such an increase were demonstrable. Suppose an ideal epidemiological inquiry had been possible; that a series of comparable community surveys of psychiatric morbidity had been done, first among the village dwellers of England before the Industrial Revolution, and then at intervals amongst the urban settlers after the Revolution. Suppose further that mental illness rates increased steadily over time. What inferences could be drawn? It would not be justifiable to attribute an increasing prevalence of mental illness to population increase. Changes would have occurred in a vast nexus of inter-related variables, such as diet, physical health, pollution, use of leisure, and so forth, and no factor could be singled out as uniquely influential.

Ecological studies

Let us turn now from the time perspective to look at mental illness in different geographical settings. A logical starting-point is to ask whether mental illness rates are higher in large, densely populated towns than in sparsely populated rural areas.

Mental illness in town and country. If one considers the true prevalence of mental disorders in the community, as distinct from referral to psychiatric services, there are no studies permitting direct comparison between town and country. Shepherd *et al.* [105] have collated psychosis rates from a number of epidemiological surveys in rural areas of the U.S.A., Japan, Denmark, Germany, and Sweden, and in urban areas of the U.S.A., Japan, and England. There is a considerable range of variation in the findings, but these discrepancies may be largely explained by the different methods of case-finding and classification employed.

If psychiatric referral rates are taken as indices of morbidity—which, as already shown, is an unreliable procedure—the findings may be anomalous [9]. In parts of Scotland, the crude over-all referral rates suggest that mental illness may be twice as common in the town as in the country. On closer scrutiny, the excess is found to be made up almost entirely of outpatients, which may simply mean that outpatient services are more accessible to town dwellers. If inpatient figures alone are considered, the rates are sometimes higher in rural areas; but this may mean that country dwellers can best obtain psychiatric treatment by entering hospital. Clearly differences between town and country in referral rates may be an artefact reflecting, amongst other things, the differential availability of services. This notion is supported by the finding that, in country areas which are well supplied with outpatient and inpatient facilities, total psychiatric referral rates are much the same as in large towns [9].

I have laboured this theme in order to emphasize the great difficulties of method which beset any attempt to study relationships between mental health and population characteristics. The point can be further illustrated by considering the hypothesis that a change from a rural to an urban way of life may cause some forms of mental illness. This could be described in terms of a move from agricultural to industrial employment, which is a relatively objective index. But the difficulty of defining relevant variables for investigation soon becomes apparent—'increasing affluence and changes in pattern of life go hand in hand with rising social and geographical mobility, a move into urban environments with less cohesion than rural ones, and a decline in the strength of traditional and religious supports. Economic advancement may bring increased monotony and boredom' [109]. The lack of tools for evaluating sociological variables of this kind is a major handicap in research.

It is, of course, popularly held that the simple rustic life is more conducive to mental health than the supposedly artificial and stressful life of the large town or city. But there is no research evidence to support this notion. Furthermore, there seems to be no bucolic community that is free from mental illness. The well-known survey of the Hutterite communities provides an example. The Hutterites are an exceptionally close-knit group of German descent who lived in Russia and migrated to the North-American Middle West about 1870. They are a fundamentalist religious sect who live in strict isolation, leading a simple agricultural life, characterized by communal ownership of property and renunciation of the mass media. It was originally supposed that the Hutterites as a group were totally free from mental illness. But the investigators Eaton and Weil [35] found that the over-all prevalence rate for mental disorder amongst the Hutterites was much the same as in urban areas. However, the distribution of types of mental illness was quite different from that of other areas in North America. There was no evidence of any kind of anti-social disorder, but depressive illnesses were strikingly common.

Mental illness in the big cities. There is some evidence that various types of pathology, such as delinquency, narcotic addiction, suicide, and possibly more formal mental illnesses accumulate in crowded areas of big cities. However, it has not been demonstrated that population density in itself is an important determinant of this increased pathology. Here again, the fundamental problem of method is to disentangle the vast number of variables that might interact. Not surprisingly, there are as yet no published epidemiological studies of mental illness which focus on population density whilst correcting for other variables.

Delinquency; narcotic addiction. It is widely recognized that delinquency is most frequent in crowded and deteriorated areas of cities. In Chicago, Shaw's classic survey showed an unequal distribution of delinquency in different districts, and identified characteristics of highly delinquent neighbourhoods [104]. Similar studies have been carried out in San Francisco [36], Philadelphia [100], Liverpool [79], Croydon [83], and London [121]. Such studies show that the majority of delinquent areas can be mapped out with some precision. Areas of high delinquency, apart from their overcrowding, are usually characterized by poor housing, low rents, and few owner-occupiers, and are usually associated with high rates of infant mortality, tuberculosis, alcoholism, and suicide.

Rates of narcotic addiction are difficult to establish accurately because many cases remain unidentified. It is clear, however, that in the U.S.A. narcotic addition is heavily concentrated in the crowded and deteriorated areas of big cities [13, 14, 87, 88].

Suicidal behaviour. Since Durkheim's epoch-making investigation of 1887, there has probably been more intensive study of the demographic and social correlates of suicidal behaviour than of any other psychiatric phenomenon. Durkheim [34] believed that suicide rates reflected patterns of social relationships within communities and had little to do with individual mental illness. Unfortunately, he overlooked many of the pitfalls of this type of inquiry. In particular, he was too ready to make inferences from statistical correlations to causes, he made little attempt to disentangle causes from consequences, and he was unaware of the complex ramifications of the sociological variables he was investigating.

Nowadays, a distinction is made between suicide and attempted suicide, which differ in many ways, although both are associated with population density. For research purposes, it is an advantage that suicide rates are recorded nationally, though it is widely accepted that under-reporting occurs for various reasons [112].

Rates for successful suicide are highest in densely populated areas of cities. A precise association between suicide and population density has been reported by Capstick [17] and Dublin [33]. It appears that there are two peaks in suicide rates; a low peak is associated with low population density, and a much higher peak with high density. It has been reported that suicide rates are highest in areas where many people live in social isolation, bereft of the support of family or other primary group [97, 112].

Suicide is thus an outstanding example of a psychiatric phenomenon to which population density and various disturbances of
social relationships appear to make a contribution. However,
amongst the causes of suicide, the relative importance of these
factors, and of mental illness, physical illness, and personality
remain to be determined.

In the same way, there can be no simple formulation of the ante-
cedents of attempted suicide. The determinants are exceedingly
complex, involving factors in the individual and his environment,
and the interaction between them. This is well summarized by
Professor Carstairs [19].

Studies of attempted suicide have shown that the most important social
correlate is overcrowding. Typically, the person who makes a non-fatal
suicidal gesture has been harassed beyond endurance by recurrent
friction within the domestic group, in cramped and overcrowded
premises. Here one can see the mutual reinforcement of multiple factors.
A majority of those who attempt suicide are relatively young men and
women, who often have had a bad start with unstable or absent parent-
figures. These patients tend to experience great difficulty in their turn,
in forming stable interpersonal relationships: they are often at the same
time demanding and inconsiderate towards others, and yet themselves
emotionally immature and dependent. Their deficiences prompt them
to seek out partners from whom they hope to derive support, but all
too often the partner whom they select is handicapped in much the
same way; so far from meeting each other's dependency needs, these
unfortunates only succeed in making each other's state worse than before. Often too, they turn to drink or drugs to allay their need for
dependence and this in turn further impoverishes their ability to form
rewarding personal relationships.

Mental illness. There are several well-known ecological studies
of the distribution of mental illnesses within the different neighbourhoods of individual cities and large towns. Often these
inquiries have been conducted with painstaking and systematic
attention to detail, and yet the methodological difficulties of case-
finding and diagnosis have been so great as to allow only tentative
conclusions.

The classical prototype study was that of Faris and Dunham [41]
in Chicago (1939). Great differences were found in the patterns of
mental-hospital admission rates for psychoses in the various
census tracts of the city. Rates were highest in the deteriorated slum
areas of the city centre, where many rootless people were to be

found. Rates declined towards the periphery; indeed, the dweller in the crowded city centre was fifteen times more likely to be admitted to a mental hospital than somebody living on the outskirts.

A more modern study in Mannheim [52] is yielding similar findings. Preliminary results show that rates of first utilization of hospitals for schizophrenia are highest in central areas of the city characterized by a low standard of housing and social disorganization.

As already mentioned, in interpreting these findings it should be borne in mind that the accumulation of mental illness is usually greatest in neighbourhoods characterized by 'adverse' socio-economic indices. For example, in a recent inquiry in North London, Mezey and Evans [80] studied the association between mental-hospital admission rates and various demographic and socio-economic factors in three adjacent boroughs. Significantly higher rates were found in the borough which had the highest percentage of the elderly, of the single and previously married, of low socio-economic groups, of people born outside the United Kingdom, of one-person households, and of poor housing conditions.

Different studies have focused attention on one or other of these sociological factors. The classical inquiry of Hollingshead and Redlich [56, 57] in New Haven, Connecticut, revealed a great predominance of identified mental illness (particularly the psychoses) in the lowest of five socio-economic classes. This study has been criticized on a number of grounds; for instance Mishler and Scotch [81] reject the findings as reflecting class bias in interviewing, in diagnosis, and in hospital admission and discharge patterns.

In Stirling County, Leighton *et al.* [67] reported a striking increase in the risk of mental disorder in communities that were classified by them as socio-culturally 'disintegrated'. It was postulated that a sense of 'psychological anomie', or alienation, was characteristic of the inhabitants of these areas and affected their mental health adversely.

Several studies have emphasized the role of social isolation in the causation of mental illness (e.g. [41]). It is suggested that, paradoxically, it is not intensity of social contact, but rather loneliness, that conduces to mental illness and suicide in big cities. In Hare's study of mental-hospital first admission rates in Bristol

[54], the highest rates for schizophrenia were in the city centre. It seemed that population density alone was not a major factor; nor was good or bad housing, as judged by rateable value. But living alone did seem to be associated with risk of illness. Hare did not conclude that social isolation was a causal factor; on the whole he thought it was more likely to result from the tendency of certain personalities to segregate themselves. A similar view was taken by Kohn and Clausen [64] and by Gerard and Houston [45] in Worcester, Massachusetts.

Migration. Another factor highlighted by ecological studies is migration. It has been frequently reported that city neighbourhoods with high rates of mental illness contain excessive proportions of migrants. Does migration carry an increased risk of mental illness?

Ødegaard emphasized the difference between emigration and internal migration. In Norway, first admission rates were significantly lower for those moving into other areas within their own countries than those who remained where they were born [7]. Particularly low rates were associated with short-distance migration, except for migration to the capital, where migrants were found to have higher rates than the city born. It was thought that 'Internal migration is less final and irrevocable than emigration. . . . Often it is a natural and well-prepared step in the progress of a young person who has acquired some special training.'

Early studies of emigration appeared to show that rates of mental illness amongst immigrants were far higher than amongst the indigenous population. In his classical study of Norwegian immigrants to the U.S.A., Ødegaard [86] attributed this finding to a selective process, that is, a special tendency of the unstable to emigrate. Some writers have emphasized rapid socio-cultural change as a determinant of increased mental illness. In a study of immigrants to the U.S.A., Srole [111] concluded that a decisive factor is not transplantation to the American metropolis as such, but rather the jump into the metropolis from a particular kind of overseas milieu—namely from the lowest socio-economic reaches in farm, village, or small towns. Srole suggested that 'to span and compress the profound socio-economic revolutions of the last 150 years within the adult years of a single life cycle would appear to exact a considerable price in psychological well-being'.

In a careful review, Murphy [84] cast doubt on the supposed association between emigration and increased risk of mental illness. As more sophisticated studies were undertaken and it became possible to control for such related variables as age, social class, employment level, and ethnic status, the observed differences diminished until, 'Today the relationship has become quite doubtful, and its meaning equally so' [84].

The problem is complex, involving such factors as the reasons leading to migration, the selection procedures enforced by the host country, and the kind of adaptation required of immigrant groups. It is perhaps not surprising that the highest rates of mental disorder have been reported in refugees and displaced persons [37, 91].

The drift hypothesis. From the foregoing comments on social isolation and migration, I would like to extract a principle that bears on any analysis of the relationship between mental illness and population characteristics, namely, that correlation does not imply causation. This is illustrated by the so-called 'drift versus breeder' controversy in social psychiatry.

If it is the case that high rates of mental illness are associated with overcrowded slum conditions, are we to infer that adverse environmental factors play a part in the causation of such illness (breeder)? Or is it that those who are disposed to mental illness move into these deteriorated neighbourhoods (drift)? Arguments for and against these alternative explanations have been many. Faris and Dunham [41] repudiated the drift hypothesis; so did Hollingshead and Redlich [56], on the grounds that psychiatric patients of high socio-economic status had always lived in 'good' areas, whilst those of low status had always lived in the slums. Morris [82], and Goldberg and Morrison [48] found that the parents of young schizophrenics did not differ in social class from the rest of the population; these authors thought that the process of schizophrenia in the patients led to occupational failure and social decline. With the development of more sophisticated statistical techniques, evidence is accumulating that the drift phenomenon does play a significant part [11].

The moral is to avoid the pitfall of confounding social vicissitudes arising from pre-morbid personality traits and early psychotic symptoms, with the causes of mental illness.

Rehousing and mental health. So far I have been discussing the mental health of people living in crowded and deteriorated areas of big cities. The question arises, what happens if, as a result of programmes of urban renewal, people move out of these areas into new housing estates? This is difficult to evaluate, but there is some research evidence that rehousing may not solve all the problems and may bring problems of its own.

Martin *et al.* [77] reported an increased prevalence of psychiatric disorder in the population of a new housing estate as indicated by utilization of psychiatric outpatient services, mental hospital admissions, and the findings of a personal interview survey.

Hare and Shaw [55] compared mental health in two districts of Croydon, a new housing estate on the outskirts and an old, poor, densely populated district at the centre. Measures of psychiatric status, social factors, personality, and physical health were evaluated. No differences were recorded in neurosis rates for the two areas, and the authors concluded that the amount of ascertained psychiatric illness was unaffected by residence in a new housing development.

Taylor and Chave's investigation [114] was in the different setting of a new town where attention had been given to community developments. This town was compared with an L.C.C. housing estate, a decaying London borough, and the national figures. Prevalence was gauged in terms of outpatients, inpatients, cases diagnosed by G.P.s, and those detected by household interviewing. There was no less neurosis in the new town nor any smaller incidence of 'sub-clinical' neurosis

Impressive evidence of the emotional impact of rehousing is afforded by Fried's study of 789 Boston slum-dwellers whose homes were demolished in an urban renewal programme [43]. They were interviewed before, and 2 years after, compulsory rehousing took place. It was found that half of them experienced a severe grief reaction which was manifest in feelings of painful loss, continued longing, general depressive tone, frequent symptoms of psychological or somatic distress, a sense of helplessness, expressions of both direct and displaced anger, and tendencies to idealize the lost place. Feelings of anger were expressed as denigration of the new environment by contrast with the idealized memory of the old. Many of the respondents expressed feelings of personal mutilation in a vivid way.

Fried emphasizes that the grief expressed by the majority of his respondents might not be found among other populations in other places undergoing other experiences of rehousing.

Urban life and the stress hypothesis

Technological developments. Apart from sociological factors of the kind reviewed above, it has been suggested that urban life is associated with technological developments which may conduce to mental illness [18]. There is little scientific evidence to support this notion, though there are some indications that various sources of excessive noise may be inimical to mental health.

According to McKennell and Hunt [75], the most distressing sources of noise to people living in a city like London are road traffic, building sites, street repairs, and aircraft. Susceptibility to such noise, they suggest, may be related to personality factors. Noise may affect proficiency at work, and town dwellers may suffer a more marked hearing loss with age than country dwellers [6]. Noise may be an important hazard to public health [128]. Davis [28] reported a high risk of breakdown in aircraft carrier crews exposed to the extreme noise levels of nearby jet planes.

A recent report suggested that excessive environmental noise may influence mental-hospital admission rates [1, 2]. A detailed demographic study was made of the relationship between admission rates and noise levels in the vicinity of Heathrow airport, taking into account other variables such as socio-economic status, migration and density rates, and admission policies. A significantly higher admission rate was found from the maximum noise area than from outside this area.

Whilst this is a suggestive finding, it should not be inferred that noise is a 'cause' of mental illness. The likelihood is that certain people, such as anxious neurotics, are specially vulnerable to excessively powerful, repetitive auditory stimulation such as that from frequent, low-flying aircraft, whilst the psychiatrically healthy are not at risk in this way [65].

The stress hypothesis. In the context of mental illness, much confusion has arisen from the lack of any clear definition of the term 'stress'. To mention but one ambiguity, the word is sometimes applied to environmental events, and sometimes to an organism's response to such events. Lazarus [66] has analysed the stress concept in great detail, emphasizing that it has physiological, sociological, and psychological referents.

Vickers [119] distinguishes three kinds of variables:

(1) the environmental situation ('stress situation'),
(2) the physiological and psychological changes which it engenders in the individual ('stress change');
(3) the behaviour consequent upon these changes ('stress behaviour').

The first two kinds of variable call for further elucidation.

The stress situation. Levi and his co-workers have described in some detail the possible role of 'urban conglomerates as psychosocial stressors' [18]. They maintain that urban life may present a great number of potent stressors including the urbanization process, the industrialization process and the urban environment— settlement density, population density, urban structure and internal differentiation, design of supply systems, etc. It is held that factors of this kind may conduce to mental illness.

This view sounds plausible, at least *prima facie*. The layman would probably accept unquestioningly that environmental conditions may subject the psyche to wear and tear, and so lead to mental illness. It is open to the scientist to doubt it. The difficulty is that it is exceedingly difficult to evaluate psycho-social stressors of the kind postulated. A given stimulus may be regarded as a stressor in one society and not in another; or it may be a stressor to one subject and not to another. Furthermore, the effects of a stressor on an individual may vary from time to time.

It is generally accepted that some extreme experiences may result in psychiatric disturbance in a large proportion of people exposed to them. In wartime it has been clearly shown that the risk of neurotic breakdown is particularly great in those exposed to injury in combat [26, 40, 47, 94, 98, 99, 124]. Various chronic psychiatric disorders are common sequelae of the extreme experience of confinement in a concentration camp [21, 38]. There was a high incidence of psychiatric breakdown amongst large numbers of people involved in the disastrous fire at the Coconut Grove Nightclub in Boston in which nearly 500 people lost their lives [4, 24] and in other civilian disasters [116, 117].

That less catastrophic life-events may give rise to mental illness, emerged from research at the University of Washington, Seattle [58, 93]. In an attempt to quantify changes in life-patterns, the research workers devised a scale made up of events concerned with occupation, residence, finance, recreations, religion, and family relationships—all events which were thought likely to impinge on an individual's 'steady state'. There was a high degree of consensus among respondents as to the relative impact of these events. An intensive study of men in the U.S. Navy showed that those who had the highest score for life-crises developed more illnesses of all kinds. That is, there appeared to be a greater risk of developing mental and physical illness following a period of psycho-social stress than following an uneventful period.

Whilst a method of this kind can be used to show a significant statistical correlation between 'degree of life change' and subsequent health change, it is difficult to see how psycho-social stressors of the kind postulated by Levi could be analysed in any comparable way. Few of the stressors said to be posed by urban conglomerates are in any sense quantifiable; they are exceedingly complex and difficult to isolate from one another.

Stress change. Carlestam and Levi [18], in their treatise on urban conglomerates as psycho-social stressors, speculate extensively about possible stress mechanisms, that is, physiological and psychological changes engendered in the organism. They invoke the well-known concept, derived from the work of Cannon [16] and Selye [103], of stress as a response preparing the organism for fight or flight. They hold that psycho-social stimuli inherent in urbanization and urban life may affect neuro-endocrine function, particularly the hypothalamo-adrenomedullary and hypophyseal-adrenocortical axes, with increased secretion of adrenaline, noradrenaline, corticosteroids, and thyroxine. Such physiological changes could, they postulate, lead to precursors of disease and to disease itself, but they acknowledge, 'We don't know under what circumstances they do so or even if they actually do so.'

Some of the physiological mechanisms cited have been studied in human subjects under systematically controlled laboratory conditions [42]. Levels of circulating adrenaline and noradrenaline were measured under conditions of overstimulation (high sensory input), understimulation (sensory deprivation, monotony), conflict, and anticipation of unpleasant experience. Consistent relationships were found between adrenal output, behavioural efficiency, and emotional reactions. Interesting as these experiments are, it is questionable how far stress situations typical of life in modern urban society may be realistically simulated in the laboratory.

Carlestam and Levi [18] further develop their theme by suggesting that the relationship between psycho-socially mediated physiological changes and disease may be greatly modified by 'predisposing or protective intervening variables', which may be psycho-social factors, constitutional factors, or mental processes. They speculate that 'the generalisation seems justified that rapid urbanization and life in the crowded slums of the largest cities does in fact comprise an increase of predisposing and a decrease of protective intervening variables as compared to rural life'. However, the authors acknowledge that this has to be taken on trust, because it is difficult or even impossible to present any statistical proof.

Summing up the hypothesis that diseases may be 'psycho-socially induced', Carlestam and Levi [18] conclude 'processes of this kind have been claimed to constitute a major factor in the causation of several diseases in the fields of psychiatry and internal medicine. Reviewing the literature in this field we find a state of suspicion, but no proof.'

In recent years the pathogenic concept of stress has attracted the attention of many clinical and experimental investigators, most of whom have been preoccupied with the intervening variable of stress change. Yet, as Kagan [61] pointed out at a recent International Congress, the pathogenic mechanism has yet to be discovered. It may be a blood-pressure rise, or pulse-rate increase, or increased adrenaline secretion; 'any of these may be in somebody's opinion a mechanism that leads to disease. But until we have shown that it is a cause of disease, we cannot say so. It might even be a cause of good health' [61]. In the context of mental illness, these remarks certainly hold.

This raises the question as to whether preoccupation with mechanisms is likely to be a fruitful research strategy in the long run. It is arguable that the need is rather for more intensive and systematic epidemiological research aimed at establishing relationships between 'stress situations' and 'stress behaviour'. Unfortunately, in the case of urbanization and the urban environment, stress situations are exceedingly difficult to disentangle.

Family size and psychological adjustment

This paper has been mainly concerned with mental health in relation to population density and urbanization. If one looks at mental health from a different perspective, that of family size, there is rather more statistical evidence, particularly in relation to the educational, emotional, and behavioural adjustment of children.

Most of the evidence comes from three major studies, two longitudinal and one cross-sectional. The two longitudinal studies are those of the National Survey cohort of children born in 1946 [31, 32], and of the National Bureau of Child Development cohort born in 1958 [27]. The cross-sectional. study is that of 10- and 11-year-old children in the Isle of Wight [96].

In all three studies, large sibship size was shown to be a handicap affecting children's achievement in school. Verbal abilities, particularly reading skills, were most affected, but impairment of mathematical abilities was also reported. Douglas [31] showed an association between large sibship and general educational retardation, whilst an association with specific reading retardation emerged in the Isle of Wight study. These associations still held when social class was controlled.

It appears that the determinants of these impairments, particularly of verbal skills, in children from large families are environmental and not genetic [95]. The damage is almost certainly done in the early pre-school years when the children are acquiring language. It is suggested that less intensive interaction with an adult during this period leads to poor acquisition of verbal skills. It also seems that parents of large families take less interest in the school progress of their children.

More severe forms of intellectual retardation causing the child to be 'unable to benefit' from normal state education are more frequent in large families. In the Isle of Wight survey, more than half of the mothers of retarded children had 4 or more children, as against only a third of the mothers of control children.

The techniques used by Rutter in analysing his data enabled individual factors to be isolated. When social class, sex, and geographical location were kept constant, children from a family with just 1 or 2 children had a 12-month reading gain over children from sibships of 5 or more. When the effects of over-crowding (number of persons per room) and of lack of household amenities were separately isolated, the number of children in the family still appeared to be the most critical factor.

When emotional adjustment was examined, children from large families were found to be less well adjusted in Rutter's study, but the effects of social class and sex were more potent. In the Isle of Wight, children with anti-social disorders were more likely to come from large families, whilst those with neurotic disorders were more associated with small families. Anti-social poor readers were particularly likely to come from large families.

Many children from large families undoubtedly suffer during their school years and may, by coming into care, be a major liability on the state [23].

Conclusions

This paper opened with a question about the possible consequences for mental health of further increases in population. Evidence of various kinds has been presented—observations of crowded animals and historical and epidemiological studies of mental illness in man—and throughout the emphasis has been on the enormous methodological difficulties inherent in studying the problem. This is because of the great number and extreme complexity of the demographic, sociological, and psychiatric variables that might be relevant; variables which are very difficult to isolate and measure.

The available evidence does not permit us to draw any firm general conclusions about possible relationships between mental health and population density. Epidemiological studies suggest the possibility that overcrowding may be associated with increased risk of mental illness, but there may be many other factors, such as socio-economic conditions, equally or more important.

There are no research findings that indicate an optimum population size or density for the maintenance of mental health. Some writers [120] forecast that population growth in the future may lead to a mass epidemic of mental illness of cataclysmic proportions. This prophecy may yet be fulfilled, but to the best of my knowledge there is little or no scientific justification for such a gloomy prognosis. I am not advocating apathy or complacency about mental health in the future; I am simply saying that there is as yet no demonstrable relationship between the mental health of a population and its size and density.

It is unlikely that hard data about these issues will be available until considerable advances are made in methods of epidemiological research in psychiatry. The requirement is for better methods of case identification, classification, and measurement. In recent years some progress has been made; for example, the development of a standard form of psychiatric examination for research purposes [122] and the setting-up of case-registers whereby data from many different agencies can be pooled.

Meanwhile, it seems indisputable that mental illnesses are widespread in the community at the present time. Norris [85], studying admission rates to mental hospitals in England and Wales, concluded 'one out of every twenty babies born is likely to require hospital treatment for a mental disorder'. In a large survey of more than fifty general practices in London, it was found that one in every seven registered patients consulted the family doctor because of a psychiatric problem [105]. Morbidity on such a scale presents many problems in relation to provision of medical care, not the least being the question as to how our limited resources are best deployed.

There is one aspect of the provision of medical services that is causing increasing concern in some quarters. It seems that in the future the delivery of care is going to be organized on the basis of ever-increasing aggregates of patients. Health Boards will be responsible for larger populations; there is a trend towards large district general hospitals and to health clinics staffed by as many as twenty general practitioners and serving up to 100 000 patients. This process of grouping into larger service units clearly brings certain advantages, notably in providing advanced technological facilities. But it also carries the risk that the practice of medicine will become dehumanized. It is hardly necessary to emphasize that, in the treatment of both psychiatric and non-psychiatric patients, the personal relationship with the doctor is a vital element. It is to be hoped that medicine, as it advances administratively and technologically, will not lose the personal touch.

operating on populations 279

REFERENCES

1. ABEY-WIKRAMA, J., A'BROOK, M.F., GATTONI, F.E.G., and HERRIDGE, C. F. (1969). Mental-hospital admissions and aircraft noise, *Lancet* **ii**, 1275–7.
2. —— —— —— —— (1970). Mental-hospital admissions and aircraft noise, *Lancet* **i**, 467–8.
3. ADAMS, H. B. (1964). Mental illness or interpersonal behaviour? *Am. Psychol.*, **19**, 191–7.
4. ADLER, A. (1943). Neuropsychiatric complications in victims of Boston's Cocoanut Grove disaster, *J. Am. med. Assoc.* **123**, 1098.
5. ALTMAN, D., LEVINE, M., NADIEN, M., and VILLENA, S. (1970). Unpublished research, summarized in MILGRIM, S. (1970). *Science* **167**, 1461–8.
6. Annotation (1969). London noises, *Lancet* **ii**, 1289.
7. ASTRUP, C. and ØDEGAARD, Ø. (1960). Internal migration and mental disease in Norway, *Psychiat. Quart.* **34**, Suppl. 116.
8. AXELROD, J., MUELLER, R. A., HENRY, J. P., and STEPHENS, P. M. (1970). *Effects of psychosocial stimulation on the enzymes involved in the biosynthesis and metabolism of noradrenalin and adrenalin.* Paper presented to American Psychosomatic Society, March 1970. Washington, D.C.
9. BALDWIN, J. A. (1971). *The mental hospital in the psychiatric service. A case-register study.* Oxford University Press, for the Nuffield Provincial Hospitals Trust, London.
10. BETTELHEIM, B. (1963). Individual and mass behaviour in extreme situations, *J. abnorm. soc. Psychol.* **58**, 417.
11. BIRCHNELL, J. (1971). Social class, parental social class, and social mobility in psychiatric patients and general population controls, *Int. Psychiat. Clin.* **8**, No. 3, 77–103.
12. BLISS, E. L. and AILION, J. (1969). Response of neurogenic amines to aggregation and strangers, *J. Pharmacol. exp. Therap.* **168**, 258–63.
13. BALL, J. C. (1965). Two patterns of narcotic drug addiction in the United States, *J. crim. law, Crimol. Police Sci.* **56**, 203–11.
14. —— and CHAMBERS, C. D. (eds.) (1970). *The epidemiology of opiate addiction in the United States.* Thomas, Springfield.
15. CALHOUN, J. B. (1963). Population density and social pathology. In *The urban condition*, (ed. L. J. Duhl). Basic Books, New York.
16. CANNON, W. B. (1932). *The wisdom of the body.* New York.
17. CAPSTICK, A. (1960). Urban and rural suicide, *J. ment. Sci.* **106**, 1327–36.
18. CARLESTAM, G. and LEVI, L. (1971). *Urban conglomerates as psychosocial human stressors. General aspects, Swedish trends, and psychological and medical implications.* Royal Ministry of Foreign Affairs, Royal Ministry of Agriculture, Sweden.
19. CARSTAIRS, G. M. (1969). Over-crowding and human aggression. In *The history of violence in America* (ed. H. D. Graham and T. R. Gurr), pp. 751–64. Praeger, New York.

20. CHEYNE, G. (1733). *The English malady: or a treatise of nervous diseases of all kinds, as spleen, vapours, lowness of spirits, hypochondriacal and hysterical distempers, etc.* London.
21. CHODOFF, P. (1966). Effects of extreme coercive and oppressive forces (brainwashing and concentration camps). In *American handbook of psychiatry*, Vol. III. Basic Books, New York.
22. CHRISTIAN, J. and DAVIS, D. (1964). Endocrines, behaviour and population, *Science* **146**, 1550–60.
23. CLEGG, A. and MEGSON, B. (1968). *Children in distress*. Penguin Books, Harmondsworth.
24. COBB, S. and LINDEMANN, E. (1943). Neuropsychiatric observations. In Management of the Cocoanut Grove burns at the Massachusetts General Hospital, *Ann. Surg.* **117**, 814–24.
25. COCHRANE, A. L. (1946). Notes on the psychology of prisoners of war, *Br. med. J.* **i**, 282.
26. CRAIGIE, H. B. (1942). Physical treatment of acute war neurosis, *Br. med. J.* **2**, 675.
27. DAVIE, R., BUTLER, N. and GOLDSTEIN, H. (1972). *From birth to seven*. Longmans, London.
28. DAVIS, H. (1968). Cited in [128].
29. DAVIS, K. (1965). The urbanization of the human population. *Scient. Am.* **213**, 40–53.
30. DE VORE, I. and HALL, K. R. L. (1965). *Baboon ecology*, In *primate behaviour* (ed. I. De Vore). Holt, Rinehart and Winston, New York.
31. DOUGLAS, J. W. B. (1964). *The home and the school*. MacGibbon and Kee, New York.
32.—— ROSS, J. M., and SIMPSON, H. R. (1968). *All our future*. Peter Davies, New York.
33. DUBLIN, L. J. (1963). *Suicide. A sociological and statistical study*. Ronald Press Company, New York.
34. DURKHEIM, E. (1897). *Suicide* (trans. 1952). Routledge and Kegan Paul, London.
35. EATON, J. W. and WEIL, R. J. (1955). *Culture and mental disorders*. Free Press, New York.
36. EISNER, V. and TZUYEMARA, H. (1965). *Interactions of juveniles with the law*. Public Health Reports, Vol. 80. U.S. Department of H.E.W., Washington, D.C.
37. EITINGER, L. (1959). The incidence of mental disease among refugees in Norway, *J. ment. Sci.* **105**, 326.
38. —— (1971). Acute and chronic psychiatric and psychosomatic reactions in concentration camp survivors. In *Society, stress and disease* (ed. L. Levi), pp. 219–30. Oxford University Press, London.
39. ESQUIROL, E. (1838). *Des Maladies mentales*, Vol. 2, Paris.
40. FAIRBAIRN, W. R. D. (1943). The war neuroses: their nature and significance, *Br. med. J.*, **1**, 183.
41. FARIS, R. E. L. and DUNHAM, H. W. (1939). *Mental disorders in urban areas*. Chicago University Press, Chicago.

42. FRANKENHAEUSER, M. (1971). Experimental approaches to the study of human behaviour as related to neuroendocrine functions. In *Society, stress and disease* (ed. L. Levi), pp. 22–35. Oxford University Press, London.

43. FRIED, M. (1962). Grieving for a lost home. In *The environment of the metropolis* (ed. L. J. Duhl). Basic Books, New York.

44. —— (1964). Effects of social change on mental health, *Am. J. Orthopsychiat.* **34**, 3–28.

45. GERARD, D. L. and HOUSTON, L. G. (1953). Family setting and social ecology of schizophrenia, *Psychiat. Quart.* **27**, 90.

46. GIBBENS, T. C. N. (1947). *The psychology and psychopathology of the prisoner of war.* M.D. Thesis, University of London.

47. GILLESPIE, R. D. (1945). War neuroses after psychological trauma, *Br. med. J.* **1**, 653.

48. GOLDBERG, E. M. and MORRISON, S. L. (1963). Schizophrenia and social class, *Br. J. Psychiat.* **109**, 785–802.

49. GOLDHAMMER, H. and MARSHALL, A. Q. (1953). *Psychosis and civilization: two studies in the frequency of mental disease.* Free Press, New York.

50. GOODALL, J. V. L. (1968). *The behaviour of free-living chimpanzees in the Gombe Stream Reserve.* Animal Behaviour Monographs (eds. J. M. Cullen and G. G. Beer). Baillière, Tindall and Cassell, London.

51. GROUP FOR THE ADVANCEMENT OF PSYCHIATRY (1960). *Preventive psychiatry in the armed forces with some implications for civilian use.* Report No. 47, Topeka, Kansas.

52. HÄFNER, H. and REIMANN, H. (1970). Spatial distribution of mental disorders in Mannheim, 1965. In *Psychiatric epidemiology* (eds. E. H. Hare and J. K. Wing). Oxford University Press, for the Nuffield Provincial Hospitals Trust, London.

53. HAMBURG, D. A. (1971). Crowding, stranger contact, and aggressive behaviour. In *Society, stress and disease* (ed. L. Levi). Oxford University Press, London.

54. HARE, E. H. (1956). Mental illness and social conditions in Bristol, *J. ment. Sci.* **102**, 349.

55. —— and SHAW, G. (1965). *Mental health in a new housing estate.* Maudsley Monograph, No. 12. Oxford University Press, London·

56. HOLLINGSHEAD, A. B. and REDLICH, F. C. (1954). Social stratification and schizophrenia, *Am. sociol. Rev.* **19**, 302.

57. —— —— (1958). *Social class and mental illness: a community study.* Wiley, New York.

58. HOLMES, T. and RAHE, R. H. (1967). The social readjustment rating scale, *J. psychosom. Res.* **11**, 213–18.

59. JANIS, J. L. (1951). *Air war and emotional stress.* McGraw-Hill, New York.

60. JONES, E. (1948). The concept of a normal mind. In *Collected papers on psycho-analysis*, pp. 201–16. Baillière, Tindall, and Cox, London.

61. KAGAN, A. (1971). Epidemiology and society, stress and disease. In *Society, stress and disease* (ed. L. Levi). Oxford University Press, London.
62. KLAF, F. S. and HAMILTON, J. G. (1961). Schizophrenia—a hundred years ago and today, *J. ment. Sci.* **107**, 819–27.
63. KOFORD, C. B. (1965). Population dynamics of rhesus monkeys on Cayo Santiago. In *Primate behaviour* (ed. I. De Vore). Holt, Rinehart, and Winston, New York.
64. KOHN, M. L. and CLAUSEN, J. A. (1955). Social isolation and schizophrenia, *Am. sociol. Rev.* **20**, 265.
65. LADER, M. H. (1971). The responses of normal subjects and psychiatric patients to repetitive stimulation. In *Society, stress and disease* (ed. L. Levi). Oxford University Press, London.
66. LAZARUS, R. S. (1971). The concepts of stress and disease. In *Society, stress and disease* (ed. L. Levi), pp. 53–8. Oxford University Press, London.
67. LEIGHTON, A. H., et al. (1959–63). *Stirling County study of psychiatric disorder and sociocultural environment*, Vols. I–III. Basic Books, New York.
68. LEMKAU, P., TIETZE, C., and COOPER, M. (1943). Mental hygiene problems in an urban district, I, II, III, IV. *Ment. Hyg.* **25**, 624; **26**, 100; **26**, 275; and **27**, 279.
69. LEWIS, A. J. (1953). Health as a social concept. *Br. J. Sociol.* **4**, 109–24.
70. LEWIS, O. (1959). *Five Families: Mexican case studies in the culture of poverty*. Basic Books, New York.
71. LEYHAUSEN, P. (1965). The sane community—a density problem? *Discovery* September 1965.
72. —— (1965). The communal organisation of solitary mammals, *Sym. R. Soc.*, **14**, 249.
73. LINDBERG, D. (1969). *Observations of Rhesus Macaque in natural habitats*. Paper presented at Department of Psychiatry, Stanford University, California.
74. McKENNA, W. and MORGENTHAU, S. (1970). Unpublished research (Graduate Center, The City University of New York), summarized in MILGRIM, S. (1970). *Science*, **167**, 1461–8.
75. McKENNELL, A. C. and HUNT, E. A., (1966). *Noise annoyance in central London*. The Government Social Survey, H.M.S.O., London.
76. MARLER, P. and HAMILTON, W. J. (1966). *Mechanisms of animal behaviour*, John Wiley, New York.
77. MARTIN, F. M., BROTHERSTON, J. H. F., and CHAVE, S. P. W. (1957). Incidence of neurosis in a new housing estate, *Br. J. prev. soc. Med.* **11**, 196.
78. MAUDSLEY, H. (1872). Is insanity on the increase? *Br. med. J.* **i**, 36.
79. MAYS, J. B. (1954). *Growing up in the city*. Liverpool University Press, Liverpool.

80. MEZEY, A. G. and EVANS, E. (1970). Psychiatric admissions from North London related to demographic and ecological characteristics, *Br. J. Psychiat.* **117**, 187–93.
81. MISHLER, E. J. and SCOTCH, N. A. (1963). Sociocultural factors in the epidemiology of schizophrenia. *Internat. J. Psychiat.* **1**, 258–305.
82. MORRIS, J. N. (1959). Health and social class. *Lancet* **1**, 303.
83. MORRIS, T. (1957). *The criminal area: a study in social ecology.* Routledge and Kegan Paul, London.
84. MURPHY, H. B. M. (1961). Social change and mental Health. *Milbank memor. Fund Quart. Bull.* **39**, 385.
85. NORRIS, V. (1959). *Mental illness in London.* Oxford University Press, London.
86. ØDEGAARD, Ø. (1932). Emigration and insanity, *Acta psychiat. neurol. scand.* Suppl. 4.
87. O'DONNELL, J. A. (1969). *Narcotic addicts in Kentucky.* Department of H.E.W., Public Health Service. National Institute of Mental Health, Bethesda, Md.
88. —— and BALL, J. C. (eds.) (1966). *Narcotic addiction.* Harper and Row, New York.
89. PASAMANICK, B., ROBERTS, D. W., LEMKAU, P. W., and KRENGER, D. B. (1959). A survey of mental disease in an urban population: prevalence by race and income. In *Epidemiology of mental disorder* (ed. B. Pasamanick). Publ. No. 60 of the American Association for the Advancement of Science, Washington, D.C.
90. PERSKY, H., HAMBURG, D. A., BASOWITZ, H., GRINKER, R., SABSHIN, M., KORCHIN, S., HERZ, M., BOARD, F., and HEATH, H. (1958). Relation of emotional responses and changes in plasma hydrocortisone level after stressful interview, *Archs. Neurol. Psychiat. (Chic.)* **79**, 434–47.
91. PFISTER-AMMENDA, M. (1955). The symptomatology, treatment and prognosis in mentally ill refugees and repatriates in Switzerland. In *Flight and resettlement* (ed. H. B. M. Murphy). UNESCO, Paris.
92. PUGH, T. F. and McMAHON, B. (1962). *Epidemiological findings in United States mental hospital data.* Atlantic-Little, Brown, Ill.
93. RAHE, R. H. (1969). Life crisis and health change. In *Psychotropic drug response: advances in prediction* (eds. P. R. A. May and J. R. Wittenborn). Thomas, Springfield, Ill.
94. REID, D. D. (1948). Sickness and stress in operational flying, *Br. J. soc. Med.*, **2**, 123.
95. RUTTER, M. and MITTLER, P. (1972). Environmental influences on language development. In *Young children with delayed speech* (eds. M. Rutter and J. A. M. Martin). Heinemann, London.
96. —— TIZARD, J., and WHITMORE, K. (1970). *Education, health and Behaviour.* Longmans, London.
97. SAINSBURY, P. (1955). *Suicide in London.* Maudsley Monograph I. Institute of Psychiatry, de Crespigny Park, London, S.E.5.

98. SARGANT, W. and SLATER, E. (1940). Acute war neuroses, *Lancet* 2, 1.

99. ——and SHORVON, H. J. (1945). Acute war neurosis: special reference to Pavlov's experimental observations and the mechanism of abreaction, *Archs. Neurol. Psychiat. (Chic.)*, 54, 231.

100. SAVITZ, L. (1962). Delinquency and migration. In *The sociology of crime and delinquency* (ed. M. E. Wolfgang *et al.*). Wiley, New York.

101. SCHNEIDER, K. (1959). Classification of clinical material and definition of illness. In *Clinical psychopathology*, pp. 1–14. Grune and Stratton, New York.

102. SCOTT, W. A. (1958). Research definitions of mental health and mental illness, *Psychol. Bull.* 55, 29.

103. SELYE, H. (1956). *The stress of life.* McGraw-Hill Pbk., New York.

104. SHAW, C. R. and MCKAY, H. D. (1942). *Juvenile delinquency and urban areas.* Chicago University Press, Chicago.

105. SHEPHERD, M., COOPER, B., BROWN, A. C., and KALTON, G. W. (1966). *Psychiatric illness in general practice.* Oxford University Press, London.

106. SIEGLER, M. and OSMOND, H. (1966). Models of madness. *Br. J. Psychiat.* 112, 1193–203.

107. SINGH, S. D. (1966). The effects of human environment on the social behaviour of rhesus monkeys, *Primates* 7, 33–40.

108. —— (1969). Urban monkeys, *Scient. Am.* 221, 108–16.

109. SLATER, E. and ROTH, M. (1969). *Clinical psychiatry.* Baillière, Tindall, and Cox, London.

110. SOUTHWICK, C. H. (1969). Aggressive behaviour of rhesus monkeys in natural and captive groups. In *Aggressive behaviour* (ed. S. Garattini and E. B. Sigg). Excerpta medica, Amsterdam.

111. SROLE, L. (1963). Chapter on migration in *Population and mental health* (ed. H. P. David). Proceedings of 16th Annual Meeting of the World Federation for Mental Health.

112. STENGEL, E. (1964). *Suicide and attempted suicide.* Penguin Books, Harmondsworth.

113. SZASZ, T. S. (1961). *The myth of mental illness.* Harper and Row, New York.

114. TAYLOR, S. J. L. and CHAVE, S. (1964). *Mental health and environment.* Longmans, London.

115. THIESSEN, D. D. (1964). Population density and behaviour: a review of theoretical and physiological contributions, *Tex. Rep. biol. Med.* 22, 266–314.

116. TYHURST, J. S. (1951). Individual reactions to community disaster: the natural history of psychiatric phenomena., *Am. J. Psychiat.* 107, 764.

117. —— (1958). The role of transition states—including disasters—in mental illness. In *Symposium on preventive and social psychiatry.* Walter Reed Army Institute, Washington, D.C.

118. VANDENBERGH, J. G. (1967). Rhesus monkey bands, *Nat. Hist.*, *N.Y.* **71**, 22–7.

119. VICKERS, G. (1958). Congress on stress and mental illness. *Lancet* **1**, 205.

120. WAGGONER, R. W. and WAGGONER, R. W., Jnr. (1964). Population crisis and the psychiatrist, *Dis. Nerv. Syst.* **29**, 231–7.

121. WALLIS, C. P. and MALIPHANT, R. (1967). Delinquent areas in the County of London: ecological factors. *Br. J. Criminol.* **1**, 250–84.

122. WING, J. (1967). The modern management of schizophrenia. In *New aspects of the Mental Health Services* (eds. H. Freeman and J. Farndale). Pergamon, New York.

123. WING, J. K., BIRLEY, J. L. T., COOPER, J. E., GRAHAM, P., and ISAACS, A. D. (1967). Reliability of a procedure for measuring and classifying 'present psychiatric state', *Br. J. Psychiat.* **113**, 499–515.

124. WITTKOWER, E. and SPILLANE, J. P. (1940). A survey of the literature of neuroses in war. In *The neuroses in war* (ed. E. Miller) Macmillan, London.

125. WOOTTON, B. (1959). *Social science and social pathology*, pp. 203–226. Allen and Unwin, London.

126. WYNNE-EDWARDS, V. C. (1962). *Animal dispersion in relation to Social behaviour.* Oliver and Boyd, Edinburgh and London.

127. ZIMBARDO, P. G. (1969). The human choice: individuation, reason and order versus deindividuation, impulse and chaos. In *Nebraska Symposium on motivation* (ed. W. J. Arnold), pp. 237–307. University of Nebraska Press, Lincoln, Nebraska.

128. BURNS, W. (1968). *Noise and man.* Murray, London.

2.4.4. Housing environments and mental health

J. K. WING

Director, M.R.C. Social Psychiatry Unit, Professor of Social Psychiatry Institute of Psychiatry and London School of Hygiene

Introduction

J. N. Morris [18], giving 'four cheers for prevention', listed a number of areas in which progress had been made since the war towards the prevention of known diseases. One of the factors mentioned as important was the building of several million new houses. Certainly the most characteristic feature of the urban landscape is its houses, and it seems obvious that any evaluation of the future size and structure of the population, particularly in a country like Britain, should take into account the interplay between housing environment and mental health. This interplay will work in two directions. On the one hand, any degree of conscious or unconscious choice will lead to assortative mating between houses and their occupants; people will get the housing they want or that others think they deserve. On the other hand, the way living units are designed and arranged must be part of and must influence the satisfactions and dissatisfactions obtainable from everyday life. Is there, in fact, any evidence that this second kind of interplay has beneficial or deleterious effects on mental health?

Measuring the housing environment

Much of the work in this field has been based upon data readily available from the national censuses, many items of which have been found to be correlated with various indices of social deviance or psychopathology. Such social variables are clustered together. For example, people moving into new housing estates tend to be young and to have young children. They are at a stage of family development when financial burdens are greatest [32]. Their expectations of a housing environment must be different from those of groups with a different age-structure. A cluster analysis of London enumeration district data by the Centre of Urban Studies produced a six-fold classification as follows: upper-class, almost suburban, local authority housing, bedsitter, stable working class, and poor. These categories when applied to Camberwell in south-east London fitted very well with the visual impressions gained from driving round the area.

However, the most interesting clusters from a psychiatric point of view have been those concerned with low socio-economic status and with social isolation and disorganization. In the early American studies these were not distinguished separately because they tended to occur maximally in the same geographical areas at the centre of large cities such as Chicago. Thus Shaw and McKay [24] showed that delinquency rates were highest in the central urban areas, and Faris and Dunham [8] came to similar conclusions using admission rates to mental hospitals, particularly for schizophrenia. This geographical contiguity is not essential, however, and in Bristol [11] and London [21, 26, 31] it can be seen that it is the areas characterized by social isolation and disorganization (as shown by the proportion of foreign-born, daily movement in and out of the district, proportion of short-term residents, proportion of single-person dwellings and boarding houses, divorce rates, etc.) which tend to have the high suicide and first-admission rates. Areas characterized by low socio-economic status but not by social isolation (such as the London borough of Southwark) tend to have low first-admission rates but high delinquency rates.

As Dr. Gath has described in his contribution, there is considerable question as to how far the social environment of the area causes conditions like schizophrenia to arise and how far the high rates are due to the movement of predisposed individuals attracted by the anonymity of the socially isolated areas [7, 11]. How far then does the housing environment make any independent contribution, and how far does it simply reflect and confirm a social status conferred by other and more fundamental forces? Perhaps the more common neurotic conditions are affected by environmental circumstances in a way which schizophrenia, at least from the epidemiological evidence, is not. The popular sentiment that a living unit should be a 'home', i.e., it should confer a sense of belonging, security, and social identity, might turn out to be important if the relevant features of the dwelling and the corresponding attitudes could be measured.

Few studies have included a detailed description of housing environment even in terms of the check lists and standards available [13, 17]. J. K. Scott, an architect, constructed a housing check list which included aesethetic and social characteristics as well as the more easily measured physical attributes, and he divided the housing environment into four aspects: internal characteristics of the dwelling, characteristics of the block or small group of dwellings, characteristics of the larger residential unit (up to 180 dwellings), and characteristics of the neighbourhood within five minutes walk. Items describing the interior of the dwelling included its homeliness, attractiveness, individuality, safety, noisiness, privacy, spaciousness, and adaptability. Some of these, such as noise levels or safety standards, could be measured fairly objectively; others could only be rated subjectively, and the reliability of ratings was likely to be considerably less. This kind of measurement, however, does allow a profile of a housing environment rather than a simple score. No doubt much sophisticated development and refinement will be required before such scales can be used effectively and reliably, but the approach does seem a sensible one [22]. Before mentioning a small pilot study carried out using the scales it is necessary to discuss in more detail the concept of mental health.

Measures of mental health and morbidity

As in the case of physical fitness [27] any statement of characteristics supposed to define mental health positively, rather than as the absence of disease, tends to become a statement of the values held by some individual or group [14]. Health is a social concept [15]. Just as a champion sprinter, weight-lifter, or fencer has simply developed one particular set of faculties towards the limits possible for the human constitution, for ends which are in the last resort social (e.g. competition against other people), so the special development of cognitive or personal abilities by a violinist, mathematician, or actor cannot be regarded as providing standards which could or should be universally emulated. Terms like the 'quality of life' do not get us out of the dilemma. It is simpler, as Popper pointed out, when acting on a large scale, to try to reduce harm rather than positively to try to do good. The absence of apparently undesirable traits, however, may also have disadvantages. Someone who felt no anxiety whatever, for example, or who never felt guilt, could not be regarded as an ideal human being.

Disease theories cut across this sort of dilemma because they are based upon well-attested theories of normal biological functioning, and it is not necessary to depend upon social values in order to say that pathology is present. (The way in which disease theories are used *is*, of course, a matter of social value.) Apart from conditions like schizophrenia, however, disease theories of 'functional' psychiatric conditions are not yet sufficiently well developed to have been used in epidemiological work. Most investigators have used empirically derived check lists of 'symptoms' such as anxiety, depression, worrying, and irritability, the scores on which measure something that might best be called 'mental ill-health'. This may be equivalent to deriving a check list of physical symptoms, including pain, fever, jaundice, itching, and the presence or absence of warts and saying that it measures physical ill-health. General practitioners' 'diagnoses', which have also been used, are basically symptomatic and equivalent to check lists. Although crude and undiscriminating, such scales do have a certain clinical face-validity and usefulness, and the studies based on them cannot be ignored.

Interplay between housing environment and mental ill-health

The main focus of investigation has been rehousing, on the assumption that differences will be most evident when people move from a supposedly poor housing environment to a supposedly good one. Measurements of the quality of housing have usually been few and couched in physical terms, apart from general subjective impressions. The four main studies, by Wilner [29], Marc Fried [9, 10] Taylor and Chave [28], and Hare and Shaw [12] all tend towards the same conclusions. They have been summarized by Gath in § 2.4.3., and I will here discuss only a number of issues raised by all of them which seem to deserve special attention.

In the first place, the rates of morbidity are usually high—between 20 and 30 per cent—and affect women more than men (particularly women with young children). Secondly, there are no important differences in symptom scores between the occupants of new and old housing estates. Thirdly, there is considerable satisfaction with housing among both groups and little difference between them. Such dissatisfaction as there is, however, is expressed in respect of different aspects of the environment. Fourthly, there is a marked association between dissatisfaction and neurotic symptoms.

The main conclusion reached by all four sets of authors is summed up by Taylor and Chave as follows:

Dissatisfaction with environment might be a cause of neurotic reaction. But it is much more likely to be a symptom, since a remarkably constant minority of people show both a measure of dissatisfaction and nervous symptoms, wherever they happen to live. Immediate environment may play a marginal part in causation; it may colour the clinical picture, and it may be blamed by the patient. But all our findings so far point to long-standing or constitutional factors.

These conclusions may be further illustrated by a small pilot study of housing environments carried out in south-east London. Scott's indices [22] were used to describe three recently erected council housing developments—a thirteen-storey slab block of internal corridor apartments, a six-storey block of maisonettes with external access balconies, and a group of terraced houses around small enclosed courts or squares. According to these indices, the slab block appeared to be most isolating and the squares most conducive to social interaction, with the maisonette block in between. The neighbourhood of the slab block was bleak, lacking in amenities and unwelcoming, compared with the neighbourhoods of the other two types of housing. On the other hand, the internal quality of the slab-block dwellings was much superior to that of houses in the squares.

Ten families were chosen in each of the three housing developments. None had been rehoused for medical reasons. Age and sex composition, length of residence, rent and income were not significantly different. In each case the mother was interviewed by Scott.

Sense of belonging to the home was correlated with the quality and amenities of the dwelling; i.e. the slab-block dwellers were most satisfied and the square dwellers least. On the other hand, sense of belonging to the block or small group of dwellings was highest in the squares and lowest in the slab block. Social interaction was also reported to be highest in the squares and lowest in the slab block. There was no difference in the amount of mental ill-health reported in the adults or children of the three groups of families [23]. These results tend to confirm those of the larger studies in that attitudinal factors were highly specific but did not, in sum, distinguish between the environments. The suggestion that architectural features may influence the degree of social interaction is worth following up.

There were complaints among the slab-block residents about the difficulty of allowing small children to play at ground level, and there seems no doubt about the importance of this specific problem [16]. Councils have probably learned this lesson by now. Douglas also showed an effect of poor housing conditions on school performance. Middle-class children seemed better able to overcome the difficulty than working-class [6].

Discussion

Clearly housing is only one among a number of environmental factors which could have some relevance for mental ill-health. A number of studies have suggested that both psychotic and neurotic conditions can be precipitated by environmental changes, among which moving house would certainly be regarded as important [2, 3, 4, 5, 20, 25]. There are some obvious methodological pitfalls, such as the accurate and independent dating of events and of onset of illness, retrospective falsification, and dependence of events on sub-clinical symptomatology, with which the authors have tried to deal. The evidence remains suggestive that precipitating events do occur. If so, there is a paradox, since it would be expected that studies of housing relocation, or of other types of supposedly precipitating events, would indicate a higher incidence of episodes of mental ill-health among those recently exposed to the precipitant. Perhaps the index of mental ill-health is at fault, being too strongly bound to traits such as worrying, irritability, and dissatisfaction, which are not necessarily measures of illness [30]. Perhaps a high check-list score on mental ill-health identifies a number of individuals who tend to find fault with their environment whatever its characteristics. Perhaps it is impossible to construct social environments which will suit more than 85 per cent of those living in them. Perhaps, however, it would be possible to swap those who are dissatisfied in one setting with those who are dissatisfied in another, so that both groups feel better. Perhaps the 'threatening' events which seemed to precipitate depression in Brown's studies [2] were not much represented in any of the housing environments mentioned earlier, in which case the two sets of investigations are covering rather different territory.

In any case, there does seem to be good reason for further study of housing environments, particularly if refined and reliable instruments can be used both to measure differences between the environments themselves and to quantify and classify the short-term and long-term dispositions and reactions of the inhabitants.

So far as the year 2001 is concerned, however, the clearest message that can be derived from a survey of the literature on housing environment and mental health, is that medical criteria cannot be used to substitute for a system of values. There is very little evidence that different types or qualities of housing much affect the level of mental ill-health of the occupants, but that need not deter planners from adopting higher standards if they think it right. Consultation with occupiers suggests that most of them would like houses and gardens rather than blocks of flats [1]. It is not necessary to wait for confirmatory medical evidence before carrying out further consumer consultation and deciding what action to take. Perhaps, after all, a high quality of life is as good a definition of mental health as can be obtained.

REFERENCES

1. Ash, J. (1966). Families living at high density, *Official Architecture and Planning*. January 1966.
2. Brown, G. W. and Birley, J. L. T. (1970). Social precipitants of severe psychiatric disorders. In *Psychiatric epidemiology* (eds. E. H. Hare and J. K. Wing). Oxford University Press, London.
3. ——, ——, and Wing, J. K. (1972). Influence of family life on the course of schizophrenic disorders: a replication, *Brit. J. Psychiat.* 121, 241–58.
4. ——, Sklaire, F., Harris, T., and Birley, J. L. T. (1973). Life events and psychiatric disorders: some methodological issues, *Psychol. Med.* 3, 74–87.
5. Cooper, B. (1973). Statistics from general practice. In *Roots of evaluation: an epidemiological basis for planning psychiatric services* (eds. J. K. Wing, and H. Häffner). Oxford University Press, London.
6. Douglas, J. W. B. (1964). *The home and the school*. MacGibbon and Kee, New York.
7. Dunham, H. W. (1965). *Community and schizophrenia: An epidemiological analysis*. Wayne State University Press, Detroit.
8. Faris, R. E. L. and Dunham, H. W. (1939). *Mental disorders in urban areas*. Chicago University Press, Chicago.
9. Fried, M. (1964). Effects of change on mental health, *Am. J. Orthopsychiat.* 34, 3.
10. —— (1965). Transitional functions of working class communities. In *Mobility and mental health* (ed. M. B. Kantor), Thomas, Springfield, Ill.
11. Hare, E. H. (1956) Mental illness and social conditions in Bristol, *J. ment. Sci.* 102, 349–57.
12. —— and Shaw, G. K. (1965). *Mental health on a new housing estate*. Oxford University Press, London.
13. Hole, V. (1972). Housing in social research. In *Key variables in social research, Vol.* 1, *Religion, housing, locality* (ed. E. Gittus). Heinemann for British Sociological Association, London.
14. Jahoda, M. (1958). *Current concepts of positive mental health*. Basic Books, New York.
15. Lewis, A. (1953). Health as a social concept, *Br. J. Sociol.* 4, 109–24,
16. Maizels, J. (1961). *Two to five in high flats*. The Housing Centre. London.
17. Ministry of Housing and Local Government (1966). *The housing condition index*. Unpublished.
18. Morris, J. N. (1973). Four cheers for prevention, *Proc. R. Soc. Med.* 66, 225–32.
19. Myers, J. K., Lindenthal, J. J., and Pepper, M. P. (1971). Life events and psychiatric impairment, *J. nerv. ment. Dis.* 152, 149–57.

20. RAHE, R. H. (1969). Life crisis and health change. In *Psychotropic drug response: Advances in prediction* (eds. May, Pond, and Wittenborn). Thomas, Springfield, Ill.
21. SAINSBURY, P. (1955). *Suicide in London: an ecological study.* Chapman and Hall, London.
22. SCOTT, J. K. (1970). Testing a housing design reference: a pilot study, *Architect. Assoc. Quart.* **2**, 23.
23. —— and WING, J. K. (1969). *The influence of housing environment on residents' attitudes and social behaviour: a pilot study.* Unpublished.
24. SHAW, C. R. AND MCKAY, H. D. (1942). *Juvenile delinquency in urban areas.* Chicago University Press.
25. SPILKEN, A. Z. and JACOBS, M. A. (1971). Prediction of illness behaviour from measures of life crisis, manifest distress and maladaptive coping, *Psychosom. Med.* **33**, 251–64.
26. STEIN, L. (1957). 'Social class' gradient in schizophrenia, *Br. J. prev. soc. Med.* **11**, 181–95.
27. Symposium on the meaning of physical fitness (1969), *Proc. R. Soc. Med.* **62**, 1155–98.
28. TAYLOR, S. and CHAVE, S. (1964). *Mental health and environment.* Longmans, London.
29. WILNER, D. M., PRICE, W. R., PINKERTON, T. C., and TAYBACK, M. (1962). *The housing environment and family life.* Johns Hopkins Press, Baltimore.
30. WING, J. K., COOPER, J. E., and SARTORIUS, N. (1974). *The description and classification of psychiatric symptoms. An instruction manual for the PSE and Catego system.* Cambridge University Press. (To be published.)
31. —— and HAILEY, A. M. (eds.) (1972). *Evaluating a community psychiatric service: the Camberwell Register* 1964–1971, Chapter 3. Oxford University Press, London.
32. WOOLF, M. (1967). *The Housing Survey in England and Wales,* 1964. H.M.S.O., Government Social Survey, London.

2.5. Reproductive performance and social constraint

2.5.1. Reproductive constraints in ecologically stabilized societies

RICHARD G. WILKINSON

IN periods when population has grown, man has been forced to increase his exploitation of the environment, intensifying his use of some resources and finding substitutes for others as they become scarce. I have tried to show elsewhere how much of the long history of economic development represents an attempt to expand output to keep abreast of a growing population [1]. But expansion has not been the norm. When we look at the current problems caused by pressure of world population on resources—such as the need for increasingly intensive forms of food production, the concern over the supply of many important minerals, or even the shortage of building land here in Britain—it is salutary to note that, throughout most of human history, man has, without the aid of modern contraceptive techniques, managed to limit his population size to within his resources.

By maintaining population size in ecological equilibrium primitive societies have escaped the problems which threaten their traditional productive methods and way of life. During much the greater part of man's history productive methods have been remarkable for their stability: hunters and gatherers have avoided overhunting, agriculturalists avoided the necessity of shortening fallow periods, etc.

As a result of the work of Lack, Wynne-Edwards, and others it is now generally recognized that many animal populations limit their numbers in relation to resources [2]. By taking no more than the maximum sustainable yield of the resources on which they depend, they are able to avoid starvation and maintain their own population at a higher level than would be possible if resources were destructively overtaxed. That primitive human populations did likewise is less well known although Carr-Saunders published a mass of evidence to that effect as early as 1922 [3].

The condition of most underdeveloped countries today gives no indication of the life of the societies I am concerned with here. Many of the cultural factors which limited primitive populations have long since been abandoned. Most of the underdeveloped countries today are suffering from population growth which appeared in comparatively recent times, often as the result of outside interference with their cultural systems while they were under colonial rule. Nor was disease the threat that it would be today if it were not for preventive medicine. People here will know much better than I do how isolated populations become resistant to the worst effects of diseases to which they are regularly exposed. They will also recall the devastating effects of some indigenous diseases on Europeans abroad and of the European diseases which were introduced to foreign populations. The evidence is that, before European contact, primitive societies were remarkably healthy [4], certainly too healthy for disease to have been an effective regulator of population size.

Evidence on primitive methods of population control comes from early reports, from people who saw societies before European contact had had a significantly disruptive influence. But even now the few social anthropologists who are lucky enough to visit the diminishing number of societies which have not got caught up in the ever-widening net of the industrial and commercial world almost invariably report the practice of similar methods of population control [5].

Carr-Saunders said that the vast amount of evidence he had amassed on primitive societies showed 'customs restrictive of increase to have been so widespread, in the form of abortion, infanticide, or prolonged abstention from intercourse, as to have been practically universal' [6]. There is no shortage of examples of these practices, but let it suffice to say that there are examples of infanticide accounting for up to 50 per cent of live births, that abortion using a variety of techniques was extremely widespread, that taboos on intercourse after a woman had given birth often extended to as much as three years, that by these means women limited the number of their children to two or three with live births sometimes as much as 5 or 6 years apart, and that in some societies other practices—such as a denial of marriage to younger children—also helped to restrict population size. In the past, practices such as these seem to have been widespread among the Australian aborigines, among the Indians of both North and South America, in many African societies, among the Eskimos, the New Zealand Maori, and in Oceania generally [7]. What is relevant to us now is the way these cultural checks worked and people's motives for using them.

In some societies people were clearly aware of the ecological necessity of population limitation. Carr-Saunders believed that this was always so, and that population limitation must therefore stem from 'the growth of the intellect' [8]. Similar practices among animal population show that this is not necessarily so, and in fact some primitive societies limited their populations so well within their resources that even the theoretical possibility of starvation was obscured [9].

Where, however, the possibility of a food shortage was the motive for population limitation, it was often regarded as a problem facing society as a whole rather than just the individual and his family. This attitude was fostered by institutions of communal production and food sharing. It would be only too easy for us to assume mistakenly that the incentives to family limitation would be stronger under a system of greater economic independence, where people were thrown back on their own resources rather than sharing in the communal product. But there is little evidence from any society that individual poverty leads to more provident and responsible behaviour [10] Perhaps surprisingly, what seems more important is the social approval and disapproval of the people round one. Great economic independence of the nuclear family means that other people are less affected by the improvidence of a particular family and so have less reason for showing any disapproval. Systems of food sharing, reciprocal gift exchange, and feelings of responsibility for poor relations or tribesmen who may call on your resources are the links which promote the formation of moral standards and expressions of approval and disapproval. The potential power of social attitudes can hardly be overestimated; we need only recall what a forceful effect the shame associated with unmarried pregnancy has had on the lives of girls in societies like our own.

There are numerous references in the literature to the part played in population limitation by moral attitudes in primitive societies. In some parts of New Guinea any woman who had children too close together, showing that she had broken the taboo on intercourse during the 2 or 3 years during which she was feeding her last baby, was apparently 'ridiculed' by older women, who threatened not to help her bring up her progeny [11]. In the Murray Islands it was once considered 'proper' to have an equal number of boys and girls, and any excess of one over the other 'were destroyed for shame' [12]. Among the Tikopia in the Polynesian Islands the problem of overpopulation was seen—especially by the chiefs and elders—as a matter of the standard of community morality and sense of responsibility [13]. At an annual ceremony the Tikopia were reminded of their responsibilities: 'contraception (mainly withdrawal) was part of the moral code of the Tikopia, publicly inculcated with the weight of the chiefs and the religious values of the occasion behind it' [14].

Apart from moral pressures to observe codes conducive to population limitation there are often more directly practical reasons for limiting the number of one's children. Among nomadic hunters and gatherers women wanting to avoid having to carry two children over long distances often abort or kill a baby if they are still having to carry the last one [15]. Even in more settled communities the reason which is often given for avoiding having children in rapid succession is the difficulty of looking after them [16].

Many societies have superstitious reasons for abstaining from intercourse during lactation or for practising infanticide [17]. These superstitions sometimes have moral overtones, but tend to be more flexible than purely moral rules would be. In special circumstances where their application would be inappropriate, people can usually take medicines or perform some ritual to ward off the evil effect of breaking the taboo [18].

In some societies there are more complicated cultural subsystems associated with population limitation. Where for instance there is a taboo on intercourse during pregnancy and lactation it has been said that women procure abortions for fear that their husbands will leave them for another woman during this period [19]. Similarly the high cost of bride prices may lead to the killing of male offspring [20].

Perhaps the single most important factor responsible for the weakening of systems of population limitation is the development of class societies and their widening ideological influence. In societies where there is relative equality in subsistence goods (if not in ceremonial goods) everyone has the same interest in population limitation from the ecological standpoint. In class societies interests tend to diverge. In many situations the upper classes have little or no incentive to limit their family sizes and may well find it to their advantage that the peasantry or working class grows in numbers and poverty [21]. After all, what is a master without servants? Where in primitive societies there is ideological pressure—moral and superstitious—to use various methods of family limitation, in class societies there tend to be religious and secular rules forbidding them. Christian missionaries have played havoc with the moral codes of some primitive societies; the Koran too says explicitly 'slay not your children fearing a fall to poverty, We shall provide for them and for you, Lo! the slaying of them is great sin' [22]. There are numerous examples from class societies of official attempts to suppress methods of population limitation which the peasantry took up when faced with growing poverty [23].

It seems that if a society is going to evolve an *effective* moral code favouring population limitation there must be a genuine community of interests underlying it. The growing acceptance of abortion and contraception in most industrial countries today represents a developing sense of concern over environmental issues which threaten us all equally. In primitive societies people's lack of economic and practical independence from each other seems to have made each person more amenable to the moral values of their society and therefore less likely to define their self-interest independently of—and so irresponsibly in relation to—the rest of the community.

REFERENCES AND NOTES

1. WILKINSON, R. G. (1973). *Poverty and progress: an ecological model of economic development.* Methuen, London. (Most of the points raised here are discussed more fully in Chapters 3 and 4 of this book.)
2. LACK, D. (1954). *The natural regulation of animal numbers,* Clarendon Press, Oxford. WYNNE-EDWARDS, V. C. (1962), *Animal dispersion in relation to social behaviour,* Oliver and Boyd, Edinburgh.
3. CARR-SAUNDERS, A. M. (1922), *The population problem,* Clarendon Press, Oxford.

4. SCHAPERA, I. (1930). *The Khoisan peoples of South Africa*, p. 214. London; *Man the hunter* (1968), (eds. R. B. Lee and I. DeVore) p. 36, Aldine Press, Chicago; DAVIDSON, A. (1892). *Geographical pathology*, p. 565, Edinburgh.

5. NEEL, J. V., and CHAGNON, N. A. (1968). The demography of two tribes of primitive relatively unacculturated American Indians, *Proc. U.S.A. natn. Acad. Sci.* **59**, 680; RING, A. and SCRAGG, R. (1973), A demographic and social study of fertility in rural New Guinea, *J. biosoc. Sci.* **5** (Jan.), 89; LEVI-STRAUSS, C. (1961), *A world on the wane*, p. 273. London.

6. CARR-SAUNDERS, [3], 483.

7. References are too numerous to list here. The most comprehensive bibliographies on these practices are CARR SAUNDERS [3], Appendix 1 which contains over 200 references, and DEVEREUX, G. (1955). *A study of abortion in primitive societies*, Julian Press, New York, which contains quotes from some 400 sources to the use of abortion in as many pre-industrial societies.

8. CARR-SAUNDERS, [3], p. 241.

9. MATHEW, J. (1910). *Two representative tribes of Queensland*, p. 166. London. On the sufficiency of food supplies, see LEE and DE VORE, [4], pp. 52 and 85.

10. Indeed, cross-sectional studies often show a negative correlation between income and fertility, but see SIMON, J. L. (1969). The effect of income on fertility, *Population Studies*, **23**, 327.

11. RING and SCRAGG, [5].

12. HUNT, A. E. (1899). Ethnographical notes on the Murray Islands, Torres Straits, *J. anthropolog. Inst.*, old series, **28**, 5.

13. FIRTH, R. W. (1960). *Social change in Tikopia*, p. 157. Allen and Unwin, London.

14. —— (1939). *Primitive Polynesian economy*, p. 45. Routledge, London.

15. BIRDSELL, J. B. (1968). Some predictions for the Pleistocene based on equilibrium systems among recent hunter-gatherers. In *Man the hunter* (eds. R. B. Lee and I. DeVore), p. 236. Aldine Press, Chicago.

16. ELLIS, W. (1827). *Narrative of a tour through Hawaii*, p. 327, London.

17. WILKINSON, [1] pp. 38–40.

18. —— [1], pp. 39–40.

19. JOHNSTON, H. H. (1908). *George Grenfell and the Congo*, Vol. II, p. 671. London.

20. DOBRIZHOFFER, M. (1822). *An account of the Abipones*, Vol. II, p. 97. London.

21. *Colonial currency reprints*, (1921). Vol. II p. 189, Boston, Mass.; CARR-SAUNDERS, [3], pp. 20–3.

22. *The Koran*, Surah XVII: 31.

23. TSUCHIYA, T. (1937). *An economic history of Japan*, pp. 162–3, Kegan Paul (Oriental Dept.), London and Tokyo; RUSSELL, J. C. (1948). *British medieval population*, p. 160. University of New Mexico Press, Albuquerque, New Mexico.

2.5.2. The Islamic sanction of contraception

BASIM F. MUSALLAM

Office of Population Research, Princeton University, and Centre for Population Studies, Harvard University.

We rode out with the Prophet to raid Banu al-Mustalaq, and we captured some female prisoners. . . . We desired women, and abstinence became hard. [But] we wanted to practise coitus interruptus, and we asked the Prophet about it. He said, 'You do not have to hesitate, for Allah has predestined what is to be created until Judgement Day.'

Tradition from the Prophet

Introduction

The Islamic attitude towards contraception is of unique significance for understanding the nature of religious reactions to birth control within the broad Jewish–Christian–Muslim Mediterranean tradition. For, while Judaism and Christianity prohibited contraception as mortal sin, Islam permitted the practice. Since the three religions have a common origin and share many of the same assumptions, their attitudes and laws, whether they agree or diverge, shed light on one another. Some years ago John T. Noonan's *Contraception* [6] appeared. Noonan's book was an excellent study of birth control from a Roman Catholic point of view, and it was followed by a book on *Birth Control in Jewish Law* by David M. Feldman [2]. This paper will attempt to amplify the picture by describing the Islamic attitudes towards contraception.

Islamic jurisprudence

In the first Islamic century the Muslim community split over the issue of succession to the Prophet and the nature of political sovereignty in the Islamic state. One group, the Sunnis (orthodox), recognized the authority of the Medinan, Umayyad, and Abbasid caliphs. The other major group, the Shi'is, came to maintain that sovereignty was a matter of divine right, residing in the descendants of the Prophet. A third group, the Kharijites (Ibadis), maintained that the leader of the Islamic community should be elected by the entire community of believers.

Among the orthodox Sunnis, four main schools of jurisprudence developed: the Maliki, Hanafi, Shafiʻi, and Hanbali schools.
These took definite shape in the third century of Islam and were
the only surviving orthodox schools after the seventh century
(A.D. 1300). Most orthodox Muslims from the tenth to the
thirteenth century A.D., and *all* of them after A.D. 1300, belonged,
for the purpose of observing the Islamic religious law, to one of
the four Sunni schools. Similarly, the main Shiʻi groups (the
Twelver Shiʻis, the Ismaʻilis, and the Zaidis) each developed its
own school of jurisprudence, and there was also an Ibadi school.
The following is a survey of the opinions on contraception of all
these historical schools of law spanning the period from the tenth
to the eighteenth century A.D.

Islamic jurisprudence assessed all human acts by a scale of
religious qualifications, the essential function of which was the
determination of whether an act was allowed or forbidden. While
the concept 'forbidden' (*harām*) was simple, the concept 'allowed'
was complex and encompassed acts which ranged from 'obligatory'
(*wājib, farḍ*), such as the religious duties of ritual prayer and
fasting, to 'blameworthy' (*makrūh*) such as coitus interruptus.
Between these two there were the concepts 'recommended' (*sunna,
mandūb, mustaḥabb*) and 'indifferent' (*mubāḥ*).

The literature of Islamic jurisprudence is the most characteristic and important achievement of classical Muslim civilization.
It is all-inclusive, in the sense that it deals with everything relevant
to Islamic religious and social life, from religious duties such as
fasting and prayer to the organization of the market place. In
jurisprudence is contained the Islamic idea of the good religious
and social life, and the attempts of Muslims to come to terms with
the problems of their history, society, and existence are reflected
in it throughout. Properly used, jurisprudence is an inexhaustible
source for the study of Islamic social history.

The opinions of the historical schools of law

Discussions of contraception in Islamic jurisprudence are
primarily concerned with one method—coitus interruptus. Historically, coitus interruptus is the most common contraceptive method
known to man. Well into the twentieth century, and until the
recent introduction of the Pill and the I.U.D., the real history of

contraception, as far as technique is concerned, is to a significant extent the history of coitus interruptus. Other methods, especially intravaginal suppositories, tampons, and their modern equivalents, mattered, but these should be seen as having been supplementary, rather than equal, to the old, venerable, and relatively effective practice of withdrawal.

The sanction of coitus interruptus for birth control was a constant fact of Islamic law in precisely the same sense that its prohibition was a constant fact of Jewish law and Canon law. Agreement on the sanction of contraception in Islamic jurisprudence was so general that the permissive view became a cultural cliché. Rare is the legal book which does not deal with it and repeat the permission [8]. One can therefore speak of a 'classical' Islamic opinion on contraception generally adopted in jurisprudence, regardless of school. *This classical opinion is the sanction of coitus interruptus with a free woman provided she gives her permission* [10]. The differences between the schools with respect to this sanction revolved around the *kind* of permission contemplated and were therefore relatively minor.

All schools of law based their sanction on the same precondition: the free woman's permission. This was essential because, according to Islamic law, a free woman had a basic right (1) to children and (2) to complete sexual fulfilment, which coitus interruptus was judged to diminish. Because of this common precondition, as one moves from one set of opinions to the next the issues of the woman's rights to children and sexual fulfilment are more and more elaborated, defined, and qualified. All the different opinions, within the orthodox camp, were deemed legitimate, that is variant but proper Islamic views, and they were recognized as such by all orthodox jurists. Since, on the subject of contraception, both orthodox and unorthodox Islamic opinions are in substance the same, I shall include both in the same discussion.

Islamic jurisprudence treats coitus interruptus under three main headings (1) with a wife who is a free woman, (2) with a wife who is a slave of another party, man or woman, and (3) with a man's own slave or concubine. These divisions are based on the varieties of sexual intercourse which are deemed legitimate by Islam: marriage and concubinage. A man may marry a free or slave woman. He may not marry his own slave. A wife who is a slave must therefore be the slave of someone other than her husband. A man may legitimately have sexual intercourse with his own female slave, but only as a concubine, not as a wife.

Coitus interruptus with a wife who is a free woman

The Shafiʻis, among the orthodox, are the only jurists who tended to permit coitus interruptus without any condition, that is to say without the woman's permission. They reasoned that since coitus interruptus itself was not a forbidden act, no conditions should be attached to its practice. Most Shafiʻis adhered to this absolute sanction, but a few adopted the classical position that the practice is licit only with the free woman's consent. Although jurists belonging to a given school of law were generally inclined to adopt the view peculiar to that school, there were always some jurists who felt free to adopt opinions from rival schools. The Shafiʻi jurist, al-Shirazi, for example, adopted the classical opinion, and was then faced with the problem of a wife who refused to grant permission. He offered two alternative judgements without committing himself to either: first, that coitus interruptus was illicit without her permission, and second that it was licit, because she had 'a right to intercourse, but not to ejaculation'.

Those Muslim jurists who argued that coitus interruptus may be practised without the woman's permission (primarily the Shafiʻis, but some others too) found it possible to by-pass the woman's rights to children. They never denied, rejected, or over-ruled her right to sexual fulfilment, but faced with both the necessity of contraception and woman's basic right to sexual pleasure, they defined the latter as *intercourse* (without necessarily including ejaculation of the male sperm) *and female orgasm*. As a result coitus interruptus was not seen to infringe the woman's sexual rights.

In contrast to the Shafiʻis, the Hanbali school insisted on the woman's permission. They reasoned that (1) children are the free woman's right, and (2) that she may suffer harm as the result of the practice of withdrawal. The harm was specified as a reduction of her pleasure in coitus. Here, sexual fulfilment for the woman is understood to depend on the completed act of intercourse, something which coitus interruptus obviously is not. Despite the Hanbali school's strict views, a few of its jurists, notably Ibn Qudama al-Maqdisi, also argued that coitus interruptus was licit without the woman's permission, similarly basing their opinion on the understanding that the woman does not necessarily have the right to male ejaculation. Nevertheless, al-Maqdisi maintained that it was preferable to ask her permission anyway for the sake of convenience and amity. The only allowance which the Hanbalis, as a school, made for the practice without the free woman's permission was the *duty* to practice coitus interruptus in infidel territories (*Dār al-Ḥarb*), for fear of Muslim children being enslaved.

The Hanafis' original position was as strict as that of the Hanbalis, they too sanctioned coitus interruptus with a free woman only with her permission. But from the later Middle Ages on, Hanafis argued that since the 'times are bad' coitus interruptus with a free woman was licit without her permission. 'Bad times' and related indications were judged to take precedence over a free woman's right to withhold consent. The later Hanafi jurists adopted this view with an expressed awareness of the school's stricter traditional attitude, but they argued that 'regulations change when the times change'.

The Maliki school, like the Hanbalis and early Hanafis, also sanctioned coitus interruptus with a free woman only on condition that she give her consent, but some Maliki jurists added a new twist by granting the woman the right of demanding and receiving monetary compensation as the price of her permission. The woman was to give her permission for a specified period of time, the compensation being a set amount of money, and she could change her mind and withdraw her permission before the end of the period. Malikis disagreed as to whether, if she did change her mind, she had to refund the whole amount or only an amount proportional to the remainder of the period, but the latter alternative was preferred.

The Twelver Shiʿi position was essentially the same as that of the orthodox schools of law: coitus interruptus with a free woman was sanctioned only with her permission. But Shiʿi jurisprudence differed from that of the four orthodox schools by allowing for the establishment of the woman's consent as a precondition in the marriage contract. After such a precondition, a husband could practice coitus interruptus without his wife's immediate consent.

The concept of monetary compensation, which had originated among the orthodox Maliki jurists, became, among the Twelver

Shi'is, 'blood money' (*diya*) to be paid the woman in the event that coitus interruptus was practised against her wishes without a stipulation authorizing it in the marriage contract. The sum was 10 Dinars (a sizeable sum) each time coitus interruptus took place under these conditions. Some Shi'i authorities insisted on the payment, others rejected it, and still others argued that, although the man did not have to pay, it was better if he did. Essentially the division seems to have been between those who saw coitus interruptus without the free woman's permission as prohibited (*ḥarām*) and those who saw it as merely 'blameworthy' (*makrūh*). The former demanded payment; the latter did not.

The Isma'ilis sanctioned coitus interruptus with the free woman's consent, and, like the Twelver Shi'is, favoured the establishment of her prior consent in the marriage contract. The Ibadi position was the classical one stated above. Zaidi jurisprudence recommended seeking the woman's permission but did not prohibit the practice when she refused to grant it. They simply reasoned that coitus interruptus 'is not worse than complete abstinence'. Again we notice that, given the necessity for contraception, the last rights to be tampered with were the rights to sex.

Coitus interruptus with a wife who is a slave of another [9]

In cases where the wife was a slave (*ama*) of another (someone other than her husband), a different set of legal opinions applied, but these opinions were generally based on the same principles as those regarding free women. The object of coitus interruptus was the prevention of children. Since a free woman had a right to her own children, her permission for coitus interruptus was generally deemed necessary, but in the case of a slave wife, the potential children belonged to her master. On the other hand, withdrawal before ejaculation was judged to reduce the woman's pleasure in intercourse, and since sexual fulfilment was held to be the right of a woman as *wife*, regardless of her legal position as free or slave, Islamic jurisprudence had to take this factor into account. Whereas the wife who was a slave had a right to complete sexual fulfilment in intercourse with her husband, the children of such a union, should any result, belonged not to her or to her husband but to her master. Some jurists based their opinions on property rights to children, others argued on the basis of a woman's right to sexual fulfilment.

The Shafiʿis, who found it possible to set aside even the free woman's right to children and to interpret her right to sexual fulfilment so as to sanction coitus interruptus unconditionally, found no difficulty in sanctioning coitus interruptus with a slave wife absolutely. For the Shafiʿis, neither her nor her master's permission was needed.

The majority of the Hanbali jurists based their position on the primacy of property rights to children, so the master's permission, and not the slave wife's, was required, but the freedom of the children born could be included as a precondition in the marriage contract. With such a precondition, the master's permission would be superfluous and therefore dropped. Although the majority opinion among the Hanbalis remained based on property rights, some Hanbali jurists, insisting on the position of the slave woman *as wife*, argued that it was her permission, and not her master's, that was needed.

For the conflict between property rights to children, which resided with the master, and marital rights to sex, which resided with the slave wife, soon became apparent. One important Hanbali jurist, Ibn Qudama al-Maqdisi, in rejecting the view that the master's consent was necessary, argued that, since it was the wife and not her master who had the right to sexual intercourse with her husband, the master could have no say as to how intercourse was to be performed. In other words, al-Maqdisi regarded coitus interruptus as nothing more than a sexual technique, a coital method.

Such an opinion is possible only when one separates the sexual act within marriage from its procreative end, which Muslim jurists were inclined to do. They believed that women had two distinct rights, one to children and another to sexual fulfilment, so that the very concept that the Muslims held of sexual fulfilment was alien to the idea that sex within marriage is legitimate only for the purpose of procreation. This contrasts sharply with Christian views, and nowhere is the contrast more clearly expressed than in the Zaidis unconditional sanction of coitus interruptus 'because it is not worse than complete abstinence'.

Hanafi jurists further eroded the position based on property rights, namely, the need for the master's permission. Although the school's original founder, Abu Hanifa himself, argued from property rights, two other early authorities of the school, Abu Yusuf and Shaybani, stressed the woman's right to sexual fulfilment and insisted on the slave wife's, and not her master's, permission. A small number of Hanafi jurists chose one or the other of these opinions, but the majority cited both without committing themselves to either.

The primacy of property rights over marital rights seems to have disappeared completely among the Malikis. Although there were Maliki jurists who adopted the view that coitus interruptus with a slave wife was permissible only with her master's consent, the more authoritative Malikis permitted the practice only with the permission of the slave wife and her master together. But in the final analysis the slave wife's permission took precedence over her master's, for in situations where the master granted permission and she refused, her husband was not allowed to practise coitus interruptus with her, and she could take him to court and seek redress on the basis of harm done to her by his withdrawal against her wishes.

The Twelver Shi'is and the Zaidis sanctioned coitus interruptus with a slave wife unconditionally. The Isma'ilis permitted the practice only with the master's consent, and the Ibadis permitted it with his or with the slave wife's permission. All these points of view are essentially parallel to those of the orthodox jurists.

Coitus interruptus with a man's own slave

Since the need to ask anyone's permission for the practice of coitus interruptus was based either on property rights to children or on marital rights to sexual fulfilment, the permission of those who had neither right was obviously not needed. *All* Muslim jurists absolutely agreed that coitus interruptus might be practised with a man's own slave or concubine unconditionally.

Female use of contraceptives

Men were not alone in their desire to control births, and it is clear from jurisprudence itself that some women practised contraception. But the way in which jurists discussed the female use of contraceptives shows that they were not concerned with it primarily as a legal problem. What they have left us are reports which are of importance principally as evidence of medieval women's actual use of a relatively effective method of birth control.

Ibn Taymiyya, the great Hanbali judge and theologian, dealt in one of his legal opinions with the case of a woman 'who inserts a suppository (*dawā'*) during intercourse, thereby stopping the semen from entering the uterus [literally, 'channels of conception', *majārī al-ḥabal*]'. The Hanafi jurist Ibn Nujaim maintained by analogy with the classical opinion on coitus interruptus that the blocking of the *os uteri*, 'as women do', to prevent pregnancy should be subject to the husband's permission. Another Hanafi jurist, Ibn ʿAbidin, disagreed and suggested that women's practice of inserting suppositories and tampons 'to block the *os uteri*' was licit without the husband's consent. He added that the difference between this practice and coitus interruptus was obvious[11]. ʿIllish, a Maliki jurist, argued in his collection of legal opinions that the practice of 'placing something like a rag in the vagina during intercourse to stop the semen from reaching the uterus is permitted, along with coitus interruptus, but with the husband's permission'. Twelver Shiʿi opinion held that, although the practice is better done with the husband's permission, it was not prohibited without it.

It is significant that the one form of female contraception reported or in any way discussed in Islamic jurisprudence was the use of intravaginal suppositories and tampons to stop the semen from reaching the uterus; in other words, only rational and relatively effective methods were mentioned.

BIBLIOGRAPHICAL NOTE

This paper is part of a larger study which will be published by Harvard University Press, Cambridge, Mass.

REFERENCES AND NOTES

1. COULSON, N. J., (1964). *A history of Islamic law*. Edinburgh University Press, Edinburgh.
2. FELDMAN, D. M. (1968). *Birth control in Jewish law*. New York University Press, New York.
3. HIMES, N. E. (1970). *The medical history of contraception*. Baltimore. (1936), and reprinted, Schocken, New York (1970).

4. MADKUR, M. (1965). *Nadhrat al-Islām ilā Taḥdīd al-Nasl.* Dar al-Nahda al-Arabiyya, Cairo.
5. MUSALLAM, B. F. (1973). *Sex and society in Islam: The sanction and medieval techniques of birth control,* Ph.D. Dissertation, Department of History, Harvard University, Cambridge, Mass.
6. NOONAN, J. T., JR. (1966). *Contraception: a history of its treatment by the Catholic theologians and canonists.* Harvard University Press, Cambridge, Massachusetts.
7. SCHACHT, J. (1964). *An introduction to Islamic law.* Oxford University Press, London.
8. In the Islamic writing on contraception, only one jurist condemned coitus interruptus absolutely. This was the Spaniard Ibn Hazm (tenth–eleventh centuries A.D.) who belonged to the Zahiri school of law, a small, short-lived, and ultimately insignificant movement. Ibn Hazm's absolute prohibition of coitus interruptus, running counter to the general Islamic opinion on the subject, became a *cause célèbre* in the Islamic legal discussions of birth control. Muslim jurists took note of the dissent of Ibn Hazm, but his views made no dent in the solid structure of permissiveness.
9. In Islam, 'the slave has rights as a person; in particular he or she can get married. The male slave may marry up to two female slaves; the female slave may also marry a free man who is not her owner, and the male slave a free woman who is not his owner'. SCHACHT [7].
10. The jurists viewed contraception as an allowed and 'blameworthy' (*makrūh*) practice. They ranked it 'blameworthy' because it was not a simple, unmixed good; since procreation was a good, abstention from it was an abstention from a meritorious deed, but such abstentions were by no means forbidden. As Ghazali (eleventh–twelfth centuries A.D., the most influential jurist of them all) explains it was a *makrūh* in the same sense it was a *makrūh* for a Muslim to sit idly in the mosque without engaging in meditation or prayer.

In addition to the scale of religious qualifications mentioned above, there was another scale which Muslim jurists applied concurrently to the same acts, that of legal validity: A deed was (1) 'valid' (*saḥīḥ*) if both its nature and circumstance agreed with the law; (2) 'blameworthy' (*makrūh*) if both aspects also agreed with the law but something forbidden was connected with it: (3) 'defective' (*fāsid*) if its nature agreed with the law but its circumstance did not, or (4) 'invalid' (*bāṭil*) if neither aspects agreed with the law. Deeds which were judged to be *saḥīḥ* or *makrūh* (1 and 2 above) always produced their legal effects and therefore *saḥīḥ* (valid), in its more general sense, was a term usually applied to both. Seen in the light of this scale of legal validity, the Muslims believed that, since the act of contraception was proper in itself, and there were good reasons to control births, contraception was lawful: both its nature and circumstance agreed with the law. But it was 'blameworthy' (*makrūh*) because the act impinged the free woman's rights to complete sexual fulfilment and progeny. However, the jurists were quite flexible in their applications of these concepts, and the act of contraception was seen, sometimes by the same jurist, and depending on the circumstances, as both 'blameworthy' and 'obligatory' (in the sense of a religious duty, *farḍ*), or not even 'blameworthy' at all.

11. He probably meant that with coitus interruptus the woman's permission was required because withdrawal impinged on two of her basic rights (children and sexual fulfilment), and it was practised by the *man*. When she gave her permission, the practice became licit. In case she herself practised a form of contraception, the same problem clearly did not exist.

2.5.3. The history of the population of France: religion, politics, and women

THEODORE ZELDIN

Dean and Senior Tutor, St Antony's College, Oxford

The history of France's population has been markedly different from that of England. This is worth reflecting on because it casts doubts on quite a number of generalizations which are sometimes made rather indiscriminately about Europe or about developed societies. Already in the mid-nineteenth century France's population was almost stagnant, contrasting very noticeably with those of England and Germany which were at that time doubling and trebling. Then in the early 1940s France experienced a revival, and its population has risen since then at a higher rate than that of any other European country. This raises some difficult problems for those who attempt to produce universal explanations about population growth or control in purely economic or political terms. The French experience deserves consideration because it shows the need for a number of reservations when dealing with demographic problems. Moreover, France is one of the countries in which demography has been studied with great ingenuity and originality, and it can suggest approaches and methodologies which may be applied elsewhere.

The increase in the French population since the 1940s has not been due to an increase in the proportion of large families. This has remained the same, as has also the proportion of families with no children. The alteration has been due mainly to there being a shift from families with one child to families with two children, and slightly less from families with two children to those with three children. This confirms the view that if you want to increase or reduce a country's population, there is no need to alter the behaviour of more than a section of it and sometimes even only a minority of it.

Thus in 1911, when France seemed to be firmly set in a pattern of very small families, 37 per cent of couples nevertheless had 3 or more children. Today, likewise, the people who produce large families are also a minority. A statistic may illustrate this. About half a million women were born in France in 1881. Twenty-eight per cent died before reaching the age of 15; 12 per cent died unmarried between the ages of 15 and 49; 6 per cent were still unmarried in 1931; 54 per cent married. Of these, 61·1 per cent produced either no children or one or two children, but these accounted finally for 25·6 per cent of the descendants of this generation. Only 6·3 per cent of these women produced 7 or more children, but they accounted for 20·9 per cent of the children.

There has been a study of some of these large families based on the records preserved by the Cognacq–Jay Foundation, which awarded prizes to families of 9 or more children. The striking fact about them is that 19 per cent of these families had at least one illegitimate child and in 22 per cent the parents had married following pregnancy. These families are distributed very unevenly over the country, as are illegitimate births in general. There are obviously numerous factors to be taken into account in explaining how families reached this size.

One must somehow relate these facts about large families with the evidence that the regions of France which have the highest birth rates are often those with the highest degree of religious practice. Now the correlation of Catholicism with large families is well known. Charles Westoff [1], for example, in his American study of *The third child*, found this to be the most important correlation he could establish among a wide range of variables he studied. But, in France, there is no definite rule in this matter. There have been regions noted for religiosity which have had low birth rates as well as high ones. The influence of the Church has not prevented religious areas from experiencing a fall in birth rates. The common generalization that the population has declined because religious belief has declined is unacceptable, not only because of these discrepancies, but, even more so because it is a myth that religious belief has declined. Recent researches in religious sociology have made it abundantly clear that, in the nineteenth century, the supposed golden age of religious belief, there were large sections of the masses in both England and France who knew virtually nothing of the doctrines of their Churches. Moreover, the content of religious beliefs is so variable that if one is to talk significantly about them in a historical context, one must do so only in combination with all other beliefs held at the same time.

It is a familiar problem in demography to find that people do not carry out in practice the opinions they profess to hold when answering questions from demographers. In France, though the population has been rising, people in general have said that they are not in favour of its rising; they are as worried about unemployment and over-population as ever; and their opinion on population trends is extraordinarily inaccurate. The recent rise in population has paradoxically been accompanied by a dramatic abandonment of the view widely held just after the war, that the population ought to increase.

Historians, and still less demographers, do not like to talk about accident or chance. But in demography this is something which is particularly difficult to interpret. A Princeton study published in 1966 stated that as much as 54–60 per cent of pregnancies investigated were either unwanted or not wanted at the time they occurred. A similar study carried out in France at the same time, showed that only:

> 85·5 per cent of the mothers questioned, who had no children, said they wanted their child when it was born (they were questioned in the maternity hospitals both before and after births);
> 64·0 per cent of mothers with 1 child said they wanted their pregnancy;
> 35·5 per cent with 2 or more children said they wanted their pregnancy;
> 10·8 per cent of mothers with 4 or more children said they wanted their pregnancy.

Though there must obviously be reservations about such statistics, they suggest that this element of 'chance' represents in itself a certain kind of attitude which deserves investigation.

One may submit to discussion that some of the most important variables in population control work both ways. The increased use of contraceptives has paradoxically coincided, in certain groups, with less foresight and caution. People who worry about the future can react either by prudence or by fatalism. The choice any particular individual makes between these is, from one point of view, something which could be called a religious choice, in that it expresses a whole set of profound attitudes. To expect identical and universal reactions to economic, political, or cultural trends is clearly not realistic.

How far governments can influence the growth or decline of populations is not proved by the French experience. It is argued that the legislation passed between 1939 and 1946, which established family allowances on a substantial scale and gave other privileges to large families, was a major cause of France's population increase. It is noticeable, however, that though the most considerable benefits were given to families of 4 or more children, the number of such families was not increased, and the changes which occurred were only quite marginal—though that was enough to produce important total results. Perhaps more convincing is the view that during the Vichy regime there was a 'revival of family values'—a wider moral, 'religious' development. This, however, affected only a section of the population. Just as it is claimed that birth control and a tendency towards small families was initiated in the seventeenth and eighteenth centuries by the nobility and the poor middle-classes, so it was probably only a similarly restricted group which reversed this trend.

One conclusion of this paper is that some groups are much more susceptible to suggestions on family planning than others, and it is only the accurate identification of these, and their careful study, that can make prediction in this delicate matter possible. Broad generalizations about the effects of religiosity, materialism, prosperity, or politics will not do.

Such a conclusion would fit in with what we know of the development of the family as an emotional unit. The history of this is still in its infancy. Historical demographers have concentrated more on the size of households than on the human relationships within them. But this is an aspect of history in which I am interested and, basing myself on my own still incomplete investigations of the French case, I should like to add a few comments.

The normal framework which discussions of this subject assume is the development of the family away from patriarchal strictness to permissive laxity or from clan loyalties to child-centredness. This is to a certain extent associated with an old view that in a previous age extended families were the rule and that they were gradually supplanted by the small nuclear family—another view which has been demolished by recent research. Historically, I think it is more fruitful to talk about behaviour within the family, during the last two centuries at least, as falling into a number of types which co-existed during this period rather than succeeded each other in an evolutionary process.

France is often regarded as a country in which the 'traditional' family, that is to say the hierarchic unit with clearly differentiated roles, has survived with particular strength. This opinion probably contains roughly equal amounts of truth and wishful thinking. France has also, simultaneously, been the country of revolt, of experiment, and of libertinism—and this reputation is equally subject to caution. Frenchmen have been arguing about how their families should be organized with the same intensity and the same lack of consensus as they have argued about their political systems —and for just as long—but they have done so less publicly, and historians have seldom been willing to chronicle their debates on a subject which is still considered private. As a French Prime Minister once said, what concerns only the private individual is no concern of history. But the revolution of 1968 was, from some points of view, a revolution against the 'traditional' family; the continuation of this revolution today in quite a few secondary schools confirms that it was no superficial outburst; but the survival of many old patterns of behaviour shows that it was no universal revolution either.

A discussion of the population in A.D. 2001, therefore, must include an analysis of the quality of life in the different varieties of families that have existed and continue to do so; and it must consider the frustrations which each of them engendered. The possibility of a conservative reaction, in some groups, cannot be ruled out. But it is even more important to examine the effects which the changing ambitions of women are likely to have. A historian cannot look on Women's Liberation as an insignificant fashion, even if only a tiny minority belong to it; it has a substantial pre-history, largely unwritten, which makes it impossible to ignore.

It is influencing a far wider range of people than it is actually converting, and it is likely to have a profound influence on women's attitudes to child-rearing and child-bearing. It seems unlikely that the parents or children of A.D. 2001 will have a wholly altered set of values, but there is bound to be a sizeable group which will reject family hierarchy, differentiated roles, and certain aspects of maternity. This seems to me to be one of the crucial— as well as one of the most elusive and least researched—factors which will affect patterns of population growth and control in the future. To ignore it is as unwise as it would have been to ignore the rise of socialism, if this conference had been held 100 years ago.

BIBLIOGRAPHY

There are two brief surveys of French population problems which are admirable introductions by leading authorities: BEAUJEU-GARNIER, J. (1969), *La population francaise*, A. Colin, Paris, and ARMENGAUD, A. (1970). *La population francaise au 20e siècle* (3rd edn.) Presses Universitaires de France, Paris. ARIES, P. (1948). *Histoire des populations francaises et de leurs attitudes devant la vie depuis le 18e siècle*, Self, Paris, is highly stimulating. BERGUES, H. (1960). *La Prévention des naissances dans la famille* (Presses Universitaires de France, Paris) is an invaluable historical study, whose emphasis, however, is on the period before the nineteenth century. The latest research is to be found, or referred to, in the periodical *Population* and in the *Cahiers* of the *Institut National d'Études Démographiques*. For an introduction to the history of human relationships within the French family, with a bibliographical guide, see the chapters on women, children, marriage, and morals in ZELDIN, T. (1973). *France 1848–1945*, Vol. I: *Ambition, love, and politics*. Oxford History of Modern Europe, Oxford University Press and the chapters on the History of psychology in vol. II (forthcoming). For religious influences on the family, see *Conflicts in French society* (ed. T. Zeldin). Allen and Unwin, London (1970), and especially pp. 13–50. GLASS, D. V. and EVERSLEY, D. E. C. (1965). *Population in history*, Arnold, London and LASLETT, P. (1972). *Household and family in past time*, Cambridge University Press, contain major contributions to French demographic history as well as very full bibliographies for demographic history as a whole.

REFERENCE

1. WESTOFF, C. E. (1963). *The third child*. Princeton University Press, Princeton, New Jersey.

2.5.4. Some factors affecting family size and spacing in recent English cohorts

G. P. HAWTHORN
Social and Political Sciences Committee, Cambridge University

N. J. BUSFIELD, and
Department of Sociology, Essex University, and

M. J. PADDON
Department of Sociology and Social Administration, Durham University

The Problem

In the late 1950s and early 1960s the crude birth rate in England and Wales was rising, from 15·0 in 1955 to 18·0 in 1964; after that it declined, to 16·2 in 1971 and even further (14·7) in 1972. This pattern, although not necessarily its timing, has been reflected elsewhere in Europe [1]. The components of the change appear to have been a cessation of the overlap between a later-marrying and an earlier-marrying generation of women as the former completed their child-bearing; an increase, in more recent marriage cohorts, in the intervals between marriage and first births and (to a slightly lesser extent) between first and subsequent births, reversing the postwar trend towards a compression of child-bearing into a shorter space of time at the beginning of marriage; and a possible reduction in the completed family size of more recent cohorts [4]. The implications of the change for population projections have been considerable, estimates of the total in A.D. 2001 varying by as much as 30 millions since 1955 [13]; as a contribution, therefore, to future projections, as well as to possible policies, it is important to try to explain it [9, 17].

Marriage

The ratio of men (in age-group $a + 1$) to women (in age-group a) affects both rates of and ages at marriage, although quite how 'is a major unsolved problem of theoretical demography' [12]. Nevertheless, as Keyfitz has argued, it seems possible that the increasing ratio of men to women in the marriageable ages in the later 1950s and early 1960s may have contributed to the acceleration at that time in the marriage rate and to the slight lowering of the mean age at marriage. But its contribution in England and

Wales was almost certainly negligible, certainly by comparison with that in the U.S.A.

Oddly, we know more about the other determinants of the rates of and ages at marriage in pre-industrial than in modern populations. The long period of relatively low rates and high ages in north-western Europe from the sixteenth century (and perhaps earlier) to the 1930s has now given way to one of high rates and relatively low ages [7]. The large proportion of the never-married and the late marriages of the pre-industrial periods appear to have been the effect of the rule that a couple should have independent means before they established a new household [6, 20]. This rule almost certainly still obtains, but the acquisition of the means is now much easier. Hence the lifting of the restriction.

Thus, it is quite understandable that a half of the couples interviewed in a recent survey [11] (whether married in the period 1952–7 or in 1962–7) said that financial considerations (apart from ones of housing) had affected their decision to marry, and that another quarter said that considerations of housing had done so, while the average length of time between 'engagement' and marriage was less than 2 years.

Motives for family size and spacing

We have indicated elsewhere that by several indicators the economic fortunes of the country declined, even if only temporarily, and relatively, in the mid-1960s [2]. At the very least, this can hardly have encouraged shorter birth intervals and higher desired family sizes, and may indeed have contributed to some extent to the longer intervals and apparently lower sizes of recent cohorts. What effect it may have had on non-economic motivations and what non-economic motivations may have been contingently associated with it (such as to cause the same effects) are even less certain. But what *is* clear is that such motivations as did arise for postponing births and reducing family size were the more able to be effected by the widespread availability from the mid-1960s of oral contraceptives, more reliable than any other, and from the early 1970s by the greater availability of abortion and sterilization. It remains however, to test these speculations against the behaviour of individual couples. This has been done, with respect to motivation, in several recent studies [3, 11, 14, 15, 18, 19], and with respect to birth control, in some of these and one other [3, 4, 14, 15, 19]. Space precludes an extensive analysis of their findings, which in any event as far as motivation goes are inconclusive, but something may be said. We restrict ourselves here to mentioning one or two pointers from our own study on the question of changing motives; and to summarizing the results of others on birth control.

First, and in line with our expectations, it does seem from what they say that economic constraints have been *slightly* more severe for couples married in the 1960s than for those married in the 1950s. This must be partly but may not be wholly due to the economic changes of the mid-1960s; it could also be that standards for the acquisition of other goods, in the broadest sense, are rising.

Secondly, the wives in more recent marriages are perceptibly more forthcoming about the constraints imposed by children, and it may be that this too, together with changes over the past two decades in the relative position of husbands and wives in marriages (which, it must be said, remain to be described in conclusive detail), has served to lengthen birth intervals and lower family sizes.

Thirdly, however, and this remains a severe qualification on what we can say at this point, no study yet analysed has managed to pinpoint any change in values since 1950 which might in part have produced the demographic trends we are trying to explain. One may, of course (and especially in the absence of evidence), speculate. One possibility is that couples marrying in the 1960s have as single people experienced more of the new and relatively affluent 'youth culture' whose standards of leisure and consumption of luxury goods lead them to divert their resources in these directions for longer after getting married. A second, indicated but by no means demonstrated in the analysis we have so far made of our own study, is that younger and more recently married couples, themselves brought up in a society which seems to them to offer rather more advantages in education and employment, in social mobility generally, than for previous generations, have higher ambitions for their children, leading them to have slightly fewer of them and to have them at longer intervals.

Finally, and as another qualification, it should be said that when asked whether, if they had had twice as much money, they would have had any more children, only about a third of couples in *either* cohort (1952–7 and 1962–7) said 'yes'. If there is an economic effect, it operates on a minority of couples as an effect on size, although it may have a more widespread impact on spacing. Even then, of course, if a third of these couples would have had more children, the period fertility would have shown a dramatically different pattern in absolute, if not relative, terms.

Birth control

Knowledge about the contraceptive practices of British couples married since the early 1950s is much more secure. All the research has shown that over 90 per cent of recently married couples had used some ˗form of birth control, the culmination of a trend recorded by Glass [4] and described in Table 2.5.1.

TABLE 2.5.1

Ever-use of birth control by year of marriage

	1941–5	1946–50	1951–5	1956–60	1961–5
All	82·1	86·7	89·7	90·6†	91·4†
Non-manual workers	88·7	88·2	95·8	93·3†	92·7†
Manual workers	76·8	86·4	86·3	89·3†	91·3†

† The interviewing was done in 1967–8; some couples may therefore have been intending to use birth control after the survey was carried out.

This is the first point at which we introduce class differentials. This is not because they are irrelevant to the question of economic and other motivations for different birth intervals and family sizes (far from it); but because we have in any study so far analysed no information on how these motivations may or may not have varied by social class.

The data in Table 2.5.1. indicate a narrowing of class differentials in ever-use of birth control. But it should not be inferred from this that contraceptive effectiveness is thus improving. 'Ever-use' is the most imprecise of all classifications of use, and it thus disguises the second important set of facts about contraception in Britain, that more than half of all couples still use male methods, that more than half use less reliable ones (not coincident, since the sheath is considered to be more rather than less reliable), and that there is a strong positive association between social class and the use of more reliable methods.

Thirdly, however, and consistent with longer intervals between marriages and first births and first and subsequent births in the marriages of the later 1960s, it does appear to be the case that more recently married couples have started using contraception earlier in their marriages. Nevertheless, and fourthly, there still appears to be a relatively large number of 'unwanted' pregnancies, although, as one would expect with such a vague and difficult concept, estimates vary. Going against the trend of fertility as a whole, moreover, they appear if anything to have increased very slightly at all but the highest parities, from perhaps 10–15 per cent for couples married in the later 1950s to perhaps 15–20 per cent for couples married in the earlier 1960s (although some estimates put the proportion as high as 45 per cent, including, as do the others, both those who did not want the pregnancy at all and those who did not want it at the time that it occurred). This increase, if it is such, remains unexplained, although it could be, and this would be consistent with the facts to be explained, that the pressure not to have quite so many children quite so frequently makes more recently married couples define more pregnancies as in some sense 'unwanted'. Finally, with respect to the practice of birth control, there is evidence that the resort to abortion and sterilization is now more frequent, and this must have prevented an increasing proportion of unwanted pregnancies from coming to term or even from occurring at all.

This is a bald summary of information which, by comparison with that so far available on non-contraceptive matters is both full and complex; we have attempted a fuller account elsewhere [10]. Nevertheless, it is sufficient to indicate that not only the availability but also the use of more reliable methods has increased in the past two decades. Together with what could be a stronger and more widespread motivation to delay and restrict fertility (which always improves contraceptive practice, whatever the available methods [16, 20]), this would certainly be adequate to explain the changes we described at the beginning of the paper.

Conclusions

It is possible to adduce evidence that at the very least is not inconsistent with the hypotheses that the components of the fall in the crude birth rate in England and Wales since 1964 are due to slightly more severe economic constraints, higher standards of leisure and consumption, greater ambition for the children themselves, and improved birth control. Three final points should be made: first, changes at the individual, as distinct from the aggregate, level have been slight, and conventional methods of social research are poor at making the necessarily fine discriminations; second, we have as yet no idea of the relative importance of the various factors; and third, it is important to match explanations produced for England and Wales against those that might be offered to account for the similar demographic changes elsewhere in Europe.

REFERENCES

1. BOURGEOIS-PICHAT, J. (1972). La dieuxième conférence démographique Européenne de Strasbourg. II. La fécondité des pays d'Europe, *Population* **27**, 422–32.
2. BUSFIELD, N. J. and HAWTHORN, G. P. (1971). Some social determinants of recent trends in British fertility, *J. biosoc. Sci.* Suppl. **3**, 74.
3. CARTWRIGHT, A. (1970). *Parents and family planning services.* Routledge and Kegan Paul, London.
4. GLASS, D. V. (1971). The components of natural increase in England and Wales. In Select Committee on Science and Technology, First Report, *Population of the United Kingdom*, HC 379, pp. 191–6. H.M.S.O., London.
5. GREBENIK, E., and ROWNTREE, G. (1963). Factors associated with the age at marriage in Britain. *Proc. R. Soc. B* **159**, 178–98.
6. HABAKKUK, H. J. (1971). *Population growth and economic development since 1750*, pp. 10–24. Leicester University Press, Leicester.
7. HAJNAL, J. (1965). European marriage patterns in perspective. In *Population in history* (eds D. V. Glass and D. E. C. Eversley), pp. 101–43. Arnold, London.
8. HAWTHORN, G. P. (1970). *The sociology of fertility.* Collier–Macmillan, London.
9. —— (1973). *Population policy: a modern delusion.* Fabian Society, London.
10. —— (1972). *Birth control in Britain: the results of some recent studies* (unpublished).
11. ——, BUSFIELD, N. J. and PADDON, M. J. *Social determinants of family size.* A study of a sample of couples, resident in Ipswich in 1969–70, married 1952–7 or 1962–7, and in which the wife was aged 44 or less and still living with her husband. Financed by the University of Essex, the Nuffield Foundation, the Social Science Research Council, and the Marie Stopes Memorial Foundation,

with computing assistance from the Department of Applied Economics, Cambridge University.

12. KEYFITZ, N. (1971). Changes of birth and death rates and their demographic effects. In National Academy of Sciences, *Rapid population growth*, Vol. II, pp. 669–74. Johns Hopkins Press, Baltimore and London.

13. OFFICE OF POPULATION CENSUSES AND SURVEYS (1972). *Population projections No.* 2 1971–2011. H.M.S.O., London.

14. PEEL, J. (1970). The Hull Family Survey. I. The Survey Couples 1966, *J. biosoc Sci.* **2**, 45–70.

15. —— (1972). The Hull Family Survey. II. Family Planning in the first 5 years of marriage, *J. biosoc. Sci.* **4**, 333–46.

16. SAGI, P. C., POTTER, R. G., and WESTOFF, C. F. (1962). Contraceptive effectiveness as a function of desired family size, *Population Studies* **15**, 291.

17. SELECT COMMITTEE ON SCIENCE AND TECHNOLOGY (1971). First Report, *Population of the United Kingdom*, HC 379. H.M.S.O., London.

18. SMITH, A. (1971). The role of family planning. In *Family poverty* (ed. D. Bull), pp. 83–92. Duckworth and the Child Poverty Action Group, London.

19. WOOLF, M. (1971). *Family intentions.* SS 408. H.M.S.O., London.

20. WRIGLEY, E. A. (1969). *Population and history*, pp. 116–19, 140–2, *passim*. Weidenfeld and Nicolson, London.

2.5.5. The effects of fertility control on human sexual behaviour

JOHN BANCROFT

Department of Psychiatry, Oxford University

The need for human fertility control stems from one simple fact: human beings engage in sexual behaviour. It is therefore crucial in understanding the problems of fertility control to understand the effects such control has on sexual behaviour. That the evidence on such an issue is in many respects confused and in others absent is no doubt a reflection of the obstacles to the investigation of normal human sexuality which have only recently begun to lessen.

This paper will be in two parts. In the first, human sexuality will be broken down into its constituent parts and their determinants discussed. This will provide the conceptual framework and the psycho-physiological basis for the second part, which will look specifically at the effects of fertility control on sexual behaviour.

Even though much of the usefulness of such a paper at the present time must be in indicating areas of ignorance, the literature relevant to both parts is extensive. It is not intended therefore to provide a comprehensive review but rather to put the subject on a rational basis which hopefully will be relevant to subsequent research in this area.

The components of sexual behaviour and their determinants

The motivation for human sexual behaviour is indeed complex. Apart from the hedonic aspects there is the need to meet expectations of normality as well as the use of sex in the control of one human being by another, an aspect which Millett [58] has succinctly labelled 'sexual politics'. First, therefore, we must attempt some clarification of our concepts.

Sexuality has been divided by Whalen [85] into the following categories:

(1) *Sexual identification.* This is better described as *gender identity* or that part of personal identity which relates to masculinity or feminity [78, 5].

(2) *Object choice* or the preference for one type of sexual partner rather than another.

(3) *Arousal and arousability.* The first refers to the state of sexual excitement or sexual desire at a point in time. The second refers to the facility to respond to sexual stimuli with an increase in arousal.

(4) *Sexual gratification* refers to the quality and intensity of pleasure or reward associated with sexual behaviour.

(5) *Sexual activity* refers to the occurrence of purposive behaviour of sexual type, i.e. engaging in sexual contact or coitus whether or not it culminates in orgasm.

One can usefully add a further category under the heading of sexual attitudes which includes individuals' expectations and beliefs as to what is 'normal', morally acceptable, or safe. This is best linked with the category of object choice forming the sexual attitudinal system (i.e. what is believed or felt to be sexually desirable).

The sexual behaviour of an individual represents a complex interaction between these various categories. This should be borne in mind when assessing changes in sexual behaviour. Frequently in studies of fertility control reference is made to changes in libido or sexual drive without specifying what such terms mean. Operationally sexual drive is often defined in terms of sexual outlet [42]. This may be misleading, however. The frequency of coitus says nothing about the quality of the coital experience. In some cases a high frequency reflects a low level of enjoyment or difficulty in achieving satisfactory orgasm in one or both partners. Between frequent acts of coitus may be periods of low sexual interest, the individual's sexual needs being adequately met by the coital experience. Low frequency, on the other hand, or the absence of a satisfactory sexual outlet may be associated with high levels of sexual interest and arousability reflecting a failure to meet that particular individual's sexual needs. Complexities such as these indicate that the assessment of change in sexual behaviour is no simple matter.

Let us now look more closely at these various aspects, their determinants, and how they interact with one another. To do this we will have to consider psychological, neuro-physiological, and neuro-endocrine mechanisms.

Gender identity. Developmentally this is the first to be considered. There is convincing evidence from studies of pseudo-hermaphroditic and other congenital anomalies that the first 3 years or so of a child's upbringing play an important part in determining gender identity, especially the 'core' gender identity or the awareness that 'I am a male' or 'I am a female' [30]. There is now a large body of evidence, however, from animal work with both rodents and primates, to indicate that adult patterns of gender-role behaviour are partly determined by endocrine factors operating at critical periods of intra-uterine development. In humans this type of mechanism remains speculative, although there is evidence resulting from the administration of large doses of progestogens to pregnant women and the observed effects on the resulting offspring which supports the importance of such mechanisms in man [62]. It thus seems likely that gender identity depends on an interaction between these prenatal and postnatal factors (for a review of this evidence see Diamond [18]). Although the most important part of gender identity development occurs in these first few years, there are also important influences both psychological and physiological which operate at later stages. Thus at puberty the physiological changes as well as the psychological impact of peer group relationships play an important part. Similarly the development of acceptable patterns of sexual behaviour in adulthood will be necessary for the maturing and maintenance of satisfactory gender identity. Cultural determinants of what is masculine or feminine will also continue to operate throughout the individual's life-span. In our society there are important differences between socio-economic groups in this respect though these are probably becoming less marked [42, 78]. The effect of changes in sexual behaviour on the gender identity and the need to maintain a certain sexual pattern in order to stabilize gender identity are issues of particular relevance to this paper. The relationship between gender identity, sexual preferences, and overt sexual behaviour is discussed at length in another paper [5]. It must suffice here to suggest that there is a reciprocal relationship between gender identity and sexual behaviour. Thus a masculine identity will determine to some extent the pattern of behaviour adopted and vice versa. In a stable state there is consistency between the two. Anything that changes either will lead to inconsistency and instability in the system.

Object choice or sexual preference. The determinants of sexual object choice in humans remain obscure. In sub-human primates the role of hormones in maintaining the attractiveness of the female is now well established. Olfactory cues known as pheromones and visual stimuli from the genital area have been shown to be oestrogen dependent [22, 56]. Ovariectomized females lose their attractiveness, which can be restored by administering oestrogens. What is not clear is the relative importance of learning in producing this responsiveness to such endocrine-dependent erotic cues. Attractiveness of a female monkey does not solely depend on these particular cues, however. Some females are rated more attractive than others by a particular male regardless of their endocrine state [57]. In humans the role of olfactory cues is difficult to assess. Undoubtedly there are some humans, both male and female, in whom particular olfactory stimuli are very arousing [54], but once again these may represent learned rather than innate responses.

Apart from cues such as these the overt behaviour of an animal may also influence its selection, by another animal, as a mate. Thus the animal who adopts the typical female receptive posture is more likely to be mounted. The gender-role behaviour of an animal may therefore render it more or less attractive. If the masculine boy is rendered more attractive to girls by virtue of his masculinity, and hence finds relationships with them more rewarding, this may facilitate development of heterosexual preferences. The effeminate boy, on the other hand, being relatively unattractive to females may, because of this obstacle to rewarding heterosexual relationships, be more likely to develop other sexual preferences such as homosexuality. A mechanism such as this would be one way in which genetic, prenatal, or early environmental factors could influence the development of sexual preferences. Apart from this, however, the limited evidence is more consistent with learning in later childhood and adolescence as the main determinant of sexual object choice. There are possibly important differences between males and females in this respect. In lower animals learning and involvement of the cortex apparently plays a much greater part in the development of normal sexual behaviour in males than in females [24].

There has been a tendency to impose the same distinction on humans; females, it is suggested, being much less responsive to visual stimuli and more dependent on tactile stimuli [43]. Kinsey's data supporting this has now been questioned, and differences between the sexes in response to erotic stimuli appear to be much less than was once thought. There is some evidence that females are more susceptible to cultural and non-sexual factors in their acquisition of preferences and, if so, this may have served to confound the issue in the past (for a review of this topic, see Bancroft [6]).

What is probably more important for this paper is the relative stability of sexual preferences once established. Are they established during adolescence and thereafter relatively fixed? Can they be influenced throughout adult life by new learning experiences? This, of course, refers not only to changes from hetero to homosexual orientation and vice versa but also changes in the type of heterosexual partner preferred. We must, however, remain uncertain on this point. Factors that determine not just who is sexually attractive but also who is desirable as a long-term partner are even more obscure. The need for greater understanding of this process of mate-selection and the stability of the subsequent sexual bond is of considerable importance in tackling the widespread problems in marriage, sexual or otherwise.

Sexual attitudes about normality, morality, and acceptability presumably result from an interaction between personality characteristics and family and sub-cultural influences. Attitudes about sex are often instilled at an early age and endowed with considerable affect, such as anxiety or guilt. It may require a long period of uninhibiting adulthood for these primitive fears and inhibitions to be dissipated and full sexual expression and enjoyment allowed.

Sexual arousability and activity. These can conveniently be considered together.

In lower animals there is a close and predictable relationship between hormonal factors, the oestrous cycle, and sexual behaviour. In sub-human primates the situation is much more complex and closer in this respect to the human: it is therefore worth considering the primates more closely. The first very fundamental point that emerges from primate data, which though it may sound obvious cannot be overemphasized, is that sexual behaviour involves two animals and the interaction of processes operating in each of them. Thus when a male and a female are put together the arousability, activity, and gratification of the male will depend on the attractiveness and behaviour of the female. Probably, though less clearly, the reverse also applies. In the female monkey, two components of sexuality have been suggested: 'attractiveness' and 'receptivity' [55]. 'Attractiveness' is a state which acts on the male's behaviour by hormone-dependent erotic cues already mentioned. 'Attractiveness' in the female will, therefore, increase the arousal of the male, his attempts to mount, and his ability to ejaculate. The 'receptive' state acts directly on the female's behaviour by increasing the frequency of invitations to mount and making less likely refusal of the male's attempts to mount. Here then is a complexity of female sexuality which may account for so much of the confusion that has reigned over this issue. Even now there is disagreement and conflicting evidence as to the determinants of these two components. Michael [55] has reported that the 'receptivity' is influenced by a direct effect of oestrogens on the hypothalamus, whereas 'attractiveness' is a more complex matter depending in part on oestrogen-dependent olfactory cues from the vagina (pheromones). Everitt and Herbert [22], however, suggest that 'attractiveness' is an oestrogen-dependent mechanism, whereas 'receptivity' is dependent on androgens secreted mainly by the adrenal cortex. They supported this by demonstrating that 'receptivity' was reduced by adrenalectomy and only restored when androgens were administered.

The evidence from human females would fit this latter interpretation. Ovariectomy in women does not usually produce any changes in sexual interest or enjoyment on the part of the woman. Clinical data of this kind, however, are usually limited so that it is not possible to be sure that ovariectomy did not in some way reduce 'attractiveness' as defined above, although in the majority of cases it did not seem to reduce 'receptivity' [11, 43]. Adrenalectomy, on the other hand, usually resulted in a general reduction of sexual behaviour and enjoyment [83]. It has also been known for some time that the administration of androgens to women frequently leads to enlargement of the clitoris and increased sexual desire [13]. Once again it is not possible from the available evidence to say whether it affects 'attractiveness' in either direction.

When cyclical changes in sexual activity are considered there are also interesting comparisons between primate and human females. Unlike lower mammals, sub-human primates vary considerably in the tendency to show cyclical patterns of sexual activity. Michael [55] described three main types of patterns: (1) those with well-marked maxima near mid-cycle, marked declines early in the luteal phase and secondary rises immediately prior to menstruation; (2) those with sustained high levels of mounting during the follicular phase, again a marked decline during the luteal phase and low levels persisting until menstruation; (3) those with generally low levels of mounting activity throughout the cycle and no signs of rhythmic changes. More than 50 per cent of the cycles studied were of the latter type.

Evidence of cyclical sexual activity in human females has produced many conflicting reports in the literature over many years [32]. Udry and Morris [81] studying three groups of women, found patterns similar to both types (1) and (2) of Michael. Hart [32] reported patterns with peaks most commonly in association with menstruation, either immediately before, after or both. Only 6 per cent of his series showed mid-cycle peaks and 34 per cent showed no pattern. Similar findings had been shown by

Davis [17]. Thus it seems likely that Michael's observations of primates show a range of variation similar to that of human females. What determines whether a cyclical pattern occurs or not, and if so which type, is not clear. Obviously other factors may be operating in relation to menstruation. Coitus may be more likely just before menstruation in anticipation of a period of abstinence. For the same reason, coitus immediately after menstruation is more likely. The association of higher rates in the first half of the cycle, with or without mid-cycle peaks, has been attributed to the relative levels of oestrogens and progesterones. It is conceivable that, in those couples where oestrogen-dependent erotic cues (e.g. olfactory) are important, this could be a factor. Several studies have demonstrated cyclical changes in a number of physiological functions, including pain tolerance, olfaction, and auditory and visual sensitivity, all being increased around the time of ovulation [19]. Such changes have been teleologically interpreted as means of increasing the likelihood of coitus at the time of ovulation. However, progesterone which increases following ovulation during the luteal phase may contribute to such cyclical patterns. This hormone appears to have a direct effect in reducing sexual drive in both males [33, 61], and females [45]. Thus a decline of activity during the luteal phase may simply be reflecting the rise in progesterone level with the pre-menstrual peak of activity reported by Michael, reflecting the pre-menstrual decline in progesterone. Hormonal cyclical changes therefore may contribute by affecting the 'attractiveness' component during the first half of the cycle and by reducing 'receptivity' in the second half.

When we also consider the amount of variation in responsiveness to different types of erotic stimuli in the male, and the effect that this will have on the coital frequency, it is not surprising that no single pattern of cyclical activity emerges. It would help to clarify the situation if we had data on the masturbation frequency of women without partners to influence their activity. Such evidence, however, is not available. One of the three groups of women studied by Udry and Morris [81] was comprised of 13 single women but the type of sexual activity appeared to be a mixture of auto-erotic and coital.

In the male the situation is probably less complex, though there is still a lack of adequate data. There is as yet no evidence to suggest that hormonal variation may affect the 'attractiveness' of the male and hence directly affect the 'receptivity' of the female. It thus seems that we are only dealing with the male equivalent of 'receptivity'. Here, however, the situation is complex enough. The involvement of androgens in this aspect of male sexuality seems to be beyond dispute, but the precise relationship is obscure and once again we must contend with data which show considerable individual variation.

The developmental aspects are probably of prime importance. First, animal work has shown that the action of androgens in masculinizing the foetal brain at critical periods not only affects the subsequent gender-role behaviour during early life [31] but also determines the sensitivity of the brain and possibly the target organs (i.e. genitalia) to the increased levels of androgens occurring at puberty and thereafter [26]. This may partly explain why the development of sexual arousability is so much more marked and rapid in the adolescent male than in the adolescent female, even though the accompanying change in androgen secretion in the two sexes is not so disparate [43]. Variation in this sensitivity will also contribute to variation amongst males in their responses to adolescent rises in testosterone.

A further complexity has to be incorporated into this developmental picture. If the pubertal increase in androgens is prevented either by pre-pubertal castration or hypogonadism then the development of sexual arousability and behaviour is seriously impaired. If castration or hypogonadism occurs well after puberty there is usually (though not always) a decline in sexual arousability, gratification, and activity, sometimes taking a year or more before reaching its maximum effect. In the case of pre-pubertal hypogonadism the administration of androgens in adult life will do little to alter the sexual pattern but with post-pubertal hypogonadism exogenous androgens will usually restore the sexual pattern to the level established before the hypogonadism developed [60]. There is substantial animal data which is also consistent with these clinical observations [47, 49]. Thus it seems that the role androgens play in establishing the adult pattern of sexuality needs to be played at the appropriate time of development—early adolescence. This suggests another 'critical period', although a much less precise one than that occurring prenatally. The observations by Kinsey *et al.* [43] that people with late onset of puberty tend to have low levels of sexual drive in adulthood would be consistent with this hypothesis. The critical nature of this stage in development may depend on the proper interaction of endocrine change, psychological development, and learning, though we must remain uncertain on this point.

Developmental mechanisms such as these may partially explain the complex and unpredictable relationships between circulating androgen levels and sexual arousability and activity in males. The administration of exogenous androgens in 'normal' males occasionally produces an increase in arousability but more often it produces no change [34]. Androgen levels in men with sexual inadequacy are very variable. Heller and Myers [35] identified a 'male climacteric' group of men with sexual inadequacy and high gonadotrophin titres. They assumed that the underlying mechanism was primary testicular failure of uncertain origin and reported a good response to the administration of exogenous testosterone, in contrast to their 'psychogenic' group who had normal gonadotrophin titres and did not respond to testosterone. How common this 'male climacteric' picture is remains obscure and no further reports of this entity have been forthcoming. Cooper *et al.* [14] have reported lower androgen levels in those males in whom sexual inadequacy (e.g. erectile impotence) was associated with long-standing loss of sexual arousability. They labelled this group 'constitutional' and distinguished them from those whose sexual inadequacy was of recent onset, secondary, and associated with the maintenance of sexual arousability (in this case sexual arousal would occur but with the absence of adequate specific responses such as erection or would only fail in sexually threatening situations such as impending coitus). These are the only two reports in which the effects of exogenous testosterone in a series of inadequate males have been related to pre-treatment endocrine status. Beumont *et al.* [10] reported a single case of hypogonadism in which exogenous testosterone conclusively increased sexual arousability. The main interest of this single case study is that the effects of treatment included an increase in arousability (measured as erection) to psychic stimuli. This does not support the mechanism of action of testosterone postulated by Perloff [68], in which increase in genital sensitivity was the main effect. If this were the case then 'reflexive erection' and not 'psychic erection' would be affected [4].

Other reports have claimed success in treating erectile impotence with mixtures containing testosterone [12, 52]. Jacobovitz [38] claimed success with a combination of testosterone and thyroid, though he also reported a high response rate to placebo. In none of these studies was the design and method of assessment used apparently satisfactory. It remains likely, however, that a proportion of males with sexual inadequacy will respond to exogenous androgens but as yet we have no idea how to identify such cases. Kuppermann [44] has claimed success in treating frigidity in women with testosterone, but no adequate clinical information was provided to back up this claim.

Recent studies of sexual offenders, in which the effects of 'libido-suppressing' drugs have been assessed, have further emphasized the complexity of these relationships between hormones and behaviour [79, 9]. Benperidol, a butyrophenone tranquillizer, ethinyl oestradiol, an oestrogen, and cyproterone acetate, an anti-androgen, were all found to affect sexual interest and behaviour although, with the doses and duration of administration involved, the effects were not marked. However, although the patterns of behavioural effects of each of these three drugs were fairly similar the endocrine effects were very different. Benperidol produced no endocrine changes whereas cyproterone acetate and ethinyl oestradiol produced marked endocrine changes in the opposite direction; the former reduced both LH and testosterone, the latter increased both. The unexpected effect of the oestrogen in this respect may be explained by the finding of higher sex hormone-binding globulin levels in association with the oestrogen. Thus the higher testosterone level was largely composed of inactive bound hormone. This underlines the importance of relating free unbound hormone to behaviour and indicates some of the substantial methodological difficulties in the way of clarifying these relationships.

Nevertheless, even if such technical barriers can be overcome there is no reason to expect a simple picture. It is unlikely that the underlying relationship between hormones and sexual arousability is a linear one. There is some clinical evidence that women experience a reduction of sexual drive if exogenous testosterone doses are very high. Similarly, the effect of testosterone in stimulating spermatogenesis in males changes to one of inhibition when high levels are involved. It seems probable that for each individual there is an optimum level of circulating hormone which becomes established as part of a complex pattern of interacting psychological and physiological factors to produce optimum levels of sexual behaviour. Anything which alters the level of that particular endocrine variable above or below its optimum would therefore impair the behavioural pattern. It is also possible that this optimum level will vary from individual to individual.

When we turn from endocrine to psychological factors the picture is no clearer and we are confronted by all the obstacles to objective measurement which are inherent in this area. We know very little about the mechanisms which mediate between psychological appraisal of a sexual stimulus and the response of sexual arousal, though clearly the limbic system is involved [51]. Psychological factors lead to inhibition as well as stimulation however. In the past this has often been naïvely explained as a result of the peripheral autonomic effects of anxiety on sexual mechanisms. The fallacy of this explanation has been discussed elsewhere [4]. However, it is true that for many individuals the presence of anxiety in a sexual situation is associated with impairment of response both in the male (with erectile impotence or premature or delayed ejaculation) and in the female (with impaired vaginal secretion or delayed orgasm). The relevant mechanisms, however, are not so clear. It seems likely that in many situations the appraisal of threat leads to both the experience of anxiety and a direct neuro-physiological inhibition of the sexual mechanism. In other cases anxiety may accompany normal sexual response or even facilitate it. The concept of sexual threat used here does not necessarily imply that either anxiety or inhibition will be associated with it. If it is something that can be avoided by avoiding the sexual act (e.g. fear of venereal disease) then anxiety may occur if the sexual situation continues. If, on the other hand, it is something that can be avoided by inhibiting sexual response (e.g. limiting arousal and hence avoiding fear of loss of control) then impaired sexual behaviour may occur without any anxiety, the impairment serving to reduce the threat. This issue has been discussed more fully in another paper [6].

Anger or resentment is also an important affective state in its effects on sexual behaviour. In many individuals unresolved anger will directly inhibit response presumably by means of psychophysiological mechanisms, in others sexual inhibition may be used as a means of expressing hostility by depriving one's partner. Occasionally anger may facilitate sexual arousal.

Gratification. As far as the quality of sexual pleasure is concerned, we are faced with a more or less complete lack of any scientifically useful evidence. In our society there has been a tendency to emphasize the importance of the orgasm. This has often resulted in a preoccupation with orgasm in both male and female to the detriment of other parts of the sexual experience. This point has been convincingly made by Masters and Johnson [54] and is borne out in clinical experience when couples report substantial increase in pleasure in the non-orgasmic aspects when their attention is distracted from the orgasm [7]. Many women in the past have tended to emphasize the enjoyment that stems from giving pleasure to their partners rather than from their own erotic responses. This again has probably been a reflection of the cultural attitudes to female sexuality which in the Victorian era most clearly separated women into those who were worthy of being loved and those who were sexually responsive [58]. Whereas female sexuality has become more acceptable since those times, women have been further confused and inhibited by the Freudian concept of vaginal and clitoral orgasms, the latter reflecting an immature stage of sexual development. This is a further myth that Masters and Johnson [53] have exploded, but its effects are still widespread.

The physiological basis to orgasm in both males and females is quite obscure. Nevertheless there is almost certainly considerable variation between individuals and within individuals in the intensity of orgasmic experience. Furthermore the pleasantness of orgasm is a subtle matter. Unduly intense orgasmic experiences can border on the painful.

For the moment, therefore, there is no objective means of evaluating sexual gratification and one must rely on subjective ratings of pleasure.

The effects of fertility control on sexual behaviour

We are now in a position to consider the effects of fertility control on the various aspects of sexuality already defined. First, the likely range of effects will be suggested and then the available evidence relating to the main methods of fertility control will be briefly reviewed. That there is very little satisfactory evidence available will quickly become apparent.

Gender identity. Motherhood and the ability to conceive is an important component in the gender identity of some women. Thus anything affecting fertility may provoke identity problems in such a woman. Such effects will presumably be more marked with irreversible methods of fertility control. In the male also the ability to father a child may be important. It has been suggested, particularly in poor, working-class groups, that the male may assert himself and bolster his masculinity by making and keeping his wife pregnant [25, 69]. Any method which relies on endocrine change in controlling fertility could conceivably affect physiological mechanisms which contribute to the maintenance of gender identity, e.g. skin texture or body shape. However, one's understanding of such mechanisms is negligible. In the male, androgens may play an important part in maintaining gender identity by facilitating assertive behaviour and increasing muscle bulk. In the female, oestrogens may affect breast size.

An aspect of identity that can be affected by fertility control, particularly in women, is the fear that with an effective control the individual may become sexually promiscuous. A further factor is how the responsibility for fertility control is allocated. In most cases either the male or the female is responsible, and there will be some individuals who will accept such responsibility more readily than others.

Sexual preferences. Subtle cues related to 'attractiveness' could be affected by fertility-control techniques particularly if hormonal mechanisms are involved. Not uncommonly the change in sexual feelings of the female using a safe contraceptive for the first time may have adverse consequences in the male partner. Thus the increase in sexual desire that sometimes accompanies the use of oral contraceptives or follows sterilization may be threatening or distasteful to the male who cannot accept sexual assertiveness in a female. Any technique that irreversibly alters the woman (e.g. tubal ligation or hysterectomy) may provoke in the man the idea that the woman has been 'spoiled' or may aggravate previously hidden fears about injuring the woman during coitus.

Of other attitudes to sex, the most important one is that which considers sex to be sinful if it does not involve the possibility of conception. This is commonly associated with religious orthodoxy.

Sexual arousability, activity, and gratification. If hormonal mechanisms play an important part in a particular individual's pattern of sexual responsiveness, then any alteration of the normal hormonal state could disturb the response pattern most probably causing a reduction in responsiveness. The removal of the threat of pregnancy is likely to increase sexual arousability by reducing psychological inhibition or anxiety. When this is important the degree of benefit will obviously depend on the degree of safety attributed to the method by the user. Other threats may be increased, however, e.g. the fear of venereal disease or distaste associated with mess or the handling of genitalia. Mechanical effects of contraceptive techniques may operate to impair responsiveness.

Let us now look at each of the main contraceptive techniques in turn.

Coitus interruptus. Although this method is frequently decried as psychologically harmful, it is still widely used. Evidence for its harmfulness is lacking, but the idea is based on the commonsense assumption that if either partner has to concentrate on withdrawal at the right time this must impair the ability to relax and fully enjoy the sexual act. Also it deprives the couple of the mutual sharing of the male orgasm. However, it is possible that there are some individuals in whom control of ejaculation is sufficiently great that withdrawal presents no problem, and there will be some who will feel happier if intravaginal ejaculation and its accompanying mess can be avoided. It should not be assumed therefore that coitus interruptus will inevitably impair sexual enjoyment.

Sheath or condom. There is little systematic data on the effects of the sheath on sexual behaviour, even though it is very widely used. A criticism that is often levelled against it is that putting on the sheath causes an unwelcome interruption in the natural course of events. That this may be so for many couples should not be doubted, but there may be others in whom the 'interruption' could become an enjoyable part of the act. A further advantage for some is that it avoids the mess of ejaculate. For this reason some women prefer their partners to wear a sheath even when they themselves are using an oral contraceptive or I.U.D. [77]. It is also widely believed that the sheath acts as a barrier to venereal disease. Its use may therefore reduce anxiety for that reason. To some, however, condoms are associated with illicit sex, and this may influence their response when they are used [48].

The most obvious disadvantage of the sheath is that it impairs the sensitivity of the penis. That this is important would seem to be substantiated by the commercial attempts to make thinner and thinner sheaths. Occasionally, if premature ejaculation is a problem, this reduction in sensitivity can be an advantage.

Diaphragm. This is again criticized on the grounds of causing interruption of the act. This disadvantage can be avoided by fitting the diaphragm at an earlier stage. This may raise further problems, however. Unless the woman routinely fits the cap she will, by using it, be revealing her anticipation of coitus. To some women it is important that they do not communicate such wishes, and they feel less inhibited if the act is initiated by the male. Other women dislike the handling of their genitalia that is involved. Occasionally in the male partner, the complaint is that the diaphragm causes mechanical discomfort during coitus [48].

Intra-uterine devices. Although I.U.D.s are being extensively used there is relatively little evidence of their effect on sexual behaviour. Herzberg *et al.* [36] in comparing I.U.D.s with oral contraceptives reported a steady increase in libido in those using the I.U.D.s. This they reasonably attributed to confidence in their efficacy and hence reduction of fear of pregnancy. Reduction in libido has been reported in a few cases [50].

The most important effect of these devices is the tendency to prolong menstruation in many women, particularly during the first few months of use [59]. This will directly reduce the opportunities for coitus. Kutner and Duffy [46] have suggested that as the I.U.D. is fitted by a doctor, its use may lessen the guilt that some women feel who consider sex to be more for reproduction than pleasure. It is also more suitable, they suggest, for those women who are not disposed to take an active role in contraception, such as is involved in inserting a cap or taking a daily pill.

Oral contraceptives. There has now been a substantial amount of research into the effects of oral contraceptives. A number of studies have investigated effects on sexual behaviour, usually with a superficiality of approach that does not permit the type of analysis outlined in the first part of this paper. The most sophisticated procedure for assessing sexual effects reported is that by Herzberg *et al.* [36], who used three simple self-rating scales, one for level of interest, one for frequency of coitus, and one for the proportion of occasions associated with orgasm.

The greater scientific interest in sexual behaviour shown in relation to oral contraceptives than that found with other methods of fertility control possibly stems from the fact that there is a hormonal mechanism involved. To pursue this point further, we should therefore consider briefly what the hormonal basis of oral contraception is.

Up to now there have been three main types of oral preparation used.

1. Combined oestrogen–progestogen preparation in which both hormones are given in combination throughout the non-menstrual part of the cycle. The relative strength and nature of the two components varies from preparation to preparation [80].
2. Sequential formulations in which oestrogens are given in the first half of the cycle and progestogens plus oestrogens in the second half, mirroring the normal cyclical changes.
3. Continuous progestogens which are given throughout the cycle and in variable dosage.

As yet our understanding of their mode of action is incomplete. It is thought most likely that both combined and sequential preparations inhibit ovulation by interfering with normal gonadotrophin production (FSH and LH). The combined preparation, however, probably acts in other ways as well, by 'inducing histological and biochemical changes in the endometrium, physicochemical changes in the cervical mucus, and changes in tubal physiology and uterine motility, [87]. Continuous progestogen probably does not consistently inhibit ovulation and may depend on other mechanisms for its antifertility effect. For these reasons the combined preparations are the most efficient.

Apart from uncertainty about their precise mode of action, there is also considerable uncertainty about their general endocrine effects on the women receiving them. Once again these appear to vary from woman to woman. As far as effects on sexual behaviour are concerned, clinical impression is consistent with the hormonal model outlined in the first part of this paper. Thus it is usually assumed that if the Pill has a hormonal effect of supressing libido it is because of progestogen effects and not oestrogen effects (similarly the progestogen component is blamed for any accompanying depression) [80]. Grant and Pryse-Davies [28] unfortunately combined depression and loss of libido in their assessment of the effects of these compounds, but found that the frequency of this combined problem was proportional to the amount of progestogen in the Pill. When more detailed studies are examined, the picture becomes confused. Westoff *et al.* [84] reported two large-scale studies in the U.S.A. in which frequency of coitus was higher in women on the Pill than in those using other methods or no method at all. Their figures were difficult to interpret as selection factors may have biased the result. Nevertheless, their findings made a widespread libido-reducing effect of oral contraceptives unlikely. No details of the types of oral preparations used were given. These authors also illustrated the confusion in this area by suggesting that the increase in sexual activity may be due to libido-*increasing* effect attributable to progesterone. Needless to say there are occasional cases in the literature where progesterone has apparently increased libido [73].

Juhlin and Liden [39] also reported a higher frequency of coitus in women using oral contraceptives than in those using other methods. El Hefnawi [21] reported an increase in coital frequency in those using oral contraceptives in Egypt. From the epidemiological point of view, therefore, the Pill would appear to increase coital frequency. It does not follow that this means greater enjoyment. It is also difficult to separate psychological effects stemming from reduction of fear of pregnancy from any direct endocrine effects on libido. Methodological problems abound and Richter [71] suggested that results will vary according to the newness of the preparation. As confidence in a preparation increases so the incidence of increased libido goes up. When a new preparation is introduced the situation reverses until confidence builds up again.

Clearly to control for psychological factors such as these, it is necessary to carry out double-blind comparative studies in which other contraceptive measures are employed, whilst oral contraceptives are compared with placebo. So far, very few such studies have been carried out. Some of these have not reported effects on sexual behaviour. Bakke [2] reported a double-blind crossover study of a combined preparation, oestrogen alone, and placebo. Twenty out of 27 women preferred one or the other of the active preparations, whilst only 3 preferred placebo. This was partly due to withdrawal effects in the placebo period. Twelve women reported increased sexual drive and 6 of them gave up the drug because of this effect. In the uncontrolled study by Grant and Pryse-Davies [28] the frequency of depression plus libido loss varied from 28 per cent with the strongest progestogen preparations to 5 per cent with oestrogen dominated or sequential preparations. It was not clear to what extent this libido change was simply a consequence of depressed mood. Kane [40] and his co-workers in a further uncontrolled study reported that 15 per cent of their group showed decreased sexual desire, whilst 7 per cent showed an increase. Thirty-four per cent experienced depression while on the Pill. Those who were most disabled by menstruation and who had the lowest frequency of sexual intercourse before starting the preparation were most at risk for these adverse changes.

Grounds *et al.* [29] compared two groups of 10 women each for 2 months; one with an active preparation and one with placebo. On the active Pill, 8 out of 10 experienced reduced libido in the first month, though only 4 out of 10 in the second month. In the placebo group 2 out of 10 showed reduction during both months, these 2 having shown evidence of neuroticism before taking the tablet. Herzberg *et al.* [36] in an uncontrolled study compared changes of sexual behaviour in a group of women using I.U.D.s, a group using oral preparations and remaining on the same pill throughout, and a third group who changed from one oral preparation to another. Whereas the I.U.D. group showed a steady improvement sexually over the period of study, the 'no-change pill' group showed an initial improvement which then flattened out, and the 'change pill' showed a slight but steady deterioration. These workers also carefully assessed mood change. Those women who changed their pill because of loss of libido were significantly more depressed than those who did not. However, their results indicated that the relationship between mood and libido was complex. They reasonably attributed the increasing sexual improvement with I.U.D.s to increasing confidence about efficacy. Because of this they concluded that the different pattern with the Pill indicated that this psychological benefit was being counteracted by some psycho-pharmacological or endocrine effect.

Cullberg *et al.* [16] found that 15 per cent of the women they studied reported mental and sexual disturbances during the first few months of taking an oral contraceptive. By 6 months, however, there was little difference from pre-treatment frequency. In the 15 per cent temporarily affected, loss of sexual interest was accompanied by contraceptive insecurity. These workers recognized the psychological complexities of 'taking the Pill', and concluded that a very different design would be required to assess psycho-pharmacological effects. Cullberg [15] then completed a further study involving four groups of 80 women each, all volunteers. They were all using other non-oral contraceptive methods and were told that they were participating in a study of the effects of female hormones on menstrual symptoms. Four separate preparations were involved, one for each group. Three were combined preparations with high, medium, and low progestogen content, the fourth was a placebo. Mild depressive symptoms were significantly more common in the active group than in the placebo group, though there was no significant difference in this respect between the different progestogen levels. These mental changes were linked with weight gain in the progestogen-dominated group and with nausea in the oestrogen-dominated (low progestogen) group.

There were no differences in sexual drive between the different types of pill and the placebo. Lowered sexual interest, however, was linked with other signs of mental disturbance. Cullberg concluded therefore that none of these preparations had a direct effect on sexual function but indirectly affected it by means of mood change.

The conflicting nature of these various reports underlines the inherent complexity and methodological difficulties that are involved. A fairly consistent point, however, is that women with mood disturbance and low sexual drive before starting oral contraceptives are more vulnerable to both affective and sexual changes of an adverse kind. Such vulnerability is not necessarily psychological alone, as it may also depend on a sensitivity to hormonal or other physiological change.

If direct hormonal effects on sexual behaviour are relevant with these preparations, it is reasonable to ask the question whether they are related to cyclical patterns of sexual behaviour as discussed in the first part of this paper. It may be that women who show cyclical variation in libido are more susceptible to exogenous hormones. Unfortunately, we have no directly relevant data on this point though Jackson [37] claims that typically the libido of the Pill-taking women 'remains perfectly placid, whereas in the old days she used to run away for one part of the cycle and demand coitus for the other part'. In other words the peaks of sexual activity are flattened out. Diamond *et al.* [19] found that the ovulatory peaks of increased visual sensitivity which, they suggested, made coitus more likely, were flattened out by oral contraceptives.

Psychological factors peculiar to oral contraceptives mainly centre round the active responsibility which lies with the women taking them [46]. In some women this role will be more consistent with their identity than for others. In some marriages sexual conflict between the couple may be expressed in conflict over responsibility for contraception. This can be a factor in 'forgetting to take the Pill' in such women [3]. Hormonal mechanisms may also produce effects that are relevant to gender identity. Kutner and Duffy [46] found that women with low femininity scores on the MMPI (Minnesota Multiple Personality Inventory) reported more symptoms of breast discomfort and swelling. This may have reflected both differing physiological change as well as differing threshold for complaint. Fear of loss of control of sexual impulses, or promiscuity, as well as fear of lasting infertility are other factors which are important for some women [88]. This fear may in part be related to the fact that they are ingesting a compound which they may interpret as being capable of producing internal change. Other types of contraceptive are 'external' and do not threaten the internal environment or personality in this way.

It seems likely, therefore, that though most women can take oral contraceptives without adverse consequences and some with benefit, there will be others in whom mood disturbance or sexual disturbance will occur. This may be due to hormonal or psychological factors, or an interaction of the two. Clearly it is desirable to select the preparation to suit the individual woman. Clinical advice concerning avoidance of some side-effects is already available [80], and Cullberg's study [15] provides some experimental support for these clinical impressions as far as non-sexual side-effects are concerned. At the moment, however, apart from finding that women with sexual difficulties at the outset are more vulnerable, there is very little guidance for choosing the right pill to suit the sexual pattern of the woman and her partner.

Finally we must consider non-contraceptive methods of fertility control, notably termination of pregnancy and sterilization in both male and female.

Termination of pregnancy. Although considerable attention has been paid to the psychiatric sequelae of therapeutic abortion very little data on the effect of this procedure on sexual behaviour are available. In earlier papers it was often assumed that the operation would have dire consequences both sexual and psychiatric [74]. From the psychiatric aspect recent evidence has been mainly contrary to such a view, and from the sexual aspect there is no evidence to support it.

Peck and Marcus [66] gave very little relevant data but mentioned that changes in sexual behaviour, both adverse and beneficial, were more likely in women who were psychiatrically disturbed before their abortion. Simon *et al.* [75] reported sexual improvement in some of their abortion cases, but only commented on those who were sterilized. They applied a test of femininity to their women, however. Using the Loeringer Family Problem Test they found that 40 per cent gave scores in the range indicating rejection of the feminine role. On the basis of the MMPI they also dubiously concluded that a high proportion showed sado-masochistic tendencies. If either of those results had any validity they were probably reflecting cultural attitudes to abortion at that time. It is highly likely that such attitudes will change as the operation becomes more widely used, and then it would be surprising if the rejection of the female biological role would be so prevalent. Baird [1] briefly mentioned that of 61 women whose pregnancies were terminated, 10 reported more enjoyable intercourse, 42 reported no change, and 9 gave answers which were too vague to classify.

Patt *et al.* [65] studied 35 women following abortion. Half of them reported no change sexually, most of the remainder were apparently improved. They noted a reduction in impulsive or promiscuous sex and the use of better contraception following the abortion. Kenyon [41] had reported slightly more promiscuity in his group prior to abortion when compared with a control group.

Peres-Reyes and Falk [67] followed up a group of girls in early adolescence who received abortion and reported that 41 per cent had resumed sexual intercourse during the follow-up period, with two-thirds of those using contraceptives. They did not give sufficient detail, however, to judge whether these girls' sexual development had been affected.

We remain very uncertain, therefore, of the effects of therapeutic abortion on sexual behaviour, though it seems unlikely that adverse sexual consequences are common. Adverse psychiatric sequelae are more marked in those who agree to the operation under pressure [67]. It would not be surprising if it was in these cases that sexual problems were most likely to develop particularly if it was the sexual partner who was pressing for the abortion.

Sterilization of the woman. The irreversible nature of sterilization makes adverse sequelae distinctly possible. Fecundity for some women plays a central part of their gender identity, and for others sex is only justifiable if conception is a possible consequence. The main evidence on this point comes from the extensive follow-up study of Ekblad [20]. He studied 225 women following sterilization. In 54 per cent enjoyment of sex was unchanged, 33 per cent reported improvement, and in 13 per cent there was deterioration. Most of those who showed improvement had experienced marked fear of pregnancy before being sterilized. Reduction of this fear was assumed to be the cause of the improvement. Fifteen women regretted having had the operation; of these, 6 became frigid. Ekblad also investigated the possibility that sterilization might produce adverse repercussions in the spouse, particularly a fear of infidelity. Five of the husbands showed increased jealousy following the operation, and 2 became jealous who were not so before. In none of these cases, however, was this jealousy the cause of serious difficulty.

There is little further evidence on female sterilization. Simon *et al.* [75] as mentioned above, noticed sexual improvement in some women who had both termination and sterilization. In a recent pilot study Bancroft *et al.* [8] followed up three groups of women, one after termination plus tubal ligation (i.e. sterilization), one after termination and hysterectomy, and the third after hysterectomy for other gynaecological reasons. The use of hysterectomy for both termination of pregnancy and sterilization is of special interest, as the uterus could have a special significance for the gender identity of the woman. Fifteen women in each group were interviewed at times ranging from $1\frac{1}{2}$ years to $2\frac{1}{2}$ years following the operation. Of the termination–hysterectomy cases 10 out of 15 reported improvement in the enjoyment of coitus, 4 were unchanged, and only 1 reported any deterioration. In all but one case, the improvement for the wife was accompanied by improvement for the husband. In the tubal ligation and termination group 8 out of 15 reported sexual improvement, 6 no change, and 1 deterioration. Nine of the husbands were in the improved category. In the simple hysterectomy group 5 out of 13 were improved, 7 unchanged, and 1 worse. These results must be interpreted with caution as the refusal rate in this follow-up study was high, and the effects in the refused group must remain uncertain. However, the results are certainly encouraging and suggest that for the majority of women sterilization, whether accompanied by hysterectomy or not, is unlikely to be sexually harmful.

In contrast, however, Richards (personal communication) in an unpublished study in general practice found that of 70 married women who had had a hysterectomy for gynaecological reasons 40 per cent reported their sexual relationship worse (usually with loss of interest and less frequent orgasm), 28 per cent unchanged, and 30 per cent improved. This group was compared with a further 40 women who had received other types of operation. Of these 77·5 per cent were unchanged, 17·5 per cent better, and 5 per cent worse. It may be possible that it is not the operation *per se* that contributes to the sexual impairment when it occurs but the problems that preceded it, particularly if the gynaecological symptoms reflected some underlying psycho-sexual problem. If so, one would expect less adverse consequences if the hysterectomy was simply used as a means of terminating pregnancy and sterilization. There is obviously a need for careful prospective studies of this question.

Nevertheless, it seems likely that the woman's attitude to sterilization will influence the reaction to it and that adverse reactions are more likely if the operation is undergone reluctantly. This point should be particularly considered when sterilization is made a condition of abortion.

Sterilization of the man: vasectomy. Vasectomy is now being widely used. A variety of hostile and conflicting views about the likely consequences of such an operation and the reasons for seeking it have been expressed in the psychiatric literature, characterized more by emotion than reason [86]. The most detailed study from the sexual point of view was reported by Ferber *et al.* [23]. They interviewed 73 men after vasectomy. Seventy-five per cent were more satisfied with intercourse following this operation, 69 per cent reported a decrease in sexual inhibition, 19 per cent reported more intense orgasm, 25 per cent reported greater control over ejaculation, and 11 per cent stronger erections. Against this there were 4 per cent who were less satisfied with coitus, 19 per cent reporting less intense orgasm, 12 per cent with less control over ejaculation, and 10 per cent with slightly weaker erections. These workers also realized the importance of possible change in the spouse, but only obtained the husband's account of the wives' reactions. On this basis there were 83 per cent of wives who were more satisfied with coitus after vasectomy, and 4 per cent less satisfied. Those men who had sexual difficulties before the operation were more likely to report adverse sexual consequences, though evidence of previous psychiatric disturbance did not appear to be a contra-indication.

These workers gained the impression that most of their men had initially regarded vasectomy as in some sense a form of castration, but had managed to satisfactorily cope with this feeling. This point was also made by Rodgers *et al.* [72], who studied attitudes to vasectomy and concluded that there was a widespread negative feeling about the type of person undergoing vasectomy. They suggested that this factor might increase the likelihood of adverse reactions, though the results of Ferber *et al.* [23] would not support that suggestion.

The Simon Population Trust [76] carried out a questionnaire study following vasectomy in 1092 men. They achieved a 93 per cent reply rate. They asked the question 'what have been the effects of this operation on your sexual life?' and 'your wife's sexual life'. Seventy-three per cent reported an improvement in themselves in this respect and 79 per cent in their wives. In 25 per cent of the men and 20 per cent of the wives there was no change, and 1·5 per cent and 0·5 per cent respectively reported deterioration. In several of these 'deteriorated' cases there were other factors operating which may have accounted for the sexual difficulties. Wolfers [86] in a further questionnaire study obtained nearly 80 per cent response. Twelve per cent admitted to some sexual difficulties following the operation. In most of these it was apparent that some sexual difficulty had preceded the operation. Nash and Rich [64] carried out a further postal questionnaire study producing a response rate of 64 per cent. Fifty per cent of respondents felt that their marriage had improved following the operation. 'Increased sexiness' was reported by 20·5 per cent, 4·5 per cent reported delayed ejaculation, 3 per cent erectile difficulties, and 1·5 per cent loss of libido. Similar results were reported by Uehling and Wear [82], though in their case the response rate to the questionnaire was even lower, at 57 per cent. These postal questionnaire studies also raise the problem of the non-responder, and their results should be interpreted with caution. A recent English follow-up survey was abandoned because of a poor response rate [27].

At the moment, however, the evidence suggests that for most men vasectomy has no adverse effects on sexual behaviour and is often beneficial. Once again, it is those with sexual difficulties prior to the operation who seem to be most at risk. Cultural attitudes to the operation are likely to change with its wider use, but it would seem advisable to look for inappropriate attitudes and attempt to modify them before the operation is carried out.

Conclusions. There is undoubtedly a lack of adequate data on the sexual effects of fertility control. In very few studies is the evidence presented more than exceedingly superficial and there is no reason to assume that the methods used in obtaining it were any less superficial. Much of the conflict of evidence may stem from such a factor in an area in which techniques of data collection are crucial.

Nevertheless, the over-all picture is surprisingly encouraging when one considers the prophecies of gloom that have often surrounded fertility control methods. Such prophecies obviously reflect the emotive nature of the subject and the fact that scientific workers in this field more than most are likely to be influenced by culturally determined attitudes which have no precise scientific basis. The possible effect of such cultural factors on the users of fertility control methods must also be taken into consideration particularly as they are likely to be ever changing.

Some of the lack of gloom in the over-all picture is probably due to the considerable and often underestimated capacity that human beings have for adapting to new situations, whether psychological or hormonal. There are some, of course, whose lives are generally affected by difficulties in adaptation, and this may well account for the commonly reported association between psychiatric disturbance and adverse reactions. It should also be considered possible that both general psychiatric and specifically sexual vulnerability may both stem from common factors which could be endocrine in nature.

Nevertheless, there is no doubt that a wide range of methods of fertility control is desirable to meet the varying needs and vulnerabilities of the population. We also need to know much more about how to fit the method to the individual, not only to avoid unpleasant reactions but also so that young people can start using the optimum method at the earliest appropriate opportunity and hence allow their sexual development to proceed without the constraints of contraceptive anxiety or other sexual impairment [63]. The existing cost in permanent sexual dysfunction that has stemmed from such difficulties at crucial stages in development is probably considerable.

Before we can obtain clarification of such indications, however, there is need for further basic research, both in unravelling the complex relationships of hormones and behaviour and also in the development of satisfactory methods of measuring or evaluating the various components of human sexuality. Both of these aims present formidable problems, but they should not be considered insurmountable, particularly if the emotional barriers to such research can be resolved. A small proportion of the research effort that has been expended on other aspects of fertility control would probably pay considerable dividends in this crucial area.

REFERENCES

1. BAIRD, D. (1967). Sterilisation and therapeutic abortion in Aberdeen, *B. J. Psychiat.* **113**, 701–9.
2. BAKKE, J. L. (1965). A double-blind study of a progestin–estrogen combination in the management of the menopause, *Pacific Med. Surg.* **73**, 200–5.
3. BAKKER, C. B. and DIGHTMAN, C. R. (1964). Psychological factors in fertility control, *Fertil. Steril.* **15**, 559.

4. BANCROFT, J. H. J. (1970). Disorders of sexual potency. In *Modern trends in psychosomatic medicine* (ed. O. W. Hill), p. 246. Butterworth, London.

5. —— (1972). The relationship between gender identity and sexual behaviour: Some clinical aspects. In *Gender Differences: their ontogeny and significance* (eds. C. Ounsted and D. C. Taylor), p. 57. Churchill Livingstone, Edinburgh.

6. —— Psychological and physiological responses to sexual stimuli in men and women. In *Society, stress and disease. Symposium No. 3. Male and female roles and relationships* (ed. L. Levi), Oxford University Press. (In press.)

7. —— (1972). *The Masters and Johnson approach to marital sexual problems in an N.H.S. outpatient setting.* Paper read at 2nd Annual Congress European Behaviour Therapy Association, September (1972). Wexford, Ireland. (In press.)

8. BANCROFT, J., BANCROFT, J. H. J., and WILLIAMS, A. *Psychiatric follow-up study of termination—hysterectomy, tubal ligation and simple hysterectomy.* (In preparation.)

9. BANCROFT, J. H. J., TENNENT, G., LOUCAS, K., and CASS, J. *Control of deviant sexual behaviour by drugs: behaviour and endocrine changes.* (In preparation.)

10. BEUMONT, P. J. V., BANCROFT, J. H. J., BEARDWOOD, C. J., and RUSSELL, G. F. M. (1972). Behavioural changes following treatment with testosterone: a case report, *Psychol. Med.* **2**, 70–2.

11. BREMER, J. (1959). *Asexualisation, a follow-up study of 244 cases.* Macmillan, New York.

12. BRUHL, E. E. and LESLIE, C. H. (1963). Afrodex, double blind test in impotence, *Med. Rec. Ann.* **56**, 22.

13. CARTER, A. C., COHEN, E. J., and SHORR, E. (1947). The use of androgens in women, *Vitam. Horm., Lpz.* **5**, 317–91.

14. COOPER, A. J., ISMAIL, A. A. A., SMITH, C. G., and LORAINE, J. A. (1970). Androgen function in 'psychogenic' and 'constitutional' types of impotence, *Br. med. J.* **3**, 17.

15. CULLBERG, J. (1973). Mood changes and menstrual symptoms with different gestagen/estrogen combinations, *Acta psychiat. scand. Suppl.* **236**.

16. ——, GELLI, M., and JONSSON, C. O. (1969). Mental and sexual adjustment before and after six months' use of an oral contraceptive, *Acta psychiat. scand.* **45**, 259–76.

17. DAVIS, K. B. (1929). *Factors in the sex life of 2,200 women.* Harper and Row, New York.

18. DIAMOND, M. (1965). A critical evaluation of the ontogeny of human sexual behaviour. *Quart Rev. Biol.* **40**, 147–75.

19. ——, DIAMOND, A. L., and MAST, M. (1972). Visual sensitivity and sexual arousal levels during the menstrual cycle, *J. nerv. ment. Dis.* **155**, 170–6.

20. EKBLAD, M. (1955). Induced abortion on psychiatric grounds. *Acta psychiat. scand. Suppl.* **99**.

21. EL HEFNAWI, F. (1966). Four year field study of oral contraceptives in Egypt. In Social and medical aspects of oral contraceptives (ed. M. N. G. Dukes), p. 33, *Exerpta med. internat. Congr. Ser.* **130.**

22. EVERITT, B. and HERBERT, J. (1972). Hormonal correlates of sexual behaviour in sub-human primates, *Danish med. Bull.* **19,** 246–58.

23. FERBER, A. S., TIETZE, C. and LEWIT, S. (1967). Men with vasectomies: a study of medical sexual and psychosocial change, *Psychosom. Med.* **29,** 354–66.

24. FORD, C. S. and BEACH, F. A. (1952). *Patterns of sexual behaviour.* Eyre and Spottiswoode, London.

25. GILL, D. G. (1971). Some socio-cultural aspects of contraception and sexual behaviour in industrial society. In *Family planning research conference*, Exeter, September 1971 (eds. A. Goldsmith and R. Snowden). Excerpta medica, Amsterdam.

26. GOY, R. N. (1968). Organising effects of androgens on the behaviour of rhesus monkeys. In *Endocrinology and behaviour* (ed. R. P. Michael), p. 12, Oxford University Press, London.

27. ANON. (1973). Vasectomy follow-up survey abandoned. In *G.P.*, 9 February, p. 3.

28. GRANT, E. C. G. and PRYSE-DAVIES, J. (1968). Effect of oral contraception on depressive mood changes and on endometrial monoamine oxidase and phosphatases, *Br. med. J.* **3,** 777–80.

29. GROUNDS, D., DAVIES, B. and MOWBRAY, R. (1970). The contraceptive pill, side effects and personality: report of a controlled double-blind trial, *Br. J. Psychiat.* **116,** 169–72.

30. HAMPSON, J. L. and HAMPSON, J. G. (1961). The ontogenesis of sexual behaviour in man. In *Sex and internal secretions* (ed. W. C. Young), 3rd edn., p. 1401. Williams and Wilkins, Baltimore.

31. HARRIS, G. W. (1964). Sex hormones, brain development and brain functions, *Endocrinology* **75,** 627–648.

32. HART, R. D. A. (1960). Monthly rhythm of libido in married women, *Br. med. J.* **1,** 1023–4.

33. HELLER, C. G., LAIDLAW, W. M., HARVEY, H. T., and NELSON, D. O. (1958). Effects of progestational compounds on the reproductive processes of the human male, *Ann. New York Acad. Sci.* **71,** 649–65.

34. —— and MADDOCK, W. O. (1947). The clinical uses of testosterone in the male, *Vitam. Horm. Lpz.* **5,** 393–423.

35. —— and MYERS, G. B. (1944). The male climacteric: its symptomatology, diagnosis and treatment, *J. Am. med. Assoc.* **126,** 472–7.

36. HERZBERG, B. N., DRAPER, K. C., JOHNSON, A. L., and NICOL, G. C. (1971). Oral contraceptives, depression and libido, *Br. med. J.* **3,** 495–500.

37. JACKSON, M. C. N. (1966). Clinical experience with oral contraceptives in England. In *Social and medical aspects of oral contraceptives* (ed. M. N. G. Dukes), p. 47. *Exerpta med. internat. Congr. Ser.* **130.**

38. JAKOBOVITZ, T. (1970). The treatment of impotence with methyl testosterone thyroid, *Fertil. Steril.* **21**, 32–5.
39. JUHLIN, L. and LIDEN, S. (1969). Influence of contraceptive gestogen pills on sexual behaviour and the spread of gonorrhoea, *Br. J. vener. Dis.* **45**, 321–4.
40. KANE, F. J. (1968). Psychiatric reactions to oral contraceptives, *Am. J. Obst. Gynecol.* **102**, 1053–63.
41. KENYON, F. E. (1969). Termination of pregnancy on psychiatric grounds: a comparative study of 61 cases, *Br. J. med. Psychol.* **42**, 243–54.
42. KINSEY, A. C., POMEROY, W. B., and MARTIN, C. E. (1948). *Sexual behaviour in the human male.* Saunders, London.
43. ——, ——, ——, and GEBHARD, P. H. (1953). *Sexual behaviour in the human female.* Saunders, London.
44. KUPPERMAN, H. S. (1959). Hormonal aspects of frigidity, *Quart. Rev. Surg.* **16**, 254–7.
45. —— (1963). *Human Endocrinology*, p. 397. Davis, Philadelphia.
46. KUTNER, S. J. and DUFFY, T. J. (1970). A psychological analysis of oral contraceptives and the intra-uterine device. (Unpublished paper.)
47. LARSSON, K. (1966). Individual differences in reactivity to androgen in male rats, *Physiol. Behav.* **1**, 255–8.
48. LEHFELDT, H. and GUZE, H. (1966). Psychological factors in contraceptive failure, *Fertil. Steril.* **20**, 110–16.
49. LEHRMAN, D. S. (1962). Interaction of hormonal and experimental influences on development of behaviour. In *Roots of behaviour* (ed. E. L. Bliss), p. 142. Harper and Row, London.
50. LIDZ, R. W. (1969). Emotional factors in the success of contraception, *Fertil. Steril.* **20**, 761–771.
51. MACLEAN, P. D. (1965). New findings relevant to the evolution of psychosexual functions of the brain. In *Sex research: new developments* (ed. J. Money), p. 197. Holt, Rinehart and Winston, New York.
52. MARGOLIS, R., SANGREE, H., PRIETO, P., STEIN, L., and CHINN, S. (1967). Clinical studies of the use of Afrodex in the treatment of impotence, *Cur. therap. Res. clin. exp.* **9**, 213.
53. MASTERS, W. H. and JOHNSON, V. E. (1966). *Human sexual response.* Churchill, London.
54. ——, —— (1970). *Human sexual inadequacy.* Churchill, London.
55. MICHAEL, R. P. (1968). Neural and non-neural mechanisms in the reproductive behaviour of primates. Proc. internat. Cong. Endocrinology, *Exerpta med. internat. Congr. Ser.* **184**, 302–9.
56. —— and KEVERNE, E. B. (1968), Pheromones in the communication of sexual status in primates, *Nature, Lond.* **218**, 746–749.
57. —— and SAAYMAN, G. (1967). Individual differences in the sexual behaviour of male rhesus monkeys (*Macaca mulatta*) under laboratory conditions, *Anim. Behav.* **15**, 460–466.
58. MILLETT, K. (1969). *Sexual politics.* Abacus, London.

59. MILLS, W. (1970). Further experience with intra-uterine contraceptive devices, *Lancet* **2**, 921–3.
60. MONEY, J. (1961). Components of eroticism in man: I. The hormones in relation to sexual morphology and sexual desire, *J. nerv. ment. Dis.* **132**, 239–48.
61. —— (1972). Use of an androgen-depleting hormone in the treatment of male sexual offenders, *J. Sex Res.* **6**, 165–72.
62. —— (1972). Phyletic and idiosyncratic determinants of gender identity, *Danish med. Bull.* **19**, 259–64.
63. MURAWSKI, B. J., SAPIR, P. E., SHULMAN, N., RYAN, G. M., and STURGIS, S. H. (1968). An investigation of mood states in women taking oral contraceptives, *Fertil. Steril.* **19**, 50–63.
64. NASH, J. L. and RICH, J. D. (1972). The sexual after-effects of vasectomy, *Fertil. Steril.* **23**, 715–18.
65. PATT, S. L., RAPPAPORT, R. G., and BARGLOW, P. (1969). Follow-up of therapeutic abortion, *Arch. gen. Psychiat.* **20**, 408–14.
66. PECK, A. and MARCUS, H. (1966). Psychiatric sequelae of therapeutic interruption of pregnancy, *J. nerv. ment. Dis.* **143**, 417–25.
67. PERES-REYES, M. G. and FALK, R. (1973). Follow-up after therapeutic abortion in early adolescence, *Arch. gen. Psychiat.* **28**, 120–6.
68. PERLOFF, W. H. (1949). Role of hormones in human sexuality, *Psychosom. Med.* **11**, 133–9.
69. RAINWATER, L. (1960). *And the poor get children.* Quadrangle, Chicago.
70. —— (1966). Some aspects of lower class sexual behaviour. *J. Soc. Issues* **22**, 96–108.
71. RICHTER, R. H. H. (1966). Planning of clinical trials with oral contraceptives. In Social and medical aspects of oral contraceptives (ed. M. N. G. Dukes), p. 53. *Exerpta Med. internat. Congr. Ser.* **130**.
72. RODGERS, D. A., ZIEGLER, F. J., and LEVY, N. (1967). Prevailing cultural attitudes about vasectomy: a possible explanation of post-operative psychological response, *Psychosom. Med.* **29**, 367–75.
73. SCOTT, J. and BRASS, P. (1966). Massive norethynodrel therapy in treatment of endometriosis, *Am. J. Obst. Gynecol.* **95**, 1166–7.
74. SIMON, N. M. and SENTURIA, A. G. (1966). Psychiatric sequelae of abortion: review of the literature 1935–1964, *Arch. gen. Psychiat.* **15**, 278–89.
75. ——, ——, and ROTHMAN, D. (1967). Psychiatric illness following abortion, *Am. J. Psychiat.* **124**, 59–65.
76. SIMON POPULATION TRUST (1969). *Vasectomy: follow-up of 1000 cases.* Newmarket Road, Cambridge.
77. SNOWDEN, R. (1971). Social and personal factors involved in the use of effectiveness of the I.U.D. In *Family planning research conference, Exeter, September* 1971 (eds. A. Goldsmith and R. Snowden), Exerpta medica, Amsterdam.

78. STOLLER, R. J. (1968). *Sex and gender.* Hogarth Press, London.
79. TENNENT, G., BANCROFT, J. H. J., and CASS, J. The control of deviant sexual behaviour by drugs: a double-blind controlled study of benperidol, chlorpromazine and placebo, *Arch. Sex. Behav.* (In press.)
80. ANON (1968). Todays drugs. Oral contraceptives—choice of product, *Brit. med. J.* i, 690–2.
81. UDRY, J. R. and MORRIS, N. M. (1968). Distribution of coitus in the menstrual cycle, *Nature, London.* 200, 593–6.
82. UEHLING, D. T. and WEAR, J. B. (1972). Patient attitudes to vasectomy, *Fertil. Steril.* 23, 838–40.
83. WAXENBURG, S. E., DRELLICH, M. G., and SUTHERLAND, A. M. (1959). The role of hormones in human behaviour. I. Changes in female sexuality after adrenalectomy, *J. clin. Endocrin. Metabol.* 19, 193–202.
84. WESTOFF, C. F., BUMPASS, L., and RYDER, N. B. (1969). Oral contraception, coital frequency and the time required to conceive, *Soc. Biol.* 16, 1–10.
85. WHALEN, R. E. (1966). Sexual motivation, *Psychol. Rev.* 73, 151–163.
86. WOLFERS, H. (1970). Psychological aspects of vasectomy. *Br. med. J.* 4, 297–300.
87. WORLD HEALTH ORGANISATION (1971). *Methods of fertility regulation. Advances in research and clinical experience.* WHO Technical Report No. 473, Geneva.
88. ZELL, J. R. and CRISP, W. E. (1964) A psychiatric evaluation of the use of oral contraception: a study of 250 private patients, *Obst. Gynecol.* 23, 657–661.

2.6. The newer medico-social technology of fertility control

2.6.1. Some medical aspects of fertility control

MARTIN P. VESSEY

Lecturer in Epidemiology, Oxford University

Introduction

IN assessing the value of any method of fertility control, the answers to three major questions must be sought. First, how effective is the method? Secondly, how safe is the method? Thirdly, how acceptable is the method?

In considering the first of these questions, a distinction is often made between 'theoretical-effectiveness' and 'use-effectiveness'. The first of these terms relates to the efficacy of a method if it is always used exactly in accordance with instructions. The second relates to the efficacy of a method as it is actually used in practice. Thus, for example, the theoretical-effectiveness of combined oral contraceptives approximates extremely closely to 100 per cent. In practice, however, somewhere between 2 and 15 women in every 1000 using the preparations experience an unwanted pregnancy in any given year, mainly because some do not always take the tablets as directed. As might be expected, the use-effectiveness of a particular method of fertility control varies considerably from study to study, depending on the characteristics of the participants. Nonetheless, the concept of use-effectiveness has, in general, proved of more value in assessing the efficacy of methods of fertility control than that of theoretical-effectiveness. Use-effectiveness is commonly expressed in terms of a failure rate per 100 woman-years of exposure, the so-called Pearl Index [40]. Since, however, higher failure rates are invariably recorded in the early months of any investigation than in the later months, because careless use of a method is quickly exposed and is self-eliminating, more sophisticated methods of analysis are desirable. A discussion of these methods will be found in an article by Potter [43].

The safety of different methods of fertility control is extremely difficult to assess. This is mainly because serious adverse effects tend to be uncommon and do not usually present any particular distinguishing features. For example, the risk of venous thrombosis and pulmonary embolism is increased in women using oral contraceptives, but these conditions also occur in women not using the preparations. Thus serious adverse effects may easily be completely missed in investigations quite adequate in design and in size for measuring the use-effectiveness of a method of fertility control. Furthermore, anxiety about the safety of some methods of fertility control, notably those employing synthetic steroids, relates in part to the possibility of long-delayed effects, such as the production of malignant disease, which might not appear for years after the subject had stopped using any method of fertility control. A detailed discussion of the problems involved in evaluating the safety of oral contraceptives will be found in articles by Seigel and Corfman [54], Tietze [64], and Doll and Vessey [9].

Assessment of the acceptability of different methods of fertility control may also prove difficult. One objective measure is provided by finding out what proportion of a sample of subjects will agree to giving a particular method a try. A second is provided by calculation of the proportion of subjects starting to use the method who continue to use it at certain intervals of time (say 1 year, 2 years, and so on) after starting. Allowance has to be made in these calculations for subjects discontinuing the use of the method for such reasons as the planning of a pregnancy. Some of the obvious factors influencing the acceptability of any method are efficacy, safety, cost, simplicity in use, and aesthetic appeal. In addition, however, characteristics of the subjects using the method, such as age, socio-economic status, and stage of family-building, are extremely important. Where a method requires medical supervision, such as with the oral contraceptives, the enthusiasm of the doctor concerned may also have a profound influence. From these considerations, it is clear that the acceptability of a method of fertility control will vary widely from one population group to another.

In this article, an attempt will be made to review concisely the methods of fertility control which are currently available and to provide some indication of the areas in which new developments are taking place. Most attention will be paid to efficacy and safety which are largely medical problems. The question of acceptability, which is of special interest to the sociologist, has already been discussed by Illsley (Chap. 1.8).

Coitus interruptus

Coitus interruptus is an ancient method of fertility control which is still very widely used. It requires neither prior preparation nor medical supervision and costs nothing. There are few reliable data on efficacy, but use-effectiveness pregnancy rates are probably in the range of 10–30 per 100 woman-years. There is little evidence that the practice is harmful among those who find it acceptable.

The rhythm method

The rhythm method is the only fertility control measure officially approved by the Roman Catholic Church and, in the opinion of some, this is its sole advantage [41]. The efficacy of the method is probably similar to that of coitus interruptus. There are no proven harmful effects in those who find the practice acceptable. Accidental pregnancies following failure of the rhythm method are, however, particularly likely to occur very early or very late in the fertile period of the menstrual cycle, and it has been suggested that this may predispose to extra-uterine pregnancy [21] and to foetal malformation [7].

Recently, there has been some interest in teaching women how to recognize the fertile and infertile days of the menstrual cycle by interpreting the cervical mucus pattern. A clinical trial utilizing this refinement of the rhythm method has been reported from Tonga by Weissmann *et al.* [73], who suggested that it was highly effective. The methods of analysis used by Weissmann and her colleagues have, however, been criticized by a number of workers [33, 46], and it would appear that the use-effectiveness pregnancy rate in the Tonga trial was 25 per 100 woman-years.

The condom

The condom is the most widely used birth-control device. Use-effectiveness pregnancy rates vary widely in different studies, but are generally within the range of 5–15 per 100 woman-years.

Amongst those who find the condom acceptable there are no important harmful effects. Men who are allergic to rubber may, however, develop a rash on the penis or scrotum. Women may also show allergic symptoms such as vaginitis. In such cases, the condom should be abandoned and another contraceptive method substituted.

An important medical advantage of the condom is that its use lessens the risk of transmission of venereal disease, especially gonorrhoea [3].

Diaphragms and cervical caps

Diaphragms and cervical caps, although still widely used, are fast diminishing in popularity. As with the condom, reported use-effectiveness pregnancy rates show wide variation, the range being of the order of 5–25 per 100 woman-years.

Rubber allergy may occur in women using diaphragms or cervical caps or in their consorts. It is also widely believed that the diaphragm may predispose to urinary tract infection in some women as a result of pressure of the rim of the device on the urethra. This belief is supported by unpublished findings in the prospective study of women using different methods of birth control which the Department of the Regius Professor of Medicine at Oxford is conducting in conjunction with the Family Planning Association.

There is some evidence to suggest that regular use of an occlusive method of contraception, such as the condom or diaphragm, may reduce the risk of carcinoma of the cervix [4, 81].

Vaginal spermicides

Vaginal spermicides are available as pessaries, jellies, creams, and foams. Ideally, they should always be used in conjunction with an occlusive method of birth control. When used alone, use-effectiveness pregnancy rates in the range of 10–40 per 100 woman-years are to be anticipated.

A new spermicidal contraceptive, C-film, which may be used by either the male or the female, has attracted considerable attention recently. This contraceptive consists of a thin, translucent, pliable, water-soluble film, 4 cm square, containing a highly active, non-toxic spermicide. Women use C-film by inserting it into the vagina up to 3 hours before intercourse. Men place the C-film on the moistened glans penis just before penetration. Insertion of the penis into the vagina then places the film in position.

This method has been extensively used in Hungary where, it is claimed, good results have been obtained [37]. C-film is now available in the United Kingdom, and the Family Planning Association is currently conducting a trial to assess the value of the method in this country.

Steroidal contraceptives

Combined and sequential oral contraceptives. In the combined oral contraceptive regimen, both an oestrogen and a progestogen are administered daily for 20–22 days in each menstrual cycle. In the sequential regimen, an oestrogen is given alone for 14–16 days, after which both an oestrogen and a progestogen are given to complete a course of 20–21 days in each menstrual cycle. In both types of regimen, the oestrogen component is invariably ethinyl oestradiol or its 3-methyl-ether, mestranol, while the progestogen component is either a derivative of 19-nortestosterone (such as norethisterone, ethynodiol diacetate, or lynoestrenol) or a derivative of 17-α-hydroxyprogesterone (such as megestrol acetate or chlormadinone acetate).

Both combined and sequential oral contraceptives act principally by inhibiting ovulation, although they also exert other anti-fertility effects which are probably of importance [79]. At the present time, the use of combined oral contraceptives represents the most effective reversible method of fertility control that is available. Thus use-effectiveness pregnancy rates in different studies have generally been within the range of 0·2–1·5 per 100 woman-years. Sequential oral contraceptives are probably slightly less effective than combined preparations.

Oral contraceptives† are known to produce a variety of minor side-effects (such as headache, nausea, and breast tenderness), which are usually of little more than nuisance value and which tend to pass off with continued medication. In addition, however, more serious adverse reactions may occur, and there is also concern about possible long-term effects which may not yet have come to light. A brief discussion of these problems is presented in the following paragraphs.

Evidence that oral contraceptives occasionally cause *deep vein*

† This general term will be used throughout the remainder of the present section to represent both combined and sequential preparations.

thrombosis or pulmonary embolism has been derived mainly from case-control studies in which the histories of affected women have been compared with those obtained from carefully matched control subjects [22, 48, 49, 68, 69]. The pooled results of these studies suggest that a healthy woman using oral contraceptives has about five times as great a risk of developing deep vein thrombosis or pulmonary embolism as a healthy woman not doing so. These studies, however, were conducted at a time when oral contraceptives containing 100 μg or more of oestrogen were in widespread use. Subsequently, evidence was obtained that the risk of thromboembolism is positively correlated with the dose of oestrogen contained in oral contraceptives [23], and this finding led to the virtual disappearance, in the United Kingdom, of preparations containing more than 50 μg of oestrogen. It therefore seems highly likely that the results of the case-control studies are no longer directly applicable to the present situation in this country; a three- to four-fold increase in risk among users of oral contraceptives is probably now nearer the truth. In absolute terms, this implies that of every 100 000 women using oral contraceptives, 20–30 will be admitted to hospital and 1–2 will die each year from venous thrombosis or pulmonary embolism attributable to the preparations.

A second, but certainly less frequent, adverse effect of oral contraceptives, is the production of *cerebral thrombosis*. The evidence for this association has been derived partly from the case-control studies to which reference has already been made, and partly from physicians who have reviewed their total clinical experience of the disease in young women over a period of years. An excellent review of this problem has been written by Masi and Dugdale [34].

Whether or not oral contraceptives increase the risk of *coronary thrombosis* is uncertain at the present time, because the existing epidemiological evidence is conflicting [12, 22, 23, 38, 69]. The preparations are known, however, to cause hypertension in some women (see below), to decrease glucose tolerance (see p. 360), and to elevate fasting serum triglyceride levels [82]. The situation must, therefore, be carefully watched over the next few years.

As indicated above, the production of *hypertension* is now a recognized adverse reaction to oral contraceptives. The most convincing evidence of the effect has been obtained in women in whom the alternate administration and withdrawal of the preparations has been associated with corresponding changes in blood pressure [29, 77]. Confirmation has been obtained from prospective studies [59, 72]. The frequency with which an important rise in blood pressure occurs in women using oral contraceptives is still uncertain, however, although it seems likely that fewer than 5 per cent are affected in this way. A possible mechanism for the production of hypertension has been provided by study of the effects of the preparations on the renin–angiotensin–aldosterone system [28].

Oral contraceptives have many effects on the liver. The most dramatic of these is the occasional production of *jaundice*. This adverse reaction appears to be extremely uncommon in the United Kingdom, but is frequently seen in Scandinavia and South America [39, 74]. The condition usually occurs soon after the preparations are started and generally resolves rapidly when they are withdrawn. The numerous changes that occur in serum proteins in women using oral contraceptives are also thought to be mediated through the liver. These include a decrease in serum albumin and an elevation in serum thyroxine binding globulin, transcortin, transferrin, and caeruloplasmin. Changes in the plasma proteins concerned as substrates in the blood coagulation, fibrinolytic and renin–angiotensin–aldosterone systems are also believed to be mediated through the liver.

Many women using oral contraceptives show *impairment of oral glucose tolerance*. In perhaps 15 per cent, this impairment constitutes 'chemical diabetes' when judged by standard criteria, such as those of the British Diabetic Association [79]. In most women this metabolic abnormality is symptomless, and its long-term significance is as yet unknown. A useful review of the effects of oral contraceptives on carbohydrate metabolism has been written by Spellacy [58].

Although there is no doubt that the great majority of women regain their normal fertility after discontinuing oral contraceptives, there is a considerable body of evidence that some experience *persistent amenorrhoea* [55]. It should be stressed, however, that a final judgement as to whether or not there is a causal relationship must await the publication of the results of controlled studies of adequate size. In the meantime, it may be noted that many of the women who experience amenorrhoea after discontinuing oral

contraceptives respond to treatment with clomiphene or gona-
dotrophins.

There has been much concern about possible *teratogenic effects*
of oral contraceptives. At the present time there is very little
information about children conceived accidentally while women
are taking oral contraceptives. On the other hand, several reports
have been published concerning children conceived after discon-
tinuation of medication [42, 45]. These have been uniformly reassuring, but much larger studies are needed.

That oestrogens and progestogens are capable of causing *cancer*
in certain experimental animals under suitable conditions is well
established [6, 19]. Indeed some progestogens (notably chlormadinone acetate and medroxyprogesterone acetate) have been withdrawn from sale in a number of countries following reports of the
development of nodules in the breasts of beagle bitches to which
the steroids were administered [79]. There is, however, no direct
evidence that oral contraceptives are carcinogenic in the human
being. Indeed, the results of one case-control study have suggested
that the risk of benign lesions of the breast, such as fibroadenoma
and chronic cystic disease, is reduced in women taking the preparations [70]. Further studies extending over a period of many
years will be required, however, before any final conclusion can be
drawn concerning the effects, if any, of oral contraceptives on
neoplastic disease.

Depression is recognized as being one of the common reasons
why women discontinue oral contraception, and a number of small
controlled studies offer some support to the view that the reaction
is attributable to the medication. Oral contraceptives interfere
with tryptophan metabolism, and some workers believe that this
may be the mechanism whereby depression is produced [47]. Most
of the depressive symptoms linked to oral contraceptives, however, are mild and reversible. It is of interest that the prospective
study of women using different methods of birth control, which
the Department of the Regius Professor of Medicine at Oxford is
conducting in conjunction with the Family Planning Association,
has not indicated so far that there is any increase in the risk of
major psychiatric illness among women using oral contraceptives.

To offset their disadvantages, oral contraceptives have a number
of beneficial actions, quite apart from their remarkable efficacy. In
many women, menstrual periods are regularized and diminished

in amount, and dysmenorrhoea is often relieved. The reduction in menstrual flow probably lessens the risk of iron-deficiency anaemia. As indicated earlier, there is preliminary evidence that oral contraceptives may also reduce the risk of benign breast disease.

The brevity of this review has inevitably led to oversimplification. In particular, reference has been made throughout to 'oral contraceptives' as though all the various preparations are equivalent. This is undoubtedly not the case, and many studies currently in progress are seeking to evaluate the effects of the different oestrogens and progestogens at various dose levels when administered separately or in combination. Another important point is that almost all the investigations into the safety of oral contraceptives have been carried out in highly developed Western countries like the United Kingdom, Scandinavia, and the U.S.A. To what extent the results are applicable in other parts of the world is largely unknown.

New developments involving the joint oral administration of oestrogens and progestogens for contraceptive purposes are very limited. First, it has been discovered that the oestrogen content of the currently used preparations is still higher than is necessary for most women. Oral contraceptives containing only 30 μg of ethinyl-oestradiol are becoming available which should be even safer than the present 50 μg preparations. Secondly, steroids that are stored in adipose tissue after absorption from the gastro-intestinal tract are being investigated as possible one-pill-a-month contraceptives. So far, clinical trials relating to only one preparation (containing quinestrol as the oestrogen and quingestanol acetate as the progestogen) have been reported. Results are not very promising. In comparison with ordinary combined and sequential preparations, systemic and metabolic effects appear to be much the same, efficacy appears to be appreciably lower, and prolonged and heavy menstrual bleeding is much more frequent.

Progestogen-only oral contraceptives. Low doses of progestogens taken every day by mouth have been extensively investigated as contraceptives. Most of the data relate to chlormadinone acetate, a steroid which has been withdrawn from use in some countries (see p. 361), but many other progestogens (such as norethisterone acetate, megestrol acetate, norgestrel, lynoestrenol, and ethynodiol diacetate) have been studied. Some progestogen-only oral contraceptives are now available commercially in the United Kingdom.

Progestogen-only oral contraceptives do not consistently inhibit ovulation, and their mode of action is still uncertain. Their efficacy is lower than that of combined or sequential preparations; use-effectiveness pregnancy rates in different studies have generally been within the range of 2–10 per 100 woman-years. A major disadvantage of progestogen-only oral contraceptives is their tendency to disrupt the normal menstrual pattern in many women, producing irregular bleeding [71]. Their main advantage is that they appear to be largely free from the undesirable metabolic effects of combined and sequential preparations [27], most of which are attributable to the oestrogen component.

Injectable steroidal contraceptives. The most widely studied injectable steroidal contraceptive is medroxyprogesterone acetate given in a dose of 150 mg every 3 months. This regimen is highly effective, comparing favourably with the use of combined oral contraceptives [53]. The principal mode of action appears to be suppression of ovulation [79].

Unfortunately, this method of fertility control has a number of major disadvantages. First, the normal menstrual cycle is completely disrupted, giving rise initially to irregular bleeding and later, in many women, to amenorrhoea. Secondly, menstruation, ovulation, and fertility are often slow to return after the injections are stopped, although it appears that these functions recover within a year in most subjects [53]. Thirdly, injections of medroxyprogesterone acetate have been shown to produce nodules in the breasts of beagle bitches. Although the relevance of this finding to the human being is unknown, medroxyprogesterone acetate has been withdrawn from general use as an injectable contraceptive in the U.S.A.

Despite these disadvantages, the method has achieved considerable popularity in some parts of the world. There is some evidence that the drug increases milk volume in lactating women, without affecting milk composition [25], an important issue in countries where the survival of children is closely associated with breast-feeding.

The monthly injection of oestrogen–progestogen combinations has also been investigated as a method of fertility control. This regimen, however, has not achieved much popularity and will not be discussed further.

Other approaches utilizing steroids. Medroxyprogesterone acetate has been used to inhibit ovulation following absorption through the vaginal mucosa [35]. For this purpose, silicone vaginal rings impregnated with the steroid have been designed. The vaginal ring can be inserted by the woman and is left in place for 3 weeks. After removal, withdrawal bleeding occurs. A new ring is then inserted for the next month, and so on. This approach appears to offer considerable promise.

The subdermal implantation of capsules made of silicone polymers and containing the progestogen, megestrol acetate, is currently under investigation. Preliminary results suggest that this method of fertility control may give rise to fewer problems than injections of medroxyprogesterone acetate (see p. 363), while still retaining a reasonably high degree of efficacy [79].

Intra-uterine devices which release progesterone into the uterine cavity have been designed [51]. As yet, it is too early to know whether these devices represent a significant advance.

Oestrogens, either steroidal or non-steroidal, given in very large doses post-coitally, may be used as an emergency measure to try to prevent pregnancy [26]. The efficacy of this procedure, however, is still uncertain, and side-effects such as nausea and vomiting are common. The use of progestogens given repeatedly throughout the menstrual cycle as post-coital contraceptives is also under investigation.

Intra-uterine devices

Intra-uterine devices are manufactured in many different shapes and sizes. Well-established types include the Lippes Loop, the Margulies Spiral, and the Saf-T-Coil. Recently, newer types of device have been developed to try to overcome the shortcomings of the established ones. The most promising of these newer devices appear to be the Dalkon Shield, the Shell Loop, the Copper-T, and the Copper-7. The first part of the following discussion relates principally to experience with the established devices, after which some of the main features of the newer devices are summarized.

Established devices. The mode of action of intra-uterine devices is still uncertain. The principal mechanism, however, appears to be the stimulation of leucocyte mobilization within the uterus which prevents the nidation of the normal blastocyst arriving from the Fallopian tube [79]. Use-effectiveness pregnancy rates with the most widely used intra-uterine devices, such as the large sizes of the Lippes Loop, the large Margulies Spiral, and the Saf-T-Coil, are in the range of 1·5–3·0 per 100 woman-years [66].

A troublesome problem associated with the use of intra-uterine devices is their spontaneous expulsion from the uterus. For all types of device, this is most likely to occur during the month after insertion; thereafter, the risk drops rapidly. Smaller devices are more likely to be expelled than larger ones. Sometimes the woman is unaware that expulsion has taken place; such an event is usually followed by conception.

Minor side-effects commonly occur after insertion of an intra-uterine device. Of these, the most important is abnormal vaginal bleeding, especially menorrhagia and metrorrhagia. After a few months, these abnormalities tend to disappear, but they may recur later. This increase in vaginal blood loss may cause anaemia in women with an inadequate intake of iron. Another important minor side-effect is the occurrence of pain, usually in the form of uterine cramps, but occasionally felt as low backache. Bleeding and pain are the commonest medical problems leading to removal of intra-uterine devices.

The two most important serious complications which may follow insertion of an intra-uterine device are uterine perforation and pelvic inflammatory disease. Reported rates of *perforation* vary between 1 in 150 and 1 in 2000 insertions [50]; experience with the Birnberg Bow has been particularly unfavourable in this respect. Early surgical removal of closed devices (such as the Birnberg Bow) from the abdominal cavity after perforation is mandatory because of the risk of intestinal obstruction. Open devices, however, rarely cause any trouble if they are left unremoved. *Pelvic inflammatory disease* occurs in 2–3 per cent of women during the first year after insertion of an intra-uterine device [66]. The incidence is highest during the early months after insertion. Most cases are mild and can be treated with the device remaining *in situ*. It should be noted, however, that severe pelvic inflammatory disease resulting in death has been attributed to intra-uterine devices in a small number of women [52].

Concern is often expressed that intra-uterine devices may *impair fertility* or may cause *carcinoma of the cervix* or *carcinoma of the endometrium*. Data are scanty on these points, but so far as they go, they are reassuring. For example, Tietze and Lewit [67] found that 88 per cent of women who had a device removed in order to become pregnant conceived within a year. These authors also failed to find any increase in the incidence of *in situ* carcinoma or invasive carcinoma of the cervix in women using intra-uterine devices during a period of observation extending up to 6 years.

Ectopic pregnancies are relatively much more frequent (1 in 15 to 1 in 20) than usual among the accidental pregnancies occurring with an intra-uterine device *in situ* [30]. This is because intra-uterine devices prevent uterine pregnancies much more effectively than ectopic pregnancies. There is no reason to believe that ectopic implantation is actually caused by intra-uterine devices.

Newer devices. The Dalkon Shield is a small, flexible intra-uterine device, specially designed to present a large area of contact with the endometrium and to reduce the risk of expulsion [8]. In contrast with most established devices, it can be inserted reasonably easily in nulliparous women. Davis and Lerner [8] claimed very favourable results with this device; further experience, however, suggests that use-effectiveness pregnancy rates are no better than those obtained with the larger sizes of the Lippes Loop [60], although expulsions and removals for medical reasons occur appreciably less frequently.

The Shell Loop is simply a Lippes Loop made of polypropylene, which is a stiffer material than the usual polyethylene. Experience so far suggests that this device is highly effective and has a very low expulsion rate [65]. Removals for medical reasons appear to be necessary about as often as with the polyethylene device.

The Copper-T and Copper-7 devices represent a new departure in intra-uterine device design. The principle is to use a device which is well tolerated by the uterus as a carrier of a substance which alters the intra-uterine milieu by interfering with metabolic processes in the endometrium. Both the Copper-T and the Copper-7 devices carry a coil of copper wire around their stems which presents a surface area of 200 mm^2.

The mechanism of action of the copper bearing devices is still incompletely understood, although much has been learned from recent studies by Hagenfeldt and her colleagues [14–17]. There is no evidence that the copper bearing devices have any systemic effects.

Experience with the Copper-T and Copper-7 devices so far is encouraging. Use-effectiveness pregnancy rates are of the order of 1–2 per 100 woman-years [2, 36, 63]. Expulsion and removal rates also appear to be favourable. Furthermore, the Copper-T and Copper-7 devices have given more satisfactory results in nulliparous women than any other type of device.

Sterilization

Male sterilization. Vasectomy is a simple surgical procedure which can be carried out under local or general anaesthesia. The operation should be regarded as an irreversible method of fertility control, although reanastomosis is sometimes successful. A man is not sterile immediately after vasectomy as mature sperm remain in the vasa deferentia and accessory glands. Accordingly, a semen specimen must be examined for the presence of sperm about 8 weeks after the operation. Some surgeons require two negative semen tests, a month apart, before pronouncing the man sterile.

Vasectomy is an extremely safe procedure and has not been shown to have any harmful long-term effects. A high proportion of vasectomized men, however, develop sperm-agglutinating and sperm-immobilizing antibodies, and some authors have expressed concern about the possible development of autoimmune conditions as remote sequelae to vasectomy [56].

Procedures are under investigation which aim to replace vasectomy by blocking the lumina of the vasa deferentia with removable plugs made of silastic or occluding the lumina by removable clips [79]. The objective of these procedures is, of course, to improve the prospects for reversibility.

Female sterilization. Tubal ligation can be carried out via an abdominal or a vaginal incision. The procedure is very safe, many large series having been reported without mortality. Such surgical procedures do, however, require immobilization of the woman for a few days and carry with them some risk of post-operative wound infection. Accordingly, the move is now towards endoscopic methods of female sterilization. Both the abdominal (laparoscopic) and vaginal (culdoscopic) routes have been extensively used. In either case, the duration of stay in hospital is reduced to a day or less. Sterilization via a laparoscope with diathermy or division of the Fallopian tubes should always be done under general anaesthesia. The technique can be used in conjunction with termination of pregnancy or during the puerperium. Sterilization via a culdoscope can be performed under local anaesthesia, but is best restricted to 'interval cases'. An excellent review of these methods of sterilization will be found in an article by Steptoe [62]. In skilled hands, they appear to be extremely safe.

As is the case with vasectomy, effective tubal occlusion should be regarded as an irreversible method of fertility control, although some successful tubal reconstructions have been reported. Some surgeons are now occluding the Fallopian tubes by the application of tantalum clips in the hope of improving the prospects of reversibility.

A number of interesting new approaches to female sterilization are under investigation. First, the introduction of the hysteroscope has made possible a direct approach to the interstitial portions of the Fallopian tubes via the cervix. If this method is successful, it will represent a major advance because the technique is quick, relatively simple, and requires only local anaesthesia. Secondly, the use of various chemical agents to produce tubal occlusion has been reported. Perhaps the most promising method is that described by Zipper *et al.* [83], in which an aqueous suspension of quinacrine is instilled into the uterus transvaginally in two consecutive cycles immediately after menstruation. If Zipper's claims for the efficacy of this method can be substantiated by other workers, this extremely simple technique will have a very wide application.

Abortion

Abortion during the first trimester of pregnancy is a reasonably straightforward procedure. The two most widely used methods are dilatation and curettage and vacuum aspiration. The latter method, which was introduced in China in 1958, has been very widely used in Eastern Europe and is becoming increasingly popular elsewhere. In the opinion of some workers, vacuum aspiration of pregnancies up to the 10th week of gestation can be safely conducted as an outpatient procedure under local anaesthesia [1, 31].

There is no completely satisfactory method of inducing abortion during the second trimester of pregnancy. Hysterotomy, either by the abdominal or vaginal route, is often used, but the operation carries an appreciable risk. Other methods include the intra-amniotic injection of hypertonic saline, glucose or urea [13, 76] or the use of abortifacient pastes [57]. Surgical intervention is often necessary after the use of these procedures to remove retained products of conception.

Recently there has been a great deal of interest in the use of prostaglandins for terminating pregnancy. These substances appear to be of particular value when used during the second trimester. Originally, they were administered intravenously, but the extra-amniotic or intra-amniotic routes are now preferred [11, 75]. Gastrointestinal side-effects, such as nausea, vomiting, and diarrhoea are frequently seen, but it seems probable that the use of prostaglandins will prove safer than other existing methods for terminating second trimester pregnancies.

Complications of abortion may be broadly classified as short-term and long-term. Numerous studies of *short-term complications* have been carried out in many different countries. It is impossible to produce a concise summary of the findings, because so many factors affect both mortality and morbidity. These include the skill of the operator, the conditions under which the operation is performed, the duration of pregnancy, associated medical or surgical conditions, the technique of abortion used, the type of anaesthetic administered, coincident sterilization, and the age, parity, and socio-economic status of the woman [20]. Taking these considerations into account it is, perhaps, no surprise that the lowest death rates for induced abortion have been achieved in countries where the operation is freely available. In Japan, for example, the rate is about 4 per 100 000, in Czechoslovakia about 2 per 100 000 and in Hungary only about 1 per 100 000 [44]. In America, data concerning 73 000 patients taking part in the Joint Program for the Study of Abortion, indicate a rate of about 8 per 100 000 [67]. The latest data available in England, which relate to the year 1971, reveal a rate of about 11 per 100 000 [5]. Reported short-term morbidity rates likewise show wide variation. For example, in the American Joint Program for the Study of Abortion, the incidence of early medical complications was about 10 per cent and only 1 in 10 of these complications was classified as 'major'. Stallworthy *et al.* [61], on the other hand, have reported their results concerning 1182 abortions carried out in Oxford, almost 80 per cent of which were undertaken at less than 14 weeks gestation (a proportion very similar to that in the American study). Nearly 17 per cent of the patients in this series lost more than 500 ml of blood, and almost 10 per cent required transfusion. Cervical lacerations occurred in 4 per cent, and the uterus was perforated in 1 per cent. Pyrexia of 38°C or more persisting for longer than 24 hours occurred in 27 per cent. Peritonitis developed in 14 patients, with paralytic ileus in 7, and 6 others had septicaemia.

More studies of the *long-term complications* of abortion are needed. There is little doubt, however, that techniques involving cervical dilation raise the miscarriage rate and the prematurity rate in subsequent pregnancies [44, 80]. It is also known that foetal erythrocytes enter the maternal circulation at the time of surgical abortion and that this can induce rhesus sensitization. It is now a routine practice in the United Kingdom to give anti-D immunoglobulin to all those women known to be rhesus negative who have induced abortions, save for those who are sterilized at the same time [5]. Other late physical effects of abortion are dominated by the sequelae of infection; these include pelvic inflammatory disease, peritoneal adhesions, ectopic pregnancy, and secondary infertility. The frequency with which such effects occur is unknown, as definitive studies have not been undertaken. Such data as have been reported, however, suggest that the frequency is likely to be low [18, 32].

Other methods

In this short review, attention has been limited to the medical aspects of those methods of fertility control which are currently in general use or which seem likely to become so in the immediate future. Research is proceeding in some other areas which may eventually produce results of practical importance. Two examples are the development of antispermatogenic agents and the investigation of possible immunological methods of fertility control. Reviews of these and other topics will be found in articles by the World Health Organization [78], Edwards [10], and Jackson [24].

REFERENCES
1. BERIĆ, B. M. and KUPRESANIN, M. (1971). *Lancet* **2**, 619.
2. BERNSTEIN, G. S., ISRAEL, R., SEWARD, P., and MISHELL, D. R. (1972), *Contraception* **6**, 99.
3. BORELL, U. (1966). *Acta Obst. Gynecol. scand.* **45**, Suppl. 1, 9.
4. BOYD, J. T. and DOLL, R. (1964). *Br. J. Cancer* **18**, 419.
5. CHIEF MEDICAL OFFICER (1972). *Annual report for the year* 1971. H.M.S.O., London.
6. COMMITTEE ON SAFETY OF MEDICINES (1972). *Carcinogenicity tests of oral contraceptives.* H.M.S.O., London.
7. CROSS, R. G. (1968). *Brit. med. J.* **3**, 253.
8. DAVIS, H. J. and LERNER, I. S. (1971). *Adv. planned Parenthood* **6**, 89.
9. DOLL, R. and VESSEY, M. P. (1970). *Br. med. Bull.* **26**, 33.
10. EDWARDS, R. G. (1970). *Br. med. Bull.* **26**, 72.
11. EMBREY, M. P., HILLIER, K., and MAHENDRAN, P. (1972). *Br. med. J.* **3**, 146.
12. FISCHER, A. and MOSBECH, J. (1970). *Ugeskr. Laeg.* **132/52**, 2480.
13. GILLMER, M. D. G., FRIEND, J. R., and BEARD, R. W. (1971) *Br. med. J.* **1**, 434.
14. HAGENFELDT, K. (1972). *Contraception* **6**, 37.
15. —— (1972). *Contraception* **6**, 191.
16. —— (1972). *Contraception* **6**, 219.
17. ——, JOHANNISSON, E. and BRENNER, P. (1972). *Contraception* **6**, 207.
18. HAYASHI, M. and MOMOSE, K. (1966). In *Harmful effects of induced abortion*, p. 36. Family Planning Federation of Japan,
19. HERTZ, R. (1968). *Int. J. Fert.* **13**, 273.
20. HUNTINGFORD, P. (1971). *Lancet* **1**, 1012.
21. IFFY, L. (1961). *J. Obst. Gynaecol. Br. Cwlth* **68**, 441.
22. INMAN, W. H. W. and VESSEY, M. P. (1968). *Br. med. J.* **2**, 193.
23. ——, ——, WESTERHOLM, B., and ENGELUND, A. (1970), *Br. med. J.* **2**, 203.
24. JACKSON, H. (1970). *Br. med. Bull.* **26**, 79.
25. KARIM, M., AMMAR, R., EL MAHGOUB, S., EL GANZOURY, R., FIKRI, F., and ABDOU, I. (1971). *Br. med. J.* **1**, 200.
26. KUCHERA, L. K. (1971). *J. Am. med. Assoc.* **218**, 562.
27. *Lancet* (1971). **1**, 25.
28. LARAGH, J. H. (1971). *Am. J. Obst. Gynecol.* **109**, 210.
29. ——, SEALEY, J. E., LEDINGHAM, J. G. G., and NEWTON, M.A. (1967), *J. Am. med. Assoc.* **201**, 918.
30. LEHFELDT, H., TIETZE, C., and GORSTEIN, F. (1970). *Am. J. Obst. Gynecol.* **108**, 1005.
31. LEWIS, S. C., LAL, S., BRANCH, B., and BEARD, R. W. (1971). *Br. med. J.* **4**, 606.
32. LINDAHL, J. (1959). *Somatic complications following legal abortion.* Scandinavia University Books, Stockholm.

33. MARSHALL, J. (1972). *Lancet* **2**, 1027.
34. MASI, A. T. and DUGDALE, M. (1970). *Ann. int. Med.* **72**, 111.
35. MISHELL, D. R., LUMKIN, M., and STONE, S. (1972). *Am. J. Obst. Gynecol.* **113**, 927.
36. NEWTON, J., ELIAS, J., and McEWAN, J. (1972). *Lancet* **2**, 951.
37. O'DONNELL, M. (1969). *World Medicine*, 25 November, 39.
38. OLIVER, M. F. (1970). *Br. med. J.* **2**, 210.
39. ORELLANA-ALCALDE, J. M. and DOMINGUEZ, J. P. (1966). *Lancet* **2**, 1278.
40. PEARL, R. (1932). *Hum. Biol.* **4**, 363.
41. PEEL, J. and POTTS, M. (1969). *Textbook of contraceptive practice.* Cambridge University Press.
42. PETERSON, W. F. (1969). *Obst. Gynecol.* **34**, 363.
43. POTTER, R. G. (1963). *Milbank memor. Fund Quart. Bull.* **41**, 400.
44. POTTS, D. M. (1970). *Br. med. Bull.* **26**, 65.
45. ROBINSON, S. C. (1971). *Am. J. Obst. Gynecol.* **109**, 354.
46. ROCHAT, R. W. (1972). *Lancet* **2**, 1027.
47. ROSE, D. P. (1970). *J. clin. Path.* **23**, Suppl. (Assoc. clin. Path.) **3**, 37.
48. ROYAL COLLEGE OF GENERAL PRACTITIONERS (1967). *J. R. Coll. gen. Pract.* **13**, 267.
49. SARTWELL, P. E., MASI, A. T., ARTHES, F. G., GREENE, G. R., and SMITH, H. E. (1969). *Am. J. Epidem.* **90**, 363.
50. SCHWARTZ, G. F. and MARKOWITZ, A. M. (1970). *J. Am. med. Assoc.* **211**, 959.
51. SCOMMEGNA, A., GEETA, N., PANDYA, G. N., CHRIST, M., LEE, A. W., and COHEN, M. R. (1970). *Fertil. Steril.* **21**, 201.
52. SCOTT, R. B. (1968). *Int. J. Fertil.* **13**, 297.
53. SCUTCHFIELD, F. D., LONG, W. N., COREY, B., and TYLER, C. W. (1971). *Contraception* **3**, 21.
54. SEIGEL, D. G. and CORFMAN, P. (1968). *J. Am. med. Assoc.* **203**, 950.
55. SHEARMAN, R. P. and SMITH, I. D. (1972). *J. Obst. Gynaecol. Br. Cwlth* **79**, 654.
56. SHULMAN, S. and SHULMAN, J. F. (1971). *Fertil. Steril.* **22**, 633.
57. SOOD, S. V. (1971). *Br. med. J.* **2**, 315.
58. SPELLACY, W. N. (1969). *Am. J. Obst. Gynecol.* **104**, 448.
59. —— and BIRK, S. A. (1972). *Am. J. Obst. Gynecol.* **112**, 912.
60. SNOWDEN, R. H. (1972). Exeter University Family Planning Research Unit, Report No. 2.
61. STALLWORTHY, J. A., MOOLGAOKER, A. S., and WALSH, J. J. (1971). *Lancet* **2**, 1245.
62. STEPTOE, P. C. (1970). *Br. med. Bull.* **26**, 60.
63. TATUM, H. J. (1972). *Contraception* **6**, 179.
64. TIETZE, C. (1968). *Clin. Obst. Gynecol.* **11**, 698.
65. —— (1971). *Studies in Family Planning* **2**, 19.
66. —— and LEWIT, S. (1970). *Studies in Family Planning* **1**, 1.
67. —— ——, (1972). *Studies in Family Planning* **3**, 97.

68. VESSEY, M. P. and DOLL, R. (1968). *Br. med. J.* **2**, 199.
69. ——, —— (1969). *Br. med. J.* **2**, 651.
70. ——, ——, and SUTTON, P. M. (1972). *Br. med. J.* **3**, 719.
71. ——, MEARS, E., ANDOLŠEK, L., and OGRINC-OVEN, M. (1972). *Lancet* **1**, 915.
72. WEIR, R. J., BRIGGS, E., BROWNING, J., MACK, A., NAISMITH, L., TAYLOR, L., and WILSON, E. (1971). *Lancet* **1**, 467.
73. WEISSMANN, M. C., FOLIAKI, L., BILLINGS, E. L., and BILLINGS, J. J. (1972). *Lancet* **2**, 813.
74. WESTERHOLM, B. (1967). *Läkartidnigen* **64**, Suppl. 4, 71.
75. WIQVIST, N., BEGUIN, F., BYGDEMAN, M., FERNSTROM, I., and TOPPOZADA, M. (1972). *Prostaglandins* **1**, 37.
76. WOOD, C., BOOTH, R. T., and PINKERTON, J. H. M. (1962). *Br. med. J.* **2**, 706.
77. WOODS, J. W. (1967). *Lancet* **2**, 653.
78. WORLD HEALTH ORGANISATION (1969). *Tech. Rep. Ser. Wld Hlth Org.* No. 424.
79. WORLD HEALTH ORGANISATION (1971). *Tech. Rep. Ser. Wld Hlth Org.* No. 473.
80. WRIGHT, C. S. W., CAMPBELL, S., and BEAZLEY, J. (1972). *Lancet* **2**, 1278.
81. WYNDER, E. L., CORNFIELD, J., SCHROFF, P. D., and DORARSWAMI, K. R. (1954). *Am. J. Obst. Gynecol.* **68**, 1016.
82. WYNN, V., DOAR, J. W. H., MILLS, G. L., and STOKES, T. (1969). *Lancet* **2**, 756.
83. ZIPPER, J., STACHETTI, E., and MEDEL, M. (1970). *Fertil. Steril.* **21**, 581.

2.6.2. The role of the general medical practitioner in family planning

GEORGE MORRIS

Doctors and Overpopulation Group, London

Family planning is not merely fitting the cap or writing prescriptions for the Pill, useful though these activities are. Worthwhile family planning must include everything concerned with fertility control; in particular the general practitioner has a key role to play in relation to contraception, sterilization, and abortion. The most splendid and refined methods of contraception will not prevent unwanted pregnancies, nor help to curtail population increase, if people do not know how to obtain or use them or if they desire to have large families. The family doctor therefore has a significant, if not quite such a central, role to play in the fields of education and motivation.

The G.P. is, perhaps of all doctors, the most closely identified with the patient's interest. Perhaps I can deal here with the fear often expressed by well-meaning people that the G.P. who is worried about over-population and pursues an active family-planning programme is in some way acting as an instrument of society, or of the state, against the needs and desire of those of his patients who wish to have children. I accept that this is a possible danger for the future. It is certainly one that is far more likely to occur if all of us, including G.P.s, do not help to control population increase by using the acceptable voluntary methods that are now available.

For, as we all know, the present issue is not of people being denied the right to have children; it is of scores of thousands of women in the United Kingdom each year having babies that they do not want [1]. Some of them at least are becoming pregnant through lack of access to contraceptives, sterilization, or abortion.

Let us consider the resulting unwanted children. Even when they are adequately fed and housed they do only too badly. The battered and abused child is often illegitimate [2] or at least unplanned or unwanted. Perhaps not so dramatically, lesser degrees of disadvantage and unhappiness exist for many unwanted children, particularly the illegitimate and the unwanted in larger families. This has been confirmed graphically in two recent books from the National Children's Bureau [3, 4]. These and other studies show that the illegitimate child, particularly when living with the single parent [5], does extremely badly from the point of view of school performance, physical fitness, and general development, as well as in its ability to adjust to society. One also sees that the first- and second-born children in large families do better than later children (presumably more of whom are unwanted). In addition to this, the first and second children from large families, in their turn, do less well than do the children of one- or two-child families.

What the G.P. can actually do

It is most important that the G.P. should consider family-planning advice to be one of his most important duties. Just as no good family doctor ever lets an at-risk, middle-aged man with a cough out of his surgery without arranging for a chest X-ray, so I would like to feel that no G.P. would allow an at-risk woman (or man for that matter) out of his consulting room without making sure that they received family-planning advice. He must take every suitable opportunity to raise the subject. Indeed, countless young parents visiting good doctors for their children's earache or flat feet have left with a prescription for the Pill or a letter for a vasectomy.

The G.P. must not only supply contraceptives, he must also take the trouble to familiarize himself with the facts about them. All too often the G.P. is the person to whom the patient confides when worried by the most recent lurid headline of teenage brides dropping dead whilst taking the Pill; he must be in a position to reassure her that it is safer to be on the Pill than to be pregnant. Indeed, a most important part of the G.P.'s work lies in prescribing the Pill. Ninety per cent of general practitioners prescribe the Pill as their first choice in contraceptives [6].

Payment for the Pill is of considerable importance. It is hoped that, very shortly, the Pill will be available on E.C.10 (i.e. a National Health Service (NHS) prescription) either free of charge or at the standard rate– currently 20p a prescription (usually for 6 months supply).

At the moment we are allowed to prescribe the Pill on E.C.10 where the health of the woman would suffer from an unwanted pregnancy.† This leaves an enormous amount to the discretion of the individual doctor. Indeed it is difficult to imagine any woman's health that would *not* be adversely effected, even if very slightly, by an unwanted pregnancy. Doctors who choose to interpret the present law liberally therefore find that they can prescribe the vast majority of their prescriptions for the Pill on E.C.10. Some courageous doctors who recently stated publicly that they intended, as a matter of policy, to prescribe *all* their Pill prescriptions on E.C.10, in fact, have run into difficulties with their local Executive Council for this political stand. However, I know of no doctor who has been questioned at all for over-liberal prescription of the Pill on a NHS form.

When one remembers that the basic NHS cost for the Pill is somewhere in the region of 15p a month it would be very surprising if there were any such trouble. For this is an infinitesimal cost compared with that of the vast majority of new drugs, and

† See p. 390.

one that pales into insignificance when compared with the £4364 estimated as the cost to society of one illegitimate birth [7]. This low cost of the Pill to the NHS is not reflected in the payment the woman herself has to make to the chemist which may be several times that of the actual basic cost. In addition to this, the G.P. is entitled, if he so wishes, to charge his NHS patients for writing a prescription for the Pill or for a routine initial examination. The British Medical Association recommends that he may charge for these respectively 70p. and £4·50, but doctors are at liberty to charge more. It is therefore not at all unusual for a woman to have to pay £5 or £6 before obtaining the Pill. Small wonder that a significant, if small, number of women do actually become pregnant having been discouraged from obtaining a prescription by financial considerations.

Fortunately more and more G.P.s are prescribing the Pill liberally on NHS prescription and more particularly are desisting from charging for writing private prescriptions.

Sterilization

Here again the family doctor has a key role to play. Even today a significant number of people are too diffident to ask their G.P. about sterilization, and many patients do not know that the newer forms of female sterilization only require an overnight stay in hospital.

Vasectomy is an even more minor procedure, but is not at the moment freely available in NHS hospitals, although some local authority clinics do provide the service. A NHS consultant, if he is sympathetic, may consider that in a particular case there are good medical reasons for the operation to be performed under the NHS. On the other hand, he may decide that no such reason exists, and may charge a fee of his own choosing. There are many cases where vasectomy requests have been turned down by NHS consultants, even in the presence of overwhelming need [8]. A great deal obviously depends on the strength of the G.P.'s letter of referral. However, many working men requesting vasectomy have still found themselves presented with a bill for up to £70 for this relatively minor procedure, even when strong medical and social reasons did exist.

The G.P. is in a very strong position to bring pressure on his surgical colleagues to liberalize their attitudes. All of us wish to be respected by our peers, and very often a friendly letter or telephone call can bring about, if not a change of policy, then at least the review of a particular case.

Vasectomy is a very suitable operation for the trained G.P. to perform in his own surgery, and the Vasectomy Advancement Society exists to train G.P.s for this useful task. In one group practice in Northumberland the doctors average 100 cases each year [9]. A most useful method of reasuring patients about sterilization is to allow them to speak to patients who have undergone the operation, and some doctors keep a list of phone numbers of volunteers. Reassurance from another patient is often more effective than from a doctor and, as we know, people are usually only too pleased to talk about their operations.

Abortion

Whether middle-aged doctors, or legislators for that matter, like it or not, young women have always resorted to abortion when other methods of family planning have failed [10]. In 1972 there were some 156 000 legal abortions in this country. This is too many, and all of us, including G.P.s, must work for more efficient prevention. On the other hand, one shudders to think of the human suffering, not to mention the resultant population pressures, if these 156 000 women had been denied safe and legal termination. Any G.P. casting his mind back a few years will remember how the septic results of badly performed illegal abortions were a common complication in general practice. I have seen none of these complications since the 1968 Abortion Act became law.

Most women requesting an abortion see their G.P. first [11]. Although we are all entitled to our opinion, particularly on this difficult subject, I do feel the doctor has to be honest. If he conscientiously disapproves of abortion he should tell the patient, but he should also explain that it is her right to obtain a second opinion. In particular, I think fair-minded people will deplore the habit of some doctors [12] who employ delaying tactics by arranging for, often unnecessary, urine pregnancy tests and who fail to expedite appointments, so that several weeks may pass and what would have been a safe, early termination of pregnancy becomes a more hazardous, and often impractical, procedure.

It is certainly the G.P.'s duty to familiarize himself with the facts about abortion. The G.P. looking at short-term complications will find that many recent papers on the subject [13, 14, 15, 16] show early abortion to be a very safe procedure [17]. Indeed this is borne out by personal clinical experience in general practice, where the vast majority of women who have terminations early on in pregnancy, in fact, do fare extremely well. The only complication I see in general practice are in the unhappy women who have been *refused* termination [18, 19].

If the G.P. is unfortunate enough to practise in an area where the consultant gynaecologists are hostile to performing abortions there is relatively little he can do other than to refer those patients who can afford it to the non-profit-making organizations such as the Pregnancy Advisory Service. Even here, though, he can make the needs and feelings of himself and his patients felt through influence and pressure at local, regional, or national level.

For a doctor whose practice is in an area where some of the consultants are liberally disposed it is obviously important to refer to those gynaecologists who are known to be sympathetic; although it must be said that even the most sympathetic of consultants is not likely to be impressed by a brief and almost illegible note.

Given the extremely doubtful assumption that any doctor knows better than the patient whether she ought to have the pregnancy terminated, the G.P. with his knowledge of the patient and her family is certainly likely to be in a better position than the consultant gynaecologist, who may well be seeing her for the very first time. In a twenty-minute interview the most perceptive consultant is unlikely to know as much of a patient as does her G.P. Indeed, as Buckle and Anderson stated in 1972:

We have in the past made it clear to colleagues in general practice that they are in the strongest position to judge a request for abortion. If we are in agreement with the request no further reference of the patient is necessary, and we have consequently been spared the hypocrisy of referring patients for a psychiatric opinion merely in order to gain a second signature. [20]

Many G.P.s in other parts of the United Kingdom would wish that they were lucky enough to work with colleagues with this degree of humility and understanding.

Aberdeen

If anyone doubts the value of vigorous family planning for our patients, they could do worse than look at the situation in Aberdeen. Aberdeen has a high proportion of people in social class V [21] and some of the worst housing in Scotland. Owing to fishing and other light industries there is a higher-than-average proportion of single young women. These are factors which lead to higher-than-average rates for illegitimate and unwanted births. To offset these disadvantages, Aberdeen has more than a quarter of a century's practice of liberal abortion policies and local-authority-supported contraception. Thus, in spite of its difficulties, Aberdeen has the lowest illegitimate birth rate, the lowest infant mortality and morbidity rates, the lowest maternity death rate, and, with the exception of Edinburgh, the lowest birth rate in Scotland [22], while Aberdeen's rate of population increase is roughly half that of the rest of the United Kingdom.

There is a lesson here for all of us. It is essentially that the committed doctor's concern about over-population and the day-to-day needs of his patients do not conflict; they go hand in hand.

REFERENCES AND NOTES

 1. CARTWRIGHT, A. (1971). *Family intentions survey: Office of Population Censuses and Surveys.* H.M.S.O., London.
 2. JACKSON, G. (1972). Child abuse syndrome: the cases we miss, *Br. med. J.* 2, 756–7.
 3. SEGLOW, J., PRINGLE, M. K., and WEDGE, P. (1972). *Growing up adopted.* The National Children's Bureau, London.
 4. DAVIE, R., BUTLER, M., and GOLDSTEIN, R. (1972). *From birth to seven.* The National Children's Bureau, London.
 5. BLAKE, P. (1972). *The plight of one-parent families.* Council for Children's Welfare, London.
 6. CARTWRIGHT, A. and WAITE, M. (1972). General practitioners and contraception in 1970–71, *J.R. Coll. gen. Pract.* 22, Suppl. 2.
 7. LAING, W. A. (1972). *The costs and benefits of family planning.* P.E.P. Broadsheet 534.
 8. Case histories—see below.

Case No. 1

Mr. P. is a 40-year-old working butcher with a wife in her early forties. They have two teenage children and considered their family complete. They have always used contraceptive measures, but unhappily the wife became pregnant and this was not discovered until too late for termination. Mrs. P. has high blood pressure and cannot use the Pill. Mr. P. did not wish there to be any risk of another pregnancy and asked his doctor to recommend him for a vasectomy. He was referred to a consultant surgeon who said that he would do it but as there were 'no medical reasons' would charge a fee of £40.

Case No. 2

Mr. and Mrs. L. are in their mid-thirties. The wife has had five babies, only two of whom are alive. Two of the babies were born dead, and the last child had severe congenital deformities and died after a few days. The wife was unable to use the Pill as it gave her headaches and made her depressed. Fear of pregnancy was causing an enormous amount of marital upset and was completely inhibiting the couple's sex-life. The family doctor, when asked about vasectomy, referred the patient to a consultant surgeon who agreed to perform the operation for seventy guineas. Mr. L. went to another G.P. and was referred to a surgeon who quite correctly did the operation free of charge under the National Health Service.

9. HOBBS, J. (1972). Vasectomy in general practice, *J.R. Coll. gen. Pract.* **22**, 583.

10. PEEL, J. and POTTS, M. (1972). *Textbook of contraceptive practice.* Cambridge University Press.

11. CARTWRIGHT, A. and WAITE, M. (1972). General practitioners and abortion, *J.R. Coll. gen. Pract.* **22**, Suppl. 1.

12. ANON (1972). *Women and abortion.* The Women's Abortion and Contraception Campaign, London.

13. LEWIS, S. C., LAL, S., BRANCH, B., and BEARD, R. W. (1971). Outpatient termination of pregnancy, *Br. med. J.* **4**, 606–10.

14. BERIĆ, B. M. and KUPRESANIN, M. (1971). Vacuum aspiration, using pericervical block, for legal abortion as an outpatient procedure up to the 12th week of pregnancy, *Lancet* **2**, 619–21.

15. TIETZE, C. (1973). *Family planning perspectives* **5**, 38.

16. ARTHURE, H. R. (1972). Royal Society of Health Conference, February 1972.

17. See also, this volume, pp. 343–4 and pp. 368–70.

18. FORSSMAN, H. and THUWE, I. (1967). One hundred and twenty children born after application for therapeutic abortion refused, *Acta psychiat. Neurol. scand.* **42**, 71–88.

19. LAMBERT, J. (1971). Survey of 3,000 unwanted pregnancies, *Br. med. J.* **4**, 156–60.

20. BUCKLE, A. E. R. and ANDERSON, M. M. (1972). Implementation of the Abortion Act: report on a year's working of abortion clinics and operating sessions, *Br. med. J.* **3**, 381–4.

21. *Registrar-General's Census of the United Kingdom, 1961.* H.M.S.O., London.

22. *Annual report of the Medical Officer of Health to City Council Aberdeen.* (1972).

2.6.3. The effect of the United Kingdom Abortion Act 1968 on the illegitimate birth rate

DAVID SOSKICE

Fellow of University College, and Institute of Economics and Statistics Oxford University.

I believe that few people would wish to advocate that the burden of population regulation should rest on a policy of induced termination of pregnancy, at least in the present state of our knowledge of methods of inducing termination. On the contrary, it is widely agreed that the burden should rest on a policy of extensive and effective use of contraceptive methods, both on account of the relatively higher morbidity associated with induced termination as compared to contraception and on account of the relatively higher costs. However, there are at least two important reasons why such a policy may require to be supplemented by a policy of induced terminations if it is desired that the aim of population regulation is to be effectively carried through. In the first place, a long period of time may be needed to bring about an effective and extensive use of contraception; and in the second place, it would be foolish to imagine that even if contraception was effectively and extensively practised that it would wholly prevent unwanted conceptions. It is not clear, of course, in either of these two cases that such a supplementary policy of legal abortion would be effective in reducing the birth rate. In general, statistics of the experience of legal abortion in other countries have been in the form of annual time series from which suggestive rather than substantiated conclusions can be drawn. However, the General Register Office has produced excellent statistics of the experience of legal abortion in the United Kingdom since 1968, which enable comparisons to be made between legal abortions and births in about 130 local authority areas in England and Wales.

This paper is primarily concerned with the effect of legal abortion on illegitimate births. The annual aggregate figures of illegitimate births in England and Wales are briefly reviewed, preparatory to a discussion of two studies [1, 2] of the relationship between legal abortions and illegitimate births derived from comparisons of the area statistics.

From 1961 when the number of illegitimate births was 48 490, the numbers of illegitimate births rose steadily until 1967 when the number was 69 928 [4]. In 1968, however, during which the Act was in force for 8 months, this rise was halted, and the number of illegitimate births fell to 69 806. In 1969 the number fell to 67 041, and in 1970 to 64 744. In 1971 the number rose to 65 678.

In themselves, these figures do no more than suggest that the Abortion Act has substantially reduced the numbers of illegitimate births. However, significant changes were occurring in the use of contraceptives by married women throughout this period, and it is likely that these changes were paralleled in the use of contraceptives by single women. An analysis of age-specific illegitimacy rates (i.e. illegitimate births per 1000 single women in

TABLE 2.6.1†

Age-specific illegitimacy rates per 1000 single women in each age-group

Year	Age-groups			
	15–19	20–4	25–9	30–44
1962	8·7	30·4	54·9	31·9
1963	9·3	31·0	58·4	34·0
1964	10·3	31·8	55·6	31·5
1965	11·4	32·6	57·4	32·3
1966	12·2	32·3	55·9	32·6
1967	13·5	31·8	56·4	33·6
1968	14·1	31·1	54·7	33·1
1969	14·2	29·4	52·4	31·8
1970	14·0	28·7	49·4	31·3

† Table 8 (p. 13) from [2].

each age-group) given by Dodd [2] (see Table 2.6.1) suggests that such a change in the use of contraceptives may have taken place among single women at least in the 20–4 age-group prior to the Abortion Act coming into operation. To get a clearer idea therefore of the effects of the Abortion Act, the author has made a detailed comparison of changes in illegitimate births and legal abortions on unmarried women in 89 local authority areas [1].

The Registrar General's Annual Supplement on Abortion gives details of legal abortions in local authority areas in England and Wales with populations greater than 100 000 [6]. The 89 areas examined comprise all the areas in England excluding the Greater London areas. For each area a comparison was made between legal

abortions in 1969 on unmarried women usually resident in the area
per 100 000 population and the percentage change in illegitimate
births between the calendar year 1967 [8] and the 12-month period
July 1969–June 1970 [9] (roughly corresponding to abortions in
the calendar year 1969). The analysis had to be restricted to legal
abortions in 1969, because to analyse those in 1970 would have
required monthly data on illegitimate births in the 89 areas in
1971; these data were not available.

The 89 areas were divided into groups according to whether the
rate of legal abortions in 1969 on unmarried women per 100 000
population was greater than 600 (12 areas); between 500 and 600
(11 areas); between 400 and 500 (18 areas); between 300 and 400
(20 areas); between 200 and 300 (21 areas); and less than 200
(5 areas). For each group of areas the average percentage change in
illegitimate births between 1967 and 1969–70 was calculated and
also the number of areas for each group in which illegitimate
births had risen between 1967 and 1969–70 and the number in
which they had fallen.

The logic of this approach was as follows. Very roughly, illegitimate births between July 1969 and June 1970 in a particular
area, say the jth ($I_{j,69-70}$) are equal to the difference between conceptions during 1969 ($C_{j,69}$) and legal abortions ($LA_{j,69}$) and illegal
abortions ($IA_{j,69}$), all relating to single women usually resident in
that area, less the proportion (S_m) of that difference accounted for
by 'shotgun' marriages; so:

$$I_{j,69-70} = (1 - S_m)(C_{j,69} - LA_{j,69} - IA_{j,69}). \quad (2.6.1)$$

(This neglects spontaneous abortion, and the fact that some illegitimate births of women usually resident in the area will take place
outside the area and conversely; it also assumes the time-lag
between births and abortions is 6 months.) If this equation is
lagged $2\frac{1}{2}$ years,

$$I_{j,67} = (1 - S_m)(C_{j,66-7} - LA_{j,66-7} - IA_{j,66-7}). \quad (2.6.2)$$

Subtracting eqn (2.6.2) from eqn (2.6.1),

$$I_{j,69-70} - I_{j,67} = (1 - S_m)(C_{j,69} - C_{j,66-7}) - \\ - (1 - S_m)(LA_{j,69} - LA_{j,66-7}) - \\ - (1 - S_m)(IA_{j,69} - IA_{j,66-7}). \quad (2.6.3)$$

We then assume (1) that $LA_{j,66-7}$ can be neglected, on the grounds
that it would be small and fairly evenly spread over the different

areas; and (2), the crucially important assumption, that changes in conceptions were distributed independently over the different areas. (2) is not unreasonable: for though it may be that to some extent increases in contraceptive use occurred in the 'less backward' areas in which abortion rates were high, it is also true that such increases would have reduced the number of abortions in those areas by reducing the demand for them. On these assumptions, the effect of legal abortions on illegitimate births can be gauged by comparing the changes in illegitimate births in those areas in which the number of legal abortions was high with the changes in illegitimate births in those areas in which the number of legal abortions was low. The magnitude of the effect on illegitimate births then reflects the extent to which legal abortions were substitutes for illegal abortions, as can be seen from eqn. (2.6.3) (as well, of course, as the proportion of 'shotgun' marriages). Thus if it was assumed that a proportion b of legal abortions in each area represented the reduction in illegal abortions in that area, then

$$b\,LA_{j,69} = -(IA_{j,69} - I_{j,66-7}), \qquad (2.6.4)$$

so that $\qquad I_{j,69-70} - I_{j,67} = -(1 - S_m - b)\,LA_{j,69}. \qquad (2.6.5)$

To make the comparisons between the changes in illegitimate births and the level of legal abortions more comprehensible, we

Table 2.6.2

Data on legal abortions and illegitimate births, 1967 and 1969–70

Legal abortions on unmarried women in 1969 per 100 000 population	Number of areas in group	Average percentage change in illegitimate births 1967 to 1969–70 in areas in group	Number of areas in group in which illegitimate births rose	fell	Percentage of areas in group in which illegitimate births rose
<200	5	+7·2 (2·56)†	5	0	100
200–300	21	−4·3 (2·28)	8	13	38
300–400	20	−7·9 (1·89)	4	16	20
400–500	18	−10·3 (2·93)	2	16	11
500–600	11	−7·5 (1·71)	2	9	18
>600	12	−15·2 (2·72)	0	12	0

† Standard errors of *average* percentage change.

compare percentage changes in illegitimate births in each area with legal abortions on unmarried women per 100 000 population in that area. The results are given in Table 2.6.2.

To my mind, these results show very clearly the significant effect of the Abortion Act on illegitimate births. In England and Wales as a whole illegitimate births *fell* by 8·0 per cent between 1967 and 1969–70. In those five areas where there were fewer than 200 legal abortions on unmarried women per 100 000 population illegitimate births *rose* on average by 7·2 per cent; and in *each* of the five areas illegitimate births rose. Conversely in the twelve areas with more than 600 legal abortions on unmarried women per 100 000 population illegitimate births fell on average by 15·2 per cent; and in *each* of the twelve areas illegitimate births fell.

To get a more precise idea of the value of $(1 - S_m - b)$ I divided both sides of (2.6.3) by $I_{j,67}$, and ran a regression of

$$(I_{j,69-70} - I_{j,67})/I_{j,67} \quad \text{on} \quad LA_{j,69}/I_{j,67}.$$

$R^2 = 0.464$ and estimated value of $(1 - S_m - b)$ was -0.362; the estimated value of the constant term was 4·66. (The regression coefficients are significant on the usual assumptions, though it is not clear that those assumptions hold in this model.) The conclusion of these results is thus, in very loose terms, that (1) three legal abortions on average have been responsible for one less illegitimate birth and (2) on average, in the absence of legal abortion illegitimate births would have risen by about 4–5 per cent p.a.

However, these conclusions [10] differ markedly from those reached by Dodd [2] in his extremely useful study of the statistical effects of the United Kingdom Abortion Act. He compared fertility rates and legal-abortion rates and changes in both, for married and single women for 129 local authority areas in 1969 and 1970; he included the Greater London and the Welsh areas in addition to the 89 English areas used in the analysis described above [1]. Fertility rates and legal-abortion rates were defined as births and legal abortions per women at risk. Table 2.6.3. shows the results obtained by Dodd. None of the correlation coefficients are significant. What has gone wrong? I believe the differences between these results and those of the previous analysis can be explained as follows.

1. *Comparison of fertility and legal-abortion rates.* If both sides of eqn. (2.6.1) are divided by the number of single women at risk,

TABLE 2.6.3

	Single women r†	Married women r†
Fertility rates in 1969 with legal-abortion rates 1969	−0·06	−0·14
Fertility rates in 1970 with legal-abortion rates 1970	0·02	−0·16
Change in fertility rates 1969–70 with change in legal-abortion rates 1969–70	−0·07	−0·17

† *r* is the value of the correlation coefficient.

and variations in fertility rates compared with variations in legal-abortion rates, the variations in conception rates and illegal-abortion rates would be very high, and thus likely to prevent any clear correlation between fertility rates and abortion rates from being observed.

2. *Comparison of changes in fertility and legal-abortion rates.* Taking changes eliminates much of the variation in conception and illegal abortion rates. However, the problem of importance is now in the timing of fertility rates, for the comparison is of the change in fertility rates between 1969 and 1970 with the change in the legal-abortion rate *over the same period*. But if, on average, legal abortions occur at the end of the first trimester then, in a particular area, a high legal-abortion rate in the second half of 1969 implies a low fertility rate in the first half of 1970, so again it is not surprising that there is a low correlation coefficient when comparing changes over the same period. In other words, if the proper correlation is between (a) the change in the fertility rate between mid-1969–mid-1970 and mid-1970–mid-1971 and (b) the change in the legal abortion rate between 1969 and 1970 then, if the change in the fertility rate from 1969 to 1970 is correlated with the change in the legal-abortion rate from 1969 to 1970, the spurious correlation between the legal abortion rate in the second half of 1969 with fertility rate in the first half of 1970 must substantially reduce the over-all correlation.

REFERENCES AND NOTES

1. SOSKICE, D. (1973). *Br. J. Hosp. Med.* March 1973.
2. DODD, N. (1972). *Abortion and fertility in England and Wales.* Dissertation for M.Sc. in Medical Demography, London University.
3. *Registrar General's Quarterly Return for England and Wales.* H.M.S.O., London.
4. Ibid. Table 1a.
5. *Registrar General's Statistical Review of England and Wales for the Year* 1969, *Supplement on Abortion.* H.M.S.O., London.
6. Ibid. Table 17.
7. *Registrar General's Statistical Review of England and Wales for the Year* 1967, *Pt. II Tables, Population.* H.M.S.O., London.
8. Ibid. Table E.
9. Monthly data obtainable from the Office of Population Censuses and Surveys, Somerset House, Strand, London, W.C.2.
10. These conclusions are supported by the results of CARTWRIGHT, A. and WAITE, M. (1972). *J. R. Coll. gen. Practrs.*, Supp. **22**, No. 1, 1972.

2.6.4. Obstacles to family planning

JEAN MEDAWAR
Margaret Pyke Centre, London

Introduction

This paper is part of a collection of similar papers intended to introduce 'a plain man' to current problems of demography. The majority of people in this country are not 'plain men' who read to learn; but anyone who does qualify for the title should know, and may even want to know, what his and his partner's reproductive behaviour has to do with these problems. He is unlikely to look at this book unless he is already anxious about the rate at which the increasing human race is consuming the Earth's diminishing resources, and wondering what he could do about it, and he will be better able to alter his behaviour if he knows something about the forces which make him feel and think the way he does.

Men and women who want to plan the number of their offspring are playing a game with Nature in which she holds most of the cards, while they are handicapped both by their biological constitution and their culture. The plain man who wants to win any of the hands, in the short time left for playing, had better understand how and why the rules of the game have evolved.

Nature's conspiracy

The major obstacles are built first into ourslves and then into public opinion and institutions. Nature has evolved an enormous conspiracy against the success of any plan but hers: the entire biological programme is directed to ensure the reproduction of the species—the human species included. Everything, especially the design of the two sexes, each with their own inherited genes, intricate tides of hormones, maternal instincts, and desires for personal immortality, drives people in the same direction; men and women are made to complement each other and, at best, do so. What Noël Coward called 'the urge to merge' is insistent and often irresistible. In the relatively recent past the forces of mortality were so fierce that human fertility had to be maintained at a high level—it was only early last century that family size ceased to be decided largely by a cruel sum in which parents added and death subtracted. Therefore, we are endowed with, and partly ruled by, a constitution selected to secure the survival of whatever was formerly an optimum number of offspring. Human fertility was moulded by forces of natural selection in conditions totally different from today when, thanks to sanitary engineering, science, and medicine, almost every child in the United Kingdom survives to have children of its own. We have either to adapt in a hurry or perish as other species have done.

Added to the legacy of our own make-up are the equally powerful obstacles of handed-down cultural beliefs. Whatever most of us say, we tend to feel—as we have been taught to feel—that it is always better for every couple to marry and to have a family rather than not. Young couples are pressed, even by acquaintances, with the question (expecting the answer 'Yes') of 'Any news yet?' This is understandable and even nice, but is an impertinence today when our present annual crude birth rate of 16 per 1000, although falling slightly, will, if maintained, increase our present 56 million population to 66 million in 39 years. At the moment 9 per cent of all families have no children; but many more have babies not because they particularly want them but because society gives them no encouragement not to. If we are to avoid a heavy-handed rationing of births the childless ought to be honoured, so that passionate potential parents can reproduce more than the national average of two and a bit children—which would keep population growth at near zero—without compounding the present substantial growth in numbers. As Gerald Leach [1] has shown, a quite small shift in the sizes of families can do it. If public opinion fully understood the options, private actions might achieve one child less in every three families, and so stabilize the present growth.

Institutional obstacles

Institutions embody and almost enshrine the attitudes of past centuries. The practice of birth control has been handicapped by technology, medicine, law, education and finance.

Technology. The first and worst obstacle is that no contraceptive or method is yet foolproof or without disadvantage: the devices are 'stone-age' compared with the sophistication of the stratagems evolved by Nature to ensure reproduction.

Medicine. Medical opposition barely exists today, but less than four generations ago a doctor wrote to the *Lancet* that birth control was 'a subject no decent man would handle with a pair of tongs— it shall never become a wing of the healing art'. It has become such a wing, but training for its practice is still not a routine part of medical education. Understandably, many doctors find it hard to change the established doctor–patient consultation, and to delegate some of their traditional procedures in order to bring help and advice to the larger numbers of couples who need it today. A few (1 in every 10) prefer not to discuss birth control with patients at all.

Legal. The legal obstacle was partly removed by the 1967 NHS Family Planning Act which empowered, but did not oblige, local authorities to provide a service for family planning.

Educational and financial. Though a fine improvement on the previous arrangements which had virtually left matters to a charity or to chance, the 1967 Act allowed two considerable checks to remain: birth control appeared to be insufficiently important or proper to be made a normal part of the Health Service, and the lack of money for information, education, and supplies prevented many from even trying to plan.

The future of the obstacles

Although no universally acceptable wonder drug or device is likely to be found, the range and safety of methods is almost certain to increase as the supply responds to the urgency of the demands [3].

The absence of money for education or even information was partly repaired in December, 1972 when the Secretary of State announced that he intended to support the Health Education Council with money for a campaign of public education. As far as reporting on the removal of the cost of supplies is concerned, at the time of writing, the Cabinet is about to decide whether or not supplies as well as services shall be free under the reorganized National Health Service.†

If both are to be freely given, the obstacle of cost and aura of disapproval will at last have been removed, as a large majority of public opinion, supplied recently by National Opinion Polls, wants. The Lords have already decided that supplies should be free, and 70 M.P.s of all Parties have given their approval. Whether supplies are made free this week, this year or next, the tide is washing this particular block away, leaving behind the older obstacles of biological constitution and culture. If these had not already been shown removable, the future would be blackly clouded; but in Aberdeen [2], a stable population, illegitimacy lower than the national average, and representation in the clinics of social classes IV and V in the same proportion as in the population have been achieved largely because Sir Dugald Baird in the Hospital, Dr. Ian McQueen in the Town Hall, and Professor Raymond Illsley in the University knew what people needed and had the energy and courage to provide accordingly [3]. They understood that most people live their sexual lives without reference to the grave ratio between populations and resources, and that personal goals are usually more influential than national. So they introduced strong and practical official approval for birth control, provided all methods with easy access, including necessary terminations, and backed the whole with a health-education programme in which

† On March 26, 1973, Sir Keith Joseph, Secretary of State for Social Services, announced that 'as from 1 April, 1974 contraceptives will be placed on the same basis as other drugs and appliances under the National Health Service—that is, family planning will become a normal part of our health service arrangements. The maximum cost to the patient will be the prescription charge.'

the health visitors, entering every home where there was a child
or children, were as important as the doctors. So the obstacles can
be overcome; public opinion wants them overcome; time is short
and the dangers are real. Perhaps we shall adapt, just in time.

REFERENCES

1. LEACH, G. (1971). *Family Planning* **19**, No. 4, 95.
2. McQUEEN, J. A. G. (1969). Community education in birth control,
   Medical officer **122**, 301.
3. ANON. (1973). *The benefits of birth control—Aberdeen's experience*
   British Birth Control Campaign, London.

THE LAW AND FERTILITY CONTROL:
AN EDITORIAL NOTE

Recent changes relating to abortion under the English civil law have been
cogently reviewed by HART, H. L. A. (1972). Abortion law reform:
the English experience, *Melbourne Univ. Law Rev.* **8** (May), 388–411 (55
refs.). University of Melbourne Press, Melbourne, Vic.; while *The Report
of the Committee of Enquiry on the operation of the Abortion Act 1967*,
under the chairmanship of Mrs. Justice Lane, is pending (H.M.S.O.,
London). For a conspectus of western views on abortion see the contributions in NOONAN, JR., J. T. (ed.) (1970). *The Morality of abortion.*
Harvard University Press, Cambridge, Mass. An account of the experiences in Eastern Europe following the legalization of abortion in the
1950s is given by TIETZE, C. (1964). The demographic significance of
legal abortion in Eastern Europe, *Demography* **1**, 123.

Restrictions on marriage due to the civil law in the nineteenth century
in North-west Europe are discussed briefly by VAN DE WALLE, E.
(1972). Marriage and marital fertility. In (eds. D. V. Glass and R. Revelle)
Population and social change, pp. 137–9. Arnold, London. The restrictions
were particularly pervasive in certain Swiss cantons, notably Lucerne:
see BICHEL, W. (1947). *Bevölkerungsgeschichte und Bevölkerungspolitik
der Schweiz*, p. 155. Zurich; and for an account of German marriage laws
see KNODEL, J. (1967). Law, marriage and illegitimacy in nineteenth-
century Germany, *Population Studies* **20** (Mar.), 279.

The historical role of religious systems. An excellent introduction to the
Judaic–Christian ethic is given by NOONAN, JR., J. T. (1972).
Intellectual and demographic history. In (eds. D. V. Glass and R. Revelle)
Population and social change, pp. 115–35. Arnold, London. See also
NOONAN, JR., J. T. (1966). *Contraception: a history of its treatment by
the Catholic theologians and canonists.* Harvard University Press, Cam-
bridge, Mass. For the Jewish view see FELDMAN, D. M. (1968).
Birth control in Jewish law, New York University Press, New York.

The paper by MUSALLAM, B. F. (1974). *The Islamic sanction of
contraception.* This volume pp. 300–10, provides a most scholarly introduction to the teachings of classical Islamic jurisprudence.

2.7. Public concern and population

2.7.1. Local attitudes to population growth in South Buckinghamshire

CAROLE MUSSON

Conservation Society, Beaconsfield, Bucks

THIS is a short report of the survey into local attitudes to population growth carried out in 1972 by the South Buckinghamshire branch of the Conservation Society [1] and which was never intended to be an academic exercise. The prime objective, if the results were favourable, was to press the Local Authority into providing a more comprehensive family-planning service in the county.

Our lack of resources, both financial and in terms of manpower, hampered us in the conduct of the survey. We were unable to employ proper sampling techniques, and no attempt at a truly random survey was tried. Therefore, the method adopted was either to interview people on Saturdays in busy shopping areas in South Buckinghamshire—High Wycombe, Aylesbury, Chesham, Amersham, and Marlow—or to leave questionnaires for individuals to complete in doctors' waiting rooms, in some schools and colleges, and on a house-to-house basis. On the whole, most people were very willing to answer the questions, and many showed a keen interest in the subject matter of the survey. We received the return of some 82·5 per cent of questionnaires distributed.

A total of 660 people were interviewed; this number was broken down by sex and age. No attempt was made to classify people by social or occupational classes, since the title given to their occupation by most people was too vague.

The results of the survey may be summarized as follows:

1. The first question—'Do you think Great Britain is over-populated or not?—produced a 74 per cent positive response. However, the second question which directed attention to the local area—'Do you think your own area is over-populated or not?'—produced only a 48 per cent positive response. The considerable disparity between the two responses may be explained by the fact that 'your own area' was interpreted by the respondent as his or her own immediate neighbourhood of residence.

2. The third question posed was an open-ended one which asked those who had given a 'yes' response to the first question to suggest possible solutions to the problem of over-population. The principal suggestions appeared to be better family-planning facilities, regional development in order to reduce the concentration of population in certain areas, emigration, and control of immigration.

3. The fourth question asked respondents to state the ideal family size. A good majority—71 per cent—thought that 2 children per family was the ideal family size, though a substantial minority —16 per cent— thought that 3 children was ideal. An interesting correlation was made between actual family size where applicable and stated ideal family size. It was found that 68 per cent of those with 4 or more children thought that the ideal family size was smaller than their own. The next group of questions dealt with the provision of family-planning services. Eighty-nine per cent of those questioned thought that advice on family planning should be more widely publicized, and 88 per cent thought that family planning should be provided free under the National Health Service. The question 'Do you think voluntary sterilization for men and women should be provided free under the National Health Service?' produced an 82 per cent positive response.

4. Questions 8 and 9 dealt with the financial aspect of population policy. Fifty-eight per cent of those questioned thought that a possible way to encourage smaller families in the future would be to pay family allowances on the first 2 children only. Agreement with this proposition increased with age. Fifty-six per cent of respondents thought that the Government should provide tax incentives to encourage smaller families. The final question asked 'Do you think that it may become necessary in the future to exert some Government control over family size?' An affirmative answer was given by 57·5 per cent of respondents, and this figure rose to above 60 per cent in the under-25 age-group.

REFERENCE

1. SOUTH BUCKS BRANCH OF THE CONSERVATION SOCIETY (1972). I. BRIGHT, C. MUSSON, H. VENNING, *Survey into local attitudes to population growth, August 1972*. South Bucks Branch Conservation Society, Kings Head House, London End, Beaconsfield, Bucks.

2.7.2. A recent survey of opinion on population problems in the Oxford and Reading districts

G. R. WHITFIELD AND J. F. FARRAR
Conservation Society Reading
(*Dr Whitfield is also a member of the Department of Applied Physical Sciences, University of Reading*)

In spite of increasing discussion of population growth and its control in academic and political circles, comparatively little is known of how the electorate feels on these matters [1]. Still less is known about how opinions on population correlate with parameters such as age, sex, religion, and occupation. The recent National Opinion Poll report [2], for example, was concerned only with the size of Britain's population, Government action to control it, and correlations with political leanings.

In late November and early December 1972, the Reading and Oxford branches of the Conservation Society carried out a comprehensive survey of personal attitudes to population and contraception in Reading, Oxford, Abingdon, and Kirtlington. The preliminary results are presented here; full statistical analysis is still in progress.

Methods

The questionnaire was designed to avoid bias in the wording of the questions, to be as simple as possible, and to be confidential.

Recipients of forms were chosen from the electoral register using random numbers. A 1 per cent sample was considered adequate, but since a pilot survey in Reading had led us to expect a return of approximately 50 per cent, 2 per cent of the electorate was selected in Reading and Oxford.

A number of volunteer distributors each delivered 20–40 forms accompanied by an explanatory letter, and collected them 7–14 days later. In the Oxford area, these were handed to the selected person wherever possible; if he or she was no longer at that address, a member of the current household of equivalent status was substituted. In Reading they were simply delivered, and the accompanying letter explained who should fill them in.

Completed forms were coded, and the data transferred to punched cards. Analysis of the Reading survey revealed a number of coding and programming errors. To facilitate the detection of such errors a check digit was added near the end of each card in the Oxford region surveys.

Results

The completed questionnaires returned varied from 50 per cent (Oxford) to 31 per cent (Kirtlington) of those sent out.

The Oxford and Abingdon results were checked for bias by comparing age and occupation with data in the census returns for 1971 and 1966 respectively. Whilst there was no apparent relation between returns and age, in both cases social classes I and II were over-, and III and IV under-, sampled.

The provisional analysis may be summarized as follows.

1. Sixty-five per cent of those questioned think Britain has too many people, and another 29 per cent think it has about the right number. Less than 1 per cent think it has too few.

2. Sixty-eight per cent consider that the Government should encourage steps to lower the birth rate, and 77 per cent that it should advertise birth control more. Twenty-five per cent are against any positive Government policy.

3. Most people feel that birth control should be freely available for married people (90 per cent) and single people (64 per cent). Whilst the majority (76 per cent, Reading only) felt that advice on birth control should be free of all charge, rather less than half considered that contraceptives should be free. In the Oxford area, three-quarters think that voluntary sterilization should be freely available under the National Health Service, and more than half would favour tax incentives for smaller families; only one-quarter think family allowances should be paid on more than 2 children.

4. Forty-eight per cent would not object if the Government advised them to have no more than 2 children, but only 24 per cent would be pleased. Twenty-six per cent would object, half of them strongly, but of these 63 per cent consider Britain to be over-populated.

5. Two children is the commonest view of the ideal family; the mean ideal family size was felt to be 2·34 children. However, the mean family size which Reading families intend to have is 2·04 children.

6. About half think Reading is about the right size, whilst 28 per cent think it should grow; only 7·5 per cent would like to live

in a larger town. Thirty per cent of people in Oxford think Oxfordshire should stop growing, and 44 per cent that it should grow more slowly.

Conclusions

A majority of people in the Reading and Oxford districts who completed the questionnaire consider that Britain has too many inhabitants and that the Government should take action to lower the birth rate.

REFERENCES

1. FREEMAN, N. M. R. (1970). Not by bread alone: anthropological perspectives on optimum population. In *The optimum population for Britain* (ed. L. R. Taylor). pp. 139–49. Academic Press, London.
2. *Population and birth control* (1973). A report prepared for National Opinion Polls Ltd. (NOP/6248), London.

2.8. Some final impressions

H. B. PARRY

*Fellow of Wolfson College and Nuffield Institute for Medical
Research, Oxford University*

The general reconnaissance

AT the final plenary session of the Workshop we attempted in a
tentative manner to ascertain whether any consensus of opinion
might emerge on the major issues which had been discussed in the
individual sessions; whether there were any areas of substantial
agreement, which could point towards the formulation of a preferred population size for the United Kingdom; whether there
were special areas of ignorance which should receive increased
research attention; and whether we could offer the 'plain man'
any simple and agreed directives to guide him in an evaluation of
population problems, and in his own personal family decisions.

The short answer is that we failed, but the pattern of our failure
bears scrutiny [4]. There were present scholars from many disciplines relevant to any proper definition of current population
problems, yet it was not possible to develop a meaningful dialogue.
One sensed that because a view, often widely held and accepted in
a general way, was not phrased in the currently acceptable terminology, nor supported by a full scholarly apparatus, then the whole
contribution tended to be disregarded, irrespective of whether
contained within it was an important, if unquantified, element of the
whole truth. In many branches of current population studies it is
often immensely difficult to assemble *contemporaneously* quantitative data across the needful range of relevant parameters. Most
studies relate to areas readily accessible to current investigation;
they do not necessarily, and frequently do not, embrace certain
parameters crucial to a proper understanding.

This diversity of view appeared to lie principally in the importance which different participants with different specialist backgrounds placed on the importance of the short-term, i.e. the next
two or three decades, as against the longer-term problem. Those

brought up in the tradition of the biomedical sciences were deeply concerned in our medium- and long-term future, although acutely aware that no acceptable quantitative definition of this 'ecological' concern [16, 28, 38] was adequately documented, and therefore open, quite properly, to many reservations [5]; however, these deficiencies should not be *allowed to obscure* the fact that the problem is a very real one. Those nurtured in the social sciences, notably economics, tended to stress the short-term position and were reluctant to concede that the long-term ecological problem was a real one, or indeed was ever likely to be of importance. To any biologically trained person with knowledge of the devastating effects of certain socio-economic systems of land use over the last 100 years, be they in North America, Australia, Africa, or elsewhere, and the consequences of such misuse on the probable potential capacity of large land areas to support stable societies in the foreseeable future, such a conflict was a cause of dismay. It provoked reflections as to why such a divergence of opinion might arise; and, more important, how the viewpoints of those in different disciplines, each highly relevant to the whole, might be reconciled; and thus provide more precise guidance towards a considered view of what may be an acceptable or optimal size of the future United Kingdom population.

In broad terms, there is much support for the view that the human population of the world is in need of restraint [3, 28, 32], and that the size of the populations of the developed countries of the Western (Atlantic) tradition, no less than those of the developing countries, should be stabilized [7, 8, 38]. Glass [20] suggests a stabilized fluctuating population for the United Kingdom; Ohlin [34] drew attention to the importance of the consumption expectation of the population, rather than their total numbers, in determining the impact of a given population on the environment, while Illsley [27] drew attention to the beneficial effects of a general acceptance of family planning and limitation in a local region upon its local government services and upon the 'quality of life' which such services are able to support.

In modern developed countries with very low mortality rates, the population size is determined almost entirely by fertility and over a time-scale measured in decades; for the rapid feedback of environmental factors on fertility which tended towards stability in more primitive communities has been lost [12, 44]. The crucial parameter is the fertility of the females in a cohort as measured by their mean completed family size (CFS), or more precisely, the Net Reproduction Rate [12]. The mean CFS of a national cohort is compounded of a vast number of individual decisions, successful and unsuccessful, which are influenced by personal, social, economic, religious, sectarian, ethnic, and regional circumstances and by plain chance happening. The cumulative effect of these factors on the fertility of those presently of reproductive age will determine the size and composition of the future population in two to four decades' time.

Noonan [33] has elegantly directed attention to the importance of the 'cluster of ideas' based on the mythological–moral values current in the populations of the Judaeic–Christian tradition on the individual decision-taking which determines family size, and which is still highly relevant in parts of Europe [41]. However, little is known of the precise impact of modern social-psychological factors on contemporary family building, apart from recent pilot studies in the United Kingdom [23], on shifts in the importance of different considerations over the reproductive life-span, and hence on the final CFS.

The biologists' battle

The history of the destruction of the original forest and vegetational cover representing stable dominant, i.e. mature, botanical ecosystems, which has followed overexploitation by human and animal populations, and the consequent soil erosion is so well documented that biologists are acutely aware of the problems of environmental damage and the immensity of the task of their correction. Biological scientists with an ecological training are often especially perceptive of the risks attached to procedures which are likely to lead away from a balanced natural environment, procedures which to others appear harmless enough because their effects are inapparent or long delayed. The biologist may appear to others to overstate his case, but then he is aware of the difficulties in re-establishing a stable self-perpetuating ecosystem and of the length of the time-scale involved—usually decades and often centuries, if it is ever fully restored. Talking to those not exposed to these problems in their daily lives and thoughts, one often realizes the conceptual and emotional barrier which separates otherwise well-informed persons. Perhaps the recent realization in Japan [24] of the seriousness of the contamination of their sea-food supplies by stable chemicals poisonous to man (especially heavy metals which are not degraded) may lead to a better understanding, towards which the biologist might prudently contribute by expressing his concern with a more muted messianic vigour.

The economists' faith

To the economists, the environmental damage and food-production deficits feared by the biologists appeared to be unwarranted, exaggerated, and unlikely to be of general quantitative significance in the foreseeable future. This reaction appeared to stem from the proposition, enshrined in the ethic of classical economic theory [19], that a continuing annual increase of the Gross National Product was a good and desirable thing, which could proceed at an annual rate of 3–5 per cent compound virtually indefinitely with beneficent advantage. Any shortages of presently used basic materials derived from non-renewable resources would be replaced by new materials developed by technological innovation. The benefits of such economic growth would indeed enrich the United Kingdom's 'life-style', but whether this 'enrichment' would serve the *real*, i.e. best social, economic, and cultural, *needs* of the people, rather than reflect the current *capabilities and desires* of industrial technocracy [19], beneficent and otherwise, was far from clear.

It was by no means self-evident to the Biomedical Working Party that this proposition was necessarily well-founded. There was no chance of examining the implications of these economic concepts, beyond the assessments for United Kingdom population sizes already considered [12]. Even in this restricted context it became apparent in the discussion of the Economics Working Party that there were wildy divergent views as to the proper assumptions, and their quantifications, which should be used as inputs for the models upon which the economic assessments relating to future population sizes were based.

Indeed, there are economists who question whether continued economic growth is inherently necessary and desirable [29], a point of view which would attract support from many biomedical scientists, and certainly from a section of the general public [36].

Furthermore, the bland assumption, implicit in much of the Workshop discussion, that the United Kingdom and other net-food-importing countries will be able to continue the practice of the past century of freely importing foodstuffs to make good any shortfall in home production, should now be viewed against subsequent commodity market developments. In June 1973, the U.S. Government suddenly placed an immediate embargo on the export of soya beans and soya-bean products with the partial cancellation of existing commercial forward contracts to sell [39]. As the U.S.A. provides the largest part of the soya beans available to the world market, which in turn forms a significant portion of the total food proteins used in Japan and, to a less extent, in Europe, the effect of this sudden cutting-off of supplies was a radical and ominous change, even if the new harvest mitigates the effects on the world protein market for the time being. With the reduction of world fish protein supplies and a declining surplus of bread grains available in world markets, the continuing availability to the United Kingdom, even if balance of payments permit, of substantial surpluses of foodstuffs from the world market over the next decade must now be open to serious question.

At the least, therefore, it seems prudent to keep under close review the basis of many of the economic projections, upon which rely current judgements of Britain's optimum population in relation to the United Kingdom's economy to the end of the century. This will be particularly so if our population should show any tendency to be other than stabilized, or if the terms of world trade in essential commodities should move substantially against us, as the recent increases in the price of bread wheats foreshadows.

The geologists' nightmare

To those concerned with the earth's resources of fossil fuels and minerals, the increasing scarcity and possible exhaustion of our main sources of many of these commodities by the end of the century is very real [31]. Their increasing under-supply of world market demands and relative cost are likely to effect materially the pattern of their availability in many parts of the world; e.g. inadequacy of oil supplies may limit India's development [15]. Yet that these developments were likely to impose severe strains on our present economic arrangements was not generally acceptable.

However, within a week of the Workshop discussions, it was publicly announced from the U.S.A. and widely recognized in the United Kingdom, that petroleum oils and natural gas were likely to become increasingly inadequate to meet the world's present and projected demands, and that a shortage of fuel [25] for internal combustion engines might well prove an important economic and political limitation on growth before the end of the century [2, 26, 31]. Should this appraisal, which is questioned [1], prove correct, the time available to develop alternative energy sources seems perilously short.

The exhaustion of metallurgical mineral resources is also a cause for similar concern [16, 31].

The doctor's role

There was a wide measure of agreement from the biomedical sessions. With the control of most infectious diseases and the alleviation of many disabling physical conditions, medicine in the United Kingdom was now in a position to pay increasing attention to positive health, physical and mental, and to the environmental factors upon which freedom from ill-health depends. Many G.P.s were deeply concerned with the individual cases in their practices, in which too large or closely spaced families placed intolerate strains on parents, especially the mothers. Arising from these family strains, the upbringing of the children tended to be unsatisfactory for their proper emotional and intellectual development and gave rise to problems in their later life. It was with the alleviation and prevention of these problems of child-rearing, especially those of a psychological nature, that the Working Parties were especially concerned. The problems with an accepted genetic basis are amenable to genetic counselling [14, 37]; it was upon the much larger group of ill-defined, but often disabling, deviant mental states and of 'sad families' with a substantial environmental component in their causation that investigative and preventive efforts should be concentrated [42].

The medical profession was in a special position to co-ordinate and to advise their patients on matters of family planning and the upbringing of their children. The family G.P. with his knowledge of family background, local conditions, and economic circumstances was in an especially favoured relationship from which to offer wise advice, and, if this work were linked with collaboration from the hospital-based consultants, an effective agency was practicable, although it was pointed out that only about $\frac{2}{3}$ of all G.P.s were as yet actively offering advice of this kind. More should be encouraged and trained to do so.

A summary for a plain man's assessment

The total population of the United Kingdom. No formal expression was made except by one distinguished demographer, who considered 35 million a suitable size at which to aim. There was widespread concern from the biomedical scientists that more active steps should be taken to watch closely, and reduce wherever practicable, the probable rate of increase, to encourage family limitation in specific instances, and to question the wisdom of the continued encouragement of *per capita* consumption of resources. Locally, there was considerable public concern regarding the effects of present population densities on public amenities and the aesthetics of the physical environment of the region, and a general view that any population increase was undesirable [36].

The completed family size (CFS). Small changes in the average number of children raised to reproductive age by each woman during her own reproductive life will have a profound effect on the future size of the United Kingdom population. Thus a shift in the probable mean CFS of 2·4 for those marrying in the 1950s to 2·16 would stabilize the population [21]. For reasons of genetic variability a spread of family size of 1–4 children is desirable [14]; but encouragement to limit the number of children *per woman* to 4 or less, especially among 'sad families', is probably desirable on social and health grounds, although the effects on mean CFS is likely to be small [21]. To move towards zero population growth (ZPG), a substantial reduction in the numbers of families with 3 and 2 children is required (see also [19]).

The planning of child-bearing. Since the Workshop was held, extended family-planning services have become available under the National Health Service in the United Kingdom, although not free of charge, which was the hope expressed at the Workshop [30]. There is thus now better provision for ensuring that every child is a planned child [14]. The very personal and private decisions which determine motherhood and family size are imperfectly charted; but the attitude of those born since 1950 and brought up in the milieu of wider education and freer discussion and less-rigid social conventions on sexuality and with access to the contraceptive pill and legal abortion is likely to be radically different from earlier cohorts. There would appear to be a very real need for sensitive and perceptive contemporary collaborative studies of a long-term or 'longitudinal' kind, i.e. over the major part of the reproductive life of the participants, to study the changing determinants of the reproductive attainment of the successive cohorts now entering their reproductive life (see [46]).

The rearing of children. Although the role of the family unit in child-rearing was not discussed specifically, it was generally recognized that the home circumstances of a child's upbringing affected substantially his or her subsequent personality, intellectual attainment, and mental health. Although it was difficult to demonstrate causal correlations in an acceptable scientific form, this failure might be due more to the insensitivity or inappropriateness of the measurements used than to the absence of a causal connection. The role of unstable relationships, both human and in the physical environment, of parental attitudes, and of family aspirations on a child's subsequent mental development warranted more detailed study, particularly in respect of families with 4 or more children; especially birth spacings, economic status, family organization and educational attainment goals, assistance outside the immediate family, and disturbed parental relationships.

The national economy and population size. There was a clear divergence of opinion regarding the relevance and importance of the economic factors which should be taken into account, especially the inputs for the model building used in assessing the economic consequences of a predicted future population size and structure in the United Kingdom, and the impact on the national economic position and standard of living of a given population level. There is urgent need that the bases of this divergence should be examined closely and defined clearly and that gaps in our knowledge be subjected wherever possible to the most careful investigation, not by economists alone, but also by others able to speak for the biomedical and sociological disciplines. Thus a clearer consensus may emerge on the probable economic consequences of varying

United Kingdom populations in the medium and longer time-scales, i.e. beyond A.D. 2011.

Perhaps we should not overlook the evidence over the very long term available in historical demographic studies [22], notably the Chinese experience over several millennia [10, 40], and take note of the 'high-level equilibrium trap' to which the loss of impetus in Chinese intellectual life and technological innovation under the Manchus may be attributed [17, 45].

Whither should we travel—some aims and objectives. The total population of the United Kingdom is an imperfect measure of man's impact upon and ability to live constructively within these islands' environmental and ecological base. The advice of demographers is for little or no planned change [12, 20, 34], partly because of the uncertain effects of population policies in the past and partly because it is the consumption demands of the population in fulfilling its personal, social, and cultural aspirations as presently perceived, which constitute the greatest single determinant of that impact [34]. Whether the fulfilment of these demands for economic opportunity for personal transport, foreign travel, leisure activities, education, and so on is compatible with an acceptable way of living for the present and projected sizes of our population depends upon individual judgement of relative values, indeed upon an aesthetic value-judgement [20, 34]

Most of us base our aesthetic value-judgement on our personal inclinations, talents and training within the aspirations and constraints of the societal mythology persuasive in our generation. Whether this is an adequate base may be doubted in the context of the rapid developments—social, physical, and organizational—which have occurred and are forecast for the next decades. Rather should we not be thinking of what sort of island in what sort of world and providing what kinds of 'life-styles' may be most desirable one, two, or three decades hence. By 'desirable' we must mean those best able to provide for, and sustain, a 'total' environment which, after meeting basic physical and social needs, is most conducive to the development of an individual's happiness and creative achievement [1318,], while ensuring ecological stability.

There will be almost as many concepts of such a desirable 'total' environment as there are individuals who articulate them. But some common base-ground will be conceded by many people.

Alleviation of non-self-righting environmental damage and pollution and of the impact of shortages of non-renewable resources; the provision of necessary wholesome food and housing, for peace and natural solitude; some amelioration of the strains of modern cities and their living conditions; the simplification of the demands of government agencies on individuals—all these could be achieved more readily if the present population were smaller. If it were much larger the point beyond which effective remedial action can succeed may well be passed, unless inconceivably draconian measures are used. So perhaps we should try to stabilize the United Kingdom population, even concede that the United Kingdom is overpopulated [38a], and aim for a modest decrease. *Pari passu* we should question the unlimited encouragement of consumer consumption under the pressure of business persuasion, and reconsider the economic ethic of growth and maximizing profits, so that the containment and phased reduction of unit consumer demand for pollutant products and scarce resources may be encouraged.

But the last, most important, and probably most influential, objective lies within the power of the individual. Contemporary society and medico-social reproductive technology now permit highly effective and usually acceptable methods of family planning, generally available to all and allowing gratification of sexual appetites and psycho-physiological needs.

Reproductive attainment, which may now be controlled so readily, now operates in a radically new socio-psychological situation. The personal challenge is to rethink the rights, responsibilities, and obligations of the individual in his reproductive behaviour to his partner and to himself, to his family, to his neighbours, and to society, contemporary and future. We must accept a restriction on our 'right' to reproduce [35], doing so only when a stable parental home is established in which a child may be successfully reared. The challenge to society is to reconsider what organizational framework can best support child-bearing and child-rearing with the greatest chance of producing stable adults, free of mental and physical ill-health, with their inherent talents flowering. Society must continue to watch closely the impact of economic and legal enactments on the pattern of family life and child development, and to discourage the jettisoning of long-established traditional methods without the most careful appraisal of the new. Indeed, society must construct a new ethos of social attitudes towards reproduction, child-rearing, and the family, and reconsider society's hitherto general commendation of the intrinsic virtue of child-birth.

We close with some guide-lines, based on those proposed by Sir Alan Parkes [35, 38*b*], setting out the obligations that present society may properly require of its members:

1. To produce only planned and wanted children.
2. Not to take a substantial risk of begetting a mentally or physically defective child.
3. Not to produce children because of irresponsibility or religious observance or merely as an unplanned by-product of sexual intercourse.
4. To plan the number and spacing of births in the best interest of mother, child, and rest of the family.
5. To give the best possible mental and physical environment to the child during its formative years and to produce therefore only children who are wanted and cherished in the course of an affectionate and stable relationship between man and woman over the whole period of the rearing and training of children to adult life.
6. However convinced the individual may be of his or her superior qualities, not for this reason to produce children in numbers, which, if equalled by everyone, would be anti-social and demographically disastrous.

REFERENCES

1. ADELMAN, H. A. (1972–3). Is the oil shortage real? Oil companies and OPEC Tax-collectors, *Foreign Policy* **9**, 16–64.
2. AKINS, J. S. (1972). The oil crisis: this time the wolf is here. *Foreign Affairs (Wash.)*, Winter No., and *Petroleum Inst. Weekly* 27 March, 1–20.
3. ANON. (1971). *Population program assistance.* Government Printing Office, Washington, D.C.
4. ANON. (1973). Britain 2001, *Lancet* **i**, 650.
5. ANON. (1973). Almost the last word on the Club of Rome, *Nature, Lond.* **242**, 147–8, NAUGHTON, J. (1974). *Encounter* **42** (Jan.), 72–7.
6. ANON. (1973). The repeated cycle of sad families. Leader in *The Times, Lond.* 28 June.
7. ANON. (1973). *Population problems and policies in economically advanced countries: Proceedings of Conference at Ditchley Park, Oxford, U.K. 29 Sept.–2 Oct. 1972*, pp. 36. The Population Crisis

Committee, Washington, D.C., and the Ditchley Foundation, Enstone, Oxford.

8. BENJAMIN, B., COX, P. R., and PEEL, J. (eds.) (1973). *Resources and population*, p. 182. *Proceedings of Symposium and the Galton Lecture (Economic Policy and the threat of doom)* by J. E. Meade, Sept. 1972, organized by the Eugenics Society, London. Academic Press, London.

9. BERELSON, B. (ed.) (1974). *Population policy in developed countries.* McGraw-Hill, New York.

10. BIOT, E. (1836). Sur la population de la Chine et ses variations depuis l'an 2400 avant J. C. jusqu'au XIII'e siècle de notre ère, *J. Asiastique* Ser. 3, **1**, 369–94; **1**, 448–72; **2**, 74–8.

11. BROWN, B. C. and RICHARDSON, G. B. (1974). This volume, pp. 201–13.

12. BRASS, W. (1974). This volume, pp. 186–200.

13. BUTCHER, H. J. (1972). *Human intelligence: its nature and assessment*, p. 343. Methuen, London.

14. CARTER, C. O. (1974). This volume, pp. 250–6.

15. CASSEN, R. H. (1974). This volume, pp. 216–43.

16. Editors of the *Ecologist* (1972). A blueprint for survival, *Ecologist* **2**, 1–43; and Penguin Books, Harmondsworth.

17. ELVIN, M. (1973). *The pattern of the Chinese past*, p. 346; Part III. Economic development without technological change, pp. 201–319, and especially p. 314 et seq. Eyre–Methuen, London.

18. FREEMAN, M. M. R. (1970). Not by bread alone: anthropological perspectives in optimum population. In *The optimum population for Britain* (ed. L. R. Taylor), pp. 139–50. Academic Press, London.

19. GALBRAITH, J. K. (1973). Economics: unequal development and the theory of social action. *Proc. R. Soc. Med.* **66**, 559–64.

20. GLASS, D. V. (1974). This volume pp. 72–87.

21. GREBENIK, E. (1972). On controlling population growth. In *Biology and the human sciences* (ed. J. W. S. Pringle), pp. 25–48. Clarendon Press, Oxford.

22. HABBAKUK, H. J. (1971). *Population growth and economic development since 1750*, p. 110. Leicester University Press.

23. HAWTHORN, G. P., BUSFIELD, N. J., and PADDON, M. J. (1974). This volume, pp. 316–22.

24. HAZLEHURST, P. (1973). Fish can maim, paralyse and deform. *The Times, London.* 3 July, p. 12.

25. HUBERT, M. K. (1969). [20], Chap. 8, pp. 157–242; and (1971). The energy of the Earth, *Scient. Am.* **225** (Sept.), 60–70.

26. HUTBER, F. W. and FORSTER, C. I. K. (1973). Sources of energy and their adequacy for man's needs. In *Resources and population* (eds. B. Benjamin, P. R. Cox, and J. Peel), Academic Press, London.

27. ILLESLEY, R. (1973). This volume, pp. 112–32.

28. MEADOWS, D. H., MEADOWS, D. L., RANDERS, J., and BEHRENS, W. W. (1972). *Limits to growth.* Earth Island Publiacations, London, see also (1974) *Nature, Lond.* **247**, 94–5.

29. MISHAN, E. J. (1973). To grow or not to grow: what are the issues, *Encounter* **40,** 9–29.
30. MORRIS, G. (1974). This volume, pp. 373–80.
31. NATIONAL ACADEMY OF SCIENCES (1969). *Resources and man: a study and recommendations.* W. H. Freeman, San Francisco.
32. NATIONAL ACADEMY OF SCIENCES (1971). *Rapid population growth: consequences and policy implications,* Vol. 1, pp. ix + 105. Johns Hopkins Press, London and Baltimore.
33. NOONAN, J. F., JR. (1972). Intellectual and demographic history. In *Population and social change* (eds. D. V. Glass and R. Revelle), pp. 115–35. Edward Arnold, London.
34. OHLIN, G. (1974). This volume, pp. 88–100.
35. PARKES, A. S. (1969). The right to reproduce in an over-crowded world. In *Biology and ethics* (ed. F. J. Ebling), pp. 109–16. Academic Press, London.
36. *Public concern and population* (1974). This volume, pp. 392–6.
37. ROBERTS, J. A. F. (1971). Genetic advice for potential parents. In *Family planning* (eds. J. Medawar and D. Pyke), pp. 233–8. Pelican Books, Harmondsworth.
38. TAYLOR, L. R. (1970). *The optimum population for Britain,* Symp. Inst. Biol. No. 19, Academic Press, London and New York; (*a*) p. vii, (*b*) p. xix.
39. *The Times, Lond.* (1973). 20 June, p. 5.
40. WILLIAMS, S. W. (1883). *The middle kingdom: a survey of the geography, government, literature, social life, arts and history of the Chinese empire and its inhabitants* (2 Vols.). Population and statistics, Vol. 1, pp. 258–88. W. H. Allen, London.
41. ZELDIN, T. (1974). This volume, pp. 310–15; Editor's Note, p. 391.
42. WEST, D. J. (1974). In collaboration with FARRINGTON, D. P. *Who becomes a delinquent?* Heinemann Educational Books, London for the Institute of Criminology, Cambridge.
43. FREJKA, T. (1973). *The future of population growth, alternative paths to equilibrium,* p. 288. Wiley, New York; and The prospects for a stationary world population, *Scient. Am.* **228** (Mar.), 15–23.
44. KUNSTADTER, P. (1972). Demography, ecology, social structure, and settlement patterns. In *The structure of human populations* (eds. G. A. Harrison and A. J. Boyce), pp. 312–51. Clarendon Press, Oxford.
45. NEEDHAM, J. (1959). Science and civilisation in China. Vol. 3, §20. Cambridge University Press, London.
46. LASLETT, P. (ed.) (1972). *Household and family in past time.* Cambridge University Press, London.

Appendix: addresses

The following is a list of those who attended the workshop discussions of the papers in this book, including those who gave the papers.

ARDENER, Mr. E. Institute of Social Anthropology, Oxford.
ARGYLE, Mr. M. A. Department of Psychology, Oxford.

BALDWIN, Dr. J. Clinical Epidemiology Research Unit, Oxford Regional Hospital Board.
BANCROFT, Dr. J. Department of Psychiatry, Oxford.
BARRETT, Dr. J. C. London School of Hygiene and O.P.C.S., London.
BARTLETT, Prof. M. S. Department of Biomathematics, Oxford.
BENJAMIN, Prof. B. Civil Service College, London.
BERELSON, Dr. B. Population Council, New York.
BONNAR, Mr. J. Maternity Department, John Radcliffe Hospital, Oxford.
BRASS, Prof. W. London School of Hygiene, London.
BROCK, Mr. M. G. Vice-President, Wolfson College, Oxford.
BROWN, Mr. B. C. Department of the Environment, London.
BRUNER, Prof. J. Department of Psychology, Oxford.
BRUNER, Mrs. c/o Department of Psychology, Oxford.
BUSFIELD, Miss Department of Sociology, University of Essex.

CAIRNCROSS, Sir A. St. Peter's College, Oxford.
CALLENDER, Dr. S. Department of Clinical Medicine, Oxford.
CARTER, Dr. C.O. M.R.C. Clinical Genetics Unit, Institute of Child Health, London.
CARTWRIGHT, Dr. A. Institute of Social Studies in Medical Care, London.
CASEY, Mr. D. Simon Population Trust, Cambridge.
CASSEN, Mr. R. H. Institute for Development Studies, Sussex.
CHEKE, Dr. A. Zoology Department, Oxford.
COLEMAN, Mr. D. A. Department of Anthropology, University College, London.
DAVIS, Mr. N. H. W. Population Statistics Division II, O.P.C.S., London.
DOLL, LADY c/o Regius Professors' Department.
DOLL, Prof. Sir R. Regius Professor's Department, Radcliffe Infirmary, Oxford.

FARRAR, Mr. J. F.	Imperial College, Field Station, Stillwood Park, Berks.
FREEDMAN, Prof. M.	Institute of Social Anthropology, Oxford.
GATH, Dr. D.	Department of Psychiatry, Oxford.
GELDER, Prof. M. P.	Department of Psychiatry, Oxford.
GIBSON, Dr. J.	Department of Genetics, Cambridge.
GOTTMANN, Prof. J.	School of Geography, Oxford.
GREBENIK, Mr. E.	Civil Service College, Sunningdale, Ascot Berks.
GUILLEBAUD, Mr. J.	Churchill Hospital, Headington, Oxford
HABAKKUK, Mr. H. J.	Jesus College, Oxford.
HAJNAL, Dr. J.	London School of Economics, London.
HANDLIN, Prof. O.	The Queen's College, Oxford.
HARRISON, Dr. G. A.	Reader in Physical Anthropology, Oxford.
HAWTHORN, Dr. G.	Churchill College, Cambridge.
HENDERSON, Mr. K.V.	Overseas Development Administration, London.
HIORNS, Dr. R.	Department of Biomathematics, Oxford.
HOBCRAFT, Dr. J.	London School of Economics, London.
HOPKINS, Prof. K.	Department of Sociology, Brunel University.
HUNT, Mr. K. E.	Institute of Agricultural Economics, Oxford.
JONES, Mr. G. T.	Institute of Agricultural Economics, Oxford.
KRAAY, Dr. C.	Vicegerent, Wolfson College, Oxford.
LANGFORD, Dr. C. M.	London School of Economics, London.
LITTLE, Prof. I. M. D.	Nuffield College, Oxford.
LORAINE, Dr. J. A.	Department of Social Medicine, Edinburgh.
LUMBERS, Dr. E.	Nuffield Institute for Medical Research, Oxford and University of Adelaide.
MACDONALD, Dr. N.	Clare Hall Hospital, Potters Bar, Herts.
MATHIAS, Prof. P.	All Souls College, Oxford.
MEDAWAR, LADY	Margaret Pyke Centre, London.
MORRIS, Dr. G.	169, Cranley Gardens, Muswell Hill, London.
MUSSON, Mrs. C.	Kings Head House, London Road, Beaconsfield.
PADDON, Mr. M. J.	Department of Sociology, University of Durham.
PAINE, Mr. G.	Registrar General, Somerset House, Strand, London.
PARRY, Mr. H. B.	Wolfson College, Oxford.
PATTEN, Dr. J.	Department of Geography, Oxford.

Peet, Dr. K.	Holton, Oxford.
Pickering, Sir G.	Pembroke College, Oxford.
Redfern, Mr. P.	O.P.C.S., Somerset House, Strand, London.
Richardson, Mr. G. B.	St. John's College, Oxford.
Seers, Prof. D.	Institute of Development Studies, Sussex University.
Short, Dr. R. V.	M.R.C. Unit of Reproductive Biology, Edinburgh.
Singer, Dr. A.	Maternity Department, John Radcliffe Hospital, Oxford.
Snyder, Dr. B. R.	Massachusetts Institute of Technology and Wolfson College, Oxford.
Soskice, Dr. D. V.	University College, Oxford.
Stallworthy, Sir J.	John Radcliffe Hospital, Headington, Oxford.
Stewart, Mr. S.	Government Actuary's Department, London.
Thompson, Miss J.	O.P.C.S., Population Statistics Division, Somerset House, Strand, London.
Varley, Prof. G. C.	Hope Department of Entomology, University Museum, Oxford.
Venning, Dr. G.	Medical Director, G. B. Searle and Co., High Wycombe.
Vessey, Dr. M.	Department of the Regius Professor of Medicine, Radcliffe Infirmary, Oxford.
Whitfield, Dr. G.	Ashdown, Basingstoke Road, Reading.
Wilkinson, Mr. R.	London.
Wing, Prof. J. K.	M.R.C. Social Psychiatry Research Unit, Institute of Psychiatry, London.
Wishner, Prof. J.	Deparment of Psychiatry, Oxford, and University of Pennsylvania, Philadelphia.
Woolf, Mrs. M.	Goldsmiths' College, London University.

Glossary

Crude birth rate (CBR): Number of live births per year per 1000 people.

Crude death rate (CDR): Number of deaths per year per 1000 people.

Rate of natural increase: Difference between crude birth and crude death rate—usually expressed as a percentage.

Rate of population growth: Rate of natural increase adjusted for (net immigration or emigration.

Fecundity: The facility with which a woman conceives.

Fertility: Number of children born to a woman during her lifetime.

General fertility rate: Number of live births per year per 1000 women aged 15–49 years; strongly affected by the age distribution of women in the 15–49 age span.

Age-specific fertility rates: Number of live births per year to 1000 women of a given age group (seven five-year age groups are commonly used: 15–19, 20–24, 25–29, 30–34, 35–39, 40–44, 45–49).

Total fertility rate (TFR): The average number of children a woman will have if she experiences a given set of age-specific fertility rates throughout her lifetime.

Gross reproduction rate (GRR): The average number of daughters a woman will bear if she experiences a given set of age-specific fertility rates throughout the reproductive ages, with no allowance for mortality over this period.

Net reproduction rate (NRR): Same as the gross reproduction rate but adjusted for mortality of women over their reproductive years.

Infant mortality rate (IMR): Annual death of infants 0–12 months old per 1000 live births during the same year.

Completed family size (CFS): Number of surviving children at the termination of a woman's child-bearing.

Life expectancy: Average number of years remaining to be lived after attaining age X by a cohort exposed to a given set of mortality rates.

Dependency ratio: Number of people of 14 years or under, plus 65 or over, divided by the population aged 15 to 64 years.

MWRA: Married women of reproductive age.

Married fertility: Number of births per year per 1000 MWRA.

DHSS: Department of Health and Social Security, Alexander Fleming House, Elephant and Castle, London, S.E.1 (01–407–5522).

DOPG: Doctors and Overpopulation Group, 169 Cranleigh Gardens, London, N.10.

FPA: Family Planning Association, 27–35 Mortimer St., London, W1A 4QW. Journal: *Family Planning*.

G.P.: General (medical) practitioner.

HMSO: Her Majesty's Stationery Office, Government Bookshop, P.O. Box 569, London SE1 9NH (01–928–6977).

IPPF: International Planned Parenthood Federation, 18, Regent St., London, S.W.1.

I.U.D.: Intra-uterine device.

K.A.P.: Knowledge, attitude, and practice of family planning.

OPCS: Office of Population and Census Su veys, Somerset House, Strand, London, W.C.1.

PIC: Population Investigation Committee, London School of Economics and Political Science, Houghton St., Aldwych, London, W.C.2. Journal: *Population Studies*.

PC: The Population Council, 245 Park Avenue, New York, N.Y. 10017. Journals: *Studies in Family Planning, Current Publications in Population/Family Planning*.

SPT: Simon Population Trust, 141 Newmarket Rd., Cambridge, CB5 8HA.

Z.P.G.: Zero population growth, i.e. a population size is stationary or declining.

LEGEARD, C. (1966). *Guide de recherches documentaires en démographie*, Presses universitaires de France, Paris, contains a great deal of information on primary sources, techniques, bibliographies, research centres, etc.

Index

Index

labour
  force, 94, 207
  shortage, 83, 237
legal abortion, 147
  and illegitimate birth rate, 381
  England and Wales, 382, 384–6
  India and South Korea, 148
life expectancy at birth, 55, 140, 141
Lippes Loop, 364, 366
Loeringer Family Problem Test, 343
lower birth rate,
  incentives in developing countries,
    145
  India, 144
lynoestrenol, 358, 362

malaria in India, 224
Malaya, 64, 104, 109
male
  castration, effects of, 330
  sexual inadequacy, 331
Maliki, 301, 303, 307
Malthus, 94, 202
Manchus, 405
Margulies spiral, 364
marriage
  and parenthood, 121, 123, 399
  patterns, 72, 74, 75
married women in full-time employ-
    ment, 86
Mate-selection, 327
Mauritius, 67, 103, 104, 109
  family planning, 153
megestrol acetate, 358, 362
mental
  disorders, 261, 262, 269, 286; *see
    also* psychoses
  health, 256, 288
    and children, 276
    and housing, 271, 285, 289
    and population size, 278
  hospital admission rates, 262
  illness, 263–72
    and excessive noise, 272
    and migration, 269
    Hutterites, 265
    in big cities, 265, 267–8
    in country and towns, 264
    stress hypothesis, 272–5
  states, deviant, 402
mestranol, 358
Mexico, 104, 109, 138–40, 142
minerals, *see* resources

Minnesota, Multiple Personality In-
    ventory, 342
models for population projections,
    192–8
Morocco, 138, 140–1
  family planning, 149, 153
mortality, 193; *see also* death rate
Murray Islands, 297
Myxomatosis, 14

National
  Committees for Health and Vital
    Statistics, 175
  Health Service and contraceptive
    pill, 375, 390
natural disasters, impact of population
    growth, 237
Nepal, 138, 140–1, 143
  family planning, 149, 153
net reproduction rate, 55–7, 59, 73,
    97, 399
Netherlands, 138–9, 140, 142
  birth control, 77
neuroses, presence in all communities,
    263
New Guinea, 297
New Zealand, 72
Nigeria, 137–8, 140–1, 143
  family planning policies, 149
non-renewable resources, 94
Noonan, J. F., 'cluster of ideas',
    Judaeic–Christian traditions, 399
noradrenaline, 260
norethisterone, 358, 362
norgestrel, 362
North Korea, 149
North Vietnam, 138, 149
Notestein, F., 95

object choice or sexual preference,
    323, 325–6
occupational classes of adults, school
    attainment and I.Q., 245
oestrogen, 358
Office of Population Censuses and Sur-
    veys (formerly General Register
    Office), 173
one-child family, 123
one-pill-a-month contraceptives, 362
oral contraceptives, 337–9, 342, 361–
    362
  adverse reactions, 359–61
  benefits of, 361